YOUTHQUAKE

Edward Paice is Director of Africa Research Institute. He was a History Scholar at Cambridge University and winner of the Leman Prize. After working for several years as an investment analyst in the City, he moved to Africa to write travel and natural history guides in Kenya and newly independent Eritrea. He is the author of *Lost Lion of Empire: The Life of 'Cape-to-Cairo' Grogan*, nominated by *The Week* as 'Best Newcomer' in 2001; *Tip & Run*, an acclaimed account of the First World War in East Africa; and *Wrath of God: The Great Lisbon Earthquake of 1755*. In 2003–4 Paice was awarded a Visiting Fellowship at Magdalene College, Cambridge. He is a Fellow of the Royal Geographical Society.

Also by Edward Paice

Wrath of God: The Great Lisbon Earthquake of 1755

Tip & Run: The Untold Tragedy of the Great War in Africa

Lost Lion of Empire: The Life of 'Cape-to-Cairo' Grogan

YOUTHQUAKE

WHY AFRICAN DEMOGRAPHY SHOULD MATTER TO THE WORLD

EDWARD PAICE

HEAD
of ZEUS

An Apollo Book

First published in the UK in 2021 by Head of Zeus Ltd
An Apollo book

9 7 5 3 1 2 4 6 8

A catalogue record for this book is available from
the British Library.

ISBN (HB): 9781 800241589
ISBN (E): 9781800241619

Typeset by Ben Cracknell Studios

Printed and bound in Great Britain by
CPI Group (UK) Ltd, Croydon CR0 4YY

Head of Zeus Ltd
First Floor East
5–8 Hardwick Street
London EC1R 4RG
www.headofzeus.com

To Steph, Ted and Artie

Contents

List of Maps

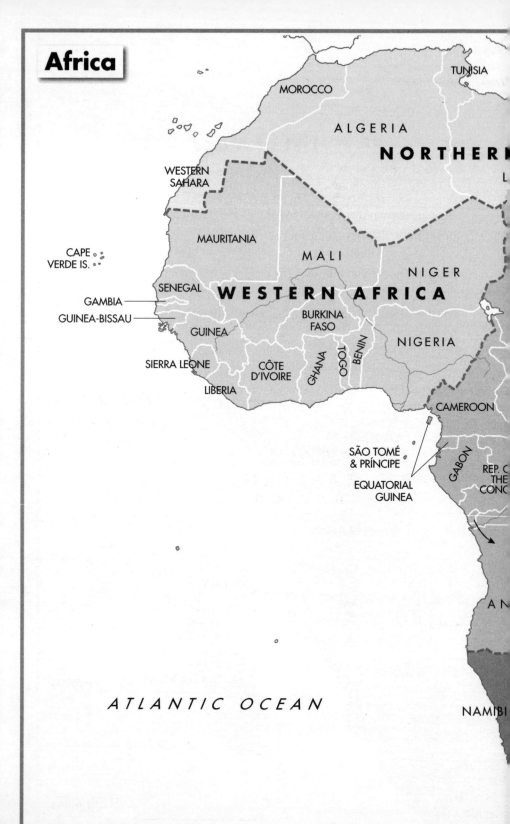

Africa

TUNISIA

MOROCCO

ALGERIA

NORTHER

WESTERN SAHARA

MAURITANIA

CAPE VERDE IS.

MALI

NIGER

SENEGAL

WESTERN AFRICA

GAMBIA

GUINEA-BISSAU

GUINEA

BURKINA FASO

NIGERIA

SIERRA LEONE

CÔTE D'IVOIRE

GHANA

TOGO

BENIN

LIBERIA

CAMEROON

SÃO TOMÉ & PRÍNCIPE

GABON

REP. O THE CON

EQUATORIAL GUINEA

A N

NAMIBI

ATLANTIC OCEAN

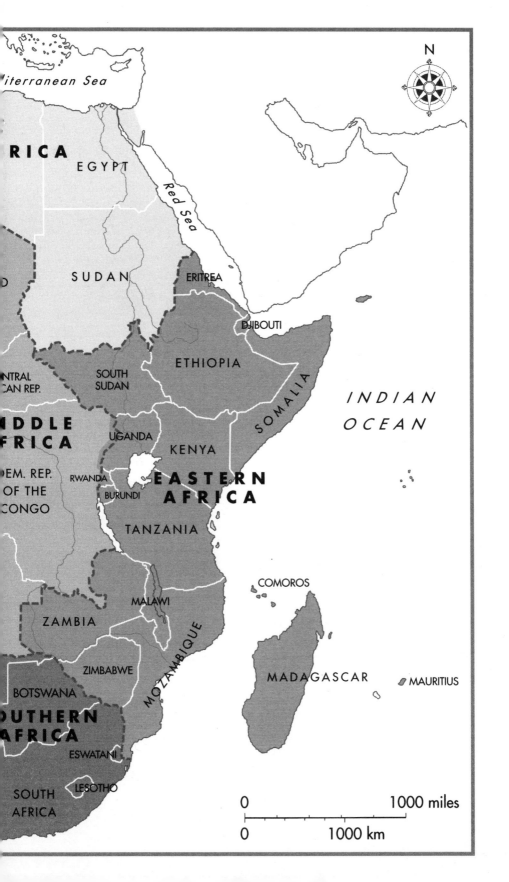

Map 2: The true extent of Africa

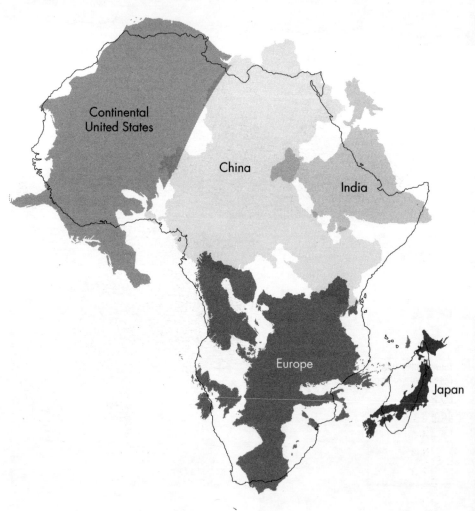

Source: Adapted from McKinsey & Company, 'Africa's overlooked business revolution', *McKinsey Quarterly*, 15 November 2018.

Map 3: Total fertility rate (TFR) in countries with 10m+ population, 2020–25

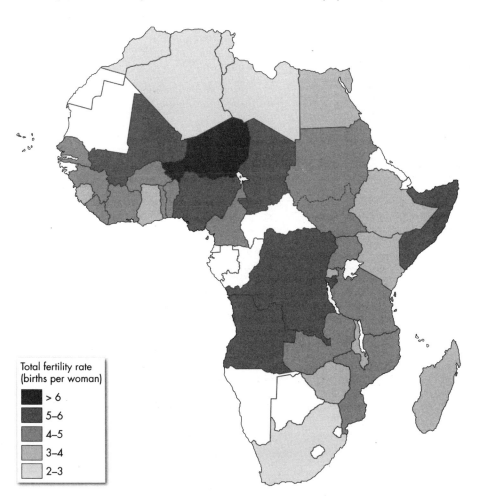

Total fertility rate
(births per woman)
- > 6
- 5–6
- 4–5
- 3–4
- 2–3

Source: UNPD, *World Population Prospects: The 2019 Revision*.

Figure 1: Africa's population pyramids in 2020, 2050 and 2100

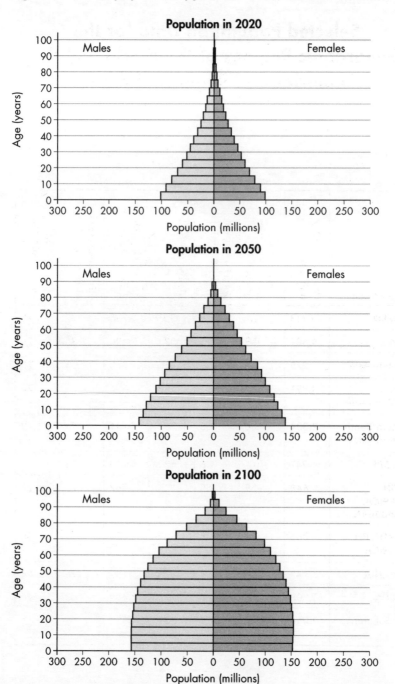

Source: UNPD, *World Population Prospects: The 2019 Revision, Vol II – Demographic Profiles.*

Selected Population Data for the Geographic Regions of the World and the Countries and Regions of Africa

Region/country	Population 2019 (million)	Average annual rate of population growth (%)	Total fertility rate, 2015–20 (births)	Median age (years)	Projected population 2050 (million)	Life expectancy at birth (years)	Population 0-14 years (% of total)
WORLD	7,713	1.1	2.5	30.9	9,735	72	25
ASIA	4,601	0.9	2.2	32.0	5,290	73	24
Western Asia	275	1.6	2.7	28.2	382	73	28
Central/ Southern Asia	1,991	1.2	2.4	27.6	2,496	69	28
Eastern/South-Eastern Asia	2,334	0.6	1.8	36.6	2,411	76	19
EUROPE	747	0.1	1.6	42.5	710	78	16
LATIN AMERICA/ CARIBBEAN	648	0.9	2.0	31.0	762	75	24
NORTHERN AMERICA	366	0.7	1.8	38.6	425	79	18
OCEANIA	42	1.4	2.4	33.4	57	78	24
AFRICA	1,308	2.5	4.4	19.7	2,489	63	40
Sub-Saharan Africa	1,066	2.7	4.7	18.7	2,177	61	42

Region/country	Population 2019 (million)	Average annual rate of population growth (%)	Total fertility rate, 2015–20 (births)	Median age (years)	Projected population 2050 (million)	Life expectancy at birth (years)	Population 0–14 years (% of total)
NORTHERN AFRICA	242	1.9	3.3	25.5	372	72	33
Algeria	43	2.0	3.1	28.5	61	77	31
Egypt	100	2.1	3.3	24.6	160	72	34
Libya	7	1.4	2.3	28.8	9	73	28
Morocco	36	1.3	2.4	29.5	46	76	27
Sudan	43	2.4	4.4	19.7	81	65	40
Tunisia	12	1.1	2.2	32.8	14	76	24
WESTERN AFRICA	391	2.7	5.2	18.2	796	57	43
Benin	12	2.7	4.9	18.8	24	61	42
Burkina Faso	20	2.9	5.2	17.6	43	61	44
Côte d'Ivoire	26	1.2	4.7	18.9	51	57	42
Gambia	2	2.9	5.3	17.8	5	62	44
Ghana	30	2.2	3.9	21.5	52	64	37
Guinea	13	2.8	4.7	18.0	26	61	43
Guinea-Bissau	2	2.5	4.5	18.8	4	58	42
Liberia	5	2.5	4.4	19.4	9	64	40
Mali	20	3.0	5.9	16.3	44	59	47
Mauritania	5	2.8	4.6	20.1	9	65	40
Niger	23	3.8	7.0	15.2	66	62	50
Nigeria	201	2.6	5.4	18.1	401	54	44
Senegal	16	2.8	4.7	18.5	33	67	43
Sierra Leone	8	2.1	4.3	19.4	13	54	40
Togo	8	2.5	4.4	19.4	15	61	41

Region/country	Population 2019 (million)	Average annual rate of population growth (%)	Total fertility rate, 2015–20 (births)	Median age (years)	Projected population 2050 (million)	Life expectancy at birth (years)	Population 0-14 years (% of total)
EASTERN AFRICA	434	3.1	4.4	18.7	851	64	42
Burundi	12	3.1	5.5	17.3	25	61	45
Eritrea	3	1.2	4.1	19.2	6	66	41
Ethiopia	112	2.6	4.3	19.5	205	66	40
Kenya	53	2.3	3.5	20.1	92	66	39
Madagascar	27	2.7	4.1	19.6	54	66	40
Malawi	19	2.7	4.3	18.1	38	63	43
Mauritius	1	0.2	1.4	37.5	1	75	17
Mozambique	30	2.9	4.9	17.6	65	60	44
Rwanda	13	2.6	4.1	20.0	23	68	40
Somalia	15	2.8	6.1	16.7	35	57	46
South Sudan	11	0.9	4.7	19.0	20	57	41
Tanzania	58	3.0	4.9	18.0	129	65	44
Uganda	44	3.6	5.0	16.7	89	63	46
Zambia	18	2.9	4.7	17.6	39	63	44
Zimbabwe	15	1.5	3.6	18.7	24	61	42
SOUTHERN AFRICA	67	1.4	2.5	27.0	87	63	30
Botswana	2	2.1	2.9	24.0	4	69	33
Eswatini	1	1.0	3.0	20.7	2	59	37
Lesotho	2	0.8	3.2	24.0	3	54	32
Namibia	2	1.9	3.4	21.8	4	63	37
South Africa	59	1.4	2.4	27.6	76	64	29

Region/country	Population 2019 (million)	Average annual rate of population growth (%)	Total fertility rate, 2015–20 (births)	Median age (years)	Projected population 2050 (million)	Life expectancy at birth (years)	Population 0–14 years (% of total)
MIDDLE AFRICA	174	3.0	5.5	17.3	383	59	45
Angola	32	3.3	5.6	16.7	77	61	46
Cameroon	26	2.6	4.6	18.7	51	59	42
Central African Republic	5	1.4	4.8	17.6	8	53	44
Chad	16	3.0	5.8	16.6	34	54	47
Rep. of Congo	5	2.6	4.5	19.2	11	64	41
Democratic Rep. of Congo (DRC)	87	3.2	6.0	17.0	194	60	46
Equatorial Guinea	1	3.7	4.6	22.3	3	58	37
Gabon	2	2.7	4.0	22.5	4	66	37

All data from UNPD, *World Population Prospects: The 2019 Revision – Data Booklet* and *Comprehensive Tables*: also custom data acquired via website un.population.org. Population figures are rounded to the nearest million. The total fertility rate is the average number of live births per woman in the period 2015-20. Median age and % of population under-14 data are for 2020. The following member countries of the African Union with populations less than 1 million are not included: Western Sahara (Sahrawi Arab Democratic Republic), Cabo Verde, Comoros, Djibouti, Seychelles, São Tomé and Príncipe.

The geographic regions referred to throughout the book are those used by the United Nations.

Although 'Africa' and 'sub-Saharan Africa' are often used interchangeably by Western institutions, here Africa refers to the entire continent and sub-Saharan Africa to all countries except those in Northern Africa.

The Africa regional designations 'Northern', 'Western', 'Eastern', 'Middle' and 'Southern' are those employed by the Population Division of the United Nations Department of Economic and Social Affairs.

Commonly Used Abbreviations

ACBF – The African Capacity Building Foundation, Harare

AFD – Agence française de développement, Paris

AfDB – African Development Bank, Abidjan

AU – African Union, Addis Ababa

CCP – Chinese Communist Party

DHS – Demographic and Health Survey

DRC – Democratic Republic of the Congo

ECA – United Nations Economic Commission for Africa (also UNECA)

FAO – Food and Agriculture Organization of the United Nations, Rome

GDP – Gross domestic product

IIASA – International Institute of Applied Systems Analysis, Laxenburg

ILO – International Labour Organization, Geneva

IMF – International Monetary Fund, Washington DC

LSE – London School of Economics

LSHTM – London School of Hygiene & Tropical Medicine

OAU – Organisation of African Unity, Addis Ababa

OECD – Organisation for Economic Co-operation and Development, Paris

SAPS – World Bank/IMF structural adjustment programmes

TFR – Total Fertility Rate

UN – United Nations, New York

UNDESA – United Nations Department of Social and Economic Affairs, New York

UNDP – United Nations Development Programme, New York

UNEP – United Nations Environment Programme, Nairobi

UNESCO – United Nations Educational, Scientific and Cultural Organization, Paris

UNFPA – United Nations Fund for Population Activities until 1987, thereafter United Nations Population Fund, New York

UNICEF – United Nations Children's Fund, New York

UNPD – United Nations Department of Economic and Social Affairs – Population Division, New York

USAID – United States Agency for International Development, Washington DC

WHO – World Health Organization, Geneva

WIC – Wittgenstein Centre for Demography and Global Human Capital, Vienna

INTRODUCTION

'You Start with the Numbers'

An unusual exchange between a businessman and an economist in Kenya highlights some of the reasons why demography matters in their country and throughout Africa. Elsewhere, people are less familiar with the continent's population dynamics. These will determine whether the global population peaks before the end of the twenty-first century – or continues to grow. Governments of the world's richest countries are more preoccupied by the prospect of their own populations ageing and declining.

'WANJIGI URGES KENYANS TO CHURN OUT MORE BABIES', ran *The Standard*'s headline one day in December 2018.[1] It was particularly eye-catching because of the identity of the speaker at what looks, in a YouTube recording of the event, to have been a church gathering. Jimi Wanjigi has been variously described in the Kenyan press as 'billionaire businessman', 'Kenya's most feared oligarch' 'kingmaker' and 'uber tenderpreneur'. He is a man who usually maintains a low profile.

Wanjigi is a compelling orator. The principal target in his 'sermon' was *wazungu* – white foreigners – who implore Kenyans 'not to make too many children', to 'get one or two each' only, because they 'don't have [enough] money, land and food'. His riposte to any suggestion that large families and rapid population growth might strain personal and state resources was forthright.

'That's fake. We have enough resources in this country to be greater numbers than we are.'[2]

The total fertility rate (TFR)* in Kenya has fallen from a world-leading level of about eight births in the late 1970s to less than four. Wanjigi need not worry too much: high fertility remains widespread in the country. Among the poorest quintile of Kenyans the TFR is still above five births, among mothers with no schooling it is above seven births, and in the country's North Eastern region women's ideal family size is more than nine children.[3] Leading demographers anticipate a likely population of close to 90 million by 2050, compared to 48 million enumerated in the country's 2019 census.[4] If that proves close to the mark, the number of Kenyans will have grown by a factor of 15 in the course of a century.

Kenya's men must do better still, Wanjigi urged. If they cannot produce more children with their wives, they must find someone else with whom to have them. Only then will Kenya 'have bargaining power like other populous countries'. Wanjigi cited China and India as examples of countries that are 'great because of numbers', and rued the fact that Kenya's population was dwarfed by that of Ethiopia, its neighbour to the north. 'You start with the numbers,' he emphasised.[5]

A few months before the Wanjigi address, the late President Magufuli of Tanzania told an audience during a tour of the Lake Zone 'not to listen to those advising about birth control, some of it coming from foreigners, because it has sinister motives'. His country is about the same size as Nigeria, but with a population only a quarter of the size. Tanzanians needed 'to keep reproducing', the president said, and anyone adopting family planning was 'lazy': it would leave them 'with two children only', simply because 'they do not want to work hard to feed a large family'. Magufuli explained that he had visited many countries outside Africa and seen 'the side effects of birth control. In

---

* Defined as the mean number of live births a woman would have during her reproductive lifetime (between the ages of 15 and 49) if she were subject throughout that period to the prevailing age-specific fertility rates.

some countries they are now struggling with declining population growth. They have no labour force.'[6]

At another public occasion Magufuli declared that 'women can now throw away their contraceptives' because 'education is now free'. They need not worry any longer about the burden of extra school fees on household expenditure. After the tour of the Lake Zone, on which he was accompanied by a presumably uneasy representative of the United Nations Population Fund (UNFPA), Magufuli banned family planning adverts on Tanzanian television and radio.[7] The president subsequently cajoled Tanzania's women to 'Set your ovaries free!'[8]

Pronatalism is embedded in most countries in Africa, especially in patriarchal societies and where religion encourages it. Suspicion about the motives of family planning organisations – invariably funded by foreign donors, as Wanjigi and Magufuli both alluded to – is widespread. It has deep historical roots. 'Population growth is a controversial topic because, in the not-too-distant past, some countries tried to control population growth with abusive, coercive policies, including forced sterilisation,' explains Professor Alex Ezeh, a Nigerian demographer and founding director of the African Population and Health Research Council in Nairobi.[9] Suspicion about motives is intertwined with antipathy to being 'told' what to do by foreigners, also alluded to by Wanjigi and Magufuli, or lectured about women's 'sexual and reproductive health and rights'.

While male politicians and family planning advocates seeking to improve the lives of women often seem to be talking past each other, the Wanjigi and Magufuli world view no longer goes unchallenged. In Kenya, a concrete manifestation of this is that almost two-thirds of married women use modern contraceptive methods, one of the highest usage rates in Africa. In Jimi Wanjigi's home region, Central Kenya, the rate is almost 75% and women there have fewer than three children on average. More prosaically, beneath the YouTube clip of Wanjigi's address, a well-known female Kenyan obstetrician and gynaecologist posted: 'I did not know such a rich man could be so daft.' A respected (male) Eastern Africa political scientist was even blunter about Magufuli's performances, tweeting that the Tanzanian president had 'taken traditional notions of women as children-production machines to an Orwellian level'.[10]

Objective discussion about population growth and the issues it raises is rare in African media. So the publication of a lengthy and considered response to Wanjigi's exhortations in a mass-circulation Kenyan daily was conspicuous. It would not have been published in Tanzania or many other countries across Africa. In his regular column for *The Nation*, Kwame Owino, director of the Nairobi-based Institute of Economic Affairs, observed that Wanjigi was 'not alone' in his 'straight-line thinking': it is common for people to equate bigger populations with bigger markets and 'national economic strength'. However, there is no evidence of 'direct links between population size and economic and political development per se', Owino informed his readers. At most, a large population is a necessary, but not sufficient, condition for power and influence on the global stage. It would be as wrong to claim that a 'failure to keep birth rates high would… condemn Kenya to lower economic development in comparison to other countries with higher fertility and populations' as it was to maintain that 'ramping up marriage and child bearing is a sure tool for the economic and political gains'.[11]

China and India, cited by Wanjigi in support of his argument that numbers confer greatness, are in fact good examples of Owino's corrective. In the second half of the twentieth century both countries were among the poorest in the world, and their influence in global affairs did not match their huge populations. In 1980, China's gross domestic product (GDP) per capita was lower than that of Chad or Malawi, two of the poorest countries in Africa (then and now). Furthermore, their increasing prominence on the world stage was primarily driven by rising national wealth, stellar in China's case from the 1980s onwards, underpinned by the possession of nuclear weapons. It cannot be attributed to population size. China has always had a substantial share of the global population, but eras of utter bleakness punctuate its history. Furthermore, there is also no correlation between population growth and economic growth: if anything, countries with very high rates of population growth have

tended to register lower rates of economic growth. Across Africa, high
fertility and rapid population growth correlates with the distribution
of extreme poverty (although the direction of causality is unclear,
that is to say it is uncertain whether high fertility causes poverty or
poverty causes high fertility).

China was a peculiar model for Wanjigi to have chosen for another
signally important reason. At the end of the 1970s, in arguably the
most notorious examples of the sort of 'controversy' referred to by
Professor Ezeh, the Chinese Communist Party (CCP) introduced its
one-child policy and other measures to try to curb rapid population
growth. 'The greatest obstacle to production and income per capita
growth is population growth,' declared demographer Wu Cangping
at the time.[12] This coincided almost exactly with the start of China's
economic 'miracle'. Furthermore, the country's TFR has fallen so far
that its population will plummet in the second half of the twenty-first
century if current trends persist. As the CCP now urgently seeks ways
to raise the national birth rate, it is confronted by the unwelcome
prospect of China going from being poor and young to becoming
'not rich, first old', or 'old before rich', as a saying goes – ageing before
its GDP per capita rises anywhere near as high as the world's rich
economies.[13]

Owino's riposte addressed more than Wanjigi's economics. The
realisation of Wanjigi's vision would 'simply condemn many more
families to pain and suffering'.[14] Maternal mortality – death within
six weeks of giving birth – has halved since 2000, but is still at a
similar level to Uganda, the neighbour to the west which Kenyans
expect to best in everything, and scarcely better than Ethiopia to
the north, categorised by the UN as one of the world's 46 'least
developed countries'.[15] The lifetime risk of a Kenyan women dying
while pregnant or in childbirth is one in 42, a toll not in keeping with
the country's lower-middle-income status and one described by the
World Bank as 'staggering'.[16]

As for their children, neonatal and infant mortality – a key
bellwether of living conditions in developing countries – are now a
quarter of what they were at independence in the 1960s, but about one

child in every 30 still dies before its first birthday and one in 20 before its fifth.[17] These, Owino explained, were average figures. In some of Kenya's 47 counties, one child in 10 dies before the age of five.[18] Better health correlates more closely with increasing national wealth than with population size.

Owino concluded by saying that it was 'irresponsible' of Wanjigi to 'cajole Kenyan mothers to go on an overdrive of conception, gestation and birth'. He 'should have been more circumspect [and] his audience less amused' by the call to 'ramp up child bearing'. To make 'Kenya's national priority an Olympics of births against neighbours and the world' would be to 'chase glory based on a fallacy'. Demographer Eliya Zulu, executive director and founder of the Nairobi-based African Institute for Development Policy, concurs: 'although leaders embrace big populations as symbols of political power, a source of global influence and a potential economic asset, it is increasingly apparent that development goals are better met through high-quality populations rather than big ones'.[19]

Government planners (and the 2012 Population Policy for National Development) have long recognised that the rate of past and projected population growth 'complicates'[20] the realisation of Vision 2030, Kenya's national development plan. It creates a need for substantial health and educational expenditure and other public goods just to maintain the existing level of service provision, while exacerbating land degradation and environmental damage. In 2010, the Minister of State for Planning estimated that with population growth still above 2.5% a year, Kenya's GDP would have to grow by an average of 12% a year to keep the budget on track to meet Vision 2030's targets.[21] At the halfway mark in 2020, economic growth had averaged 5–6% a year, and about 40% of government revenue is required to service Kenya's mounting debts.

There are other significant ramifications to population growth that attract little attention abroad. It is possible that Jimi Wanjigi did not have all Kenyans in mind. In countries where voting is substantially along ethnic or regional lines, the public is acutely aware of 'the numbers'. A few months before Wanjigi's address, an article in *The Standard* suggested that within two decades the Somali population was set to rise from its current sixth position to become one of Kenya's top four ethnic groups.[22] With a TFR above six births per woman and population growth above 3% a year, Kenya's ethnic Somalis are certainly outpacing Wanjigi's Kikuyu and others. While it is statistically unlikely that they will catch up with any of Kenya's 'big four' – the Kikuyu, Luhya, Kalenjin and Luo – the article served as a potent reminder that, in addition to its influence on human development, national finances and the environment, demography is political. Similarly, on the day that the preliminary results of the 2019 census were published, all Kenyan newspapers ran articles comparing the total population and other demographic data with the country's neighbours; as Tanzania's last headcount was held in 2012 it was possible, with a little sleight of hand, to portray Kenya as the most populous country in the region. Demography matters.

Outside Africa, scant public attention is paid to the continent's population trends. Headline growth and totals are periodically quoted in Western media, usually with adjectives like 'explosive' and 'startling' attached, but constraints of space or interest make presentation of detail rare. Coverage in Europe is mostly concerned with the thorny issue of migration. Even in the output of Africa specialists, demography is often absent when its inclusion might be expected. It is common to find no mention of local population trends in country or regional political analyses, even in connection with all-important elections; or to find no papers with demographic themes being presented at African studies conferences. Even the best social, anthropological and historical studies often omit reference to population dynamics. Much commentary from Western investment and consultancy firms uncritically and without differentiation labels 'Africa's demographics' as 'superb'.

In a sense, this is unsurprising. Most Western news coverage and commentary on Africa is reductionist and stylised, crisis-infused and bereft of nuance. Familiarity with the basic physical geography of the continent is not widespread, and knowledge of the rich history of pre-colonial Africa is almost non-existent. Africa remains substantially *terra incognita*, as much of the continent was labelled on ancient maps. It is even referred to frequently as if it were a single country, rather than a continent comprising 54 (or 55) sovereign states* – more than a quarter of the world's countries, which are home to one in six of the world's citizens. Standard 'flat' maps diminish Africa's true dimensions. At 30 million km², one-fifth of the world's land mass, the continent covers a greater area than China, India, the US and most of Europe combined (see Map 2). India, soon to overtake China as the world's most populous country, would almost fit into Northern Africa neighbours Libya and Chad. Africa's two largest countries, Algeria and the Democratic Republic of the Congo (DRC), are each more than four times the size of metropolitan France. The Congo Basin Forest, the second-largest tropical rainforest in the world after the Amazon, is a similar size to Mexico; and after the Arctic and Antarctica, the Sahara is the world's largest desert. Sheer scale is one of many good grounds for familiarity with Africa's geography, and the same can be said of its population dynamics.

Africa's demography has not always been so overlooked. For much of the second half of the twentieth century, media and public attention around the world was repeatedly engaged by talk of a global population 'explosion'. Between 1960 and 2010 the number of people in the world rose from 3 billion to 7 billion, the 'most rapid expansion in our 50,000-year history' according to Carl Haub, for many years the senior demographer at the Population Reference Bureau in Washington DC.[23] The chief catalyst was improvements in public health in the developing countries of the so-called 'Third World'. As the 'explosion' drama opened, Africa's population growth was not the prime focus of Western policymakers – the numbers involved in Asia were far greater, and Latin America was the US's backyard. But in time, Cold War politics and the persistence of rapid growth in Africa placed the continent centre-stage as well.

---

* The United Nations recognises 54 sovereign states. Nine of the states are small island territories. The African Union additionally recognises Western Sahara.

**Figure 2: World population and annual growth rate, 1950-2020
(estimates) and 2020-2100 (medium-variant projections and 95%
probability range)**

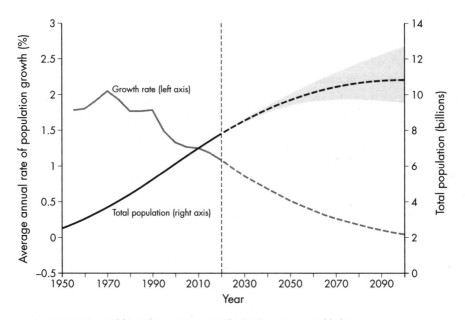

Source: UNPD, *World Population Prospects: The 2019 Revision - Highlights.*

Explosion fever waned in the 1990s. By then it was clear that global
population growth had peaked in the late 1960s, at just over 2%
annually, a rate at which a number doubles in about 35 years. Thereafter
it had eased steadily as increases in Asia moderated. With the end of
the Cold War as well, the global 'population question' was no longer
deemed a priority by Western governments and international finance
institutions like the World Bank. By 2020 the global growth rate was
half the level of its peak 50 years earlier. Other 'existential' crises
have taken the place of the population explosion. After 9/11 it was
the 'global war on terrorism'. To the fore nowadays – not for the first
time – is the environment: global warming, climate change (natural

and human-induced or -exacerbated), depletion of natural resources and the destruction of biodiversity. Global narratives fashioned in the West wax and wane.

With the exception of migration, any interest in population matters today among governments of industrialised and post-industrial countries is focused on the antithesis of an explosion. After more than eight decades of sustained population growth in almost every country of the world, across much of Europe, North America and East Asia ageing and shrinking populaces are the zeitgeist. The International Monetary Fund (IMF) has warned that the detrimental economic and social consequences will soon constitute a global crisis.[24] Think (according to some) declining consumption, demand for investment and government revenues; a diminishing pool of savings capital as growing numbers of elderly people seek to fund longer retirement; labour shortages (or surpluses); ballooning healthcare costs; abandoned towns and rural areas. Not all experts are convinced that the consequences will be so dire; nor was everyone convinced that the population explosion was a real phenomenon whose (equally) dire consequences could be predicted with certainty.

The preoccupation with population shrinkage in the West, Eastern Europe and East Asia does at least have firm foundations in current demographic trends. Almost half the population of the world now live in countries where the TFR is below 2.1 births. This is the 'replacement-level' fertility rate at which population growth will be zero if mortality – the death rate – is at developed-country levels.[25] It means that by mid-century, more than 50 countries worldwide are likely to have declining populations.[26] In most of them it is hard to envisage migration on a large enough scale to offset the declines, if desired. In China, for example, if the current TFR of 1.5 births were unchanged for the rest of the century, the population would fall from a peak of a little under 1.5 billion in 2030 to just above 500 million. The extent to which this projection proves merely theoretical will become evident by mid-century. It implies a contraction in population size even greater than that which is believed to have occurred in the thirteenth century, following the Mongol conquest of Jin-dynasty

China. This is a possibility, at the very least, so alarming that the CCP has started to address it vigorously. However, few countries have ever seen fertility bounce back to two births or higher after falling significantly below replacement level. Inducing Chinese families to have more children may not prove as straightforward for the CCP as ensuring they had fewer.

In many countries population decline is already well advanced, even precipitous. In Eastern Europe, Ukraine's current trajectory suggests that its population could halve this century, from 48 million to 24 million people. Bulgaria's headcount has fallen from 9 million to 7.2 million since the end of communist rule in 1989, and is projected to slide to 5.4 million by 2050. In Western Europe, Italy recorded the lowest number of births and highest number of emigrants ever in 2018. By mid-century, Europe's population will have declined from more than 20% of the global total in 1950 to about 7% – bit-part status in demographic terms.

In East Asia, Japan's population is shrinking by about one person every minute. The number of births has fallen well below a million a year to a level last seen at the end of the nineteenth century; it is now comparable to that of the UK, which has a population little more than half the size of Japan's. By 2050, what was a population of 128 million at the start of the twenty-first century is projected to be as low as 106 million. About 40% of Japanese citizens will be aged 65 or above. By the end of the century, South Korea's population is projected to drop from 51 million to 30 million, a level last seen in the early 1970s. Its TFR is now below one birth per woman, the lowest of any populous country in the world.

This narrative of population implosion is re-emergent, not new. Even in the modern era, the 'depopulation of civilised nations' – depopulation being defined as 'the cessation of increase of population' – was highlighted by Dr H.R. McKlveen in the *Journal of the Medical Association of America* in 1895. France's predicament at the time was considered particularly dire, the author noting that 'every method has been tried to increase the birth rate... but all in vain'.[27] In the 1930s, the last time that declining populations were a major concern in the West, John Maynard Keynes was to the fore, like the IMF today, in warning of the potentially deleterious consequences of this phenomenon for many of the economies of Northern Europe.

Table 1: Global population growth rate, TFR, births, deaths and net addition, 1950-2050

	1950-55	1970-75	1990-95	2010-15	2030-35	2050-55
Annual rate of growth p.a. (%)	1.8	2.0	1.5	1.2	0.8	0.5
Total fertility rate (births per woman)	5.0	4.5	3.0	2.5	2.3	2.2
Births (annual average, million)	98	122	134	140	140	140
Deaths (annual average, million)	51	47	50	55	72	95
Additional population (annual average, million)	47	76	83	85	68	44

Source: UNPD, *World Population Prospects: The 2019 Revision.*

Despite this resurgent scare for the world's richer countries, the global population tally keeps ticking upwards (see Table 1). Many who (with diverse motivations) vigorously denied the notion of a population explosion neglected to acknowledge – or failed to understand – that a slowing growth rate would not mean an almost instantaneous end to population growth. When the annual growth rate peaked in the late 1960s, the net addition to the world's population – births minus deaths – was about 73 million people. This continued to climb for another two decades, peaking at almost 90 million a year in the late 1980s. Although the annual growth rate had fallen to just 1% by 2020, more than 80 million people were still being added to the global tally every year, a number one-third higher than when the annual growth rate peaked and equivalent to adding the entire US population every four or five years. Talk of a 'baby bust' is also baffling:[28] the number of births worldwide remains at an all-time high of about 140 million every year. It has been at that level for more than a decade, and will still be thereabouts in mid-century. Only by excluding Africa and a great many developing countries from consideration – a somewhat partial view of global demography – does the term 'baby bust' have any resonance.

The mathematical alchemy that sustains population growth long after the growth rate has peaked is succinctly explained by John Weeks, Distinguished Professor Emeritus of Geography and director of the International Population Center at San Diego State University: 'We're building on an ever bigger base of people, so even a low rate of growth adds a lot of people.'[29] Furthermore, even if the TFR in a high-fertility country were hypothetically to drop overnight to replacement level, it is possible for its population to continue growing for several decades and to double in size if it has a sufficiently youthful age structure. Both these points are singularly pertinent to the demography of many African countries; and it is Africa, more than any other continent, which will determine whether the global population stabilises and starts to fall this century or continues to grow. This is the new 'population question'.

Stabilisation is a highly emotive issue. A century or more will have elapsed between the 1960s, the decade in which the rate of global population growth peaked, and the point at which authoritative sources of demographic projections and forecasts consider population increase most likely to cease. In that time the world's inhabitants will have more than doubled in number from just under 4 billion people, and possibly almost tripled if it reaches 10.9 billion, the 'medium variant' projection by United Nations demographers. In the face of this prospect, population 'optimists', determined to strangle any suggestion that the population explosion may not be over after all, or that a secondary explosion is now evident, continue to emphasise that the global growth rate peaked long ago and fertility will fall faster than leading demographers expect – so there is nothing to worry about. This is somewhat disingenuous given the scale of continuing growth, even if the concept of a population 'explosion' was controversial and the noun misleading. Environmental activists – usually portrayed as the main population doom-merchants – and others take a very different view.

The go-to source of population projections is the Population Division (UNPD)* within the United Nations Department of Economic and Social Affairs. Its *World Population Prospects* publication (see text box) is usually revised every two years and the headline figures are closely scrutinised, not only by demographers but also by the diverse interest groups seeking evidence to buttress narratives about population growth being a non-issue or an out-of-control threat to the future of the planet. The disputes and rancour over global projections underscore that demography is a highly politicised – and divisive – science. Non-demographers often overlook or suppress important details when deploying it; and even among the ranks of respected demographers there are some who have long offered or opined on global predictions seemingly without availing themselves of any of the expertise on population dynamics in Africa possessed by their Africa-focused peers within and outside the continent. As Africa is now a key determinant of the global trend this century, this must surely start to change.

In a great many African countries, the direction of demographic travel could not be more different from that of the ageing rich countries. While the rate of global population growth has slowed to 1% a year, the number of African citizens is growing at 2.5% a year. That rate will not fall below 2% until mid-century. How the Wanjigi/Owino 'debate' – overt or covert pronatalism versus human capital development – plays out country by country, district by district, will substantially determine the answer to the new population question: when – or if – the global population will stabilise in the second half of the century. It will also materially affect the lives of hundreds of millions of Africans.

---

* The acronym is also used for the United Nations Procurement Division. The context of this book should avert any confusion. The United Nations Population Division should not be confused with the United Nations Population Fund (UNFPA), formerly known as the United Nations Fund for Population Activities.

'Many of the world's biggest questions about fertility and economic growth now center around Africa, and we really don't know what the answers are going to be,' a Bloomberg columnist correctly observed in 2018. 'How exciting (if also a bit frightening)!'[30]

The numbers people

UNPD has been making global, regional and national population projections since the 1950s. Other reputable sources include the World Bank, the US Census Bureau, the Washington DC-based Population Reference Bureau and the International Institute for Applied Systems Analysis in Austria.

Fertility is the prime variable in modelling country projections, followed by mortality and then, usually of relatively minor significance, migration. In a projection further than 30 years out, the assumed trend in fertility will typically account for three to four times the degree of error of mortality assumptions. In other words, accurate population projections rest substantially on accurate assumptions about fertility trajectories based on as many relevant sources as possible.

Projections are not technically forecasts or predictions, although the terms are often used interchangeably. They set out the consequences of future fertility, mortality and migration based on a statistical extrapolation of past trends. There is often no indication of the likelihood of a projection proving correct. A forecast denotes the most likely outcome and usually involves expert (but necessarily subjective) assumptions about future trends. However, UNPD's medium-variant – or 'most likely' – population projections are often treated as forecasts. In recent years, it has also introduced probabilistic projections. UNPD's global population projections have proved vastly more reliable over two to three decades than most forms of forecasting, for example in comparison with economic forecasting.

UNPD's medium-variant projection for the global population in 2050 envisages an increase from 7.7 billion to 9.7 billion, with a

95% probability assigned to a range of 9.4-10.1 billion. This level of certainty is underwritten by the fact that mid-century is only one generation away. More than half of the world's 2050 population has already been born, and changes in reproductive behaviour and mortality tend to be quite gradual. As a recent UNPD note stated, '[t]he size of the world's population over the near future is relatively certain'.* For most countries, fertility and mortality can also be projected with reasonable accuracy over two to three decades, although the trajectory of fertility in high-fertility countries is notoriously difficult to anticipate.

The margin of uncertainty in projections to 2100 is far greater. They involve assigning numbers based on historical data to the reproductive choices and behaviour of unborn generations. UNPD's current medium-variant projection for 2100 stands at 10.9 billion, with a 95% probability of the outcome being between 9.4 and 12.7 billion people and an 80% probability of it being in the range 9.9-12 billion. The likelihood of the global population stabilising before 2100 is estimated by UNPD to be 27%.

In an interview with *National Geographic*, John Wilmoth, director of UNPD, captured the level of uncertainty regarding the end of the century by saying that 10.9 billion 'may still be off by two billion'.†

Population projections have always been controversial, and contested on empirical and ideological grounds.

* UNPD (2019e), *How Certain Are the United Nations Global Population Projections?*, Population Facts No. 2019/6, p. 3.   † John Wilmoth quoted in Robert Kunzig, 'A world with 11 billion people? New population projections shatter earlier estimates', *National Geographic*, 19 September 2014.

1

'Think Africa!'

Africa is said to be 'in the midst of the greatest demographic upheaval in human history'.[1] Its population growth since 1950 is certainly unprecedented in the modern era.[2] Moreover, in Eastern, Western and Middle Africa the rate of growth in 1980–2015 surpassed that of 1950–80.

'This is Africa's century,' South Africa's president, Cyril Ramaphosa, declared in September 2019. 'The future is great, it looks very bright for the African continent, and if ever there was a time when Africa can definitely be said to be on the rise, this is the time.'[3] There is stiff competition to his claim from the East: in 2020, for the first time since the nineteenth century, the economies of Asia were larger than those of the rest of the world combined.[4] However, if Ramaphosa was referring to Africa's population expansion, his assertion is incontestable. The numbers are remarkable. This alone will be sufficient to guarantee the continent's increased prominence on the world stage.

In the second half of the twentieth century the population of Asia, the world's most populous continent, seldom grew by more than 2% a year. India's growth never exceeded 2.25% a year. Africa's was rarely below 2.5%. The consequences of seemingly small annual differentials are magnified over decades. During Europe's great expansion in the nineteenth century the population merely doubled.[5] In India's rapid phase of growth, between 1920 and 2020, its population increased by just over five times. Between 1950 and

2050, Africa's population will have expanded by a factor of 10. That of North America also multiplied tenfold in the nineteenth and early twentieth centuries, but in-migration from Europe was the significant driver. Africa's growth is almost entirely the product of natural increase, the surplus of births over deaths.

Table 2: World population by region, 1950–2050

	1950 population (million, estimated)	2000 population (million, estimated)	2050 population (million, medium-variant projection)	Growth factor, 1950–2050
World	**2,536**	**6,143**	**9,735**	**3.8x**
Asia	1,405	3,741	5,290	3.8x
Africa	228	811	2,489	10.9x
North America	173	312	425	2.4x
Latin America/ Caribbean	169	522	762	4.4x
Europe	549	726	710	1.3x
Oceania	13	31	57	4.4x

Source: UNPD, *World Population Prospects: The 2019 Revision.*

Africa's rate of growth is rapidly driving its global share higher. A 'great rotation' is well under way. In 1980, one in 10 people in the world were African. In the space of 40 years, as the continent's population nearly tripled from less than 500 million to an estimated 1.3 billion, that share rose to about one in six. Over the next 30 years, the populations of more than half of the continent's 54 countries are set to double or more, according to UNPD. This will give Africa 2.5 billion inhabitants by 2050 – equivalent to the population of the world in 1950. At that point it will account for more than a quarter of the global total.

For more than a decade it has been clear that Africa is now the main engine of continuing global growth. More specifically, sub-Saharan countries will add the most people – about 1.1 billion by

2050, compared to 200 million in Northern Africa.* The combined total – 1.3 billion – will account for two-thirds of the 2 billion increase projected for the world by mid-century. Nine African countries are on course to have at least 15 times the number of citizens in 2050 than in 1950. Among them, Côte d'Ivoire will have expanded by a factor of 20 and Niger by a stupendous 25 times (see Table 3).

Figure 3: Contributions of demographic components to population growth of world regions, 2010–50

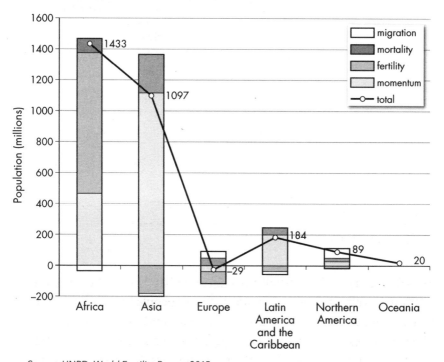

Source: UNPD, *World Fertility Report 2015*.

By the end of the century, UNPD's medium-variant projection is for Africa to account for 40% of the world's 10.9 billion people. If this scenario is realised, the continent will have contributed 3 billion of a 3.2

---

* UNPD's Africa regional designations are used throughout the book – Northern, Western, Middle, Eastern and Southern. The constituents of each region are listed in the 'Selected population data' in the front matter.

billion increase in the global population between 2020 and 2100. Africa is sometimes portrayed as being on the brink of a population explosion. In fact, it is experiencing a mega-surge that has been under way for more than half a century and will last for another 50 years or more.

Table 3: Nine African countries are projected to have populations in 2050 that are 15 times larger (or more) than in 1950

Country	Africa region	Estimated pop 1950 (million)	Estimated pop 2020 (million)	UNPD medium-variant projection – 2050	Growth factor 1950–2050
Niger	Western	2.6	24.2	65.6	25x
Côte d'Ivoire	Western	2.6	26.4	51.3	20x
Uganda	Eastern	5.2	45.7	89.4	17x
Angola	Middle	4.5	32.9	77.4	17x
Tanzania	Eastern	7.7	59.7	129.4	17x
Zambia	Eastern	2.3	18.4	39.1	17x
DRC	Middle	12.2	89.6	194.5	16x
Somalia	Eastern	2.3	15.9	34.9	15x
Kenya	Eastern	6	53.8	91.6	15x
Comparators					
World		2,500	7,794	9,735	4x
Africa		228	1,341	2,489	11x
Sub-Saharan Africa		179	1,094	2,117	12x
Thailand		20.7	69.8	65.9	3x
India		376	1,380	1,639	4x
Mexico		27.9	128.9	155.2	6x

Source: UNPD, *World Population Prospects: The 2019 Revision.*

Today, there are only eight countries in the world whose populations are growing by 3% a year or more, a rate which implies doubling every 24 years. All are in Africa.[6] Eleven countries worldwide have a

Figure 4: Africa – percentage population increase by country, 2015–50 (UNPD medium-variant projections)

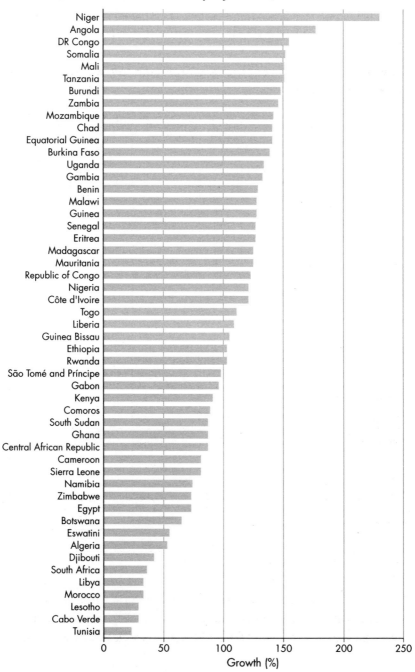

Source: UNPD, *World Population Prospects: The 2019 Revision.*

TFR of five births or more. All are in Africa,[7] with Niger registering the highest fertility rate in the world: on average, Nigérienne women have more than seven children. In most sub-Saharan countries childbearing begins at a young age and continues for decades. Nearly half of births worldwide to women and girls aged 15–19 occur in the region; the proportion of all births to women in their forties is also the highest in the world.

Table 4: African countries among the top 20 contributors to global population growth by 2050

Country	2019 pop estimate (million)	2050 medium-variant projection (million)	Additional population 2019–50 (million)	Ranking in global growth tables, numbers added 2019-50*
Nigeria	201	401	200	2
DRC	67	194	127	4
Ethiopia	112	205	93	5
Tanzania	58	129	71	6
Egypt	100	160	60	8
Angola	31	77	46	10
Uganda	44	89	45	11
Niger	23	67	44	12
Kenya	52	91	39	13
Sudan	42	81	39	14
Mozambique	30	65	35	16
Madagascar	26	54	28	20
Total	786	1613	827	

*The eight non-African countries in the top 20 are India (1), Pakistan (3), Indonesia (7), USA (9), Philippines (15), Iraq (17), Bangladesh (18) and Mexico (19). *Source:* UNPD, *World Population Prospects: The 2019 Revision - Highlights*, p. 13.

Of the 20 countries projected to add the most people by 2050, 12 are in Africa (see Table 4) Nigeria is currently the only African country to rank among the world's 10 most populous, and is the fastest-growing in that group. By 2050, as Nigerians pass the 400 million mark, their country will have overtaken the US (projected to be 379 million) to sit behind India (1.6 billion) and China (1.4 billion) as the third most populous country in the world. Ethiopia (205 million) and DRC (194 million) will also have entered the global top 10 by mid-century. Five countries in Eastern Africa alone – Kenya, Uganda, Tanzania, Mozambique and Ethiopia – will have larger populations than Russia, currently the ninth most populous country in the world. By mid-century, Eastern Africa's population, like that of Western Africa, will have soared past those of Latin America and Europe.

By 2100, based on current trajectories, five of the 10 most populous countries globally would be African. Today, these five – Nigeria, DRC, Ethiopia, Tanzania and Egypt – have a combined population of 538 million. By the end of the century that would have almost quadrupled to 1.9 billion. Whether or not these projections prove accurate, it is already clear that in terms of global demography in the twenty-first century 'the big story will be Africa'.[8]

The most striking consequence of rapid and sustained growth is the 'chronic youthfulness',[9] as one leading demographer has termed it, of the populations of almost all of Africa's countries (see text box). The median age is a little below 20 years old, about 10 years less than in Latin America and Asia and more than 20 years less than in Europe and China. This is sometimes referred to as if it were quite a new development. In fact, the median age has been below 20 for the past 70 years. Similarly, the proportion of Africans under the age of 25 is much the same as it was in 1980, at about 60%. In six countries – Uganda and Somalia in Eastern Africa, Angola and Chad in Middle Africa, and Mali and Niger in Western Africa – the median age has hardly risen in 30 years and remains less than 17 years. In Niger it is

Africa: the (very) young continent

- By 2050 about 40% of all children born worldwide each year will be African.

- One-third of African countries have an under-18 majority in their population.

- The number of under-18s in Africa will exceed 1 billion by mid-century – about 40% of all under-18s in the world. By 2100 half the world's under-18s will be African.

- By 2050 one-third of the world's 'youth', the designation given to young men and women aged 15–24, will be African.

- More than 1.5 billion babies will be born in Africa between 2020 and 2050.

- Almost half of the 62 million births worldwide to adolescent mothers aged 15–19 are in sub-Saharan Africa. 'Children having children continues to be a sad reality in Africa,' states the United Nations Economic Commission for Africa.

- In the mid-2010s, almost one in five women in Western Africa aged 20–24 were married by the age of 15. In Eastern, Western and Middle Africa more than 40% of women aged 20–24 were married by the age of 18 (and 11%, 17% and 12% respectively by the age of 15). In Northern and Southern Africa less than 20% and about 5% of women aged 20–24 respectively were married by the age of 18.

- More than 50% of children in sub-Saharan countries live in extreme poverty, subsisting on the equivalent of an income of US$1.90 a day.

- The number of primary-school children in African countries will expand by one-third to about 250 million between 2015 and 2030. There will be about the same number of African primary-school children as the combined populations of Germany, France, the UK and Spain.

- By 2050, the number of young people in sub-Saharan countries below the age of 24 will exceed 1.1 billion, the total population of the region today.

Sources: UNPD, *World Population Prospects: The 2019 Revision - Data Booklet;* UNECA, *The Demographic Profile of African Countries* (2016); UNICEF, *Generation 2030 Africa* (2014), and *Generation Africa 2.0* (2017).

close to 15. There and in Eswatini (formerly Swaziland) the median age has even dipped below 15, in 2015 and the mid-1980s respectively – a very rare occurrence anywhere in the world in the modern era. A 'youthquake' is perhaps a more apt analogy for what is occurring than an 'explosion'.

Since the 1960s, children under the age of 15 have accounted for at least 40% of all Africans. Today, their number is equivalent to the total population of the continent 40 years ago and they are more numerous than the *combined* populations of the US and Mexico. In high-fertility, high-growth individual countries and the Middle Africa region children make up as much as 45% of the population. Nigeria exemplifies this age structure. Almost two-thirds of Nigerians are under the age of 25 and about 45% are under 15. In the next-youngest continent – Asia – less than a quarter of the population are children, while in Europe children constitute only about 15% of the population and are now outnumbered by the elderly.

In 2050, all but two of the world's 40 youngest countries will be African.[10] The number of births across the continent has reached 44 million a year and the figure will exceed 50 million by 2050. Meanwhile, the annual number of deaths has remained between 10 and 11 million since the mid-1990s. This is only about 60% higher than in the early 1950s, while the population has grown sixfold. Even after taking into account increased life expectancy, 'death control', as it is sometimes referred to, has been truly remarkable in Africa. Children will still comprise one-third of the total population in mid-century: in the Eastern, Western and Middle regions more than half of the population will still be under the age of 25. By the end of the century the continent's children and youth alone will be twice as numerous as the total population of Europe and will constitute about half of all under-25s globally.[11]

At the other end of the age scale, less than 4% of Africans are over the age of 65, compared to 9% in Asia and nearly 20% in Europe. As recently as 1980, there were only 15 million over-65s in the entire continent. Today Germany alone has a similar number. In sub-Saharan countries the number of over-65s will triple in the next 30 years but will still not exceed 100 million, comprising less than 5% of the region's total population and less than 7% of the global total of over-65s.

'Youth' is a specific age category defined by the International Labour Organization (ILO), UNPD and many other international bodies as between the ages of 15 and 24 (inclusive). These years generally mark the transition from childhood to adulthood. It is the age group in which young men and women commonly finish schooling and either move on to further education or start work. In most African countries about 20% of the population is in this important and challenging stage of life, a high proportion relative to other parts of the world and one that is likely to remain largely unchanged over the next three decades. However, for many in Africa, early cessation of schooling, early marriage, unattainability of higher education and other factors confound stereotypical life courses.

'Working age' is defined as 25–64. Again, this can be anomalous when applied to Africa: all but a tiny minority of young men and women need to work before the age of 25. Furthermore, the upper age bracket exceeds the continent's average life expectancy at birth. If the size of youth cohorts in Africa is compared to that of working-age populations, some astonishing 'bulges' become apparent. Among the countries with populations of more than 10 million, there are a dozen* where the youth population (spanning a decade) is more than 60% of the entire working-age population (spanning four decades). In Uganda, Chad and Niger the figure is almost 70%. If this were represented in a café in which there are 17 people, seven of them would be aged between 15 and 24, and 10 of them between 25 and 64. This is not true of all African regions: youth populations in Northern Africa are typically less than 40% of the size of working-age populations.

---

* Burundi, Ethiopia, Malawi, Mozambique, Uganda, Zambia, Angola, Chad, DRC, Burkina Faso, Mali, Niger.

Figure 5: Percentage of population by age group for the world and by region, 2017

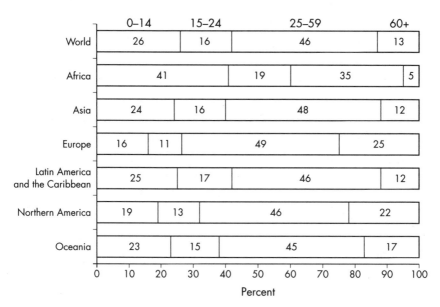

	0–14	15–24	25–59	60+
World	26	16	46	13
Africa	41	19	35	5
Asia	24	16	48	12
Europe	16	11	49	25
Latin America and the Caribbean	25	17	46	12
Northern America	19	13	46	22
Oceania	23	15	45	17

Percent

Source: UNPD, *World Population Prospects: The 2017 Revision.*

The African Union's (different) definition of youth is anomalous, spanning the ages of 15–34. There have been national leaders around the world who would fall into this category, and many of the revered African figures of the independence and post-independence eras – Patrice Lumumba, Amilcar Cabral, Thomas Sankara – would by this definition have been 'youths' when at their zenith. Using this wider bracket, youth constitutes about one-third of Africa's 705 million-strong working-age population, and the number is set to increase by 30% by 2030.[12] Whichever age range is used for youth, in every country on the continent its magnitude is not to be overlooked.

The youthfulness (see text box on page 24) of African populations confers a huge burden of dependency (see overleaf). Over the past three decades the working-age population has comprised about a third of the total in sub-Saharan regions of the continent.[13] In theory, this means that one-third have to support the other two-thirds, the

Dependency

International organisations calculate dependency ratios in different ways.

In *World Population Ageing* reports, UNPD defines the working-age population as everyone aged 20-64. In the biennial revisions of *World Population Prospects* a 25-64 age bracket is used. The AfDB and the World Bank use 15-64 to calculate dependency ratios in Africa. Even by this measure, Africa's dependency ratio is higher than that of Latin America and Asia in 1990 - and it will still be so in 2050, despite having improved from about 85 dependants to every 100 people of working age to 60 dependants to every 100 people of working age.

None of these can give more than a rough impression of dependency, and there is considerable variation between countries. Most young men and women in Africa are considered 'working-age' well before they reach their early twenties; many children work, even while also attending school. Furthermore, 'dependants' often include relations and others who are neither children, youth nor aged. Individual incomes and needs vary through lifetimes.

The National Transfer Accounts Project based at the East-West Center and the Center on the Economics and Demography of Aging at the University of California, Berkeley, devised a means to quantify dependency more precisely. The methodology has been adopted in a number of African countries. It calculates economic support ratios - the ratio of producers (workers) to consumers (those with needs) in all age groups - as opposed to basic dependency ratios. In theory, decline in the economic support ratio frees up funds and other resources which can be invested or spent, thereby fostering development and boosting economic growth. Like the basic dependency ratio, albeit more indicative of economic reality, economic support ratios are declining, but not as fast as in Asian countries where fertility declined rapidly at the end of the twentieth and beginning of the twenty-first century.

Sources: AfDB, *Creating Decent Jobs: Strategies, Policies, and Instruments, 2019*, p. 238; National Transfer Accounts Project www.ntaccounts.org; UNPD, *World Population Ageing 2015*, pp. 34-7.

very young and the old. Although peak dependency in Africa as a whole occurred in the 1980s, and in some sub-Saharan countries the dependency ratio is improving quite fast, in many high-fertility countries the ratio of the working-age population to dependents has continued to worsen.[14] By 2050 the working-age population of the region will still be well below half of the total – and it may not exceed half the century (see Table 5).[15] In East and Southeast Asia today, about 55% of the population is working-age.

Table 5: Dependency in selected countries with annual population growth exceeding 2.5%, 2020–50

Country*	Pop. aged 0–14 years, 2020 (%)	Median age, 2020 (years)	Total child + old-age dep. ratio, 2020 (%)*	Pop. aged 0–14 years, 2050 (%)	Median age, 2050 (years)	Total child + old-age dep. ratio, 2050 (%)**
Niger	50	15.2	110	41	19.0	78
Uganda	47	16.7	92	31	24.8	55
Angola	46	16.7	95	38	20.7	71
DRC	46	17.0	95	36	22.1	66
Burundi	43	17.3	91	36	22.7	64
Tanzania	44	18.0	86	36	22.3	67
Mali	47	16.3	98	32	21.5	67
Burkina Faso	46	17.6	88	35	22.7	64
Chad	47	16.6	96	36	22.0	65
Mozambique	45	17.6	88	35	22.9	62
Zambia	44	17.6	86	35	22.8	64
Nigeria	44	18.1	86	35	22.4	65
Average	46	17.1	86	3.1	22.2	66
Comparators						
World	26	30.9	53	21	36.2	59
Africa	41	19.7	78	32	24.8	61
Sub-Saharan Africa	42	18.7	82	33	23.9	61
Northern Africa	33	25.5	63	25	31.1	58

*Countries are listed in descending order of average annual population growth rate, 2015–20.
**Children 0–14 years + adults 65+ years/population 15–64 years. A total dependency ratio of 100% indicates that every working-age adult has one dependant. The global average in 2020 was about two working-age adults to every dependant (53%). *Source:* UNPD Data Download Centre.

The statistics recording Africa's population growth and the continent's 'chronic youthfulness' are by any measure extraordinary – and their durability is starting to cause increasingly widespread alarm in the West. 'Africa's population – can it survive such speedy growth?' asked *The Economist* in 2014.[16] Four years later, the Bill & Melinda Gates Foundation added an influential voice to the chorus of concern with the publication of its 2018 *Goalkeepers* report. A tweet by the Vox news site announcing Bill Gates's appearance on *The Ezra Klein Show* said he had been invited to explain 'one of the biggest problems the world is facing: rapid population growth in Africa… and what it will take to turn it around'.[17] Shortly afterwards, *The Economist* announced that 'demography is one of the biggest reasons for gloom… The most helpful development would be an unexpected decline in birth rates in sub-Saharan Africa.'[18]

Sceptics of the alarmism of the 'first' population explosion in the second half of the twentieth century will have none of it. According to this camp, Africa's population growth will ease sooner and faster than anticipated by UNPD projections. The principal logic used by its proponents to buttress such a claim is that fertility in Africa will 'inevitably' fall as fast and as far as it did in other developing regions from the 1960s onwards; the continent has simply embarked on this path a few decades later than others. Meanwhile, UNPD is accused of always overestimating for 'political reasons'. Global population growth will level off and then start to decline sooner than UNPD and other experts anticipate. These are bold claims, as we will see, often made for ideological reasons by commentators with little knowledge of the specifics of demography in Africa, or who have become famous for combating 'negativity bias'. Measurements of poverty, conflict, life expectancy, education, health services – you name it – have all improved in Africa over the past three decades, and the inference is that this will 'inevitably' continue. 'The data' supposedly supports this contention and forecloses debate on the issue. Aggregate global data will of course be increasingly influenced by the development indicators for Africa and its constituent countries. This may not have quite the impact that standard-bearers of perpetual progress would want.

Figure 6: Total dependency ratio for the world and regions, 1950-2050

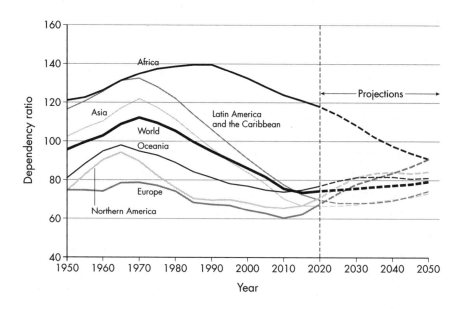

Source: UNPD, *World Population Prospects: The 2015 Revision.*

The cornucopian – or Panglossian – take on population growth and Africa's future is popular in Africa and among those whose job it is to promote a confident outlook. 'Think of a continent that will have the same population as India and China taken together by 2050,' urges Akinwumi Adesina, president of the African Development Bank (AfDB). 'Think of a continent with a rising middle class, rapid urbanisation and that will have the youngest population on earth by 2050... Think Africa!'[19] At the 2018 Africa Investment Forum held in Johannesburg, the continent's 'growing demographic' was presented as its prime attraction to investors. The authors of a book launched at the event, titled *Africa's Business Revolution,* cited the fact that 'Africa's population is young, fast-growing and urbanising' as number one of their positive 'Big Five Trends'.[20] Some forecast a colossal 'demographic dividend' resulting from Africa's youthful age structure, amounting to hundreds of billions of dollars a year – of which more later.

The widespread belief in Jimi Wanjigi's demographic determinism – his assertion that burgeoning, youthful populations equal economic growth and increasing wealth – is puzzling. None of Africa's five richest countries measured by GDP per capita – Equatorial Guinea, Seychelles, Mauritius, Gabon and Botswana[21] – has a population above 2.5 million, while in the continent's most populous country and biggest economy, Nigeria, about half the population lives in extreme poverty – one of the highest rates in Africa. With so much else that is contentious about demography in Africa, and becoming more so, analysis of the *detail* is essential. As the American sociologist, historian and political demographer Jack Goldstone says, 'no general statement about African demography is true'.[22]

In addition to scrutinising generalisations, received wisdom and wishful thinking, it is important to know the history of these narratives; whether the figures for the future presented by demographic institutions are likely to prove correct; and what appears to be happening to population trends across Africa *right now*. Only then is it possible to attempt some informed speculation about how population dynamics over the next two to three decades might interact with other trends – social, political, economic, environmental – in Africa's countries. This will determine the future of the continent, region by region, and will impact on global affairs; but the outcomes of this interaction cannot be known with the degree of certainty some would claim possible.

2

Museveni's 'Miracle': An African Perspective

A speech by a prominent African president in 2018 provides a different perspective to Western narratives about population growth in Africa. In the 1970s, population matters were politicised as the concept of a global population 'explosion' took hold.

President Museveni of Uganda opened his annual Address on National State of Affairs in 2018 by declaring that the country's population had grown from 'about 14 million' in 1986 to 40 million. Annual growth had averaged 2.5% between 1969 and 1986, the year his thirty-plus-year reign commenced, but it had now reached a new peak above 3.5%. For Museveni this was a 'miracle', the result of 'security of life and property and better healthcare' provided by the National Resistance Movement (NRM) government. 'Uganda is beginning to gallop,' the president declared. The population 'will be 102 million by 2050'.[1]

The forecast is easily justified. Uganda has one of the lowest median ages in the world – just short of 17 years. Three-quarters of Ugandans are below the age of 30, more than half are below 18, and children of primary-school age – between the ages of six and 12 – make up 20% of the population.[2] Recalling Professor John Weeks's remark about population momentum, this is some 'base' on which to build. According to economist Ramathan Ggoobi at Uganda's Makerere University Business School: 'Ugandans are still producing children using calculus – "let me produce six; three might die and I remain with the three". Yet children no longer die the way they used to; hence all the six survive and exert a huge dependency burden on the parents.'[3]

On average Ugandan women have five children. Only 25% of those who already have three want no more, and the proportion of young women aged 15–19 who are pregnant or have given birth shows no sign of decline.[4] Meanwhile, as Ggoobi says, infant and child mortality rates have plummeted since the early 1990s and maternal care has improved significantly. So far the rate of growth shows no sign of flagging: in the last two intercensal periods – 1991–2002 and 2002–14 – the population grew by about 45% in just over a decade.[5]

For Museveni, this is a triumph of 'development'. In the 1980s Uganda was a country ravaged by war and the depredations of his predecessors Idi Amin and Milton Obote. GDP per capita* had halved since the early 1970s. Soon afterwards it fell victim to the HIV/AIDS epidemic as acutely as any country in the world. By 1994 life expectancy was the lowest globally, at 37 years. The US Census Bureau estimated at the time that it would fall to just 31 years by 2010, and the population would diminish by almost one-third.[6] For a leader with a keen sense of history and a long memory, Uganda's demography is also a triumph over Western doom-mongers.

By coincidence, 2018 – the year of this national address of Museveni's – was the fiftieth anniversary of the publication of *The Population Bomb: Population Control or Race to Oblivion*. This book was to have an immense impact around the world and marked the real beginning of the population explosion era. Throughout the so-called 'Third World', nowadays referred to as the developing world, intense and sustained pressure to curb population growth was brought to

---

* According to the World Bank, GDP per capita 'does not completely summarize a country's level of development or measure welfare' but it 'has proved to be a useful and easily available indicator that is closely correlated with other, non-monetary measures of life, such as life expectancy at birth, mortality rates of children, and enrolment rates in school'. Its limitations include insufficient measurement of informal economic output and inequality.

bear by Western governments and institutions. In Africa, this has not been forgotten by Museveni's generation.

The Population Bomb was the work of Stanford University evolutionary biologist Paul Ehrlich.* Its initial reception was muted, but it soon became a blockbuster selling many millions of copies and making Ehrlich a media superstar. The book has been cited as one of the most influential of the twentieth century. The central thesis was that the planet was so overpopulated, and overconsumption so extreme, that it was only a matter of time before it was engulfed by mass starvation and environmental collapse. The bleak, notorious opening sentences of the prologue give a flavour:

> The battle to feed humanity is over. In the 1970s hundreds of millions of people will starve to death in spite of any crash programs embarked upon now. At this late date nothing can prevent a substantial increase in the world death rate, although many lives could be saved through dramatic programs to 'stretch' the carrying capacity of the earth by increasing food production and providing for more equitable distribution of whatever food is available.

The youthfulness of the world's population was the seed of its destruction, in Ehrlich's view. 'One of the most ominous facts of the current situation is that over 40% of the population of the underdeveloped world is made up of people *under 15 years old*,' he wrote. 'They are the gunpowder for the population explosion.'[7] No country would be spared. In a speech to the British Institute for Biology three years after publication, Ehrlich said that 'by the year 2000 the United Kingdom will be simply a small group of impoverished islands, inhabited by some 70 million hungry people'. 'If I were a gambler,' he added, 'I would take even money that England will not exist in the year 2000.'

In the 1960s, the threat – or occurrence – of famine was frequently

---

* Although co-authored by Anne Ehrlich, authorship was credited to her husband alone.

in the news. Tens of millions are estimated to have died in China at the start of the decade. In 1966 the US shipped a quarter of its wheat harvest to India to stave off starvation. During Nigeria's three-year civil war – the Biafran War – ghastly images of malnourished children in the breakaway republic were transmitted around the world; and in 1968, the first of a series of droughts hit Africa's arid and semi-arid Sahel* region, more than 2.5 million km^2 stretching from the Atlantic to the Red Sea roughly between the latitudes of 10°N and 20°N. Demographers John Caldwell and Chuchuke Okonjo warned in *The Population of Tropical Africa* – published in the same year as *The Population Bomb* – that annual population growth rates of 3% or more were 'hardly rates of growth with which weak economies, yielding many of the world's lowest per capita incomes, can easily cope; and certainly not rates which would allow incomes to be raised quickly enough to secure reasonable living standards in the foreseeable future'.[8] Simultaneously, the global population passed the 3 billion mark, almost double its level at the start of the twentieth century.

This milestone was the cause of immense consternation in the West. Furthermore, *The Food Problem of Developing Countries*, published by the Organisation for Economic Co-operation and Development (OECD) in 1967, projected a global population of an unthinkable 11 billion by 2050.[9] In November 1967, the US Senate Subcommittee on National Security and International Operations, whose members included a 43-year-old future president, George H. W. Bush, commenced an inquiry into the global 'population crisis'. It was told, among other things, that President Lyndon Johnson had spoken on the topic no fewer than 41 times in the previous two years. In 1969 his successor, Richard Nixon, warned Congress that the pressure of 200 million people was putting democracy in jeopardy in America. Stabilising numbers at home and abroad became policy: by the mid-1960s, the US began to fund family planning programmes. This, then, was the backdrop to the launch of *The Population Bomb*

---

* Derived from the Arabic word for shore, or coast, and referring to the southern reaches of the Sahara.

and the start of many years of extreme pressure on African leaders and newly independent governments to curb population growth.

Ehrlich was convinced that global food production was bound to fall 'catastrophically behind population growth'. He welcomed the advances in agricultural technology and practices being hailed as the 'Green Revolution' – the introduction of improved and high-yield seed varieties, and extensive use of irrigation and fertiliser in Mexico, India and elsewhere in the southern hemisphere – but did not consider that these would be sufficient to provide a lasting panacea to ubiquitous undernourishment.[10] Norman Borlaug, the American agronomist credited with being the principal architect of the Green Revolution, appeared to agree. In his Nobel Prize acceptance speech in 1970 Borlaug warned that higher yields had merely 'given Man a breathing space', perhaps for three decades. 'But', he added, 'the frightening power of human reproduction must also be curbed, otherwise the success of the Green Revolution will be ephemeral only. Most people still fail to comprehend the magnitude and menace of the "Population Monster".'[11] Borlaug's biographical entry on the Nobel website reads: 'Borlaug is a warm adherent of birth control. The object is to strike a balance between population growth and food production.'[12]

There was no mistaking Ehrlich's message. He used phrases like 'the cancer of population growth… must be cut out' and 'we will breed ourselves into oblivion'. Furthermore, he suggested that the food aid being sent in what seemed like ever-rising quantities from the West to the 'Third World' should be tied to population-control measures. This was a solution also advocated by William and Paul Paddock's book *Famine 1975!*, published a year before *The Population Bomb* with the chilling subtitle *America's Decision: Who Will Survive?*

'Controversial' and 'polarising' do not do full justice to how *The Population Bomb* was perceived. It was one of those books on which everyone had an opinion even if they had not read it. Marxists, for whom the term 'Malthusian' is an unbridled insult, regarded Ehrlich as being as unconscionably 'anti-poor' and as ahistorical as the reverend himself (see text box). The Stanford professor was portrayed

'The original population scaremonger'*

The essence of *The Population Bomb* – that the world had finite natural resources and human 'carrying capacity' – was not a new contention. In many respects, the book seemed to echo – or amplify – the assertions of the Reverend Thomas Malthus more than a century earlier. In *An Essay on the Principle of Population*, published in 1798, Malthus proposed the theory that population growth, if unchecked, is geometric whereas food production increases arithmetically. More intensive use of more land can bridge the gap only for so long before poverty and misery escalate and population is checked by rising mortality. This can occur through the 'positive checks' of 'vice and misery' – including high infant and child mortality, and the consequences of poverty, disease and war – or through 'moral restraint' in the shape of delayed marriage or chastity.

According to Malthus, the poor and 'lower classes' were destined to bear the brunt of the exactions of 'natural law' when population exceeded the resources needed to sustain it. He regarded intervening to assist them as pointless and ineffective. At best, intervention merely delayed the inevitable.

Ehrlich popularised Malthus, whose name was really only familiar to demographers and geographers. He was also influenced by the more recent work of the ecologist and ornithologist William Vogt, director of the Planned Parenthood Federation of America in the 1950s. In the immediate post-war years Vogt declared that the world was 'full' and warned of an imminent civilisational crash due to overpopulation and environmental devastation. In his hair-raising and deeply depressing book *Road to Survival*, published in 1948, Vogt envisaged this crash wiping out three-quarters of the human race.

Vogt died in 1968, the year *The Population Bomb* was published.

* Brendan O'Neill, 'Burying Malthus to save Malthusianism', *spiked*, March 2010.

as the voice of the ruling classes devising new means to exploit the world's dispossessed and preserve the status quo. Others cast him as a publicity-seeking sensationalist and misanthrope, or criticised him for straying (and extrapolating) too far from biology, for having no grasp of economics, for attributing the depredations of capitalist social institutions on the poor to 'natural' factors, and for being racist. Ehrlich even received death threats.[13]

The Population Bomb was also extremely popular. Given that eminent demographers of the time like Kingsley Davis spoke of the 'population plague', Ehrlich's call for population control hardly marked him as a lone wolf. Fictional books about overpopulation, its looming consequences and the measures that would have to be taken to counter them abounded, including John Brunner's multiple prize-winning *Stand on Zanzibar*, published the same year as Ehrlich's book (with one plotline involving the fictional African state of Beninia seeking to do a deal with a sinister American super-corporation to take on its management in order to accelerate its development). To many, *The Population Bomb* was the forthright statement of good sense they had been waiting for; and in Ehrlich, many ecologists, conservationists, environmental activists and 'Greens' saw a respected, high-profile scientist delivering a forceful call to arms in the desperate, intensifying battle to save the planet.

Ehrlich advocated population control in the US and other developed countries, as well as poorer regions, to stabilise the global headcount at a level below 4 or 5 billion. In the mind's eye of Western policymakers and influential individuals, however, the real overpopulation problem was in the 'Third World', evidenced by the concentration of poverty there, the teeming cities and seemingly annual famine scares. This was certainly the view of the leading proponents and financiers of population control from the 1950s onwards, most of whom were middle-aged, white male American tycoons and philanthropists (and some of whom were more well intentioned than others). By 1970 Z.P.G. – 'Zero Population Growth' – was an influential movement co-founded by Ehrlich: at the annual meeting of the Population Association of America that year it was

noted that the concept had 'caught the public by storm'.*[14] Two years
later it was also the title of a film starring Oliver Reed, one of a host
of dystopian movies *The Population Bomb* inspired.

As the Cold War intensified, and population growth showed no sign
of abating, the US and other Western governments also feared that it
would lead to even more poverty and increasing landlessness. More
people meant more potential recruits for the 'Commies' in Asia, Latin
America and Africa. Ever-larger sums of money were deployed by
American philanthropic foundations, birth-control organisations and
think-tanks to counter the threat. Many had roots in, or been closely
associated with, the global eugenics movement earlier in the century,
whose prime objective to 'improve' the quality of the human race
and tackle poverty came to be associated with proposals for selective
breeding and prevention of 'racial degeneration'. In the inter-war
period, this was considered an unexceptional and progressive cause
in the West, supported by adherents of all political and ideological
persuasions, and the medical and scientific establishments.

Until the mid-1960s, the population 'crusade', as it has been
dubbed,[15] remained essentially a private enterprise. It moved
mainstream with the declaration by 30 world leaders that unplanned
population growth was a global threat. By the end of the decade, US
government-backed birth-control programmes began to proliferate.
The United Nations Fund for Population Activities (UNFPA)
was founded in 1968 and began operations the following year.† A
United Nations publication remarked that 'Changes in the general
international climate of opinion as regards national family planning
programmes... are in some measure due to the moral influence of

---

* It is interesting to note that fertility in the US reached replacement level in the
early 1970s and the country was therefore on its way to achieving zero population
growth (excluding migration).

† It was ironic that 1968 was also the year of the Teheran (Tehran) Proclamation of
the United Nations International Conference on Human Rights. This upheld that
'parents have a basic human right to decide freely and responsibly on the number
and spacing of their children'. However, a warning was issued to member states at the
conference 'to give close attention to the implication for the exercise of human rights
of the present rapid rate of increase in world population'.

the United Nations and the specialised agencies, and the role of these international bodies in legitimizing or reinforcing the respectability of such policy.'[16] Ehrlich's book caught the wave perfectly, and magnified it. In an era of escalating paranoia, Ehrlich observed that 'the interlocking crises in population, resources, and environment [were] the focus of countless papers, dozens of prestigious symposia, and a growing avalanche of books'.[17]

Asian drama

Asian Drama: An Inquiry into the Poverty of Nations by the Nobel Prize-winning economist Gunnar Myrdal was published in 1968. It was an epic, running to three volumes and 2,284 pages – about 10 times the length of *The Population Bomb*, published the same year, but just as bleak: Asia was regarded by the West as a 'basket-case' as well as a vital front in the war against the expansion of communism.

'This book has been received in the West with decided dis-comfort, not to say horror,' wrote one reviewer, 'while in the underdeveloped countries of Asia it has caused consternation and pain: horror in the West for fear that Myrdal is saying the billions spent on development aid over the last 20 years have been wasted; pain in Asia for fear that he is saying the whole economic and social mess is really the fault of the Asians themselves. Myrdal is saying both.'

Myrdal showed up the prevalence of false statistics and the self-interested or opportunistic character of much of the research undertaken in Asia by Westerners at the time. He did not see this as inevitable, but considered there was a 'real danger... in the application of Western economic theories to areas where these theories are all but worthless or totally irrelevant'.

Myrdal concluded that what rich countries did to help underdeveloped countries was of marginal benefit; and that economic development would not take place in the poor nations 'unless social reforms are carried out which will motivate the apathetic masses and dignify labour'. On both counts, he was not optimistic. Myrdal saw laziness and a lack of self-discipline everywhere; and considered many national leaders to be complacent and have a tendency 'to blame economic stagnation on the system inherited from the vile colonial rulers and the inadequacy of the flow of capital from the rich nations'. He lamented the lack of skills, overpopulation, hypocrisy and vulgarity of ruling elites, and the dearth of manufacturing and agricultural reform. These were all charges which would soon be levelled at African countries.

Source: Joel H. Busch, review of *Asian Drama: An Inquiry into the Poverty of Nations* in *The Australian Quarterly*, Vol. 40, No. 4, Dec. 1968, pp. 118-21.

Although birth control or 'family planning' was presented in the US 1971 Family Planning Services and Population Research Act and other legislation as progressive, a basic human right and voluntary, the reality was often different in developing countries. The World Bank increasingly tied aid for health programmes in the 'Third World' to the adoption of population-control measures. Notorious abuses occurred, most notably during India's forcible sterilisation programme, funded by the World Bank and other Western agencies; and with the imposition in China of its one-child policy. Reflecting on the impact of *The Population Bomb* in its 50th anniversary year, bestselling science writer Charles Mann wrote in *Smithsonian Magazine* that the book 'gave a huge jolt to the nascent environmental movement and fueled an anti-population-growth crusade that led to human rights abuses around the world'.[18]

Population growth in Africa was as rapid as anywhere in the world, but its sheer size – and the fact that in the West its prospects were considered brighter than Asia's – meant that the main attention was focused elsewhere in the 1970s, particularly on India. At about 350 million, Africa's population was two-thirds the size of India's – but its land mass was more than nine times greater. Furthermore, India was one country. There were some 50 governments to deal with in Africa, and no country's population was among the top 10 globally. Even by the mid-1980s three-quarters of the 48 countries in sub-Saharan Africa had fewer than 10 million inhabitants. Almost half had fewer than 5 million*; 10 had fewer than a million inhabitants; 13 had a land mass of less than 50,000 km²; and 14 were landlocked.[19] Only Nigeria (with an estimated 100 million people), Ethiopia (42 million) and Zaire (today's DRC, 32 million) could justifiably be labelled populous. In the first of the 1979 Reith Lectures on BBC Radio, the Kenyan academic Ali Mazrui remarked that Africa was 'a continent large enough to be Jonathan Swift's Brobdingnag, but inhabited by minute Lilliputians'.

The legacy of colonial-era geographical fragmentation is often cited as an important factor in the political, economic and social development of post-independence sub-Saharan Africa, one that made it arguably the least integrated region in the world. The demographic ramifications are less often considered – but African leaders were acutely aware of them. With nation-building the priority[20] (alongside political survival and the defence of sovereignty) there was near-unanimity that this would require more people, and that raising population issues would risk inflaming religious and tribal sensitivities. In the 1960s, only Kenya and Ghana adopted population policies aimed at reducing population growth. To some extent this was because in both countries the governments regarded themselves as 'modernisers', and family planning was depicted as a 'modern' practice by many developing nations in parts of Asia. They were also genuinely concerned about financing the development of their countries, given that Kenyan and Ghanaian women were on average bearing eight and seven children respectively. In Kenya, GDP had grown by 6% a year between 1960 and 1980,[21] one of the best rates of any developing country in the world, but this was substantially dragged down in per capita terms by population growth.

Museveni was in exile in Tanzania, working to unseat Idi Amin, when the campaign to control population growth in Africa began

---

* For comparison, the population of the UK, a minuscule territory, was greater than 55 million at the time; Denmark and Finland had populations approaching 5 million.

in earnest. At the first World Population Conference in Bucharest, Romania, in 1974, African delegates forcefully rejected the proposition that population control had merits, arguing that contraception was neither 'African' nor conducive to development and that demography was essentially neutral. It was also reminiscent of colonial-era population policies and widely regarded by post-independence leaders as a Western conspiracy to retain political and economic domination. Fred T. Sai, a Ghanaian physician later referred to as the 'godfather of family planning',[22] was present at the conference and described how '"development is the best contraceptive" was a theme which was sung and re-sung all over the place [by Africans]'.[23] At the time, the official position of three countries – Madagascar, Malawi and Zambia – was that they needed to *increase* the birth rate, while in Côte d'Ivoire and Upper Volta (today's Burkina Faso) the sale of contraceptives had been made illegal. A UN publication commented that 'low density and the attendant problems of providing adequate services for a sparsely settled population are the reasons generally given [in sub-Saharan Africa] for policies favouring higher fertility'.[24]

Despite African opposition, a 'World Population Plan of Action' was endorsed in Bucharest by the 130 national delegations, all but three of which were headed by men. It was just one of many global action schemes launched at the behest of the World Bank and United Nations that attested to their growing reach and aspirations. The 1970s also spawned the 'World Plan for Agricultural Development', a 'World Employment Programme', a 'World Plan of Action for the Application of Science and Technology to Development' and a 'Programme of Action and Declaration on the Establishment of a New International Economic Order'. However, staunch resistance by African leaders, intellectuals and media to Western intervention regarding population matters continued throughout the 1970s. For most of them, demography was an issue of national sovereignty, and family size a personal choice.

In *Black Africa*, published in 1978, the Senegalese polymath Cheikh Anta Diop articulated another prevalent belief – that Africa's so-called 'population problem' was one of having too few people and not multiplying fast enough. Diop criticised 'influential American groups' seeking to have US and other donor aid made conditional on agreement to limit birth rates and declared that 'our continent, with its demographic emptiness, has an imperative duty to apply a systematic policy of intensive repopulation in optimum time'. Jimi Wanjigi's refrain can be heard in Diop's assertion that 'Black Africa contains sufficient sources of natural energy, raw materials and foodstuffs to feed and sustain such a population.' Diop was also intensely concerned that Africa's 'demographic emptiness' did not result in it 'becoming the receptacle for the rest of the world's human overflow'.[25]

In another televised speech in 2018, Museveni declared that 'Africa has been suffering from underpopulation... We are sorting that out.'[26] Forty years after Diop, the belief in Africa's 'demographic emptiness' remains powerful and widespread. When Museveni was a child in the early 1950s the total population of British-administered East Africa – today's Kenya, Tanzania and Uganda – was just 19 million. This was 2 million less than the population of Thailand, for example, a country with a land mass barely one-third as extensive. At independence there was consensus among educated elites in the Eastern, Western and Middle regions of Africa that a great deal of 'catching up' with the rest of the world was imperative.

Some research suggests that at its zenith in relative terms Africa – in modern times – accounted for about 15% of the global population. This was three or four centuries before the peak of the Atlantic slave trade.[27] Some caution is required, as this coincides with a period between the middle of the fourteenth century and beginning of the sixteenth century when the 'Black Death' and subsequent cycles of plague reduced the population of Europe, Northern Africa and much of Asia by about a third, but left sub-Saharan Africa relatively unaffected.

The magnitude of the impact of the Atlantic and East African slave trades on population numbers in different parts of the continent is also hotly debated. Received wisdom follows the contention of the influential Guyanese historian, Pan-African activist and author of *How Europe Underdeveloped Africa*, Walter Rodney, under whom Museveni studied in Dar es Salaam in the late 1960s, that it was disastrous. In the early 1990s another historian, Patrick Manning, made the case for the population of Africa in the nineteenth century having been half what it would have been without slavery. Data is scarce and some of it unreliable – population estimates for Africa in 1500, before the intensification of the Atlantic slave trade, range from 50 million to 100 million. Some demographers have also argued that high birth rates would have largely compensated for the number of victims: the population of Europe, after plummeting by between a third and two-thirds in the century after the Black Death first struck, largely recovered those losses during the following two centuries. 'Whether the several slave trades caused Africa's population to decline is still unclear,' says Shane Doyle, Professor of African History at the University of Leeds and an authority on the continent's demographic history, 'but they must certainly have acted as a major obstacle to growth.'[28] It is more certain that wars, famine and disease epidemics in the late nineteenth century caused severe population decline in parts of Africa, probably reducing it to as little as 7% of the global total.[29] Today Africa, with one fifth of the world's land mass, is home to about one sixth of its people.

For Museveni and many of his generation, the case for their continent still being underpopulated is clear. If population density is used as the yardstick, this appears to be fully justifiable (see text box). On a map of global densities, it is Asia, and in particular India, that stands out as being densely populated. Moreover, it is a point that needs constant reiteration. Museveni's generation well remembers how carrying capacity, measured simplistically by population density and local food supply, was deployed to counter population growth in Africa. After persuasion failed at Bucharest, contentious data was legitimised and weaponised, and used instead.

A sparsely populated continent

Although Africa's population has multiplied by a factor of six since 1950, its current size – 1.3 billion – implies a density of 44 people per km². This compares to a global average of 59 people per km². Asia's population density, and China's within it, is more than three times that of Africa.

Even in Western and Eastern Africa, the two most populous regions, population density is only slightly greater than the global average, at 65 people per km². The three other regions – Northern, Southern and Middle Africa – are what can only be described as sparsely populated with densities of 32, 25 and 27 people per km² respectively. On the face of it, the continent of Africa and three out of five of its constituent regions are among the most thinly populated inhabited areas globally.

The same can be said of almost all of Africa's countries. If small and island states are excluded only five countries have population densities of close to 200 people per km² or higher: Rwanda (512 people per km²), Burundi (449/km²), Museveni's Uganda (222/km²), Nigeria (221/km²) and Malawi (198/km²). Even these countries hardly appear densely populated or overpopulated by comparison with Bangladesh (1,291/km²), and they are all less densely populated than South Korea (517/km²). Rwanda is the only African country to exceed India's population density (460/km²).

There are a number of quite populous African countries which appear to be sparsely inhabited: in Angola, South Sudan and Zambia there are fewer than 30 people per km², comparable to Brazil, Argentina and many of the other more populous Latin American countries.

Among countries classified by the World Bank as 'lower-middle-income'* – a little under half of Africa's total – the average population density is less than one-third of the 142 people per km² global average for countries in this income category.

* Average gross national income (GNI) per capita between US$1,036 and US$4,045 (calculated using the World Bank Atlas method). *Source:* UNPD, *World Population Prospects: The 2019 Revision – Data Booklet.*

The carrying capacity of the planet, its continents and individual countries had obsessed scientists, environmentalists and futurists for generations before Ehrlich used the term in the opening passage of *The Population Bomb*. Thereafter it became a familiar trope. In Africa, it was interpreted as not-so-subtle code for 'your growth is too fast, there are too many of you on the land to survive'. It was also redolent of the 1950s, when colonial authorities in many countries decided that soils were so exhausted that population-control measures would have to be taken or famine was certain. Although there were rural locations where dire soil degradation was indisputable, the application of the term to whole countries and even regions was proved by the passage of time to have been disingenuous, the more so given the results of Green Revolution technologies elsewhere in the world. To many, this confirmed their suspicion that population density was first and foremost an instrument of control.

While carrying capacity may be measurable with reasonable accuracy for livestock on a particular tract of land, its application to humans is more problematic (and controversial). 'Some researchers suggest that a [global] population based on two people per arable hectare is sustainable, and with 1.6 million arable hectares, the planet can support 3.2 billion people'[30] is an example of a 'back-of-the-envelope' calculation that seems to encapsulate its shortcomings. There may be a theoretical (and real) limit to the number of people that the planet can feed, but assertions like this – which are commonplace – are at best speculative and at worst nonsense. Human beings are not cows, and more has to be taken into account than simple agricultural production. Even when it is, a great deal of speculation and generalisation tends to persist.

Population density may reveal much of interest about its distribution and other things, but as a measure of carrying capacity, and therefore over- or underpopulation, it is deficient (see text box). It could be said that Nigeria, Africa's most populous country, cannot possibly be underpopulated when it has double the population density of, say, France. Yet Nigeria is no more populous than the Indian state of Uttar Pradesh, has about five times its land mass, and has double the proportion of people living in towns and cities. Indeed, with populations above 100 million the Indian states of Bihar and West Bengal are more populous than all but three of Africa's countries; in both, densities are higher than 1,000 people per km². India itself has a land mass similar in size to the combined area of Angola and Sudan, yet a population about the same as the whole of Africa. Singapore, one of the richest nations in the world, with exports exceeding those of India, has a population density matching those of huge slum districts all over the world.

Carrying capacity: how long is a piece of string?

In a 1995 survey of 65 historical data-based estimates of the 'earth's maximum supportable human population', the eminent population scientist Professor Joel E. Cohen, Professor of Populations at Columbia University, identified six different methodologies. Most were 'deterministic and static', making 'no allowances for changes in exogenous or endogenous variables or in functional relations between variables'.

Using extrapolations of population density and food supply is simple and crude. For one thing, it assumes that the food supply is dependent on what is grown locally. Not only does this vary enormously, but such a measure takes little account of other essential requirements including 'energy, biologically accessible nitrogen, phosphorus, fresh water, light, soil, space, diseases, waste disposal, nonfuel minerals, forests, biological diversity, and climatic change'.

Cohen noted that the various methods used in basic and applied ecology were not 'adequate' for the task of determining human carrying capacity. He indicated why this was the case in the following passage:

Human carrying capacity depends both on natural constraints, which are not fully understood, and on individual and collective choices. How many people the earth can support depends in part on how many will wear cotton and how many polyester; on how many will eat meat and how many bean sprouts; on how many will want parks and how many will want parking lots. These choices will change in time and so will the number of people the earth can support.

Even the basic question about human carrying capacity is problematic. Cohen continued:

The deceptively simple question 'How many people can the earth support?' hides a host of thorny issues: How many people with what fashions, tastes, and values? How many people at what average level of material well-being? With what distribution of material well-being? With what technology? With what domestic and international political institutions? With what domestic and international economic and demographic arrangements? In what physical, chemical, and biological environments? With what variability or stability? With what risk or robustness? What standards of personal liberty will people choose? How many people for how long?

Source: Joel E. Cohen, 'Population growth and Earth's human carrying capacity', Science, Vol. 269, 21 July 1995, pp. 341-6.

Even introducing the refinement of using arable land instead of total land mass to calculate density, Museveni's statement about underpopulation in Africa appears to hold good. By this measure, the population density of Africa is – again – almost exactly the same as the global average of 535 people per km². It is true that there are countries that by this measure are substantially more densely populated than the global average. They include Egypt (3,350/km²), DRC (1,188/km²), Rwanda (1,091/km²), Burundi (987/km²), Kenya (878/km²), Côte d'Ivoire (859/km²), Ethiopia (711/km²) – and Museveni's Uganda (639/km²).[31] But again, this says more about population distribution than carrying capacity or sustainability. Arable land comes in many forms and with hugely variable productivity depending on rainfall and the quality of the soil, seeds, fertiliser and other inputs as well as the use of technology. Furthermore, the amount of land classified as being used for agriculture in any country is usually far greater than that classified as arable, and this extra land is usually also used for feeding people. The land utilised for agriculture in DRC, for example, is more than three and a half times its arable land, in Kenya it is almost six times and in Ethiopia more than two and a half times.[32] Refinements can radically alter perceptions of density and carrying capacity, one way or another.[33]

In the early 2000s, a major study on long-term population projections by UNPD pointed out that '[l]and area is of course a weak proxy for the natural resources available to a country'.[34] However, carrying capacity remains an influential concept, and population density a prominent metric today in reports from the Food and Agriculture Organization of the United Nations (FAO), the World Bank and countless other international organisations. Among Africans who were alive in the 1970s and 1980s, the suspicion persists that these are still being used to establish the 'fact' that Africa is overpopulated: population density has hung like a sword of Damocles over the continent for decades, even centuries. Museveni's reference to Africa's underpopulation was considered and deliberate.

The president's statements about population matters in the national address and elsewhere during 2018 were also clearly directed as much at *wazungus* as Ugandans. Politicians in many African countries certainly consider pronatalism to be popular ground among rural audiences in countries where large families are the norm. But referring to the 'miracle' of rapid population growth in Uganda under the NRM and the ongoing need to reverse underpopulation in Africa was also underscoring how population matters have loomed large in the political history of the nation: pronatalism should not be attributed solely to 'cultural factors'. Furthermore, the view that population growth in Africa over that past seven decades is, in the context of centuries, simply a 'rebalancing' is not confined to the continent. Some cite the fact that, despite being the world's

second-largest continent, Africa has only generated one-fifth of global
population growth since 1950 – about 1 billion out of 5 billion. Writing
in *The New York Review of Books* in 2018, the author, former senior
correspondent at *The New York Times* and Professor of Journalism at
Columbia University, Howard W. French, remarked that 'Africa has
finally overcome its long-term population deficit in comparison with
other continents, and is now barreling into a globally unprecedented
demographic takeoff'.[35]

It is conceivable, given Museveni's reputation for being a
consummately canny politician, that there was also a very specific
message about family planning. For more than a decade, international
– Western – family planning organisations had waged a campaign
to mobilise Museveni as a standard-bearer. Initially, the results were
disappointing. In 2010, as host at a UN conference on family planning
in Kampala, the president barely alluded to any need for the greater
availability and use of modern contraception. At the time, he was
wont to tell student meetings, as did President Magufuli in Tanzania,
'your job is to produce children'.[36] At the Kampala conference, the
First Lady actively promoted Moon Beads, a natural birth-control
product said to help women avoid sexual relations at the time of peak
fertility.

At the 2012 London Summit on Family Planning, however,
Museveni was to the fore. The president talked up the benefits of
voluntary family planning, especially for 'the peasant women', and
pledged to increase funding for it. In 2014, he agreed for population
issues to be incorporated into national planning. Then, on World
Population Day in 2016, he advised Ugandans to be careful only to
have the number of children they could adequately care for. By then
the country's TFR had fallen from 6.7 to 5.4 births in the course of
a decade, and the proportion of women in Uganda using modern
contraceptive methods had increased from about one in four to one
in three. 'Steady progress' is a catchphrase of Museveni's. It is likely
that the 2018 address was a reminder to *wazungus* not to push too
hard, that Uganda's population size and rate of growth is a matter
for Ugandans.

3

A Message from the West

As political and economic crises mounted in the 1980s, Africa's 'lost decade', the message from Western governments and institutions became increasingly firm: population growth will cause disaster. One influential African institution concurred.

Another Western publication was almost as influential in putting the carrying capacity and population density of Africa (and the world) under the spotlight as *The Population Bomb* was on population growth. By coincidence, *The Limits to Growth* was commissioned in the same year as Ehrlich's book appeared. Its sponsor was the Club of Rome, a newly founded network of businesspeople, scientists, academics and others who might today be termed 'thought leaders'. The principal authors, a team at the Massachusetts Institute of Technology, were asked to assess 'the predicament of mankind' based on five key trends: accelerating industrialisation, rapid population growth, widespread malnutrition, a deteriorating environment and depletion of non-renewable resources. It was the first attempt to model the future of the 'world system' with the intention of determining what might make it sustainable.

The report was published in 1972. Its 'business-as-usual' scenario concluded that, due to the limits to growth inherent in a world with finite resources, a 'sudden and uncontrollable decline in both population and industrial capacity' would be evident within a century. According to this scenario, global industrial output would peak by 2008, global food per capita availability by 2020 and the global population would start to fall by about 500 million people a decade by 2030. Of the 13 presented in the report, it was the 'Doomsday' scenarios that inevitably attracted by far the most attention. Others that presented more sustainable futures if appropriate action was taken rapidly were deemed less newsworthy.

Like *The Population Bomb*, *The Limits to Growth* sold many millions of copies worldwide and attracted vehement criticism. Together, in the 1970s they moved to the fore controversy over the concept of 'overshoot' which both publications articulated and, at the other extreme, the assumption that population growth and the Earth's finite natural resources could generate industrial and economic growth indefinitely. Often derogatively referred to as 'neo-Malthusian', *The Limits to Growth* attracted criticism from both right and left of the political spectrum, from the world of industry and the Catholic Church, and from economists certain that 'Mr Market' would 'sort everything out' and that the idea that economic systems were subject to physical-resource limits was absurd. The basic assumptions, methodology, data and conclusions were rubbished by critics. Despite the criticism, the concept of the world's resources being finite became increasingly influential among Western policymakers, aid donors, academics and environmentalists. Concern that population growth might constitute an existential crisis for the world turned to certainty.

Doomed

In the 1970s and 1980s, population growth and the impact of overpopulation on the environment were depicted in Western media and public discussion with strikingly similar rhetoric to the climate crisis today. The alarm, sense of urgency and certainty behind the headlines were no different. 'Climate change: 12 years to save the planet? Make that 18 months' ran a headline on the BBC website in 2019. Beneath it followed the assertion that 'the sense that the end of next year is the last chance saloon for climate change is becoming clearer all the time'.* An article in *The Geographical* tells us that 'during this decade humankind will either decide to steer clear of the climatic maelstrom, or to plunge into it'. It continues: 'we find ourselves on a sick and overpopulated planet. Will human civilisation dodge the biggest, overarching problem ever met in its amazing 200,000 year-long adventure? Or will it just surrender to the prospect of a "sixth extinction"?† The veteran American environmentalist Bill McKibben has announced that 'we're reaching the endgame on the climate crisis'.‡

More dramatic still, a co-founder of Extinction Rebellion claims that 'science predicts' that climate change will kill 6 billion people this century,§ a death toll greater than any envisaged by *The Population Bomb*. In *MIT Technology Review* Roy Scranton, author of *We're Doomed. Now What?* and *Learning to Die in the Anthropocene: Reflections on the End of a Civilization*, predicted a 'climate apocalypse' by 2050 which '[i]n all likelihood… will be worse' than the Little Ice Age of the mid-fourteenth to mid-nineteenth centuries that is thought to have reduced the global population by one-third (although it is well-nigh impossible to disentangle its impact from that of the Black Death and other crises of the period).¶

Paul Ehrlich remains prominent today. The Intergovernmental Panel on Climate Change has arguably superseded the Club of Rome as guardian of the concept of limits to growth, the Zero Population Growth movement has been replaced by the pursuit of net zero emissions, and catastrophism is as irresistible to Western news media as it was 50 years ago.

* Matt McGrath, 'Climate change: 12 years to save the planet? Make that 18 months', BBC News website, 23 July 2019.
† Marco Magrini, 'Climatewatch – Why 2020 marks the start of a crucial decade for the environment', *Geographical*, 1 January 2020.
‡ Bill McKibben, 'The climate crisis', *The New Yorker*, 15 April 2021.
§ Roger Hallam on BBC *HARDtalk*, 15 August 2019.
¶ Roy Scranton, 'Lessons from a genocide can prepare humanity for climate apocalypse', *MIT Technology Review*, 24 April 2019.

Within a decade the influence of *The Population Bomb* and *The Limits to Growth* was fully apparent. Robert S. McNamara, formerly US Secretary of Defense, took over as president of the World Bank the year *The Population Bomb* was published. By 1984 he was declaring that 'short of thermonuclear war itself, population growth is the gravest issue the world faces over the decades immediately ahead'. In the early 1980s the FAO undertook a 'detailed investigation of the potential carrying capacity of the world's farmlands', its purpose being to determine 'the number of people the world can feed at… standards for a minimum daily diet at various levels of farming technology'.[1] Although population growth in Asia was still the focus of the keenest attention, interest in the situation in Africa dramatically increased during the decade. One reason for this was that whereas rapid fertility decline was clearly under way in most Asian countries, in Africa there was no let-up whatsoever.

The FAO forecast that if treated as a single unit, with all land with agricultural potential devoted to growing food and similar technological inputs to those deployed in Green Revolution countries, sub-Saharan Africa could at most support 1.6 times the population projected at the time for the year 2000 (at minimum nutrition standards).[2] That projection was 730 million people, implying a carrying capacity of 1.2 billion.* Fourteen countries in sub-Saharan Africa, accounting for half of its population, were deemed to be already exceeding their carrying capacity. These included Nigeria, Ethiopia and Kenya. A further seven were forecast to be in the same position by the year 2000. Of these 21 African countries in all, it was stated that seven would 'not be able to feed themselves' even if they adopted equivalent technology and agricultural inputs to those deployed in Latin America and Southeast Asia.

The FAO conceded that its study was only a 'rough guide to a country's ability to feed itself'. It did not take into account the

---

* The population projection for 2000 turned out to be more than 100 million too high. The estimated carrying capacity of 1.2 billion is about 100 million higher than the population of sub-Saharan Africa in 2019.

possibility of importing food with earnings from exports, but reservations were expressed about the ability of 'much of Africa' to generate sufficient foreign exchange from its exports to do so.[3] The statutory glimmer of hope required by such reports was provided by saying that if the use of technology and inputs in agriculture were to match levels employed in 'more advanced' countries of Southeast Asia and Latin America, sub-Saharan Africa could probably support a hypothetical maximum population of 4.2 billion in the year 2000.

Among the countries assigned the bleakest outlooks was Burundi. In 1983, while Museveni was fighting the Bush War to topple Milton Obote, a further report – this time by the World Bank – analysed its carrying capacity and labelled population density as 'generally extremely high', at 154 people per km^2. This was three times the level of Museveni's Uganda and nearly eight times that of Tanzania. The report concluded that Burundi 'does not have the agricultural and financial resources to support more than about double its present population [of 4 million] over the foreseeable future', and recommended an optimum population size of no more than 8 or 9 million 'over the next 30 years'.[4]

Hard on the heels of these reports came the FAO's *The State of Food and Agriculture* in 1984. It was published just as what was billed as 'the worst drought of the century' reached its peak in the Sahel, and also parts of Eastern and Southern Africa. According to the report, 'entire ways of traditional living, which had endured for centuries, were on the verge of collapse'. In the first paragraph of the foreword the FAO's director-general wrote: 'We note grimly, [that] well over 30 million men, women and children, in 21 African countries, were directly threatened by starvation... the skeletal figures of starvation victims in Africa became a recurring feature on television screens.' It continued: 'More than ever before, it was obvious that increased global production alone would not automatically secure access to available food for those in greatest need.' Africa became 'the focus of world attention' for tragic reasons.[5]

By the mid-1980s, when Museveni came to power in Uganda, population growth was portrayed by the Bretton Woods institutions,* Western donor governments and demographers as crippling the prospects of sub-Saharan Africa and their own efforts to reduce poverty globally. In 1986 the World Bank published *Population Growth and Policies in Sub-Saharan Africa*, which was to be a highly influential 'policy study'. In his foreword, the Bank's senior vice-president (operations) wrote: 'At no time in history has any group of countries faced the challenge of development in a situation of such rapid population growth.' Latin America's population growth had peaked in the early 1960s at 2.9% a year, and South Asia's at 2.5% in the late 1960s. In sub-Saharan countries, however, it was still growing by an 'extraordinarily rapid' 3% a year on average in the mid-1980s – and showing no signs of slowing. In every decade since the 1950s the region's population had expanded by close to 30%. Africa's underpopulation was certainly being 'sorted' (as Museveni would allude to many decades later).

Mortality was now declining rapidly from very high levels in most countries in sub-Saharan Africa. Infant mortality had fallen from almost one in five in the early 1950s to about one in nine and life expectancy at birth had risen to almost 50 years from 36 in 1950.[6] But beyond Southern Africa, only in Zimbabwe was there any real sign of fertility decline, a development usually expected to follow improving mortality. Meanwhile, the populations of Kenya, Côte d'Ivoire and Zimbabwe itself were growing by more than 4% a year, an astonishing rate at which a population doubles in less than 18 years. Many countries had TFRs that exceeded the peak rates recorded anywhere else in the world and only about 3–4% of women used modern contraceptive methods. At the start of the 1980s women in most countries in Eastern Africa were having more than seven children on average – and in Rwanda, eight. In the World Bank's

---

* So-called after the conference at Bretton Woods, New Hampshire, in July 1944 at which the post-war framework for US-led economic order and international 'structured co-operation' was debated, and the plans laid for the creation of the World Bank, the IMF and The General Agreement on Trade and Tariffs (GATT).

opinion, such rapid growth was 'neither desirable nor necessary'[7] and it caused 'deep concern'.[8]

Concern was compounded not only by drought, but by the impact of the global oil-price spikes, commodity-price collapse, global recession and inflation of the 1970s. Up to the mid-1970s, average GDP growth in Africa was above 3% a year and the best performers matched the best East and Southeast Asian countries. Between independence in 1964 and 1973, for example, Zambia's GDP grew by an average of 15% annually; between the late 1960s and the end of the 1970s Kenya's GDP growth matched that of Malaysia; and Côte d'Ivoire's record equalled that of Indonesia.[9] When conditions turned for the worse, the results were dramatic. In Ghana, whose economy had been one of Africa's stellar performers since independence, GDP contracted by an average of 3% a year in the 1970s. Côte d'Ivoire's economic miracle imploded. External factors could not be fingered as the only cause of economic disaster in many countries. In some, 'hungry' political elites were establishing themselves and subverting the operation of the state. Nigeria (profligacy with oil revenues) and Tanzania (a villagisation programme in rural areas, abolition of co-operatives and crushing of business enterprises) might be termed examples of self-harm. The World Bank observed that the setbacks jeopardised the region's capacity 'to maintain even the living standards already attained since independence' in the 1960s and 1970s.[10] According to Professor John Iliffe, author of *Africans: The History of a Continent*, 'Africa's share of world trade probably fell to its lowest point for a thousand years.'[11]

Colossal indebtedness was a further problem. As the decade progressed, international banks awash with Middle Eastern petrodollars actively sought borrowers in Africa. Encouraged by external advisers at the World Bank and other institutions, most countries borrowed increasing sums externally to fund development expenditure. This strategy went badly wrong in those with flexible exchange rates when inflation started to rise sharply worldwide. The US increased interest rates in response, and the dollar consequently strengthened. African debtor countries had to borrow more to service their loans, and when the oil price plummeted in 1982, triggering a debt crisis throughout the 'Third World', they were joined by oil exporters like Nigeria who had been beneficiaries of high oil prices. In a little over a decade Africa's debts had increased from US$11 billion in 1970 to more than US$120 billion as the world prices for all the continent's major exports fell.

In his book *What Is Africa's Problem?*, written shortly after taking power in Uganda, Museveni wrote: '[t]here is no way that Africans can emancipate themselves from poverty and backwardness without carrying out an industrial revolution. As long as we continue exporting cheap, raw, primary commodities, our present situation will not change.'[12] Many African governments did implement industrialisation policies in the 1960s and 1970s, but their initiatives were a further casualty of the 1980s. Manufacturing would account for the same proportion of GDP in 2005 as it had in 1975 – about 10%. The fact that about 70% of the population of sub-Saharan Africa remained reliant on 'peasant' or subsistence agriculture attested to the lack of diversification or investment in pro-poor 'developmentalism' on the scale that was under way in many Asian countries.[13] In other sectors of national economies job creation was too weak, and education too limited in extent and quality, to stimulate significant rises in productivity and incomes. Another undesirable consequence was a 'brain drain' of the best-educated and technically qualified. One reputable institution estimated that 30% of Africa's 'high-level manpower' – or 70,000 people – had taken jobs in Europe by the end of the 1980s. This is considered an underestimate: in a single three-year period more than 110,000 skilled Nigerians – doctors, nurses, engineers and university staff – left the country.[14] These were the shifting sands beneath what has become known as Africa's 'lost decade'.

If South Africa was excluded, almost half a billion people in sub-Saharan Africa were generating a combined GDP equivalent to that of Belgium, whose population was 10 million. 'Population assistance' – through more widespread education and more extensive use of voluntary family planning – became the World Bank's highest priority in Africa, alongside implementation of 'market reforms' and 'structural adjustment' measures in the growing number of heavily indebted economies. These combined austerity measures and economic liberalisation by curtailing state expenditure in the name of fiscal discipline, privatising state-owned enterprises, ending or reducing subsidies, liberalising internal and external trade regulations and a host of other reforms. Free markets and free trade – it was envisaged – would then remedy the damage wrought by 'irresponsible' and 'corrupt' states. Curbing 'explosive' population growth and enforcing fiscal austerity went hand in hand, but the World Bank was far from convinced that these would prove sufficient. After analysing the seeming plethora of challenges, its 1986 report concluded that the outlook in coming decades, 'although not hopeless', was 'grim'.[15]

In the decade following the first World Population Conference in Bucharest, in 1974, the views on population growth of governments and leading institutions in Africa seemingly underwent a volte-face. At Bucharest, most African governments had staunchly resisted any attempts by the US, in particular, to foist population control on their continent, many of them regarding it as an attempt at colonialism by the back door. Northern African countries felt less threatened: Egypt, with a population of 35 million in the mid-1970s, regarded population growth as the single biggest threat to development if allowed to continue unchecked. Outside Northern Africa, however, by 1970 less than a third of countries had population policies targeting lower growth.[16] Meanwhile, in Ethiopia, Cameroon, Gabon and Sudan more than 50% of the population was under 15, and many others were adamant that they were underpopulated.

At the second World Population Conference, in Mexico City in 1984, African governments all recognised the importance of family planning as a health measure and human right. The importance of integrating population matters in national planning was also acknowledged, and it was noted that UNFPA had conferred its Population Award on the head of China's family planning programme the previous year (a decision that would cause considerable embarrassment subsequently). However, the Reagan administration offered room for manoeuvre for leaders who wanted it. It was announced at the conference that the US government considered population growth to be neither negative nor positive, but a 'neutral phenomenon'. Furthermore, it introduced the 'global gag rule', prohibiting UN agencies, NGOs and family planning organisations from receiving any US government funding if they 'performed or actively promoted abortion as a method of family planning'. Fertility and growth would fall as liberalised markets in Africa and elsewhere in the 'Third World' worked their economic and developmental magic. In developed countries too, the scare about population growth was held by the American conservatives now in a position of influence to be 'merely a delusion of leftwing infantilism'.[17]

By the end of the 1980s – the Reagan decade in the US and the 'lost' decade in Africa – it was reported that two-thirds of African governments thought population growth was too high and half stated they had policies in place to curb it. Even Nigeria's Muslim president, General Buhari, said publicly that the rate of population growth was compromising development; his successor, General Babangida, advised families to have no more than four children. At the time, almost one in three Nigerian girls were married by the age of 15, although its TFR, at 6.3, was actually the lowest in Western Africa.[18]

The desperate economic straits that most African governments found themselves in was one catalyst for their apparent volte-face. In 1960 average GDP per capita in sub-Saharan Africa was double that of Southeast Asia; in 1980 the two were similar; by the early 1990s, GDP per capita in Southeast Asia was double that of sub-Saharan countries.[19] Only four countries in sub-Saharan Africa – Cameroon, Republic of Congo, Lesotho and Botswana – had recorded sustained growth in GDP per capita over three decades. Delivering promises made at independence became increasingly difficult for presidents and their governments. The expansion of health and education could not keep pace with the rapidly growing number of users, and structural adjustment programmes (SAPs) simultaneously required the withdrawal of subsidies for items like food and fuel.

The threat to the stability of many nations posed by the precarious food situation was another catalyst. During the 1970s cereal imports to sub-Saharan Africa increased by 10% a year, and by the end of the decade agricultural production in the region had fallen to 80% of its per capita output in 1960, 20 years earlier.[20] The Lagos Plan of Action for the Economic Development of Africa drawn up by the Organisation of African Unity (OAU) in 1980 was described at the time as 'the philosophy for Africa's future'. The Plan emphasised the urgent need for greater economic self-reliance in – and closer co-operation between – Africa's states to reduce dependence on Western governments and institutions. In this context, it is significant that the first statement of the first chapter recognised that 'over the past two decades… the food and agriculture situation in Africa has undergone a drastic deterioration; the food production and consumption per person has fallen below nutritional requirements'.

While it seemed that there was a growing consensus among presidents and at the highest level of governments that agricultural production and the rapidity of population growth would need to be addressed simultaneously, it is a moot point how genuine it was. Throughout sub-Saharan Africa in particular, the top priority for most presidents was to ensure, one way or another, that funding from international donors continued. If this involved saying what Western donors wanted to hear about population growth, that was a price worth paying. Only Kenya, Ghana, Botswana and Senegal were listed by the Population Council, an influential New York-based non-governmental organisation, as sub-Saharan countries with 'strongly anti-natalist policy'.[21] Uganda was also starting to take steps to reduce growth, and in Rwanda – with a TFR higher than eight births per woman – concern among government officials about the political and security ramifications of high population density intensified almost monthly as interpersonal and inter-communal conflict proliferated.[22] But even in these countries, with the exception of Botswana, policy was failing for various reasons to secure significant results. Kenya and Ghana still had TFRs higher than six and seven births respectively, despite having launched national population policies in the 1960s; Senegal's TFR was flatlining at more than seven births and Rwanda's was rising. Furthermore, after Mexico City it appeared as though the cost of non-compliance would be negligible. In Nigeria, the population policy which came into effect in 1988 was seemingly designed and 'implemented' in a way almost guaranteed not to disturb the status quo.

Whatever the real views of presidents, one of the most respected African institutions certainly shared the alarm prevalent among Western donors and financing institutions about population growth and food supply. Adebayo Adedeji, executive secretary of the United Nations Economic Commission for Africa (UNECA or ECA), based in Addis Ababa, acknowledged the role of these linked factors in the continent's 'sombre situation'. Published three years before the grim prognoses of the World Bank 1986 report, *ECA and Africa's Development 1983–2008: A Preliminary Perspective Study* is every bit as revealing a historical document. Even in the 1960s and 1970s, when GDP growth in many sub-Saharan countries had been quite good, it had only narrowly outpaced population growth. As economic growth evaporated, populations continued to burgeon (in contrast to most other regions of the world). Furthermore, job creation was simply not keeping up. Almost half of the 33 million people added to the region's workforce in the 1970s 'found no access to remunerative employment', and 70% of Africans were classified as either 'destitute' or 'on the verge of poverty'.

The ECA, like the World Bank, envisaged 'almost a nightmare' scenario arising if high population growth and stagnant or falling incomes continued. Adedeji also concurred with the FAO that 'Africa's food situation is by now the single most critical area of concern in the region'. If agricultural output did not improve materially, much of the continent would end up dependent on foreign food aid indefinitely – provided that was forthcoming. In the meantime, the economic and social cost of high population growth was deemed so great that without improvement 'all services would deteriorate in terms of quantity and quality' and fewer people would have access to education, healthcare or water.

The ECA was not merely sharing the position of the international financial institutions and agencies on whom Africa was becoming increasingly reliant out of simple pragmatism. Although technically a United Nations agency, it was founded as – and remains – an African institution. Adedeji himself had been the architect of the Lagos Plan of Action. This explains why, in addition to acknowledging various shortcomings and mistakes of African states post-independence, and their dire consequences, Adedeji launched a blistering attack on the role of the 'present world economic order' and the 'Bretton Woods order' in exacerbating Africa's difficulties. Adedeji argued forcefully that – given 'perverse international financial and monetary arrangements, increasing domination of the developed countries through, inter alia, transnational corporations, monopolistic technology markets, and stagnant or declining prices of raw material exports from the developing countries while prices of manufactured imports from the developed countries are continually increasing' – it was extremely difficult for Africa to 'get the equity it deserves'.

In the ECA's 'nightmare scenario', Adedeji and his colleagues set out how much worse things would be in 2008 'if present trends continue without conscious change':

> The potential population explosion would have tremendous repercussions on the region's physical resources such as land and the essential social services – education, health, housing, nutrition, water, etc. At the national level, the socio-economic conditions would be characterised by a degradation of the very essence of human dignity. The rural population, which would have to survive on intolerable toil, will face an almost disastrous situation of land scarcity whereby whole families would have to subsist on a mere hectare of land. Poverty would reach unimaginable dimensions since rural incomes would become almost negligible relative to the cost

of physical goods and services. The conditions in the urban centres would also worsen with more shanty towns, more congested roads, more beggars and more delinquents. The level of the unemployed searching desperately for the means to survive would imply increased crime rates and misery. But, alongside the misery, there would continue to be those very few who, unashamedly, would demonstrate an even higher degree of conspicuous consumption.

In the 'overpopulated shanty towns' of Africa's expanding cities, 'riots, crimes and misery would be the order'. In just 25 years, 'self-reliance and independence would, to the generation of 2008, sound [like] slogans of the past'.[23] The very sovereignty of African states would be in jeopardy. In many respects, large parts of Adedeji's text could almost have been written by Paul Ehrlich.

Many African intellectuals remained unconvinced about the so-called perils of population growth. Published in the early 1970s, *The Myth of Population Control*, by the Ugandan intellectual Mahmood Mamdani, was particularly influential throughout the explosion era. The book used evidence from rural India to show that population growth was a consequence, not the cause, of poverty and that having large numbers of children maximised the options of families trapped in poverty.

Professor Mwesiga Baregu at the University of Dar es Salaam was one of those who took issue with the World Bank's 1984 publications *World Development Report* and *Towards Sustained Development in Sub-Saharan Africa* for focusing on the 'rising tide of people' in the 'Third World', and claiming that population growth was the single biggest long-term threat to Africa's economic advancement. In his paper 'The African "population problem": Situational versus world historical perspectives', Baregu dismissed the Bank's prognosis as evidence of a narrow, 'situational' view, rather than acknowledging the longitudinal trend. He pointed out that not only had Africa's growth lagged behind that of Europe and other continents for centuries, but that the European 'population invasions' of the continent in the so-called 'Scramble for Africa' had further retarded the continent's development and technological innovation. Armed with this historical perspective, Baregu countered that high population growth could stimulate both. African governments were therefore right to be reticent when urged by the West to 'sell' population control to their citizens.[24]

In Zimbabwe, a 1983 report by the Whitsun Foundation, a creation of three of the country's largest white-owned businesses, called for urgent action on the population 'problem'. To many, this seemed especially tactless – and suspicious – just two years after independence. At the University of Zimbabwe Nelson P. Moyo, like Baregu, challenged the claim that population pressure was the prime cause of poverty. For Moyo, it was 'capitalist development policies that have removed from rural people the means to produce their own subsistence' and radical structural and institutional changes to the white settler economy were what was required to spread the benefits of development – not large-scale birth-control programmes. 'Policy makers', Moyo concluded, 'will have to address the cynicism brought about by the colonial regime's genocidal efforts in the 1960s and 1970s to introduce birth control measures.'[25]

There were even signs in the reports of the World Bank itself and other international institutions that many of their economists and experts were unconvinced that population growth hindered development and regarded family planning programmes as a low-priority policy. In her paper for the Bank's Fifth Agriculture Sector Symposium in 1985, the economist Teresa J. Ho spoke of Africa's 'low population densities', the small proportion of arable land being used and the 'vast population supporting capacity' of many countries.[26] The influential FAO report highlighting Africa's limited carrying capacity also stated that Sudan alone could support 'up to a billion people' – twice the population of Africa at the time.[27] Another World Bank report, published in 1983, was clear that 'it would be wrong to attribute the growing food deficit to population pressures per se'.[28] Yet that, by and large, was what came across in the pronouncements of senior officials at the Bretton Woods institutions and Western policymakers, donors and charities. The same report even confirmed, revealingly, that 'the message that Africa faces a population problem has come mostly from the West, and in many quarters it has been dismissed as either irrelevant or mischievous'.[29] Its author concluded that 'national leaders show little enthusiasm about tackling this question and those few who have tried to do so regard the population issue as a political liability'.[30]

At the end of the 1980s, the World Bank reiterated its disquiet about the 'extraordinary challenge to the development community' from the predicament of most countries in sub-Saharan Africa. In his introduction to the new report, the Bank's president, Barber Conable, noted that the economic crisis 'had continued to deepen' as a result of 'weak agricultural growth, a decline in industrial output, poor export performance, climbing debt, and deteriorating social indicators, institutions and environment'. Most people in the region were 'almost as poor as they were 30 years ago'.[31] In Baregu's Tanzania, for example, GDP per capita more than halved between the mid-1970s and the late 1980s, taking it back to the same level as in 1960 and making the country the second-poorest in the world. Even countries that had made social welfare and economic gains in the immediate aftermath of independence in the early 1960s had seen them wither. There were sub-Saharan countries in which school enrolment and nutritional indicators were declining; in which a quarter of children died before their fifth birthday; and where unemployment in urban areas was reaching shocking levels, especially among educated young people. Conable concluded that 'the difficulties facing Africa are formidable, the margin for manoeuvre is slim indeed. The risks are devastating in human terms.'[32]

Population growth remained a central focus of the new report, ostensibly compounding the 'difficulties' and 'risks' facing many countries. 'Never in human history has population grown so fast,' it declared, and warned that if current trends persisted Africa's total population would double to 1 billion by 2010, with grave consequences. Improvements in living standards would be impossible and the region would be 'increasingly unable to feed its children or find jobs for its school leavers'.[33] Alongside the costs of educating children and the investments needed to create basic infrastructure and jobs, the threat of inadequate food production retained the prominent position it had occupied in the 1986 report. Despite talking of Africa's 'vast underpopulated regions' and its 'rich agricultural potential',[34] the thrust of the report was – how exactly are these countries going to feed their burgeoning populations amid 'accelerating environmental degradation'?[35]

The World Bank reflected the consensus of population experts at the time. For example, the influential Australian demographers John and Pat Caldwell, who had researched extensively in Africa over many decades, were unequivocal. In *Scientific American* they declared: 'the persistence of high fertility in sub-Saharan Africa, while all other regions have been able to control population growth, represents a grave threat'.[36] For African governments there were more pressing concerns. Most countries were mired in economic crisis. More than 30 were experiencing the deleterious effects of 'neoliberal' reforms and austerity imposed by the World Bank and IMF SAPs, ostensibly to put their economies on a better footing. Crippling national debt levels continued to rise while, as the Malawian economist Thandika Mkandawire put it at the time, 'two or three IMF experts sitting in a country's reserve bank have more to say than the national association of economists about the direction of national policy'.[37] Meanwhile, the HIV/AIDS epidemic was threatening to ravage a number of countries.

The British environmentalist Norman Myers also examined the 'population question' at the end of the 1980s. 'Of course population growth is not the only factor [affecting the development of sub-Saharan Africa],' he wrote. 'Also to blame are the generally harsh environment, its unreliable climate, its adverse trade terms, its weak infrastructure and its faulty development policies. But there is much agreement that the list of problems is headed by population growth.'[38] Such was the dominant narrative throughout the explosion era. The claim that absolute numbers were not the most important issue, but that the rate of population growth jeopardised food security and meant that Africa's economies had to 'sprint ahead for living standards even to stand still'[39] sounded rather disingenuous – and not entirely convincing – to African critics of Western institutions.

4

Revolution in Cairo

In the 1990s the concept of a population 'explosion' evaporated. Western priorities shifted and the worst prognostications about population growth in Africa were not realised.

There were some influential voices in the West who were unconvinced by population alarmism. Among the most prominent opponents of Ehrlich's population-explosion thesis was Julian Simon, a libertarian University of Maryland professor later labelled 'The Doomslayer'. Simon challenged the ascendant view that rapid population growth had negative economic and environmental consequences and would exhaust the planet's natural resources. He regarded people as 'the ultimate resource', the title of his book published in 1981, and asserted that human brain power was capable of finding a technological work-around to any challenge or resource limitations it confronted. A memorable line in the introduction to a later book, *The State of Humanity: Steadily Improving*, contrasts strikingly with the opening lines of *The Population Bomb* and epitomises Simon's differences with Ehrlich: 'we have in our hands now – actually in our libraries – the technology to feed, clothe, and supply energy to an ever-growing population for the next seven billion years'. This is the optimism embraced by Jimi Wanjigi, by the late President Magufuli and by cornucopians worldwide.

As the 1990s opened, most African governments were largely beholden to the economic diktats of the World Bank and IMF as the price for 'stabilisation' of national finances and the funding with which to stay afloat. About three-quarters – 40 countries – had adopted SAPs. However, debt levels remained crippling and, with the exception of Ghana and Museveni's Uganda, SAPs did not have the swift positive impact on growth envisaged by the Bretton Woods institutions and Western donors. 'IMF riots' shook a dozen countries. In many cases the reforms aggravated the very problems they were supposed to alleviate, inequality worsened, and women and children – the principal beneficiaries of government expenditure on health and education – were disproportionately affected. This was not only down to economics: the central importance of politics was ignored by those who designed SAPs, and in Africa the scarcity of financial resources is widely thought to have undermined 'developmentalism' and underpinned the emergence or entrenchment of widespread cronyism and patronage politics.

The end of the Cold War brought further turmoil. The benefits of patronage of one or other of the adversaries enjoyed by governments since independence abruptly ceased. 'The wind from the east is shaking the coconut trees,' observed President Bongo of Gabon.[1] Soon the whole continent became associated with regime overthrow, conflict and instability. Calls from the West for the immediate introduction of multi-party politics further threatened autocratic leaders in situ for decades. DRC, one of the countries worst affected by the vicissitudes of the post-independence era had been 'wrecked by a perfect storm of kleptocracy, Cold War geopolitics, structural adjustment and chronic civil war'.[2] Meanwhile, beyond the countries of Northern and Southern Africa, no matter what resolutions were approved by African leaders at the Mexico City population conference, there were few signs of lower fertility or easing population growth. In fact, the rate of expansion of the continent's population had increased in the 1980s to 32% from 31% in the previous decade and 28% in the 1960s.

Battered by the multiple crises of the 'lost decade' and the ongoing external pressure to curb population growth, in the early 1990s the OAU and ECA announced in a joint publication, *Population and*

Development in Africa, that the continent faced 'a major population explosion in the near future'; and in the 1992 Dakar/Ngor Declaration African governments universally acknowledged that population growth was adversely impacting development and committed to reduce it to 2.5% a year by 2000 and 2.1% by 2010. Objectives were also set for infant, child and maternal mortality rates, for life expectancy and for an increase in the use of modern contraception from less than 10% of married women to 40% by 2010. 'The underlying assumption' of African governments, according to the ECA, was 'the need for the African people to commit themselves to an evolutionary process characterised by a significant reduction of mortality and fertility'. Infant mortality rates of about one in 10 were two and a half times those of Latin America (although rates in Northern and Southern Africa were comparable). In the poorest continent in the world, Eastern Africa was the poorest region with GDP per capita of less than US$200.[3]

Meanwhile, having played a key role in ensuring that population growth was regarded in the West as the leading challenge to development, the environment and biodiversity, Paul Ehrlich relaunched and reiterated his original thesis. In *The Population Explosion*, published in 1990, he maintained that the US was now within 50 years of exhausting its soil and fresh-water resources. Africa featured, but not in great detail – the main observation being that the consequences of overpopulation and defective agricultural policy were readily visible in sub-Saharan Africa.

Another voice attracted equal, if not greater, attention and was very much focused on Africa, in particular Western Africa. 'The coming anarchy', an essay by the American writer Robert D. Kaplan in *Atlantic Monthly* in February 1994 that was subsequently turned into a book, read like a combination of *The Population Bomb* and the ECA's 'nightmare scenario' for 2008. It seemed to fill a gap left by the almost complete absence of analysis of Africa in Samuel P. Huntington's post-Cold War treatise 'The clash of civilizations', published in *Foreign Affairs* a year earlier. Picking up on this omission, one reviewer remarked: 'Africa is the missing piece in what

Huntington claims is a global analysis. This is important, for a holistic attempt that cannot account for fifty countries and nearly a billion people seems curious, at the very least... The fact that Africa is riven by war, civil conflict, poverty and disease hardly makes the continent less important.[4] This checklist of horrors encapsulates the Western view of the continent by the early 1990s, a low point of which leaders like Museveni were all too aware. Africa was either ignored, or written off in its entirety as a basket case. The euphoria and optimism of the post-independence years was long forgotten. For the more ambitious and ideological among them, there was something to prove – in their own way, and in their own time.

Kaplan's dystopian vision of the future envisaged a 'bifurcated world' in which 'nature is coming back with a vengeance, tied to population growth'. Most of its inhabitants would be condemned to a life that is 'poor, nasty, brutish and short', like Hobbes's First Man. The post-modern world was now in 'an epoch of themeless juxtapositions, in which the classificatory grid of nation-states is going to be replaced by a jagged-glass pattern of city-states, shanty-states and anarchic regionalisms'. In the post-Cold War era, Kaplan reckoned that 'Africa's immediate future could be very bad.' He predicted that a 'coming upheaval, in which foreign embassies are shut down, states collapse, and contact with the outside world takes place through dangerous, disease-ridden coastal trading posts, will loom large in the century we are entering'. This suggested that the continent 'may be as relevant to the future character of world politics as the Balkans were a hundred years ago', and that 'Africa's distress will exert a destabilizing influence on the US.' 'Afrocentrists', Kaplan concluded, 'are right in one respect: we ignore this dying region at our own risk.'

For Kaplan, Western Africa provided 'an appropriate introduction to the issues, often extremely unpleasant to discuss, that will soon confront our civilization'. The region was 'becoming the symbol of worldwide demographic, environmental and societal stress', a 'prism' through which 'disease, overpopulation, unprovoked crime, scarcity of resources, refugee migrations, the increasing erosion of nation-states and international borders, and the empowerment of private armies, security firms, and international drug cartels' were 'most tellingly demonstrated'. Here, as much as anywhere, one could witness 'the withering away of central governments, the rise of tribal and regional domains, the unchecked spread of disease and the growing pervasiveness of war' and a reversion to 'the Africa of the Victorian atlas'. As a consequence, 'the demographic reality' of Western Africa was one of 'a countryside draining into dense slums by the coast'.[5]

'The coming anarchy', subtitle 'How scarcity, crime, over-population, tribalism, and disease are rapidly destroying the social fabric of our planet', was as much commented on as *The Population Bomb*, *The Limits to Growth*, *The Clash of Civilizations* (published in book form in 1996) and the other 'Big Idea' books of the era. It was perceived by its detractors as neo-Malthusian, pessimistic to an extreme, misanthropic and demoralising. Some delighted, even years after publication, in rubbishing the whole text because such-and-such a prophecy had been proved wrong. Others could not see what this fuss was all about. At the time, Kaplan's view of Africa's 'immediate future' was hardly unique among Western commentators. In the UK, a New Year piece in *The Independent* in 1994 opened with the line, '[m]ost people outside Africa will continue to wish or pretend the continent did not exist because it will produce another crop of horror stories'. This article and Kaplan's essay appeared just months before genocide was unleashed in Rwanda in which as many as 800,000 people were killed, mostly by hand; they appeared almost alarmingly prescient, especially the former, which included the line: 'Zaire and the central region of Africa will provide horror stories of starvation and death early in the year.'[6]

As far as population growth was concerned, the OAU and ECA continued to stress in a 1994 report that Africa 'faces a major population explosion in the near future'.[7] To some observers, Rwanda was a warning – a catastrophe triggered in part by competition for resources in Africa's most densely populated country. Yet that same year renewed optimism was sparked by another momentous event.

A Web search for 'Africa 1994 events' does not typically show the Rwandan genocide on the first page of results. Instead, all items feature the end of apartheid, a joyous election and the beginning of black majority rule in South Africa, with Nelson Mandela installed as the country's president.

The mid-1990s, and 1994 in particular, brought other occurrences which collectively had a marked impact on high-level international engagement with the issue of family planning within Africa. In development organisations and international finance institutions like the World Bank, the concept of 'intensification' began to gain influence following the dissemination of research on the so-called 'Machakos Miracle' in Kenya. According to researchers from the UK's Overseas Development Institute and the University of Nairobi, whereas the population density of Machakos District had increased by between three and five times since the 1930s (depending on the type of land), food production per km^2 had increased by a factor of 11.

Their paper *More People, Less Erosion* asserted that population growth had had *positive* effects in Machakos, spurring innovation, adaptation, job creation, greater co-operation within the community and the adoption of new technology to counter the vicissitudes of a harsh local environment. Furthermore, the sustainability of the agricultural systems in Machakos had improved, and soil degradation had visibly diminished since the 1930s.[8] The researchers were influenced by the work of the Danish economist Ester Boserup in the 1960s, in particular her emphasis that population growth is a catalyst for invention that can spur agricultural development and improvements in productivity. Her belief that carrying capacity was elastic, her faith in the power of human ingenuity and conviction that numbers alone did not determine the consequences of population growth were echoed by Julian Simon – and were the antithesis to neo-Malthusian doom-laden narratives regarding population sustainability.

The findings from Machakos flew in the face of received wisdom that high population density usually hindered rural development and that drylands had relatively inflexible population-carrying capacity. They underscored the fact that the relationship between population and food security is complex, depending on a plethora of dynamics, and variable. Moreover, the researchers stated that Machakos was not a one-off: examples in other countries were cited.

The 'Machakos Miracle' proved as controversial in development circles as *The Population Bomb*, *The Limits to Growth* and Julian Simon's *The Ultimate Resource* had among a broader readership. Critics disputed the extent to which increasing population density had played a role in improving livelihoods in Machakos, whether the poorest in the community had benefited from improvements in the same way as those with land and assets, and the extent to which any of the lessons of Machakos's experience could be applied elsewhere. Some pointed out that even after the 'miracle' Machakos was not self-sufficient in food production. Experts galore in various related fields scrutinised the methodology and findings, aligning as much according to individual ideological or political bent on neo-Malthusianism as on the basis of empirical evidence and appraisal. A seismic shift in theory regarding population growth, food security, economic development – in 'development theory' – was under way.

Of even greater influence was a revolution unleashed at the third International Conference on Population and Development in September 1994. Held in Cairo, the agenda pushed by a decisive proportion of delegates was the promotion of 'sexual and reproductive health and rights', with an emphasis on putting women and girls, gender equity and the primacy of individual rights 'at the centre of global development'. Maternal and child health were prioritised and family planning was relegated in importance, or at least rebranded as a component of maternal health.

The implication of the new 'rights-based approach' signalled at Cairo was that population growth would take care of itself if women were empowered through education, property rights, equal access to financial services and the workplace and greater political representation. It seemed that women had finally been brought into the decades-long, impassioned debate about population growth. Cairo was hailed as a triumph for feminists, women's groups and human rights activists, and their 'victory' was consolidated at the huge UN World Conference of Women in Beijing in 1995, chaired by Tanzania's Gertrude Mongella.

The historic revision of outlook and policy marked by the Cairo conference was facilitated by many factors, and their individual importance is still debated. In its aftermath, Professor John Cleland of the London School of Hygiene & Tropical Medicine (LSHTM) considered the key factor to have been 'a feeling that the population problem was largely solved and that radically new goals were required to prevent UNFPA from sliding into irrelevance'.[9] Others cite the ascendancy of the notion that 'population control' and family planning were inherently coercive. In an influential paper published in 1994 a World Bank economist argued that the key factor in fertility reduction was the number of children desired by a woman, and that this was a function of her education, income and infant-survival rates more than the availability of family planning and modern contraception.[10] Many European nations and Japan were starting to become rather more preoccupied with their sub-replacement-level fertility, population ageing and the prospect of decline than with global population explosion.

As far as the all-important link between population growth and food insecurity that had underpinned calls to control the rate of growth for decades was concerned, the situation appeared to be not quite so clear-cut any more. In addition to the influence of the 'Machakos Miracle' in development circles, famines became much rarer in the 1990s. Significantly, the year before Cairo the World Bank also reported that world prices of all agricultural commodities were at their lowest levels ever, that crop yields everywhere were continuing to rise faster than population growth, and that globally cereal yields had increased more in the 1980s than in the previous two decades combined. Meanwhile, global population growth continued to slow

– and some demographers even detected signs of possible fertility decline in Eastern, Western and Middle Africa.

In the aftermath of Cairo, reputable scientific institutions were as much in the firing line as family planning advocates and organisations. A 'Population Summit of the World's Scientific Academies' had been convened in New Delhi prior to the conference to decide on the scientific foundations for resolutions to be put to delegates in Cairo. The main resolution, underpinned by the belief that the global population was set to double within 50 years, was for a goal of 'zero population growth in the life of our children'. The statement was drafted by The Royal Society, the US National Academy of Sciences, the Royal Swedish Academy of Sciences and the Indian National Science Academy and signed by 58 of the world's leading scientific institutions. Opponents of the 'myth' of continuing population growth took aim at the funders of the New Delhi meeting, the Rockefeller, Ford, Packard and MacArthur 'population control foundations' (as one critic dubbed them) and various Western 'industrial interests'.[11]

To a far greater extent than its two predecessors in Bucharest and Mexico City, Cairo brought the vitriol that had exemplified the population explosion battle into the open. It was a stark reminder of how politicised population issues had become, and how people and organisations of very different political persuasions found themselves on the same 'side'. Political and religious conservatives found common cause with feminists, human rights activists, anti-racists and anti-capitalists. Family planning advocates were in the same camp as anti-natalist 'eco-fascists'. 'Greens' and environmentalists were bitterly divided over the issue of consumption and whether it should even be included in the debate about population, as this was entirely the fault of rich, developed economies, not the 'Third World' countries where population growth was occurring. The divisions were complex, but there was no doubting which side 'won' this round of a long-running battle. A decade afterwards, Martha Campbell at the University of California, Berkeley, School of Public Health put

it succinctly: '"Malthusian" and even "demographic" became
derogatory terms describing anyone still expressing an interest
in, or concerned about, population growth.'[12] 'Population-shaming'
became commonplace in Western academic institutions – and
many other places besides.

A radically different narrative to that of population explosion also
gained traction after Cairo: population collapse. In the late 1980s,
the PBS TV commentator and self-styled 'data-driven amateur
demographer' Ben Wattenberg published *The Birth Dearth*. In 1997,
he wrote in *The New York Times Magazine* that 'for 30 years one
notion has shaped much of modern social thought: that the human
species is reproducing itself uncontrollably, and ominously'. Now it
was time to put an end to the decades of 'persistent alarm' and declare:
'The population explosion is over' – the title of his article. His main
evidence was his interpretation of UNPD's recently published *World
Population Prospects: The 1996 Revision* which 'proved' that fertility
was in 'free-fall' all over the world – and that demographers had been
'caught with their projections up'.[13]

In many African countries, according to Wattenberg, fertility rates
were 'plunging': the last frontier of high fertility rates in the world was
finally following the lead of every other continent. Tunisia had shown
the way, reducing its TFR from 7.2 to 2.9 births in just three decades.
'Modernisation', in the shape of urbanisation, education and rights
for women, legal abortion, higher incomes, better access to modern
contraceptives, lower infant mortality rates and higher aspirations,
was going to bring about similar change south of the Sahara. In
Jimi Wanjigi's Kenya, 'once regarded as the premier demographic
horror show' when the TFR briefly touched nine births in the late
1970s, things were changing dramatically.[14] For Wattenberg, UNPD's
recently introduced low-variant projection, which envisaged the
global population peaking at 7.7 billion by 2050, looked far closer to
the mark than its medium variant of 9.4 billion.

Wattenberg was a maverick commentator, and his main preoccupation was the threat posed by low or declining birth rates to the US
and the rest of the 'civilised' world. He was also keen to counter the

use of the population explosion as an 'Archimedean lever' by activists drawing attention to global warming. But others, for various reasons, shared his scepticism about projections. In October 1997, *The Wall Street Journal* carried an article titled 'The population implosion' by Nicholas Eberstadt, who, like Wattenberg, was a visiting fellow at the American Enterprise Institute, a conservative think-tank; Eberstadt was also a respected scholar and visiting fellow at the Center for Population and Developmental Studies at Harvard. The two men shared the opinion that global population growth would end within four decades, and Eberstadt claimed that 'some of the world's best demographers... are now seriously considering the possibility that the world's population will peak in our lifetimes'.[15] On the left there were also commentators who considered that UNPD's projections were too high, part of a Western imperialist conspiracy to maintain the myth of population explosion and thereby justify the imposition of birth control in developing countries.

At the New Delhi summit of scientists, African resistance to radical population control measures continued: the African Academy of Sciences dissented. The statement issued by its chair, the Kenyan entomologist Dr Thomas Odhiambo, recognised that population growth and size might be a cause for concern in some countries but declared that a one-size-fits-all declaration on global population growth was not in Africa's interests. Not only were its people 'an important resource for development, without which the continent's natural resources will remain latent and unexplored', but the role of the economic and development policies of 'the North' in Africa's 'population predicament' needed to be acknowledged. The statement continued:

> To imply that family planning is the panacea for fertility regulation, and even development, is at least simplistic. An understanding of the social and cultural milieu of African

societies is central to an analysis of the success or failure
or the intrinsic value or otherwise of family planning
programmes. In Africa, many of the so-called impediments
to family planning have a rationality which require careful
assessment.[16]

This was a thoughtful and firm rebuttal by African scientists that was
redolent of the broadside against the 'present world economic order'
from ECA executive secretary Adebayo Adedeji a decade earlier.
Africa, by and large, was sticking to the mantra 'development is the
best contraception'.

After Cairo, the pressure on African governments eased and
soon, in the words of Professor Alex Ezeh, 'population was removed
from the development vocabulary altogether'.[17] In 1995 Joel E. Cohen
remarked that there was 'no believable information to show which
approach will lower a country's fertility rate the most, now or a
decade from now, per dollar spent'.[18] Furthermore, the long-running
debate as to whether population growth had a significant positive or
negative effect on economic growth had also reached stalemate with
no conclusive evidence one way or another.

When the United Nations Millennium Development Goals were
drawn up in the year 2000, population growth and dynamics were
conspicuously absent. By then, the only population issue in Africa
was, for once, of equal concern to Western policymakers and donors,
and African governments and people: the ravages of the HIV/AIDS
epidemic. By the year 2000 about 70% of the world's cases were in
Africa, causing average life expectancy to plunge in the worst-affected
countries. Donor funding for healthcare increasingly shifted to meet
this new challenge, and to reducing maternal and child mortality.
Financial commitments to family planning programmes fell by about
a third in the decade after Cairo. To all intents and purposes, the
population bomb and its explosion were old hat.

Massimo Livi Bacci, Emeritus Professor of Demography at the
University of Florence, sums up how the population battle of the 1970s
and 1980s appeared to those on the receiving end of Western theories,

advice and coercion: 'in the best of cases [the] advocacy for reduced rates of population increase appeared to be an act of paternalistic preaching – rich countries taking down to poor ones. In the worst of cases it appeared as an arrogant imperialist attitude, prompted by fears that the third world could grow too much.'[19] Some would argue that, Cairo notwithstanding, much the same applies today.

If President Museveni read the World Bank reports of the 1980s, and even that of the ECA, he might have smiled wryly in recent years. It is perfectly possible he *did* read them because their pessimism regarding population growth is so clearly addressed in his 2018 speeches. In 2010, Africa's population reached the 1 billion mark projected by the World Bank 30 years earlier, a size that it had warned would have grave consequences and that characterised the ECA's 'nightmare scenario'.[20] In that scenario, the ECA had warned of socio-economic conditions 'characterised by a degradation of the very essence of human dignity', of disastrous land scarcity 'whereby whole families [will] have to subsist on a mere hectare of land', and of poverty reaching 'unimaginable dimensions'.[21] At the time, the sub-Saharan region in particular was in the midst of a sustained economic upswing and had weathered the global financial crisis of 2007–8 as well as anywhere. In many countries the outlook was brighter than it had been since independence. GDP growth in Uganda averaged 7% a year during the 1990s and 2000s, and the proportion of Ugandans living in extreme poverty had been cut from about 60% almost to 20%.

Food (in)security is certainly still a policy priority throughout Africa, but Western experts have mostly ceased presenting it as an existential threat. The World Bank estimates that Africa has 200 million hectares of suitable land not being used for crops – almost half the world's total, and more than the cultivated area of the US.[22] The continent has sometimes been cast as a potential breadbasket of the world. In 2019, in a blog by a World Bank demographer noting that the population of sub-Saharan Africa had passed 1 billion and that its share of the global population would reach almost a quarter by 2050, there was no sign of the words 'overpopulation', 'crisis' or 'devastating risks' amid the many statistics and charts.[23] Nevertheless, the battle over the management of population growth in Africa has been rejoined, as Museveni's speeches attest.

Burundi, to the south-east of Uganda, is one of the countries most in the spotlight – as it was in the early 1980s. The country's population then was about 4 million and the World Bank estimated its carrying capacity in 2010 at no more than 8 or 9 million. Its population density was deemed 'extremely high', at 154 people per km², three times that of Uganda. Today the population is almost 12 million and will reach 16 million by 2030. If an 'explosion' caused in part by population pressure were to occur anywhere, Burundi would be one of the leading contenders in Africa.

Living conditions in Burundi are extremely exacting for all but a fortunate few. About 90% of the population rely on subsistence agriculture and livestock-rearing; three-quarters live below the extreme poverty line of US$1.90 a day; and 85% of the population face daily food insecurity.[24] In 2018 the United Nations World Food Programme listed the country as having the highest 'hunger score' in the world. The rhetoric of the population explosion era is even deployed by some Burundians. In 'Burundi under Malthus' scrutiny', Louis-Marie Nindorera warns that 'as the demographic time bomb ticks away, the Malthusian noose tightens' around his country. It is, according to Nindorera, 'a textbook case of Malthus' thesis'. Farm sizes now average just half a 'less and less fertile' hectare and population projections for 2050 imply population density among the almost exclusively rural-dwelling population of 1,000 people per km². The government response, to land management and population distribution, is characterised by 'apathy', while in the countryside interpersonal disputes and conflict multiply year by year.[25]

Malawi is another country sometimes said to have reached its population limit relative to the productivity of agricultural land and other resources. Yet Bangladesh, synonymous with abject poverty in the 1970s and 1980s and a poster child for *The Population Bomb*, has a land mass only about a third larger than Malawi, is also predominantly agrarian, and supports a population nearly *nine times* larger than Malawi's 19 million. There has been a 20% improvement in the average calorific intake of Bangladeshis since the mid-1990s and a 50% increase in GDP per capita. It looks set to be struck off the United Nations list of almost 50 'least-developed' countries by the mid-2020s.

Just as population matters faded from Western political and economic discourse, it soon became increasingly obvious to some African experts that, in the words of Professor Alex Ezeh, 'we need to talk frankly about our rapid population growth in Africa if we want to beat poverty'.[26]

5

African Transitions

Fertility transitions in Africa have occurred at different times and different paces. There is no 'Africa pattern'. In most countries in Eastern, Western and Middle Africa fertility decline has been erratic and seldom rapid when compared to other developing regions of the world.

As it drew to a close, the second half of the twentieth century was described by UNPD's director as 'demographically unprecedented in the history of humanity'.[1] Increasingly effective 'death control', especially in developing countries, brought about a sharp fall in mortality. The global fertility rate followed suit, declining from more than six births per woman to 2.7. But whereas the crude death rate almost halved between 1950 and 2000, the crude birth rate only fell by about 20%.[2] The result of this disparity was a surge in the world's population from 2.5 billion to 6.1 billion, an average increase of 1.8% a year over 50 years. During the population boom that accompanied the Industrial Revolution in England, the highest growth rate was 1.25–1.5% a year. It is estimated that the average growth rate of the global population between AD1 and 1700 was just 0.06% a year.[3]

The 'unprecedented' needed explanation, *definition*. The first outline of 'demographic transition' theory was suggested by the American demographer Warren Thompson in the 1920s, although Adolphe Landry was the first to use the term in his 1934 book *La Révolution Démographique*.[4] A 1945 article – 'Population: The long view' – by Frank Notestein, founder of Princeton University's Office of Population Research, is usually credited with being the first formal definition of the transition.[5] A couple of years later Notestein became the first director of the nascent UNPD.

The theory was based on the eighteenth- and nineteenth-century demographic history of Europe and North America. Transition in these regions was slow and varied, taking a century or more in most countries. In France, for example, it began in the eighteenth century and lasted for two centuries. In North America and many European countries the TFR was above seven births when the transition commenced, comparable to the highest fertility countries in Africa today. The theory describes the process by which 'modernising' populations move from having high mortality (death rates) and high fertility (birth rates), with the two roughly in balance and little population growth, to lower mortality rates, rising life expectancy and high fertility, during which population growth will accelerate; to low mortality and fertility, when populations will stabilise. 'For some, transition theory lies at the centre of modern scientific demography,' wrote Notestein's fellow American demographer Dudley Kirk in 1996; '[to] others it is a non-theory to be dismissed as an unproved generalization unworthy of much discussion'.[6]

Notestein attributed the stimulus for demographic transition to social and economic factors associated with modernisation. In the first phase, mortality declines due to medical advances, better nutrition and sanitation, and rising incomes. In the next phase, desired family size – typically large in pre-industrial, agrarian societies – starts to fall as the costs of raising children in a developing society increase and their value as labour or carers for elderly family members diminishes. The transition ends when fertility rates reach replacement – 2.1 births, the level at which a population stabilises if mortality is neither abnormally high nor low.

Replacement-level fertility and stabilisation are anomalous end points. Stability and equilibrium have not been characteristics of human population history, or that of any other species. Furthermore, the theory does not encompass what is now happening in many countries around the world, with deaths exceeding births and fertility rates well below replacement level. To claim that shrinking populations will be a global phenomenon any time soon, as some do, is only plausible if one assumes that the populations of African countries are about to follow suit imminently. As most countries in Eastern, Western and Middle Africa have not completed stage two of demographic transition it is fanciful to expect a conclusion to the process in a couple of decades.

Notestein was confident that as poorer countries industrialised, urbanised and became richer they would follow a similar demographic trajectory to 'First World' countries. But there are no hard-and-fast 'rules', and most leading demographers consider the relationship between socio-economic indicators and transition to be 'typically a loose one'.[7] Michel Garenne has pointed out that in Europe fertility decline was 'virtually unrelated to socio-economic indicators and it affected different countries at different levels of development as measured by income per capita, education level and level of urbanisation'.[8] It also took place before modern contraceptive methods were freely available. A historical perspective underscores just how extraordinary what happened in the 'Third World' in the second half of the twentieth century was. The interesting possibility that the demographic trajectory of 'inter-tropical' Africa – the territory between the Tropic of Capricorn and the Tropic of Cancer – may not strictly conform to theory is seldom raised.

Extensive research undertaken since the 1970s has demonstrated that the main triggers for, and characteristics of, changes in fertility during demographic transitions are far from identical in every location. Rapid fertility declines have occurred in high- and low-income countries, in industrialised and non-industrialised countries, in countries of different faiths and in countries with markedly different levels of urbanisation. Some demographers have stressed the significance in the modern era of the diffusion of ideas and societal interaction in influencing fertility decline.

There are quite a number of predominantly poor, rural countries where rapid declines in fertility have occurred, notably Bangladesh and Indonesia. In Bangladesh the TFR dropped from seven births in the early 1970s to about replacement level in four decades. In Iran, following the 1979 revolution which installed a conservative Muslim theocracy, the TFR fell from 6.5 births in the mid-1980s to below replacement level in just two decades. To put these declines in perspective, a sustained fall of 0.1 a year, or one birth in a decade, is generally considered a rapid fertility transition.

Notestein could not have foreseen the speed and extent of health improvements that started to take root in many developing countries in the 1950s. In the space of two decades, between the early 1950s and early 1970s, global life expectancy at birth rose from 47 to 58 years. Hard on the heels of this remarkable development, modern contraceptive methods became widely available. As a consequence, the demographic transition in most of the developing world proceeded far, far faster than it had in Europe and North America. This entailed very rapid population growth in the transition's early stages.

Figure 7: Simplified phases of demographic transition

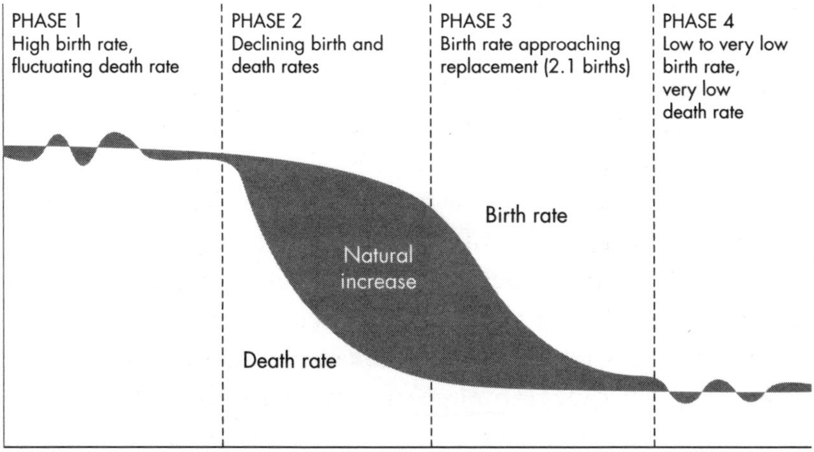
PHASE 1
High birth rate, fluctuating death rate
PHASE 2
Declining birth and death rates
PHASE 3
Birth rate approaching replacement (2.1 births)
PHASE 4
Low to very low birth rate, very low death rate
Birth rate
Natural increase
Death rate

Source: Population Reference Bureau, *2011 World Population Data Sheet.*

Between the early 1960s and 2010, Asia's TFR fell from 5.8 to 2.3 births. Fertility decline began in East Asia. In Japan, an extensive programme to make modern contraception freely available was implemented, in part to counter the alarming prevalence of abortion after the Second World War. The TFR fell from 4.5 births in 1947 to just 2.5 a decade later and Japan completed its fertility transition by the early 1960s. In South Korea, another example of a country where fertility started to fall sharply well before economic 'take-off' and widespread improvements in living conditions, the TFR fell from 5.6 births in the early 1960s to replacement level in the early 1980s. In China, the TFR was above six in the early 1960s, but there too it reached replacement level in the early 1990s.

By the end of the 1970s, fertility transition was under way right across Asia, almost without exception. The pace varied considerably, but by 2010 it was either complete or nearly so in most countries. Very few still have a TFR above three births, most notably Pakistan and Iraq; only Afghanistan and Timor-Leste are above four. In Latin America and the Caribbean fertility also peaked in the early 1960s, and by 2010 the TFR fell from just under six births to 2.3, close to replacement level. Here too there was variation between countries, but, as in Asia, most progressed from high fertility to replacement level (or very close) within a single generation. This was as unexpected to demographers as it was astonishing. In predominantly Catholic Brazil, the most populous country in the region and one without a national population policy, the TFR fell from six in the early 1960s to 1.9 by 2010.

Fertility has not followed a similar downward path yet in most of Africa. At 6.7 births, the TFR in the early 1960s was almost one birth higher than Asia's and Latin America's, but not of a completely different order of magnitude: all three regions were categorised as 'high fertility'. It declined by less than two births to 4.9 in the course of the next five decades. However, the continental fertility rate masks substantial regional differences. Although often referred to for reasons of convenience, there is no such thing as an 'African' demographic trajectory, transition or profile.

In Northern Africa, the TFR was higher than in sub-Saharan regions at nearly seven births per woman in the early 1960s, but a decade later it started to fall quite quickly and the decline was sustained. In fact, between the early 1980s and early 1990s the region's fertility decline was the fastest in the world, led by Algeria with a decline from 6.4 births to 4.3 births – a fall of more than two births in a single decade. By 2010 Northern Africa's average TFR had fallen to three births and in Tunisia, Morocco and Libya was at, or close to, replacement level. Egypt, the region's population heavyweight, had reduced its TFR from almost seven births in the 1950s to three. With a TFR of five, Sudan was the only conspicuous outlier.* Overall, the speed and extent of Northern Africa's fertility decline over half a century did not quite match that of Asia and Latin America/ Caribbean, nor was it quite complete everywhere – but it was still definitive.

In Southern Africa, the fertility transition was comparable to that of Northern Africa. In the early 1970s, South Africa's TFR was the first in the region to register a decline, from a level above six births. The TFR began to fall elsewhere a decade later. Between the early 1980s and 2010, Botswana's TFR halved from nearly six births to 2.9, Namibia's fell from 6.2 to 3.6 and Lesotho's from 5.4 to 3.4. Even in Swaziland, today's Eswatini, with a polygamous monarch and other distinctive traditions that arguably underpin fertility levels, the TFR halved from almost seven births in the early 1970s. By 2010 South Africa's TFR was 2.6 births. As it accounts for 90% of the region's population the regional average was similarly close to replacement level.

Although transitions occurred in Northern and Southern Africa, in 'inter-tropical' Africa – the Eastern, Western and Middle regions – there was still no sign of pervasive fertility decline by the 1980s. Life expectancy in sub-Saharan Africa had shown a dramatic and sustained increase from 36 years in 1950 to 49 years in the early 1980s; infant, child and maternal mortality were also falling sharply, although not nearly as fast as in much of Asia. Yet this did not trigger the fertility decline envisaged by demographic transition theory (and

---

* UNPD used to place Sudan within Eastern Africa, but the country is now included in Northern Africa.

demonstrated by other developing regions of the world). Change was most evident in some of Africa's island nations: Seychelles was demonstrably following the example of Mauritius, where the TFR had halved from more than six births to three in a single decade between the early 1960s and early 1970s – one of the most rapid fertility transitions ever.[9] In many mainland countries, especially in Middle Africa, the TFR actually increased as widespread infertility – usually associated with a high incidence of gonorrhoea – became less common.

Figure 8: Total fertility rate by world region, 1950-55 to 2015-20 (live births per woman)

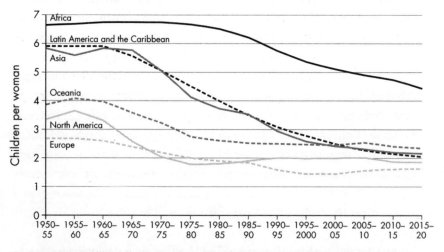

Source: UNPD, *World Population Prospects: The 2019 Revision.*

The 1988 *World Development Report* showed that just four countries in sub-Saharan Africa had a TFR below six births – Gabon, Central African Republic, Chad and Lesotho; and in the first three of these, and possibly Lesotho as well, pathological sterility was a leading factor, not the onset of a fertility transition.[10] The average population growth rate in the region rose inexorably from about 2% a year in 1950 to 2.7% in 1970 to more than 3% in 1990. At that date, the TFRs of Eastern and Western Africa were largely unchanged over two decades at seven births and 6.6 births respectively, while in Middle Africa the

TFR had risen from 6.1 births to 6.7 births. Meanwhile, the median age of the region had dropped to just 16.4 years.

A country-by-country analysis shows that in 1950 none of the 39 mainland sub-Saharan countries had a growth rate above 3%; and 29 countries had a TFR above six. By the late 1980s 23 countries were growing at more than 3% and 32 countries had a TFR above six. Burkina Faso, Mali, Niger, Chad, Burundi, Uganda, Angola and DRC had fertility rates close to or above seven births.[11] In Kenya and Niger, the cumulative fertility rate at age 50 exceeded nine births per woman in the late 1960s and early 1980s respectively, briefly challenging the 'world record of outstandingly high fertility' held by the Hutterites of North Dakota, an Anabaptist sect originally from Moravia, in the 1920s and 1930s.[12] In Rwanda as well, the TFR almost reached nine in the late 1970s and was still above eight (and rising again) at the start of the 1990s. Furthermore, there was no sign of let-up. The 10 countries with the highest adolescent birth rate in the world were all African, headed by Angola, where one in four births were to mothers aged between 15 and 19, and followed by Niger, Chad, Museveni's Uganda, Mali, Mozambique, Gabon, Guinea, Cameroon and Sierra Leone.[13] What was occurring, in inter-tropical Africa at least, was as conspicious as the rapid fertility decline spreading through Asia.

Soon after the Caldwells warned in 1990 that population growth was a 'grave threat' to sub-Saharan Africa – even graver than in earlier decades – there was confirmation that fertility was falling in a few of the inter-tropical countries. In Kenya and Zimbabwe the evidence was indisputable. The Kenya 1989 Demographic and Health Survey (DHS) showed a dramatic fall in the TFR from eight births a decade earlier to 6.7 births; the 1998 DHS recorded a further drop to 4.7 births. In just 20 years, Kenya's TFR had reduced by more than three births. This was remarkable, and exceptional. Potential early signs of a fertility transition detected in Tanzania, Senegal, South West Nigeria, Northern Sudan, Burundi, Mali and Togo were all far more modest.

Nevertheless, by the mid-1990s many leading demographers thought that quite widespread, rapid fertility decline may have begun as sub-Saharan countries started to 'catch up' with other developing regions.

Demographic detail

The Demographic and Health Surveys (DHS) Program has been running since 1984, conducting more than 400 surveys in over 90 countries. It evolved from the World Fertility Surveys carried out in the 1970s and 1980s. The programme is implemented by strategic consultancy ICF International, based in Maryland, and partners; it is primarily funded by the United States Agency for International Development (USAID). The objective is to collect high-quality, representative demographic and health data to inform policy development and national and local planning.

DHSs are widely acknowledged as a transparent, reliable and extensive resource. Reports are routinely used by governmental institutions and planners, development agencies and researchers. About half of all surveys have been carried out in Africa. They are produced in close collaboration with national statistics offices and government departments such as health ministries. National institutions conduct, and are ethically responsible for, surveys. Technical support is provided if and where required, thereby strengthening statistical capacity and capabilities.

Statisticians decide how many women should be interviewed in each region to secure representative results; less populous regions are oversampled. As the number of women interviewed in each region will not match the actual distribution of women in the country, it is then weighted to resemble the actual distribution of the population. Surveys are conducted over a number of months, usually using the national census as the sample frame. Households from all regions are selected for interview through an 'equal probability systematic selection process' designed to yield a nationally representative results.

Sample sizes are substantial, with more than 90% of selected households typically agreeing to participate. All women aged 15-49 and all men aged 15-59 who are permanent residents of the selected households or who stayed in the households the night before the survey are eligible for interview. DHS use a woman's questionnaire, a man's questionnaire and a household questionnaire. These solicit answers to a broad range of questions relating to personal backgrounds, fertility, contraception, maternal and child health, nutrition and gender issues. Information is also gathered about the characteristics of each household – what the home is made of, sources of water, sanitation and possessions. Questions are standardised, making them comparable to previous surveys and between countries.

Responses are collected through face-to-face interviews with women and men. Interviewees choose which language they are questioned in. For example, in Zambia, where the 2018 DHS was carried out by 22 teams of seven members, respondents could choose from Bemba, Kaonde, Lozi, Lunda, Luvale, Nyanja and Tonga, as well as English.

Source: The DHS Program www.dhsprogram.com

There was some uncertainty, and lively debate. The DHS Program (see text box) was new – was its data comparable to the World Fertility Surveys that preceded it? How complementary was its data to census reports that were steadily improving in number and quality? Some demographers suggested that conflict and ongoing economic crises in the region might be acting as a catalyst to lower fertility, contrary to the long-prevalent orthodoxy that extra children provided an insurance policy in tough times, particularly in rural communities.[14] Others, like Ronald Lesthaeghe and Carole Jolly, remained cautious about what was occurring:

It would be totally premature to conclude that the experience of Botswana, Zimbabwe or Kenya inaugurates a continent-wide fertility decline, and that the continuing economic crisis would have an undifferentiated positive effect on the start of the fertility transition. As the economic and political crises deepen to the point that entire regions are returning to a subsistence economy (or to below subsistence level in areas with military operations), one cannot rule out a substantial postponement of the fertility reduction. Rising mortality (other than AIDS-related) and emigration, i.e. the old Malthusian spectres, may then take the upper hand. Hence, further close monitoring of each specific situation is an absolute necessity. The only positive news is that a fertility decline has at last proven to be a possible outcome in sub-Saharan areas...[15]

It would transpire that caution was merited, but that was not immediately apparent. By the end of the 1990s, in addition to Botswana, Kenya and Zimbabwe, there appeared to be more examples of rapid fertility transitions emerging. In Western Africa, despite usage of modern contraceptive methods by married women being no higher than 20%,[16] the TFR in Côte d'Ivoire had declined from 7.4 births to 4.5 between the mid-1970s and mid-1990s, and the TFR in Ghana had fallen from 6.7 births to 3.8. Demographer Paulina Makinwa-Adebusoye, a former president of the Population Association of Nigeria, identified the onset of a fertility decline 'among all sub-groups of the Nigeria population (rural, urban, educated and non-educated and irrespective of geo-political location'). She considered that 'fertility decline may come more rapidly than would otherwise appear' in Africa due to 'profound socio-economic changes', and that it might be time to 'qualify the notion that sub-Saharan Africa... is different from the rest of the world'.[17] There were also half a dozen countries in Eastern and Western Africa where the fertility rate was unchanged in half a century, but many of them were affected by conflict and it was unlikely that *all* populations in these two regions would have started a fertility transition virtually simultaneously.

At the start of the new millennium the World Bank launched *Can Africa Claim the 21st Century?*, more upbeat in tone and outlook than its doom-laden reports of the 1980s. It was described as a 'landmark prospectus for African development'. The Bretton Woods institutions and Western donors were keen to support a 'new beginning' for Africa, and the causes of what was referred to as its 'stalled development' and lack of economic progress were being exhaustively debated. As a *Foreign Affairs* reviewer of the report pointed out, renewed interest in the continent seemed to involve very little self-examination on the part of the Western governments and agencies apparently queueing up to 'save' it. Referring to the economic reforms imposed on more than half of Africa's countries since the 1980s and the co-responsibility of Western financial institutions in Africa's indebtedness, the reviewer noted that 'the worst effects of structural adjustment are barely mentioned, and only two pages are devoted to the urgent need for debt relief'.[18] The report contained a familiar caveat about the continent's 'exceptional' demography: 'if Africa is to claim the twenty-first century, it must reverse this late 20th century pattern of rapid population growth'.

Soon afterwards, evidence began to emerge that the nascent fertility transition in sub-Saharan Africa was not proceeding quite as some had expected. Using the data from DHSs conducted either side of the millennium, John Bongaarts vice-president at the Population Council wrote first about fertility 'stalls' in Ghana and Kenya; and then, in a subsequent paper, argued that this phenomenon seemed to have been experienced in at least a dozen countries – Cameroon, Côte d'Ivoire, Ethiopia, Ghana, Kenya, Mozambique, Nigeria, Rwanda, Tanzania, Uganda, Zambia and Zimbabwe. Among them were countries that had been classified as 'mid-transition' as their fertility declines had appeared to be well advanced, as well as others in the early stages of transition.[19] While fertility stalls had occurred in Asia and Latin America, and those in Bangladesh and Egypt at the end of the 1990s had attracted particular attention from demographers, in most countries in the developing world the fastest rate of decline had occurred in the early stages of transition.

There was no consensus regarding exactly how many African countries were stalling, partly due to the use of different definitions to determine whether a fertility transition had commenced in the first place and what constituted a stall. Michel Garenne identified possible stalls in Ghana, Kenya, urban Madagascar, Nigeria, rural Rwanda and rural Tanzania.[20] David Shapiro and Tesfayi Gebreselassie identified stalls in eight out of 24 early- and mid-transition countries for which there were multiple DHSs – Ghana, Kenya, Cameroon, Guinea, Mozambique, Rwanda, Senegal and Tanzania.[21] Bruno Schoumaker, at the Université catholique de Louvain, found evidence of a stall only in Kenya and possibly Rwanda.[22] A 2010 DHS Working Paper by Kazuyo Machiyama at LSHTM re-examined the survey data from either side of the millennium to identify in which of nine sub-Saharan countries specific data limitations may have distorted TFR figures. Setting aside 'fluctuations' in countries with a TFR above five births – the case in Tanzania and Uganda, for example – Machiyama concluded that the evidence for a stall in Kenya, Benin, Rwanda and Zambia was 'compelling'.[23] Although Garenne considered stalls to be 'uncommon in African countries' and 'minor accidents in the course of the fertility transition', he warned that 'if they last longer, they could have serious consequences for long-term demographic dynamics, especially when they occur at relatively high levels of fertility'. He added that, as is always the case with fertility, 'anything could happen in the future'.[24]

Some of the countries identified as having stalled regained momentum. By 2010, Ethiopia's TFR was again falling and DHS data showed an overall decline from 6.5 births to 4.9 over 20 years. By 2020, it was close to 4 births. In Rwanda, following the introduction of a new population policy, the government succeeded in encouraging a one-third fall in the TFR, from 6.1 births in 2005 to 4.2 a decade later, an 'astonishingly rapid transformation' in the words of LSHTM's John Cleland.[25] The proportion of Rwandan women with three children already who expressed the desire to have no more doubled from a quarter to more than half during the 2000s.[26] The results of government commitment and a modern contraceptive-usage rate rising to almost 60% were also evident in the island nation of Cabo Verde, where the TFR had fallen to just 2.5 births from six in the late

1970s. However, there was no discernible uniformity across inter-tropical Africa, or if there was it supported a picture of a very slow transition advancing in fits and starts.

By 2005–10, 35 out of 42 sub-Saharan countries with sufficient data had technically commenced a fertility transition, in that the TFR had fallen 10% from its peak (a common measure of the start of transition). But the region's TFR had still only declined from 6.5 births in 1985–90 to 5.4 births – just over one birth in two decades. Furthermore, fertility declines appeared to be almost exclusively an urban phenomenon, and the most recent DHSs showed that desired family size among women aged 20–35 across sub-Saharan Africa was stable at a level above five children.[27] In Western Africa, among women aged 15–49 the desired number of children remained above six until the late 2000s.[28] This measure is not perfect, in that it is open to bias, but many demographers regard it as the 'least problematic'[29] indicator of fertility preferences.

John Bongaarts estimated at the end of the 2000s that if the current rate of fertility decline in inter-tropical Africa continued, it might take 'more than a century' to reach a desired family size closer to two children. If so, 'massive population growth' would be inevitable.[30] Outside Northern and Southern Africa, the only mainland African countries with a TFR below four births in 2010 were tiny Djibouti in the Horn of Africa and Zimbabwe (which many consider should be included in the Southern Africa region anyway). In most of sub-Saharan Africa, instead of the catch-up assumed by commentators hailing the waning support for the concept of a population explosion, fertility transition looked considerably slower and more turbulent than in Asia or Latin America/Caribbean.

Africa-focused demographers have continued to pay close attention to stalling fertility transitions. A 2013 analysis of the latest DHS data for 12 high- and intermediate-fertility countries* identified that although the trend was slowly downwards, in six of them – Benin, Burkina Faso, Cameroon, Chad, Guinea and Mozambique – the TFR had

---

* Benin, Burkina Faso, Cameroon, Chad, Guinea, Mozambique, Zambia, Zimbabwe, Lesotho, Mali, Niger and Nigeria.

actually risen between the two most recent surveys.[31] Furthermore, in Niger, Gabon, Cameroon, Chad and Nigeria women were still expressing the desire to have more children than the national TFR, an unusual phenomenon even in high-fertility countries. Another study showed that in Angola, Gambia and Uganda it had taken 40 years for the TFR to fall by 10% from its peak and thereby supposedly signal the start of a fertility transition.[32] Meanwhile, in Northern Africa – where transition was considered well advanced – the TFR rose in Algeria and Egypt in the first decade of the century. More recently, the TFR in Rwanda, having declined from 6.1 births to 4.6 births between the 2005 and 2010 DHS, appeared to stall above four births during the 2010s.

In 1986, the World Bank had argued in *Population Growth and Policies in Sub-Saharan Africa* that the region simply had not reached the level of socio-economic development necessary for sustained fertility decline. This was a surprising and anomalous contention even at the time, given that most countries in East and Southeast Asia had lower GDP per capita and worse development indicators than Africa and sub-Saharan Africa when they had started their fertility transitions in the 1960s and 1970s.[33] Moreover, many of the fertility stalls mentioned occurred when most African countries had succeeded in registering the longest period of growth in GDP per capita in many decades. In 2012, the AfDB highlighted Uganda, Tunisia, Malawi, Egypt and Burkina Faso as having increased GDP per capita by more than 3% a year for periods ranging from five to 13 years; Rwanda had managed more than 4% growth for over a decade; and Mozambique recorded in excess of 5% growth between 1996 and 2008 as it began to recover from a protracted civil war.[34] In 20 of the 24 countries analysed by the AfDB, poverty reduction was also under way, albeit 'modestly'; infant and child mortality rates were declining; and the gap in primary-school enrolment with other regions had narrowed considerably since the late 1990s. Yet almost all the countries named above had been cited by at least one leading demographer as experiencing a fertility stall.

The research into fertility stalls and new DHS data were closely followed by UNPD. When Kenya's 2003 DHS showed a stall, the medium-variant projection for 2050 was raised at a stroke from 44 million to 83 million.[35] In 2009, a UNPD study analysing fertility trends in the 31 African countries categorised as 'least developed' presented further evidence that although technically a transition was under way – the TFR in these countries had fallen by 10% to 5.8 births between 1995 and 2005 after little change in the preceding three decades – other indicators did not point to the onset of rapid, sustainable decline. Adolescent birth rates were unchanged at 130 per thousand, and the use of either modern or traditional methods of contraception, although having doubled in a decade, remained extremely low: only about one in 10 married women were using modern contraceptive methods.[36] All this was to have a dramatic impact on projections presented in the 2010 and 2012 *World Population Prospects* reports.

6

Inconvenient Truths

UNPD is regarded as the 'go-to' source of population projections. Its record for global projections over a timespan of two to three decades is good. This has proved inconvenient for commentators claiming that the global population will stabilise within a few decades and then start to fall. Furthermore, Africa's demographic trajectory this century has caught everyone out.

In 1968, the year of *The Population Bomb*, Philip M. Hauser, president of the American Sociological Association, the American Statistical Association and the Population Association of America, predicted a global population of 9.7 billion in 2018.[1] His figure was comparable to UNPD's high-variant* projection at the time (and its current medium-variant projection for 2050). Hauser was decidedly pessimistic. For the US, 1968 was the year of Martin Luther King Jr's and Bobby Kennedy's assassinations, the birth of the women's movement, race and anti-war riots, 'Commies' under every bed, and the shock of the Tet Offensive in Vietnam. Rebellions and revolutions erupted in numerous countries around the world. 'Given the present outlook,' Hauser opined, 'only the faithful who believe in miracles from heaven, the optimistic who anticipate superwonders from science, the parochial fortunate who think they can continue to exist on islands of affluence in a sea of

---

* High-variant projections assume a TFR 0.5 births above the medium variant over most of the projected period, low variants assume 0.5 births less than the medium variant.

world poverty, and the naïve who anticipate nothing can look to the future with equanimity.'[2] The figure proved to be about 2 billion too high, substantially due to the rapid and sustained fertility decline in most of Asia described in the previous chapter, particularly in China. At the end of the twentieth century UNPD was frequently under fire for alleged overestimation.

When UNPD presented *World Population Prospects: The 1998 Revision* it reduced its medium-variant projection for the global population in 2050 by a substantial 0.5 billion, from 9.4 billion to 8.9 billion. This meant that in the few years since the Cairo conference in 1994 almost a billion people had been shaved off the mid-century figure. With annual population growth falling to its slowest rate since the Second World War, the claims of Ben Wattenberg, Nicholas Eberstadt and others that the population explosion was over looked justified. The demographer Gerhard Heilig at the International Institute of Applied Systems Analysis (IIASA) in Laxenburg, Austria, noted that 'some mass media' had been led 'to jump to the conclusion that world population growth will be over soon' and warned that 'this rash judgment would be premature'.[3] Heilig would prove correct, and the demography of Africa would play a major part in that being the case.

When UNPD published *World Population Prospects: The 2000 Revision*, the medium-variant projection for 2050 was raised back to 9.3 billion. Joseph Chamie, UNPD's director, told the Commission on Population and Development at the United Nations, 'I am hoping that our population projections for the future are wrong.'[4] Assumptions for fertility decline in least-developed countries, many of them in Africa, were proving too optimistic. Some of UNPD's most ardent critics charged that the organisation was nothing but an agent for the family planning advocacy of UNFPA and was trying to stoke population alarmism again to justify corrective action by imposing coercive birth-control measures in developing countries.

Within two decades of the *1998 Revision* – less than half the time predicted by Wattenberg and Eberstadt – the global population reached 7.7 billion. Hauser's 1968 prediction for Africa's headcount in 2018 proved accurate despite his global figure having been way too high. Far from having gone into 'free-fall', as Wattenberg anticipated, the global TFR has decreased from 2.8 to 2.5 births in the twenty-first century, a rate of 0.15 births per decade. UNPD low-variant projections for 2050 made in the mid-1990s have already been exceeded by half of the 12 countries listed at the time as likely to be the most populous in mid-century; China and the US already surpass their mid-century low-variant projections by 20%.

Ironically, only a mortality catastrophe on the scale of the Black Death in the fourteenth century could now make Wattenberg's prediction for the world's population to peak at 7.7 billion correct – and he envisaged that peak occurring in 2050, not 2020. Today, UNPD's medium-variant projection for the global population in 2050 stands at 9.7 billion, compared to 9.4 billion in 1996. It has remained in a range of 8.9–9.7 billion for a quarter of a century, a difference between low and high of less than 10%.

Many of UNPD's detractors and population optimists simply paid too little attention to Africa. This is perhaps unsurprising. The population of the continent was no greater than that of Europe (including Russia) in the mid-1990s. It was often simply assumed that fertility would drop soon and fast, as it had done in most other parts of the developing world. If specific knowledge of African demography was limited to quite a small cohort of experts, however, no one could fail to know that HIV/AIDS was exacting a great toll on many of its countries. This *was* on the front pages of newspapers, and commentators tended to assume that it would hasten the end of population growth in large parts of Africa. This, some claimed, was a key factor being missed by UNPD.

UNPD was not 'missing' the impact of HIV/AIDS, of course. In 2000 its demographers revised average life expectancy downwards in the 29 worst-affected African countries, by seven years to 47. In some of them, a quarter of the adult population was HIV-positive. In Zambia and Zimbabwe life expectancy at birth fell below 33 years, the same level as 50 years earlier. This introduced additional difficulty to the business of making projections, especially in the absence of a readily available 'cure'. How bad might the situation become?

Simultaneously, the complications arising from stalling fertility declines were preoccupying Africa-focused demographers.

At this juncture of considerable uncertainty, UNPD's record was subjected to examination by a group of eminent demographers appointed by the US's National Research Council. The Panel on Population Projections published its report in 2002 and UNPD's record was found to be a creditable one. In 1958, its medium-variant projection for the global population in the year 2000 was 6.3 billion. At the time this seemed fantastical – even apocalyptic – to many: it implied that the number of people in the world would triple between the end of the Second World War and the start of the new century. In 1966 the projection stood at 6.1 billion. In 1996, three decades later, it still stood at 6.1 billion, 220 million – or 3.6% – lower than the projection made in 1958 but matching the one made in 1966.[5] The actual outcome in 2000 was 6.145 billion.

Over four decades UNPD global projections for the year 2000, and also those of demographers at the World Bank, erred by amounts considered by the Panel to be 'quite modest', although 'not statistically insignificant': between 1% and 4% with only one exception, a 7% variance in the 1968 projection.[6] All variances were on the high side, mostly due to more rapid falls in fertility than anticipated in a number of countries, particularly in Asia. The degree of accuracy in the global projections is striking, especially considering that China's TFR fell from almost five births in the early 1970s to about 1.5 by 2000, a rapid rate of decline that could not have been foreseen in the 1960s and 1970s. This was balanced by slower fertility declines elsewhere. The accuracy of projecting for high-fertility countries inevitably involves swings and roundabouts.

Sceptics might label projections 'fictitious models of what may transpire', a tongue-in-cheek remark once made by Philip Hauser. While this was certainly true of his own 50-year global projection made in 1968, most in the demography profession are complimentary about UNPD's record. 'One might quibble with this or that assumption but the UN projections have had an impressive record of success at the global level,'[7] Professor Ronald Lee at the

University of California, Berkeley, wrote in the journal *Science*. 'Over a horizon of a few decades, UN projections have a good record of predictive validity at global and regional levels,'[8] LSHTM Professor John Cleland concurs. *The Economist* describes UNPD as 'the world's most important watcher of human tides'.[9]

UNPD also convened its own expert meeting in 2002 to discuss guidelines for fertility change used in projections for intermediate-fertility countries – those with TFRs in the range from 2.1 births to five births. Until the 2000s, medium-variant projections assumed that fertility in such countries would not fall below replacement level – 2.1 births – by 2050. But in an increasing number of developed and developing countries, the TFR had fallen below replacement and stayed there. In some cases, the TFR 'floor' was well below replacement, closer to one birth than two. In 2002 a decision was taken to recognise this reality by projecting for fertility in intermediate-fertility countries to converge on a floor of 1.85 by 2050, and for fertility in all countries eventually to fall (or rise) to that level. Projection models incorporating this new determinant were introduced in *World Population Prospects: The 2004 Revision*.

Within UNPD the adoption of the new assumption was considered a 'momentous change'.[10] It denoted the statistical recognition that fertility was falling further in much of the world than had previously been modelled. However, some demographers pointed out that there was little evidence for fertility recovering to 1.85 in countries where it had fallen well below that level. The significance of this difference of opinion was material: if global fertility were to fall further than was being anticipated, the global population would inevitably start to decline in the twenty-first century. If it also fell faster than UNPD anticipated, decline would start sooner. That possibility was seized upon by some commentators and cast as a certainty. Not all of them read the caveats delivered at the same time as the 1.85 birth-fertility floor was introduced.

UNPD emphasised that, despite the modification, it was more or less inevitable that the global total would increase by 3 billion people by the middle of the century, an increase of 50% to about 9 billion; and that the speed of decline in the growth rate would slow as lower levels of fertility were reached. In his keynote address at the 2002 expert meeting, the veteran Australian demographer John Caldwell expressed concern that 'governments of developed countries seemed to be losing interest in the population issue', despite this 'huge population growth' over the next half-century. It is a moot point to what extent this was due to the publicity attracted by the claim that the population 'explosion' was over, or to the as yet unquantifiable impact of HIV/AIDS.

'The immediate challenge', in Caldwell's view, was 'to maintain some of the attitudes, policies and foreign assistance expenditures that had so far sustained the fertility decline in the developing world.' He warned that if this was not the case, the global population could rise to 10, 11 or even 12 billion. At these levels the human burden on the planet would be 'environmentally unsustainable'. It would lead to migration pressures on developed countries 'probably far greater than... those countries desire', and living conditions in the burgeoning number of large cities around the world would become a serious problem, especially for the health of the poor.[11] To population optimists this was pure scaremongering. It had all been heard before.

While the UN's global projections for the year 2000 made in the preceding four decades had mostly proved quite accurate, the margin of error in regional population projections was greater. The Panel on Population Projections report found that on average the divergence was about 8% in 15-year projections and 15% in 25-year projections – mostly on the high side. The principal exception was Africa, which continued to meet or exceed the highest projections made for the continent.[12] Although projection remained challenging against a backdrop of the HIV/AIDS crisis and erratic fertility rates, the volume and quality of data was steadily improving with the conduct of more regular, and better, censuses and the DHS Program.

As for individual country projections, and projections for discrete age groups, the Panel found that the 'length effect' of using an incorrect baseline was the cause of even larger errors – sometimes as great as 50%. These were progressively eradicated as data improved. By the new

Figure 9: UNPD forecasts 1957-98 for the world population in the year 2000

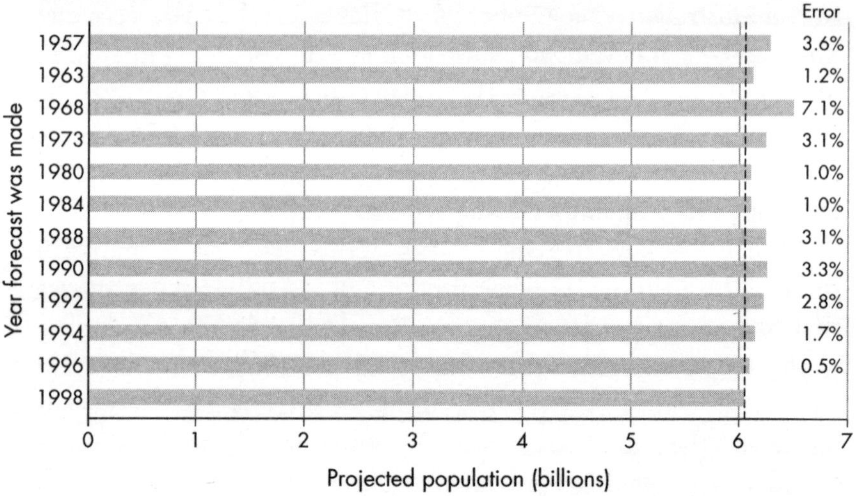

Year forecast was made	Error
1957	3.6%
1963	1.2%
1968	7.1%
1973	3.1%
1980	1.0%
1984	1.0%
1988	3.1%
1990	3.3%
1992	2.8%
1994	1.7%
1996	0.5%
1998	

Projected population (billions)

Source: John Bongaarts and Rodolfo Bulatao (eds) (2000), *Beyond Six Billion: Forecasting the World's Population*, The National Academies Press, Washington DC.

millennium the error in country populations averaged 4.8% in five-year projections but a far-from-negligible 17% in 30-year projections.[13]

Despite its record on global projections in particular, there was no let-up in the volume of criticism directed at UNPD demographers for overestimation as the 2000s progressed. For example, in a paper published in 2004 – 'Global Population Projections: Is the UN Getting it Wrong?' – an Australian professor of economics charged that 'the changes in the most important factor of all – the fertility rate – are hardly understood [by UNPD] and have been very poorly forecast'. Like Wattenberg a few years earlier, the author argued that if this had not been the case, 'maybe we could have been spared some of the more outrageous claims by proponents of population control and, more recently, by those concerned about environmental issues'. In his opinion, UNPD still appeared 'to be underestimating the future decline in fertility rates, despite all evidence to the contrary'.[14]

Leading demographers familiar with Africa knew that there was no sign of Wattenberg's fertility 'free-fall' there. In 2001, echoing Gerhard Heilig's earlier scepticism about pronouncements that global population growth was coming to an end, Jean-Pierre Guengant and John F. May warned that 'Sub-Saharan fertility rates will not necessarily decline as rapidly as has been experienced elsewhere in the world.'[15] They were not the only ones to hold this opinion. As evidence accumulated, population optimists scrambled to adjust their narrative as the evidence disproving their claims accumulated in the new century, or simply carried on – like King Canute – as if they were still right in believing that 'peak population' was imminent.

In August 2009, *The Economist* headlined an article 'Africa's population: The baby bonanza'.[16] It was an early sign that after a decade of limited interest media attention was starting to refocus on the continent's demography. In July 2011, UNPD published its biennial *World Population Prospects: The 2010 Revision*. This revealed that since 1999 the global population had increased by more than 15%, from 6 billion to 7 billion in the space of just 11 years. The medium-variant projection for the global population in 2050 was raised from 9.15 billion to 9.3 billion. An upward revision of the mid-century projection for Africa by 10%, to 2.2 billion, more than accounted for the increase in the global figure.

The likelihood of the world adding the equivalent of another China and India by mid-century was increasing, in turn making stabilisation of the global population by the end of the century less likely. This high-profile and contentious issue was further addressed by UNPD in its presentation for the first time in *World Population Prospects* of projections to 2100. The medium-variant projection for the end of the century was 10.1 billion, 800 million people higher than in 2050. As usual, some rubbished the suggestion that stabilisation would not occur around the middle of the century, as they expected. The removal of the fertility floor of 1.85 births for countries with below-replacement fertility seemed to acknowledge that fertility, once lower than the floor, might stay there, and encouraged them in their belief that UNPD was still overestimating global fertility levels in its projections.

A closer look at sub-Saharan Africa revealed the opposite problem. The use of 'standardised global trajectories' in projections, whereby a country's trajectory was based on trends in fertility elsewhere, was being found deficient for many countries. It had the effect of assuming that fertility decline would be more rapid than was actually likely, especially in the case of countries where no decline at all was apparent. In 2010, Gerhard Heilig, by now chief of UNPD's Estimates and Projections Section, reiterated the caution he had expressed a dozen years earlier, when some were trumpeting the end of the population explosion. The unpredictability of human behaviour always needed to be borne in mind, he warned, and it was important to remember that '[w]hile the past decline in fertility in most countries strongly indicates a general trend towards low fertility, it is possible that some populations might not follow these trends'.[17] There were now

Figure 10: Mean absolute error in UNPD country population projections 1957-98 for the year 2000 (by projection length and region)

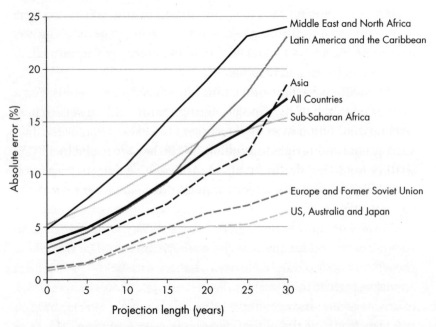

Source: John Bongaarts and Rodolfo Bulatao (eds) (2000), *Beyond Six Billion: Forecasting the World's Population,* The National Academies Press, Washington DC.

clear signs that the methodology of UNPD, so often charged with overestimation, was *under*estimating in sub-Saharan Africa.

World Population Prospects: The 2010 Revision marked a major milestone for Africa, and its potential influence on global projections. The continent's population now surpassed 1 billion and was, as Museveni would say of Uganda, 'beginning to gallop'. The population of the sub-Saharan countries had increased by a factor of more than 4.5 times since the 1950s, from 186 million to 856 million, and had overtaken that of Europe, which had only expanded by 35% to 738 million. Even Northern Africa's population had almost quadrupled in size since 1950, despite the fact that the TFR in most of the region's countries had fallen considerably since the 1970s. For comparison, Asia's population had 'only' tripled, from 1.4 billion to 4.2 billion, and Latin America's had expanded by 3.5 times, from 167 million to 590 million. Whereas in 1960 Asia's population was six times that of Africa, the differential had narrowed to about 3.5 times and by 2050 Asia's headcount was set to be only twice that of Africa. In horse-racing parlance, Africa was demonstrably 'coming up fast on the inside' with little sign of 'fading'. Fertility aside, average life expectancy in Africa, at 55 years, was still 15 years lower than in any other world region, creating further potential upward pressure on population projections. By 2010, the impact of HIV/ AIDS was deemed to have peaked.

The medium-variant projection for Africa in 2050 envisaged a further doubling of its population to 2.2 billion. If, however, there were no diminution in average fertility – UNPD's 'constant-fertility' variant – it would triple to 3 billion. While few, if any, believed that fertility would not decline at all, the UNPD high-variant projection of 2.5 billion, based on a TFR of 3.5 births in 2050 rather than three, was not so easily dismissed.

World Population Prospects: The 2012 Revision involved an Africa 'reset' – or, for some, bombshell. The medium-variant global projection for 2050 was raised again, this time to 9.6 billion. This was almost as high as the projection made in 1994, before the succession of downward revisions that prompted the unofficial declaration in Western media of the end of the population explosion. The 2100 projection was raised by more than 700 million to 10.9 billion. The population balloon seemed to be well and truly reflating, to the irritation of some, the disbelief of others and the concern of many.

Over 80% of the increase in both the 2050 and 2100 projections was attributable to Africa. The 2010 round of African censuses had confirmed mounting evidence from other sources of slower than expected declines in fertility in many countries – and the caution of Heilig and other demographers. In 15 countries, most of them African, estimates of current fertility rates had to be raised by about a quarter of a child, with a knock-on effect on projections. In all, censuses confirmed that half the population of Africa lived in countries with a higher fertility rate in 2010 than anticipated by UNPD; and less than 15% lived in countries where the fertility rate was lower than anticipated.

In a significant paragraph of the main section of the *2012 Revision*, UNPD confirmed that the use of standardised trajectories had been shown to be 'rather optimistic in the face of the recent empirical evidence' in sub-Saharan Africa. It confirmed that a 'different combination of factors (in terms of different patterns of female education, union formation, length of birth intervals, ideal number of children, adoption of modern contraceptive methods)' was at work in the region, and this meant that projections based on 'the general path... experienced in other regions', including Northern Africa, did not reflect an appropriate degree of uncertainty.[18] A short explanatory briefing note about 'the role of fertility in Africa' in the upward revision of global population projections was also issued.[19]

In a 2004 publication, *World Population to 2300*, UNPD had projected a medium scenario for 2050 of 8.9 billion, a peak in the global population at 9.2 billion in 2075, and a slight easing to 9.1 billion at the end of the century. Less than a decade later the medium scenario for 2050 was 9.6 billion, rising continuously to 10.9 billion at the end of the century. In that decade the projection for Africa's population in 2050 had risen from 1.8 billion to 2.4 billion, and for 2100 it had almost doubled from 2.3 billion to 4.2 billion. Instead of the continent adding about 1 billion people in the first half of the century, as envisaged in 2004, it would add 1.6 billion; and in the twenty-first

Figure 11: Comparison of UNPD medium-variant population projections from 1981 and 2017

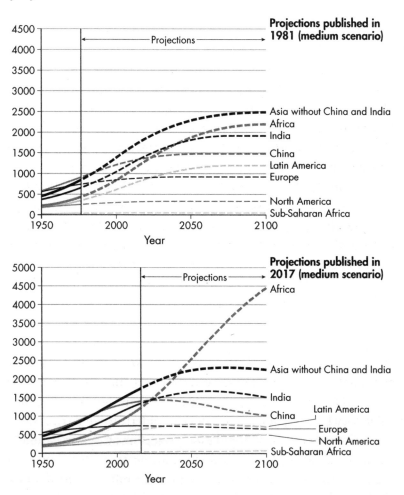

Source: Adapted from Gilles Pison, 'There's a strong chance that one-third of all people will be African by 2100', *The Conversation*, 10 Oct 2017.

century as a whole it would add 3.4 billion people, compared to 1.5 billion envisaged in 2004. 'It seems scarcely possible that sub-Saharan Africa could feed two billion people,' the publication stated, a familiar reprise of Western scepticism about the prospects for food security ever since the 1970s.[20]

The order of magnitude of the increase was so astonishing as to be, for some, literally incredible. With almost half the world's population living in countries with sub-replacement fertility in 2010, how was it possible – given that the population explosion was over – that the global population was going to grow by more than 50% in the first half of the century and by more than 80% over the whole century? One thing was certain. After a brief lull post-Cairo the term 'population explosion' was again being used by some demographers and in Western media headlines.

As far as African country projections were concerned, since the start of the century the medium scenario for Nigeria's population in 2050 had risen from 125 million to almost 400 million; for Malawi, a population of 50 million was now envisaged compared to 30 million in 2000; and for Tanzania, 140 million against 80 million. Since the *2008 Revision* the mid-century projection for Burundi had been raised from 14 million to 27 million, that for Ethiopia from 145 million to 188 million, and for Cameroon from 38 million to 49 million. Downward revisions of projections for the populations of African countries in 2050 have been quite rare in the twenty-first century.

The current trajectories of Burundi, Malawi, Niger, Nigeria, Somalia, Uganda and Tanzania imply that their populations could increase fivefold by 2100. Globally, just six countries account for more than half of the global population increase projected by the end of the century. Alongside India and the US, four are African: Nigeria, DRC, Tanzania and Uganda. In an interview with the *Los Angeles Times* after release of the *2012 Revision*, John Bongaarts at the Population Council remarked that the higher projections were 'a warning sign that people in Africa are in more trouble than we thought'.[21]

Some commentators continued to ignore or dismiss the output of 'the world's most important watcher of human tides' as politically biased, engineered or even incompetent. In *Peoplequake*, published at much the same time as the *2010 Revision*, science writer Fred Pearce suggested that the global population 'getting to eight billion could take 20 years or more years if we get there at all'.[22] In other words, it would happen by the mid-2030s. By 2019, eight years later, the global population had already increased by 10% from 7 billion to 7.7 billion. It is a near-certainty that it will have reached 8.5 billion by 2030. More egregiously, a global strategist at Deutsche Bank attracted extensive media attention the same year for an article in which he declared that UNPD's projections 'misrepresent underlying demographic dynamics'. China and India were mentioned in the piece, but not a single African country or even, quite remarkably given its ever-growing demographic significance, the African continent.[23]

Two years later, after the *2012 Revision*, the Deutsche Bank strategist had branded himself a 'rogue demographer' and claimed that the fertility rate was falling in 'many' developing countries much faster than UNPD was acknowledging; and that its projections therefore 'simply cannot be credible'. The *Financial Times* described the claim as 'a stunning act of *lèse-majesté*'.[24] In a note for Deutsche Bank's clients the rogue demographer stated that the global TFR would reach replacement level by 2025. This was literally impossible, a demographic 'howler'.

Africa was again barely mentioned in this second article. However, the rogue demographer did say that he expected fertility to fall much faster in Nigeria than UNPD did. The justification was that 'it would be odd if birth rates did not fall sharply as Nigerians begin to notice how crowded it was getting'.[25] On that scientific basis, 400 million was summarily shaved off UNPD's projection of 914 million people for Nigeria in 2100. John Weeks, director of the International Population Center at San Diego University, remarked on the 'projections' of the rogue demographer as follows: 'there is always the possibility that [he] will be right and the UN demographers will be wrong. But I wouldn't bet on it. Why not? The UN demographers are highly qualified experts with a long history of knowledge about how the world works demographically.'[26] In its next report on global population growth, produced after the rogue demographer had moved on to pastures new, Deutsche

Bank considered discretion to be the better part of valour and adopted UNPD's projections.[27]

Random, speculative population guesstimates at one extreme or the other attract attention; and they will always find amplifiers. 'The end of global population growth may be almost here – and a lot sooner than the UN thinks,' ran a headline on the website of the ever-hopeful American Enterprise Institute, referring to the 'calculations' of the Deutsche Bank strategist.[28] 'Population growth forecast from the UN may be too high', trumpeted *The New York Times*;[29] 'debunks the popular narrative that population growth is still raging away unchecked', wrote the *Financial Times*'s 'Alphaville' column.[30] Attracting attention is, of course, precisely the objective – for ideological reasons, commercial gain or self-interest of some sort. It is a reminder to be wary of demography-related newspaper and magazine headlines.

Figure 12: Population momentum, 2020–50

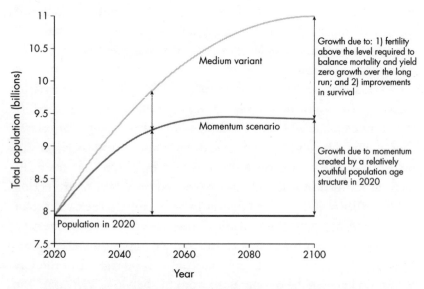

Source: UNPD, *World Population Prospects: The 2019 Revision.*

As 2050 approaches, whatever changes are made to country and regional projections in the meantime, population momentum underpins the UN's global population projections for the next two or three decades. Projections beyond 2050 involve assumptions about the fertility and reproductive behaviour of people who are not yet born. But more than two-thirds of the global growth in numbers to 2050 is implied by current age structures and reproductive behaviour, in particular the concentration of people in, or approaching, their childbearing years. It would occur even if global fertility converged immediately at the replacement level of 2.1 births and mortality rates remained at 2010–15 levels. In sub-Saharan Africa, population momentum supports 58% of projected growth by 2050.[31] This is worth bearing in mind for anyone conjuring projections. As the Russian demographers Julia Zinkina and Andrey Korotayev say with regard to Africa: 'It is critically important to understand that population increase is already inevitable (for some countries, very considerable), due to the colossal demographic inertia gained in the recent decades of very high (stalled) fertility.'[32]

7

Is Africa Different?

The demography of Africa is usually portrayed as 'exceptional'. Averaged and aggregated fertility data are partly the cause. Caution is required about generalisations, especially as the determinants of fertility transition vary country by country, and within countries. In the long run Africa will probably look less exceptional than is claimed today.

In a 2007 journal article, 'Africa's lagging demographic transition', the authors stated: 'we still lack a good understanding of why some countries have experienced significant reductions of fertility rates, while those in Africa remain with very high fertility rates'. This was the nub of what they referred to as 'the African question'.[1] John Bongaarts has been more influential than any other leading demographer in establishing the notion of African exceptionalism. He sums up sub-Saharan Africa's fertility transition as being 'later, earlier, slower, and higher'[2] than other developing regions in the past half-century on the basis that it commenced about two decades later; at lower levels of development – measured by indicators such as GDP per capita, education enrolment levels, life expectancy and urbanisation level – and therefore 'earlier' than elsewhere; it has proceeded more slowly; and the TFR is higher, modern contraceptive use lower, and desired family size larger relative to the region's development than anywhere else.[3]

Bongaarts has also isolated a 'substantial Africa effect'. After controlling for socio-economic indicators like income per capita and education levels, and demographic indicators such as mortality, fertility was higher in sub-Saharan countries than non-African developing countries by 1.1 births per woman in 2010. Bongaarts attributes the effect to the influence of 'traditional pronatalist social, economic and cultural practices' on contraceptive use and desired family size. The extent of this effect and its causes are vigorously debated, but there is now 'near-consensus' among leading demographers that, from a historical perspective, 'when it comes to fertility decline Africa is different'.[4]

The use of the word 'Africa' is problematic when linked to exceptionalism. While Bongaarts makes it clear that he is referring to sub-Saharan Africa, this qualification is often lost when his conclusions are being cited. 'Africa' is a label used by many demographers (and others) to describe only a part of the continent. The World Bank also uses the designations Africa and sub-Saharan Africa interchangeably. Northern Africa is often attached to the Middle East (as in the MENA designation), or even Western Asia. Geographical agglomerations can be useful, but they are false constructs that can also be misleading. As we know, in Southern Africa – part of 'sub-Saharan Africa' – the fertility transition is almost complete. In Northern Africa – part of 'Africa' – it is well advanced, with a TFR of around three births. These two regions may have started their transitions a little later than East Asia and Latin America, but the transition in the United Nations Sustainable Development Goals region 'Northern Africa and Western Asia' was even more rapid than that in East and Southeast Asia.[5] In a demographic context, 'Africa' and 'sub-Saharan Africa' produce generalisations to be wary of.

Of course, the distortion of aggregation does not apply to Africa alone. Indicators on 'Asia's' fertility transition are averages derived from multiple countries covering 30% of the world's land mass and 60% of its current population. They incorporate individual transitions as diverse in speed and extent as the ones in South Korea – where the TFR fell unusually rapidly and has now been stuck at about one birth for decades; in Pakistan, where the TFR has fallen from 6.6 births in the early 1960s to 3.5 today; and in China, where birth control of various types was enforced to hasten fertility decline to a greater degree than anywhere else in the world. The notion of 'Europe's' fertility transition is equally problematic, or arguably meaningless.

There are other anomalies in Africa's sub-regional designations. Zimbabwe, a country where the TFR fell from a peak of 7.4 in the early 1970s to 3.7 by 2000–05, is included in Eastern Africa by UNPD. Yet everywhere else Zimbabwe is included in Southern Africa, where its quite rapid fertility transition would have appeared less unusual. Mozambique, where the TFR remains above five, is also included in Eastern Africa, whereas, like Zimbabwe, it is a member of the 16-country Southern African Development Community. Both countries have substantial proportions of their land mass on the same latitudes as Namibia, which UNPD includes in Southern Africa. Michel Garenne captured the pitfalls of drawing conclusions from geographical aggregations in a 2008 DHS Working Paper focusing on sub-Saharan countries:

> The fertility dynamics vary greatly by country, with some experiencing a steady and rapid fertility decline, others a steady and slow decline, others a small rise followed by a rapid decline, and still others a major rise followed by a slow decline. Identifying a typology would be difficult because the number of different scenarios is the same as the number of countries due to the different dynamics and determinants in each country.[6]

Garenne further underscored complexity. At the time, the fertility transition in rural Uganda was as slow as that of the Sahelian countries, while that of urban Burkina Faso, Togo, Senegal and Mozambique had been as fast as that of Zimbabwe and Botswana. This is an altogether more nuanced analysis than simply declaring a country's fertility transition to have commenced when the TFR has fallen 10% from its peak. It does not necessarily render the use and comparison of aggregated geographical units totally nebulous, but suggests caution regarding overarching conclusions. It is instructive that 'Africa' has in the past been subdivided differently by some Africa-focused demographers: regions once used for analysis like 'Horn of Africa', 'Zambezi countries', 'Great Lakes', 'Sahel' and 'West African littoral' might not only be more logical subdivisions but also bring new insights.

Not all demographers agree with the received wisdom that fertility levels in sub-Saharan Africa and the speed of their downward trajectory are even particularly unusual. From a historical perspective, the high TFRs of many countries in Eastern, Western and Middle Africa today are certainly not unique. Some European nations had fertility rates above eight births before their transitions in the nineteenth and early twentieth century, and there were plenty of countries in Asia and Latin America/Caribbean in the 1950s, 1960s and 1970s with fertility rates as high. Garenne points out that the fertility transition of sub-Saharan Africa may look slow compared to East Asia or China and Thailand, but it is comparable to that of India and Pakistan – and of eighteenth-century France.[7] The fact that in most – but by no means all – of Africa the fertility transition began a couple of decades later than in Asia and Latin America/Caribbean may, in the *longue durée*, come to be seen as a relatively minor demographic curiosity, a timing issue alone. Fertility transitions in Northern America and Europe typically took several decades or more. In this sense, it is arguably East Asia and Latin America that were exceptional, not sub-Saharan Africa. It would arguably have been altogether more remarkable if Africa's fertility transition had kept precisely in lockstep with those of Asia or Latin America/Caribbean.

In similar vein, Lyman Stone, a research fellow at the Institute for Family Studies in Charlottesville, Virginia, contends that 'African fertility' is 'right about where a rational forecaster would predict' based on child mortality levels as a proxy indicator for socio-economic development, and 'not extremely high when compared to benchmarks that reflect actual material conditions, not just an arbitrary assumption by demographers about how fast fertility should fall'.[8] Stone observes that Ethiopia has a lower TFR than South Korea did at a similar level of child mortality, and that in African countries where this has fallen to 75 deaths per thousand or less, the TFR has fallen rapidly to 'average or below-average fertility'. For example, Senegal has among the lowest infant and child mortality rates in Western Africa and its TFR was 4.4 births in 2018 – a little below the average for sub-Saharan Africa and more than one birth below the average for Western Africa.

There are other reasons to be wary of the tag of exceptionalism. Difference over a few decades may be a passing phenomenon, whereas exceptionalism is a permanent state. The distinction is an important one, rather than mere semantics. In some quarters, 'Africa's' – usually referring to sub-Saharan Africa's – fertility transition is depicted as (another) manifestation of the continent's 'under-achievement':[9] according to this narrative Africa has 'failed' to reduce fertility rates in the 'modern way' at the same time and as rapidly as other developing regions, just as it has 'failed' to emulate the economic growth of much of Asia over the past half-century. This is a predominantly Western narrative, supported by media and news outlets, and it would be unwise to treat it as either accurate or permanent. Africa's 'cultural exceptionalism' is also emphasised by many demographers, but 'culture' is not immutable – even the most fixed beliefs evolve in all societies.

'Is it that Africans are just different,' asks the Senegalese statistician and population scientist Cheikh Mbacké, 'or could the persistence of high fertility be a rational response to current socio-economic conditions and the weakness of the support typically provided by well-functioning states in terms of security and other basic services?' He continued:

> I would argue that, just as in the past, the current reproductive behaviour of African societies is highly rational. One reason for persistent high fertility can be found in the prevailing high levels of poverty and insecurity... the majority of African populations still face economic insecurity and uncertainty, which tends to reinforce the hold of traditional norms.[10]

Mbacké could well have added 'as highly rational as in any other societies around the world'. This truism is often overlooked, sometimes ignored, the implication being that high fertility – and therefore 'Africans' – are irrational in a modernising world. Mbacké's vantage point is a good one from which to consider the many and varied explanations advanced for the persistence – so far – of high fertility in many African countries (as opposed to 'in Africa'); and for recent stalls in fertility declines.

There is no disputing that high fertility – a national TFR above five – is more prevalent in Africa than anywhere else in the world; and it is unusual for the TFR to be above five when the infant mortality rate is below 100 deaths per 1,000. But explaining the fact is difficult for the simple reason that there is no agreement between experts regarding the causes of fertility change. The 'proximate determinants' of fertility are largely agreed on, and are closely monitored by, demographers. These are the biological and behavioural factors with a direct influence on fertility. First developed in the 1970s by John Bongaarts, and refined in 2015, the 'Bongaarts model' can be used to ascertain the relative contribution to fertility decline of changes in the four most significant proximate determinants, or to ascertain likely changes in the fertility rate, especially in high-fertility countries. The four determinants are:

- the proportion of women aged 15–49 who are married or in a marital union plus sexually active women who are not in a union (evidenced in DHS surveys by being pregnant, reporting sex in the last month, using contraception or being post-partum infecundable)
- post-partum infecundability, due to sexual abstinence or breastfeeding after childbirth
- usage of modern contraceptive methods
- the incidence of induced abortion

According to Bongaarts, 'fertility differences among populations and trends in fertility over time can always be traced to variations in one or more of the proximate determinants. If accurately measured and modeled, the proximate determinants should explain 100% of variation in fertility.'[11] In other words, the model is not predictive, but is effective in explaining past fertility trends as its constituent elements can be measured with reasonable certainty.

The 'background' determinants of fertility are far more numerous and contested. These have been the focus of a huge volume of research – and vigorous debate – since the 1960s. Emphasis has been placed on different determinants, with little consensus even on the most impactful, although it is generally agreed that lower mortality is a necessary precondition for fertility transition. The degree of disagreement can be seen in the efforts to explain the fertility stalls in sub-Saharan Africa described in Chapter 5.

Some demographers attributed stalls they had identified to political and economic turmoil in the 1980s, exacerbated by the introduction of World Bank/IMF SAPs and increasing poverty. Austerity measures undertaken by the worst-affected countries included swingeing cuts to health and education budgets considered vital to sustaining fertility decline. Improvements in infant and child mortality stalled, significant because improved child survival rates are strongly associated with declining fertility; and according to one authoritative study, budget constraints led to a higher proportion of uneducated and poorly educated women entering their childbearing years in the late 1990s and early 2000s than would have been the case otherwise. In other words, Africa's fertility stalls were the by-product of crises and an associated 'education stall'.[12]

Others have cited the impact of HIV/AIDS on maternal and child mortality, and the diversion of funding for family planning to tackling the pandemic. In Eastern Africa the use of modern contraceptives declined in the late 1990s, and desired family size and adolescent fertility increased in Kenya, Tanzania, Uganda and Zimbabwe.[13] In addition to the Cairo conference and the HIV/AIDS epidemic, the declarations that the population explosion was over influenced funding, as did the increased traction of the anti-abortion lobby in the US during successive Republican administrations.

'It has become clear that a great deal remains to be learned about the determinants of fertility in Africa,' wrote Etienne van de Walle, Professor of Demography at the University of Pennsylvania, in the conclusion of a 1990 World Bank report, *Fertility in Africa* (focusing on sub-Saharan Africa only), which reviewed the current state of knowledge about the drivers of fertility. Much the same is true today. A 2010 review of evidence regarding the determinants of high fertility noted that 'one can reasonably protest that while the amount of knowledge about fertility determinants is extensive it is undifferentiated. It is a challenge to distil a few key lessons from this overwhelming body of research.'[14]

In addition to mortality and educational attainment (especially among young women), a plethora of other factors appear to have varying degrees of influence on desired family size. Many emphasise, in keeping with classical demographic transition theory, the influence of 'modernisation', in the form of increasing urbanisation and industrialisation, services provided by mobile phone networks, and improved access to electricity, piped water and health services. Before the World Bank published *Fertility in Africa* its orthodox 'one world' view held that lower socio-economic indicators – such as incomes, education, health and urbanisation levels – in high-fertility African countries than in most of Asia and Latin America explained the fertility differential. All that was required was for Africa to 'catch up' in development terms and its fertility rates would converge as people decided they wanted fewer children, choosing 'quality' over 'quantity'.

This logic was based on a mistaken premise. Development indicators in the early 1960s were higher in many African countries than in other developing countries which were commencing a fertility transition, and there were over 20 African countries in which GDP per capita grew at more than 3% a year through that decade in spite of population growth of 2–3% annually.[15] It became increasingly untenable as the 1980s progressed, as new research established that fertility declines could occur at different stages of development and that socio-economic indicators were not especially predictive of declines. Most experts agree that socio-economic factors are important, but not essential drivers of fertility decline. In Africa the correlation between them and fertility is considered to be 'typically a loose one',[16] certainly by comparison with other developing regions. However, for many commentators 'Africa's' apparent suspension in a 'low-income, high-fertility' trap is still considered a sufficient explanation.

If the idea that fertility was all about incomes was waning when *Fertility in Africa* was published, the argument that social and cultural factors were the leading factor sustaining high fertility in Africa was fast replacing it in terms of influence. Research published at much the same time by John and Pat Caldwell argued that 'African exceptionalism' – widespread pronatalism – could be largely attributed to 'African culture' and sexual and reproductive 'systems'. Some of the salient features identified were the primacy of lineage and kinship networks over the nuclear family, the practices of sharing childcare and child-fostering (which facilitate having larger numbers of children), the economic and social value of children, a 'fundamental belief in the power of ancestral forces which encourage high fertility', a 'horror of infertility'[17] and communal land-tenure systems.

Van de Walle was sceptical from the outset about some of the conclusions drawn by the Caldwells, in particular regarding the 'primacy of religious influences'. 'Thus,' he concluded, 'the Caldwells claim to have identified the ultimate cultural source of the failure of family planning programmes. There are, however, serious questions about their theory.'[18] Among these, van de Walle cited the fact that there was 'little direct evidence that ancestor cults are still uniformly important in the sub-Saharan region', the claim that 'barrenness is the ultimate catastrophe for a woman', and the assertion that abortion and sterilisation were 'generally unacceptable' in the region. He agreed with the Caldwells, however, on the significance of high desired family size to fertility levels – but an explanation for this remained elusive. For the Caldwells, Africans simply prized children more than anyone else in the world.

Figure 13: The Bongaarts framework analysing the proximate determinants of fertility

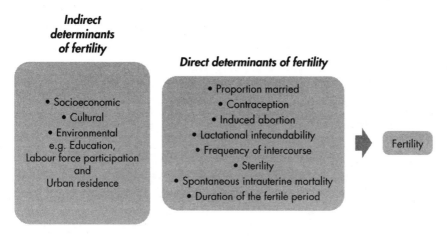

Source: K. Johnson, N. Abderrahim and S. Utstein (2011), *Changes in the Direct and Indirect Determinants of Fertility in Sub-Saharan Africa*, DHS Analytical Studies 23, ICF Macro, 2011.

Other cultural 'exceptionalisms' remain the basis for claims of inter-tropical Africa's 'unique' pronatalism, among them the prevalence of early and almost universal marriage and more widespread acceptance of premarital sex than was the case in pre-transition Asian countries. Fascinating and important research continues in this field, but again alarm bells should ring about using labels like 'African culture' for a continent of thousands of ethnic groups and indigenous languages. Even claims of a large degree of cultural homogeneity within regions are easily overstated.[19]

Africa's environmental and evolutionary history has also been invoked by some demographers seeking to explain high fertility. This line of argument encompasses theories that endemic warfare and the very high mortality rates associated with a plethora of parasitic and infectious disease accounted for a predisposition to high birth rates for survival. In similar vein, Andrey Korotayev and colleagues argue that the predominance of hoe (as opposed to plough) agriculture largely explains high fertility in sub-Saharan Africa:

Hoe agriculture, with much larger participation by women, was typical because of low population density and poor soils which encouraged shifting cultivation, whereas in Europe and Asia plough agriculture [predominated]. Higher levels of labour force participation raised the economic value of women and encouraged polygyny, which in turn leads to large extended families providing child care and facilitating maintenance of the higher levels of fertility typical of hoe agriculture.

The authors contend that, given the demographic legacy of this history of agricultural development, tropical Africa will need 'much stronger measures of sociodemographic policy (both in the field of family planning and education promotion) than in other world regions to facilitate fertility decline'.[20] Most theories about evolutionary and environmental history are dismissed as speculative, though some are more plausible than others. Again, Cheikh Mbacké asks rhetorically, 'why would a system that is no longer needed to ensure survival and demographic growth persist to the detriment of economic development?'[21]

Governance and its impact on the introduction or efficacy of family planning programmes have also been thoroughly scrutinised. In Western and Middle Africa, in particular, few governments have ever firmly committed to launching and sustaining effective and extensive initiatives to support the reduction of fertility levels. Family planning and modern contraceptive methods alone cannot drive a fertility transition, but since the 1960s nowhere in the world has a transition occurred without them.

Gender relations and female empowerment are indisputably important factors. In most African countries women have lowly legal status, suffer discrimination with regard to schooling and employment, experience high levels of violence, have limited workforce opportunities, and are poorly represented in national politics, business and academia. Their ability to take decisions regarding reproduction is often severely compromised. This will be looked at further in Chapter 11. The endemic economic insecurity and uncertainty alluded to earlier by Cheikh Mbacké is an equally plausible factor, not least due to the near-absence of adequate social and employment safety nets. As cultural demographer Jennifer Johnson-Hanks wrote in 2007:

> Parents cannot reliably trade child quality for child quantity, or predict that the foreign models of reproduction that now appear promising will not fall apart tomorrow. Prices for schooling, healthcare, or housing are extremely unstable, as are wages; even government employees are not paid reliably in some countries. Most employment opportunities are filled through social networks or kin relations, rather than according to formal skills or job experience; few people have access to formal credit. Buses do not run on schedule. Electricity and running water go out regularly, even in capital cities. In the rainy season, roads get washed out. Insect-borne diseases like malaria seem to strike more or less at random; the water-borne and sexually transmitted ones, from cholera to HIV/AIDS, only marginally less so. Mortality rates at all ages are high, and death often unpredictable.[22]

This list is not exhaustive. The effects of climate change and other risks could have been added.

All – or most – of the factors mentioned above can exert an influence on fertility, but the cocktail must differ by location. There can be no single overriding explanation for declines (or rises) in fertility levels, and there are anomalies to every explanation. For example, female secondary education is widely considered to be a game-changer, but Nigeria and DRC have long had some of the highest rates of female secondary-school attendance in sub-Saharan Africa and yet still have a TFR above five births and six births respectively. Similarly, much-improved economic performance between 2000 and 2015 seems to have had no really accentuated effect on national TFRs anywhere in Eastern, Western or Middle Africa, even in countries where high growth was sustained over a number of boom years, as was the case in Nigeria, Mozambique and Côte d'Ivoire. In some countries, infant mortality, life expectancy, GDP per capita and female educational enrolment have all improved markedly since the 1990s, yet fertility rates have barely reacted. Development is seemingly not always 'the best contraceptive'.

Some things can be said with certainty about fertility transitions in Africa. Firstly, as Goldstone and Korotayev have pointed out, 'forecasting of Africa's demographic trajectory based on expectations that it would follow the pattern of other regions has... been badly misleading'.[23] Secondly, whatever the disparate forces influencing fertility location by location, it is not certain that two-child families will become the norm in all African countries within the next 50 years or so. The 'Africa effect', and the apparent uniqueness of pronatalism in parts of Africa and of the fertility transition in sub-Saharan Africa, are grounded in observations over just four or five decades and benchmarked against the demographic transition envisaged by Notestein. But that 'quasi-universal phenomenon'[24] is already showing that its usefulness as a theoretical framework is fraying at the edges.

No scientific law determines that the end point of the demographic transition that commenced in Europe and North America in the eighteenth and nineteenth centuries is global convergence on a norm of about two children per family and a stable population; nor that the fertility transition of high-fertility countries should be a continuous, smooth process of similar duration everywhere (with a few exceptions); nor what happens to fertility in societies with a TFR closer to one birth than two for decades. In South Korea, where the TFR is below one, the government has already spent more than US$120 billion over the past 13 years trying to arrest population decline which is likely to commence in a decade, with little success.[25] It is a sum equivalent to the annual GDP of Morocco, Africa's fifth-largest economy. Taiwan and Singapore also offer birth subsidies. China's population will halve in the twenty-first century if the TFR continues to hover around 1.5 births. Japan has taken the first tentative steps to seeing whether allowing immigration might prove beneficial.

From the vantage point of the end of the twenty-first century, 'Africa's' – or even 'sub-Saharan Africa's' – demographic exceptionalism is likely to prove overdone. By then, conventional demographic transition theory will have been rewritten or superseded. Africa will inevitably play a central role in this revision, perhaps at the other end of the current fertility spectrum to South Korea, China and Eastern Europe, but either way will no longer be regarded as any more 'exceptional' than those countries and regions.

In this context, 'Africa' is the correct term because it refers to almost all countries in the continent. To date, among its populous countries only three have reached a TFR close to replacement level – South Africa, Morocco and Tunisia. It is interesting to ponder just how dissimilar these countries are in the context of tremendous variety in historical, political, geographical, economic, social and cultural legacies of regions and states designated as such by European colonial powers: it underscores the diversity of demography across the continent. This is far greater than is revealed by regional or continental aggregated statistics, and will remain substantial even as the range of fertility rates narrows. In some countries fertility may fall very low, while in others three children (or more) may remain the norm. As Massimo Livi Bacci points out in his book *Our Shrinking Planet*, it would be 'rather unrealistic' to think that demographic behaviour worldwide will harmonise any more than economies will, 'for many various and obvious reasons'.[26] A new, or rewritten, demographic transition theory must surely be in the offing in the twenty-first century, with Africa considered differently, not as an outlier – a puzzling curiosity – but as a key component.

8

Africa Galloping

The increases in UNPD's projections for Africa rekindled the long-running antagonism between commentators certain that the global population growth will soon stabilise and others who regard that as a remote possibility. Evidence is sometimes subordinated to ideology in this debate.

In 2014, 14 of the world's leading demographers, including John Wilmoth, incoming director of UNPD, reiterated in a journal paper titled 'World population stabilization unlikely this century' that the global population was likely to continue growing in the second half of the twenty-first century, rather than stabilise or commence a slow decline.[1] The question of stabilisation or continued growth was as contentious as ever. UNPD had flagged its position in *World Population Prospects: The 2012 Revision*, published the previous year, with its medium-variant projection of a population of 10.9 billion people by the end of the century. Nevertheless, its reiteration was generally presented in Western media as a bombshell. The headline in *National Geographic* read: 'A world with 11 billion people? New population projections shatter earlier estimates.' Beneath, in bold, followed: '**Warning: The twenty-first century may get a lot more crowded than previously thought**'.[2] Wired.com confusingly announced: 'BOOM! Earth's population could hit 12 billion by 2100'.[3]

The succession of upward revisions to projections for African regions that had caused UNPD materially to raise its global projections since the end of the 2000s was not the focus of the paper. UNPD and demographers from other institutions were for the first time presenting official 'probabilistic' population projections for all countries to the end of the century.[4] The purpose of the new methodology was to depict uncertainty by presenting a range. An 80% probability was assigned to the likelihood of the global population in 2100 being between 9.6 and 12.3 billion; and there was a 95% probability of it being between 9 and 13.2 billion.[5] The paper also reiterated that 'much of the increase... is expected to happen in Africa', and only 'unprecedented fertility declines in most parts of Sub-Saharan Africa still experiencing fast population growth' would improve the diminishing likelihood of the global population stabilising in the twenty-first century.[6]

The progressive adoption by UNPD of a probabilistic methodology was a significant refinement. It sought to address the perceived shortcoming that its conventional deterministic projections – the high, medium and low variants – potentially understated uncertainty in population growth, particularly in developing and least-developed countries where data was patchy or unreliable and fertility declines less predictable; and overstated the uncertainty of global projections and projections for low-fertility countries. The future trajectory of fertility in a country projection had also depended in the past on a judgement as to which of a set of predetermined paths the country in question was going to follow. Now probabilities were assigned to likely fertility trajectories. UNPD began incorporating probabilistic projections in full in *World Population Prospects: The 2015 Revision*, not only for the global population but for regions and almost 200 countries as well.

Another advantage to the new 80% and 95% ranges for the global population was that they were considerably narrower than the difference between the traditional high and low variants, which assumed the global TFR to be 0.5 births higher and lower respectively than the medium variant. For 80% of countries worldwide there was a difference of less than 10% between the medium variant and the median probabilistic projections for 2050. However, variances were considerably larger for the remaining 20% of countries, most of which had high fertility levels or had experienced a recent rapid decline in fertility. Many African countries were (and remain) in this category. For example, the 80% probability projection for Burkina Faso's population in 2100 was 41–126 million, a far wider range than between the low and high variants, and the 95% probability projection was much wider still.[7] Nigeria's 80% probability range was between about 500 million and 1.5 billion, compared to the 540 million to 1 billion range between the low and high variants in the *2012 Revision*. In effect, UNPD was providing narrower ranges for the global total at the end of the century while simultaneously attempting to quantify the very high level of uncertainty in long-term projections for some individual countries, particularly high-fertility ones in Africa. The 95% probability range for Africa's total population was given as 3.1–5.7 billion, with a median figure of 4.2 billion, similar to the medium-variant projection.

The authors of the journal paper assigned only a 30% probability to world population growth ending in the twenty-first century. If the global population reaches 12.3 billion, the top end of the 80% probability range, it would mean that the world had added more people in the twenty-first century than in the twentieth century. These were both statistical possibilities that some commentators, for different reasons, were not prepared to countenance. In 'The new population boom could easily be a dud', an article published in *The Wall Street Journal*, Nicholas Eberstadt at the American Enterprise Institute charged that 'concern, even alarm, about global population growth may have been reawakened' by the probabilistic projections. The methodology was, in his view, 'all but certain to reignite Malthusian debates about the race between mouths and food, and to re-energize the international population-planning activists who castigate governments and aid donors for their complacency about the global demographic threat'.[8]

Eberstadt was persistent. In 1998 he had confidently predicted that global population growth would end within four decades – a prediction that by 2014 was looking less sound with each passing year. But he was correct in pointing out that probabilistic projections did not actually increase the accuracy of long-range forecasts, given that there was no reliable method for predicting fertility trajectories over many decades and that demographers were 'hard-pressed to explain historical fertility patterns'. Eberstadt noted Africa's increasing significance in global projections, but was not convinced that sub-Saharan Africa would necessarily 'remain a demographic exception for generations'.[9]

Some critics of UNPD chose to continue simply disbelieving their projections. This was particularly true of commentators claiming that the global population would peak imminently. However, UNPD's track record on global projections over a few decades remained creditable. Its medium-variant projections for 2020 made in 1982, 1984, 1988, 1990, 1992 and 1994 were all in a narrow range between 7.81 billion and 8.05 billion. Those made in the biennial revisions of *World Population Prospects* between 1996 and 2000 were lower, at 7.67 billion, 7.5 billion and 7.58 billion. The estimated outcome for 2020 announced in the *2019 Revision* was 7.8 billion. To reprise the judgement made in the Panel on Population Projections' 2002 report, the margins of error in the global projections made over the preceding four or five decades are 'quite modest'.

The volume and quality of data informing each new edition of *World Population Prospects* improves continually. This is the raw material underlying John Weeks's opinion that 'the UN demographers are highly qualified experts with a long history of knowledge about how the world works demographically'.[10] For the *2019 Revision* UNPD assessed 1,690 censuses conducted between 1950 and 2018, information on births and deaths from vital registration systems for 163 countries, and demographic indicators from 2,700 surveys. However, the raw material is not comprehensive. Even in the world's richest countries, capture of complete demographic information in a central register is uncommon. In 2017 it was estimated that worldwide the births of 'roughly three-quarters' of children younger than five were registered, but in least-developed countries the proportion was under half.[11] Similarly, less than 50% of worldwide deaths are officially recorded.

Regional and country projections also remain susceptible to larger margins of error than global ones. In high-fertility countries, quite small or sudden variations in fertility can require substantial alterations to projections, particularly those for several decades in the future. In the *2019 Revision*, for example, the 2100 medium-variant projection for Uganda was lowered from 214 million to 137 million, news that may not have pleased President Museveni. However, any sign that the recent downward trend in the country's TFR was stalling could potentially lead to a significant upward revision.

Figure 14: UNPD projections for the global population 2020–2100

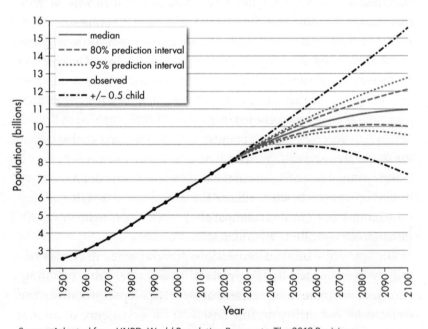

Source: Adapted from UNPD, *World Population Prospects: The 2019 Revision.*

It is sometimes alleged that data for 'most' African countries is so inadequate as to make estimates of current, and projections of future, populations completely unreliable. There are gaps in fertility data for one or more decades since 1950 for almost all countries. There are only three in which coverage of death registration exceeds 90%;[12] and only eight have a birth-registration system with coverage of over 90%.

As birth registration is UNPD's preferred source of data on fertility, this is a definite hindrance. Nigeria – the continent's most populous country – has not had a census since 2006, and arguably has not staged a credible census since independence in the early 1960s. In DRC, the fourth most populous country, the last census took place in 1984. While most countries now conduct regular and credible censuses, almost half of the continent's population lives in countries that have not held a census in the last decade.[13]

Despite these shortcomings, the availability and quality of demographic data is improving in Africa. About 80% of countries were classified by UNPD as having 'timely data available' in 2015, meaning that relevant fertility data had been collected at some point since 2010.[14] Life-expectancy data is estimated to have the lowest measurement error of the three indicators in the United Nations' Human Development Indicator.* Technology is driving change (Malawi used tablet technology for its 2018 census), and not only in the richer countries (in Mali 90% of births are recorded by the age of five, compared to less than 50% in Nigeria). Even when a country conducts the first credible census for some time and reliable data from other sources has been scarce, UNPD estimates are usually in the right ballpark. In 2014 Angola held its first census since independence from Portugal in 1975. It revealed a population of 24.3 million compared to UNPD's estimate in the *2012 Revision* of 21.5 million, an underestimation by 13%.

Big revisions of 2050 projections for countries in Africa have mostly been caused by the availability of better data, enabling a base-year estimate to be revised, or by UNPD's use of standardised trajectories of fertility decline based on the experience of multiple other countries. These will continue to occur. For example, there are a number of countries – including Niger, Mali, DRC and Angola – where quite rapid fertility decline is projected between 2020 and 2050 despite there being no sign yet of it having started.

---

* GNI per capita has the highest measurement error. The third indicator measures education. See Simone Ghislandi et al. (2019), 'A simple measure of human development: The human life indicator', *Population and Development Review*, Vol. 45, No. 1, p. 220.

Even where census or vital registration data is lacking, other important sources can fill gaps. DHSs, and the Multiple Indicator Cluster Surveys and Malaria Indicator Surveys also carried out under the auspices of the DHS Program, are all conducted regularly and on a large scale in most countries in Africa. Models have been developed that estimate current fertility for Western Africa countries from multiple imperfect data sources.[15] It would be bold to dismiss 2050 projections for Nigeria and DRC as being 'obviously' overestimated, as some commentators have done. But as probabilistic projections now show, the medium-variant projection that their combined population will be 1.1 billion by 2100, about 10% of the *global* population, is a good deal less certain than the global projection for the end of the century.

The pitfalls of very long-range projections aside, the UNPD medium-variant global projection for 2050 in *World Population Prospects: The 2019 Revision* was largely unchanged from the *2012 Revision* – at 9.7 billion. Even if the global TFR fell from the 2015–20 average of 2.5 births per woman to the replacement level of 2.1 *immediately*, the global headcount would still reach 8.9 billion in 2050 due to population momentum,[16] a phenomenon seemingly overlooked by Deutsche Bank's rogue demographer a few years ago. 'It is difficult to imagine a global population below 9 billion in 2050,' says the French demographer Henri Leridon, director of research emeritus at the Institut national d'études démographiques; he continues, 'except by envisaging catastrophes of a magnitude never before experienced on the world stage.'[17] UNPD's demographers concur: only in 'exceptional circumstances' such as 'a natural or manmade disaster leading to a catastrophic increase in the... death rate, or the implementation of draconian and efficacious policy measures to suppress the... birth rate' would the 2050 population be below 9 billion.[18] This is a very, very important point, based on simple mathematics, that is frequently ignored. 'Catastrophes' and 'exceptional circumstances' may occur, but they are presumably not what any population optimist trumpeting an end to global population growth in the 2030s or 2040s is counting on to make their prophecy come true.

As far as the medium-variant global projection for 2100 in the *2019 Revision* was concerned, this too was the same as in the *2012 Revision* at 10.9 billion. The addition of 300 million people to this total in the *2017 Revision* – almost an entire US – was reversed. This was not the start of a new trend: the probability given to the global headcount stabilising or declining before the end of the century was just 27%. This was lower than in 2014, indicating that it was considered even less likely. Following publication of the *2019 Revision* an analysis by the Pew Research Center noted, a little bizarrely, that 'For the first time in modern history, the world's population is expected to virtually stop growing by the end of the century.'[19]

UNPD may be 'the world's most important watcher of human tides', but the Wittgenstein Centre (WIC) for Demography and Global Human Capital, based in Austria, is an equally respected source of projections.[20] In 2014, the same year as UNPD announced its roll-out of a probabilistic methodology, WIC published a 1,056-page tome titled *World Population and Human Capital in the Twenty-First Century.* The projections it contained were based on opinions canvassed from hundreds of demographers and other population experts, many with country-specific knowledge. It was also the first major publication to incorporate educational attainment data in demographic scenarios, as well as age structures and sex. Its modelling was based on 'substantive reasoning and assessments of alternative arguments', as opposed to UNPD's reliance 'mainly… on statistical extrapolation'.[21]

The publication built on the work over many years of the eminent demographer Wolfgang Lutz, WIC's founder, concerning the 'functional causality' between education levels and lower mortality and fertility. Access to primary and secondary schooling is widely considered as important an influence on family size as family planning or economic factors. Female education, in particular, is associated with fertility declines globally – the better-educated a woman is, the fewer children she tends to have and the greater their chances of survival. Sensitivity to development outcomes is a key reason for the widespread appeal of WIC's projections.

It was arguably not any aspect of its methodology that led to WIC's adoption by population optimists as their champion, but its divergence from UNPD regarding when the global population would start to decline. Ten years earlier, Lutz and two colleagues had published *The End of World Population Growth in the 21st Century*. For some, the title of the book was all they needed to read. Building on an earlier article in *Nature*, the authors suggested that the likely end to population growth 'in the foreseeable future' was 'welcome news for efforts towards sustainable development'. This was an upbeat message, with a probability of 85% assigned to population stabilisation during the century and even a 15% probability of the population being less at the end of the century than at its start. This was exactly what population optimists wanted to hear, rather than doom and gloom about growth possibly continuing throughout the century.[22]

Ten years later, in the 2014 publication, WIC's 'middle-of-the-road scenario'[23] envisaged peak population in 2065–75 at around 9.4 billion people, a number that would then decline to less than 9 billion by the end of the century.[24] Central to the divergence with UNPD's long-range outlook was WIC's forecast for Africa: a total population of 2 billion by 2050 (compared to UNPD's 2.4 billion in its recently released *2012 Revision*) and 2.6 billion by 2100 (as opposed to 4.2 billion projected by UNPD). This was a further reminder, if any were needed, that the highly charged and emotive issue of the global population trajectory in the twenty-first century hinged on what would happen in Africa.

The difference between WIC's forecasts and UNPD's projections for Africa's population at the end of the century – 1.6 billion – exceeded the entire current population of China. This was a material divergence, to say the least. Inevitably, it rested on differing assumptions regarding the rapidity of fertility decline in high-fertility African countries. Nigeria provided the largest single component of the difference in figures regarding the timing of the peak in global population. WIC saw the most populous country in Africa increasing in size by a factor of 3.6 by 2100 (from 158 million in 2010 to 576 million) rather than quintupling, as projected by the *2012 Revision*, from 174 million to 913 million, a figure that had tripled since the *2002 Revision* and which Lutz and his colleagues described as 'unrealistic'.[25] By the *2019 Revision* it had been reduced to 733 million.

Additionally, WIC rejected UNPD's adherence to 'universal replacement level fertility'. In UNPD projections this entails global convergence on a TFR close to two births per woman at the end of the century, after which the global population would supposedly remain more or less stable. WIC argued that this assumption had no scientific basis whatsoever: it was merely the traditional 'end point' of a theory of demographic transition largely formulated in the 1940s. Apart from being inherently implausible, the notion that the global population might settle into an era of equilibrium overlooked the fact that in many regions of the world fertility levels have been well below replacement level for decades, as was mentioned in the previous chapter. For WIC, it is equally unimaginable that the TFR of all 'less developed countries' will also converge on two births.

WIC's middle-of-the-road scenario was only one of a number of possibilities presented. Lutz emphasised that the forecast fertility declines in Africa were 'far from being a certainty'.[26] For example, if Africa's average TFR only declined to two births by 2070, instead of 2050, WIC's end-of-century population forecast for the continent would be 2.9 billion instead of 2.6 billion. Furthermore, its 'stalled development' scenario – with much lower levels of educational attainment and higher population growth, in Africa in particular – saw the global population reaching 10 billion by 2050 and 12.8 billion by 2100.

Despite the presentation of various scenarios in *World Population and Human Capital in the Twenty-First Century*, population optimists and anyone who regarded UNPD's recent upward revisions as fuelling population alarmism – or even catastrophism – seized on WIC's middle-of-the-road scenario as 'evidence' that UNPD's projections were plain wrong. They underscored in red the contention by Lutz and two colleagues in 2013 that 'most projections agree that global growth

is likely to end in the second half of this century with 8–10 billion'.[27]
Some went even further. In 2011 the author of *Peoplequake* had claimed
that the global population might not even reach 8 billion. He added that
'Wolfgang Lutz in Vienna sees a peak as early as 2040, at closer to seven
than eight billion, followed by a strong downward slide taking us as low
as five billion by 2100.'[28] As far as the figure of 5 billion is concerned,
Lutz responded that WIC 'did a lot of alternative scenarios with partly
some quite extreme and unlikely assumptions' but 'never published
such a low medium/most likely variant'.[29] Even the 'rapid development'
scenario in *World Population and Human Capital in the Twenty-First
Century* – which assumed that all developing countries would roll out
education at the speed of South Korea and Singapore – only envisaged
peak population after 2050, and an end-of-century global population of
6.9 billion. In the battle over global population stabilisation, figures are
sometimes selected according to whether they fit the argument – and
sometimes conjured out of thin air.

In 2018, WIC's projections forecasts were updated in *Demographic
and Human Capital Scenarios for the 21st Century: 2018 Assessment
for 201 Countries*. The 'medium development scenario' for the
global population in 2050 – the most likely from a contemporary
perspective – had been increased from 9.2 billion to 9.4 billion, the
figure previously presented for 15–25 years later. The same scenario
envisaged that the global peak of 9.8 billion would be reached in
2070–80, about five years later than in the 2014 forecast and with
an additional 400 million people. It would then decline to 9.5 billion
people by the end of the century, 500 million higher than in the 2014
forecast[30] – and more than 1 billion higher than the 'median forecast'
made by Lutz and colleagues in 2004.[31]

Although the methodologies of WIC and UNPD are radically
different, and there is disagreement regarding whether or not the
global population will stabilise by the end of the century, if like is
compared to like there is in fact less variance between the range of

outcomes posited by the two institutions than some commentators like to claim. As with UNPD's upward revisions in the past decade, WIC's higher projections were largely attributable to an increase in the medium development scenario figures for Africa. These had to be raised from 2 billion to 2.25 billion in 2050 (compared to UNPD's medium-variant projection of 2.5 billion) and from 2.6 billion to 2.9 billion in 2100 (compared to UNPD's 4.3 billion) for the simple reason that base data on population size is taken from UNPD.[32] In other words, the 2018 publication involved rebasing the data, but WIC's fertility and mortality assumptions remained the same.

By 2020, the relentlessly increasing weighting and prominence of Africa in global demography was hard to overlook. In the first two decades of the twenty-first century UNPD's medium-variant projections for the continent's population in 2050 had been raised by almost 40%, a development that simply did not chime with an end to global growth and the population explosion. The upward revisions reflected two more decades of high fertility in a substantial number of sub-Saharan countries, and stalling declines there and in Northern Africa. These two decades have made for a 'much bigger base', hence the eye-popping 90% increase in the medium-variant projection for the end of the century.

Beneath the headline numbers for the continent and regions, half of the 37 African countries with a population greater than 5 million grew by more than 30% in the decade between 2009 and 2019 (see Table 6). The populations of Sahel countries Burkina Faso, Mali, Niger and Chad grew on average by almost 45%, taking their combined population to almost 80 million – equivalent to that of Germany, Western Europe's most populous country. By 2019, 20 African countries had already exceeded the UNPD medium-variant projections made just 10 years earlier for 2025; others are likely to do so by the end of 2021. The 2050 projections for 13 countries* are now 30% or more higher than in the *2008 Revision*; only for two countries in

---

* Angola, Burundi, Cameroon, Rep. of Congo, DRC, Madagascar, Mali, Mozambique, Nigeria, Senegal, Somalia, South Africa, Sudan/South Sudan.

the whole continent are they lower – Libya and Uganda (see Table 7). While it would be an exaggeration to say that the upward pressure on projections has been across the board, it has been generated by multiple countries.[33]

Table 6: By 2019 half of the 37 African countries with a population > 5 million had already equalled* or exceeded their medium-variant projection for 2025 contained in *World Population Prospects: The 2008 Revision*

	Estimated population in 2009 (million), WPP 2008 Revision	Estimated population in 2019 (million), WPP 2019 Revision	Growth 2009-19 (%)	WPP 2008 Revision medium-variant projection for 2025 (million)	2025 medium-variant projection equalled or exceeded by 2019? (Y/N)
Algeria	35	43	23	43	Y
Angola	19	32	68	27	Y
Benin	9	12	33	14	
Burkina Faso	16	20	25	25	
Burundi	8	12	50	11	Y
Cameroon	19	26	37	26	Y
Chad	11	16	45	17	Y
Rep. of Congo	4	5	25	5	Y
Côte d'Ivoire	21	26	24	30	Y
DRC	66	87	32	98	
Egypt	83	100	20	105	Y
Ethiopia	83	112	35	120	
Ghana	24	30	25	32	
Guinea	10	13	30	15	
Kenya	40	53	32	58	
Liberia	4	5	25	6	

	Estimated population in 2009 (million), WPP 2008 Revision	Estimated population in 2019 (million), WPP 2019 Revision	Growth 2009-19 (%)	WPP 2008 Revision medium-variant projection for 2025 (million)	2025 medium-variant projection equalled or exceeded by 2019? (Y/N)
Libya	6	7	17	8	
Madagascar	20	27	35	29	Y
Malawi	15	19	27	23	
Mali	13	20	54	19	Y
Morocco	32	36	12	38	Y
Mozambique	23	30	30	31	Y
Niger	15	23	53	27	
Nigeria	155	201	30	210	Y
Rwanda	10	13	30	15	
Senegal	12	16	33	18	
Sierra Leone	6	8	33	8	Y
Somalia	9	15	67	14	Y
South Africa	50	59	18	54	Y
Sudan/ S.Sudan**	42	54	29	57	Y
Togo	7	8	14	9	
Tunisia	10	12	20	12	Y
Uganda	33	44	33	53	
Tanzania	44	58	32	67	
Zambia	13	18	38	19	Y
Zimbabwe	12	15	25	17	

*'Equalled' means that by 2019 the country was already within 5% of the medium-variant projection made in 2008 for the year 2025.   **Sudan and South Sudan were a single country in 2009.   *Source:* UNPD, *World Population Prospects: The 2008 Revision* and *World Population Prospects: The 2019 Revision.* All numbers are rounded.

Table 7: Medium-variant projections for many African countries in the year 2050 have increased substantially since *World Population Prospects: The 2008 Revision.* **Reductions have only occurred for two of the 37 countries with a population > 5 million.**

	WPP 2008 Revision medium-variant projection for 2050 (million)	WPP 2019 Revision medium-variant projection for 2050 (million)	Increase/(decrease) in medium-variant projection for 2050 between 2008 and 2019 (%)
Algeria	50	61	22
Angola	42	77	83
Benin	22	24	9
Burkina Faso	41	43	5
Burundi	15	25	67
Cameroon	37	51	38
Chad	28	34	21
Rep. of Congo	7	11	57
Côte d'Ivoire	43	51	19
DRC	148	195	32
Egypt	130	160	23
Ethiopia	174	205	18
Ghana	45	52	16
Guinea	24	26	8
Kenya	85	92	8
Liberia	9	9	-
Libya	10	9	(10)
Madagascar	43	54	26
Malawi	37	38	3
Mali	28	44	57
Morocco	43	46	7
Mozambique	44	65	48

	WPP 2008 Revision medium-variant projection for 2050 (million)	WPP 2019 Revision medium-variant projection for 2050 (million)	Increase/(decrease) in medium-variant projection for 2050 between 2008 and 2019 (%)
Niger	58	66	14
Nigeria	289	401	39
Rwanda	22	23	5
Senegal	26	33	27
Sierra Leone	12	13	8
Somalia	24	35	46
South Africa	57	76	33
Sudan/ S.Sudan*	76	101	33
Togo	13	15	15
Tunisia	13	14	8
Uganda	91	89	(2)
Tanzania	110	129	17
Zambia	19	39	105
Zimbabwe	19	24	26
ALL AFRICA	1934	2430	25

*Sudan and South Sudan were a single country at the time of the *2008 Revision*. Source: UNPD, *World Population Prospects: The 2008 Revision* and *World Population Prospects: The 2019 Revision*. All numbers are rounded.

A comparison of the continent-wide and regional populations in 2020 with the medium-variant projections of the *1996 Revision* is equally instructive in the context of the charge of overestimation levelled at UNPD at the time (and ever since). To recap, that revision was compiled just as some were declaring the population explosion to be definitively over. In Africa, additionally, the ravages of HIV/ AIDS were having an ever-growing impact on mortality. There were even credible suggestions that the epidemic could stop population growth altogether within two or three decades. Projections for 28

African countries were revised downwards in the *1996 Revision* (and only 15 raised). Yet, as can be seen in Table 8 the variances between actual figures and the projections for Africa made a quarter of a century ago are modest. The accuracy of the Western Africa projection is particularly striking. The reason for the succession of upward revisions to projections for 2050 and 2100 is simply that in 1996 UNPD anticipated that in almost all African countries, replacement-level fertility would have been reached by 2050. That is now impossible, and for anyone still unconvinced of the numerical consequences it is an arresting thought that Nigeria alone is now projected to have the same population in 2050 as the whole of Western Africa does today.

Table 8: UNPD's mid-1990s population projections for Africa's regions were dismissed by many as ridiculously high. For the continent and most of its regions they have proved quite accurate.

Region	WPP 1996 Revision medium-variant projections for 2020 (million)	WPP 2019 Revision medium-variant projection for 2020 (million)	Variance 2019 projection for 2020 vs. 1996 projection for 2020 (%)
Africa	1,317	1,341	+1.8%
Eastern Africa	431	445	+3.2%
Middle Africa	166	180	+8.4%
Western Africa*	402	402	0.0%
Northern Africa	241	246	+2.0%
Southern Africa	77	67	-13.0%

*Western Africa's exact projections for 2020 made in 1996 and 2019 were 401,741,000 and 401,861,000 respectively. In other words, the 1996 projection was almost exactly correct.   Source: UNPD, *World Population Prospects: The 1996 Revision* and *World Population Prospects: The 2019 Revision*.

The 2010s were not very obliging to commentators convinced that the global population would stabilise within the next few decades. The demographic trajectory of substantial parts of Africa, either overlooked or simply ignored by most of them, was largely to blame for this. It was a reminder that guesswork and wishful thinking are risky. As Wolfgang Lutz and a colleague recently put it, like John Weeks before them, 'the scientific discipline of demography has a rather elaborate and powerful toolbox for studying population dynamics and produces detailed population projections according to different assumptions about the future trend in fertility, mortality, migration and other drivers of changing population composition'.[34] Even respected demographers who still envisage peak population a few decades earlier than UNPD have had to revisit their projections.[35] To varying degrees, Africa has caught everyone out (see Table 8).

Remarkably, given current trends and the evidence, sceptics of population growth lasting much longer continue to appear, Polyanna-like. *Empty Planet: The Shock of Global Population Decline* by the Ipsos pollster Darrell Bricker and John Ibbitson, a political columnist at Canada's *The Globe and Mail*, is a cheerily upbeat and hopeful antithesis to Ehrlich's *The Population Bomb*. Like others before them, the authors claim that a 'growing body'[36] of demographers take the view that UNPD medium-variant projections are too high, and that in most regions fertility rates are falling faster than projected due to the influence of female empowerment and education, urbanisation and increased affluence. This is apparently even true of sub-Saharan Africa, which will have been news to Africa-focused demographers. According to Bricker and Ibbitson, the global population will peak in 'three decades, give or take',[37] and return to its current level – 7.7 billion – by 2100. 'The biggest neo-Malthusian of them all is an institution, and a highly respected one at that,' the authors say of UNPD.[38] *Empty Planet* was endorsed by professional optimist, psychologist and popular-science author Steven Pinker.

There are some incongruous inclusions among the supporting cast of population 'experts' cited in *Empty Planet*. Six years after Deutsche Bank discarded his back-of-the-envelope conjectures in favour of UNPD's projections, the rogue demographer is recycled as an authority. With only five years to go until he expected the global TFR to fall to replacement level, it is to be hoped that the unimaginable catastrophe required to bring that about does not occur. The Cambridge University climate strategist Professor Jørgen Randers, one of the authors of *The Limits to Growth*, is also cited. Randers is a distinguished scholar, but in 2012 he 'guessed' (his own words), in an exercise he labelled one of 'crystal-ball-gazing', that the global population would peak in 2040 at 8.1 billion because 'fertility trends will continue downwards at the stupendous rate that has occurred over the past 40 years'. At the time the global TFR had fallen 'stupendously' from 4.7 to 2.5 births in four decades. However, in the past decade, substantially because of the ever-increasing weighting of Africa, and even though more than half the global population lives in countries with sub-replacement fertility, the global TFR has declined by 0.1 births. A reduction of more than 0.3 births by 2050 is impossible to support at present. Even the worldwide imposition of a what Randers alarmingly refers to as Deng Xiaoping's 'wise one-child policy'[39] would not be sufficient to save his guess for 2040, quite apart from the fact that the description is akin to referring to China's Cultural Revolution as 'wonderful'. A demographer would add for good measure that China's rapid fertility decline was actually well under way before the one-child policy was introduced.[40]

Amid the plaudits for a highly readable book, the most technically astute review of *Empty Planet* describes it as 'moving from an optimistic premise to unwarranted conclusions'. The reviewer correctly pointed out that Wolfgang Lutz and WIC/IIASA were 'misrepresented', as they frequently are; and that Randers and the rogue demographer are 'outliers' whose 'forecasts' are increasingly 'diverging from (estimated) reality'. Randers, the reviewer points out, even had to revise his forecast for peak population upwards to 8.3 billion in 2016 (and is likely to have to do so again).[41] 'The authors' confidence that they have better insight than the UN (and IIASA) demographers,' the reviewer concludes, 'seems to arise from three sources: personal conversations, polls, and a simplistic theory.' The demographer

Paul Morland, complimenting the book for being 'sparkling and entertaining', remarked that it had 'the positives but also the pitfalls of works written by journalists'. 'Surely,' Morland suggested, 'it is worth noting that in Africa's behemoth, Nigeria, fertility rates have hardly fallen at all so far, despite intense urbanisation?... Perhaps their predictions should have a few more caveats than the authors allow.'[42]

9

Swings and Roundabouts

Africa will 'add a US' in the 2020s and its additional population will be greater every decade until the 2050s. The number of births will exceed 500 million in the 2030s and continue rising until the 2070s. Since the substantial increases to projections for Africa in UNPD's *2010 Revision* and *2012 Revision*, any downward revision of a country projection is cited by detractors as 'evidence' that fertility levels are falling faster than UNPD anticipates, or of error. Upward revisions to 2050 projections still occur, but receive less attention.

The UNPD medium-variant projection for Africa's population growth in the 2020s envisages an increase of a little over 25%, to 1.7 billion. This compares to decadal growth rates since the 1960s between 28% (in the 1960s and 2000s) and 32% (in the 1980s). The rate of growth is gently easing but still entails the addition of about 350 million people in the 2020s – a number greater than the population of the US – compared to 301 million in the 2010s (see Table 9). The 2030s will see a further 393 million added. This is a reminder that a slowing growth rate can still be accompanied by a rising number of additional people, a phenomenon often misunderstood or overlooked. The net additional population is projected to peak in the 2050s, with about 420 million added during the decade. However, the number of births will continue rising until it peaks at about 640 million in the 2070s and 2080s, the equivalent of the total population of Latin America/ Caribbean today. That is a long way off. In the meantime, the margin of uncertainty about the 2020s and 2030s is small.

Table 9: Births, deaths and population growth in Africa by decade, 1950s-2020s

Decade	Births (million)	Deaths (million)	Net population addition (million)	End of decade population (million)	Decadal population growth (%)
1950-60	121	64	57	283	24
1960-70	151	68	83	363	28
1970-80	191	74	117	476	31
1980-90	241	83	158	630	32
1990-2000	285	101	184	811	29
2000-10	344	110	234	1039	28
2010-20	411	103	308	1340	29
2020-30	464	111	353	1688	26
2030-40	520	127	393	2077	23
2040-50	566	150	416	2489	20

Source: UNPD, *World Population Prospects: The 2019 Revision.* Population total may not tally exactly due to migration and other factors.

The scale of the upward revisions to UNPD's projections for sub-Saharan Africa and Africa as a whole since 2000 needs reiteration. They are unprecedented since the agency started forecasting in the 1950s. At 2.5 billion the medium-variant projection for 2050 is now almost 40% higher than in the *2002 Revision.* It almost exactly matches the high-variant projections for the continent made in the *1996 Revision,* just before the population explosion faded from the news, and in the *2010 Revision.* This step-change from tracking the medium variant to matching earlier high variants is equally unprecedented among the regions of the world.

Turning to Africa's regions, the projections for 2050 for all five have been subjected to substantial upward revisions since the *2002 Revision.* The medium-variant projections for Northern and Southern Africa are 21% and 85% higher than two decades ago.[1] Such large increases are quite unusual for regions where fertility is approaching replacement level. In the case of Northern Africa, whose projection has increased from 322 million to 372 million since 2010, the TFR of the region's seven countries has stalled above three births. By 2050 the population of Northern Africa, mostly concentrated close to the Mediterranean and the Atlantic coastline, will comfortably surpass the current population of Southern and Western Europe (and that of the US).

In Southern Africa, the medium-variant projection has increased from 67 million to 87 million since 2010. The incremental population is almost entirely accounted for by South Africa and is attributable to improving mortality, with better survival rates and more widespread treatment of people afflicted by HIV/AIDS. The implications for government planning and financing of acquiring 20 million extra people over the next three decades are immense.

Since 2010 the medium-variant projections for Eastern, Western and Middle Africa in 2050 have all increased by about 40%.[2] Eastern and Western Africa's populations are now set to rise from 450 million and 570 million to 850 million and 800 million respectively between 2015 and 2050. Before 2050, the populations of these two regions will overtake those of Europe (c.750 million) and Latin America/ Caribbean (c.650 million).

Despite the marked impact on projections for Southern Africa of improved mortality, the key driver of growth for the more populous regions is still fertility. In mid-century projections for Africa, fertility accounts for about 90% of population increase.[3] More than 40% of the projected growth in sub-Saharan Africa (and two-thirds of global growth) is also 'baked in': it is underpinned by current age structures and would occur even if the TFR fell to replacement level overnight. The medium-variant projection for Africa assumes that the TFR will fall steadily from 4.4 births in 2015–20 to 3.1 births in 2045–50; for sub-Saharan Africa a reduction from 4.7 births to 3.2 births is envisaged in the same time frame (see Table 10). The magnitude of these decreases over the next three decades – 1.3 and 1.5 births respectively – matches those that have occurred in the past three decades, implying a slightly faster pace of decline.

The speed of the first stage of the fertility transition in sub-Saharan Africa is often depicted as slow by comparison with East Asia. At the current rate of progress it will take 34 years for the TFR in sub-Saharan Africa to fall from six births to four. In East Asia this transition took 24 years. If this is what occurs, a difference of 10 years will appear minor by 2050. Furthermore, East Asia experienced the fastest regional fertility decline in history; and most fertility transitions in European countries were very drawn out.

Table 10: TFR for Africa and its regions, 1990-2100, and UNPD medium-variant population projections, 2020-2100

	TFR 1990-95	TFR 2015-20	2020 population (estimated, millions)	TFR 2045-50	2050 population (projected, millions)	TFR 2095-2100	2100 population (projected, millions)
Africa	5.7	4.4	1,341	3.1	2,489	2.1	4,280
Sub-Saharan Africa	6.2	4.7	1,094 (84% of Africa total)	3.2	2,117 (85% of Africa total)	2.2	3,775 (88% of Africa total)
Eastern Africa	6.4	4.4	445 (34%)	2.9	851 (34%)	2.1	1,451 (34%)
Western Africa	6.9	5.2	402 (31%)	3.5	796 (32%)	2.2	1,484 (35%)
Middle Africa	6.7	5.5	180 (14%)	3.1	383 (15%)	1.8	746 (17%)
Northern Africa	4.2	3.2	246 (19%)	2.5	372 (15%)	2.2	505 (12%)
Southern Africa	3.6	2.5	68 (5%)	1.9	87 (3%)	2.0	94 (2%)

Source: UNPD, *World Population Prospects: The 2019 Revision*. Projected population figures refer to medium-variant projections.

The likelihood of upward revisions for the population of Africa whole (or sub-Saharan Africa) by 2050 of the same magnitude as occurred with the *2010 Revision* and *2012 Revision* diminishes by the year. It would need the TFR to remain largely unchanged for the next three decades. Although this may occur in some countries, it would be extraordinary were it to happen across the board. If it did, Africa's population would reach 3 billion, as mentioned earlier, half a billion more than currently envisaged by the medium-variant projection. Conversely, if fertility started to fall at the same rate as that of 21 countries around the world that completed their transitions rapidly, sub-Saharan Africa's population in 2050 would be 1.9 billion instead of the 2.1 billion currently projected, a difference of about 10%. The possibility of that occurring is assessed at less than 5% – UNPD's 95% probability range is 2.0–2.2 billion for sub-Saharan Africa and 2.4–2.6 billion for all Africa.[4]

Although the total population for Africa and for sub-Saharan Africa in 2050 can now be projected with reasonable certainty within quite narrow bounds, projections for individual high-growth, high-fertility countries are more precarious. Substantial revisions are almost inevitable at this geographical level. The influence they may individually have on the continental total by 2050 may be limited, but their significance to the countries themselves will be immense. Some governments and national leaders have paid little attention to substantial upward revisions of population projections for their countries in the past decade. In Egypt, Rwanda, Ethiopia, South Africa and others – high- and intermediate-fertility countries alike – the ramifications of changes are carefully scrutinised and incorporated in national planning.

The *2012 Revision* report provided an instructive illustration of the difficulties, focusing on Nigeria. As there was no established trend in fertility decline at the time, the TFR having remained around six births for half a century, a projection assuming the timing of a fertility decline was problematic enough. Pinning down the timing of the start of this decline and its speed is well-nigh impossible with even the slightest degree of certainty. The TFR could stay the same for decades, or a decline may have already just started. When a fertility transition commences, how can its speed be judged at the outset? What is the likelihood of a stall? The use of high and low variants for Nigeria did not adequately capture this level of uncertainty: the newly introduced 80% probability projection had a range of 2.5–5 births for the TFR in 2050 – far wider than the one birth separating the high and low variants.

Almost a decade after the *2012 Revision*, the outlook for Nigeria is scarcely clearer. At present the medium-variant projection assumes a decline in the TFR to 3.6 births by 2050. But there is no clear sign when the TFR might fall below five births, or even if it will do so by 2050. If fertility remained unchanged for three decades and mortality expectations stayed the same, Nigeria would only add 83 million to Africa's total population in 2050 of 2.5 billion – a little over 3%. But, for Nigeria, it would mean a population of half a billion, 25% more than is currently anticipated, and the real possibility of challenging the 1 billion mark before the end of the century.

In the 1990s and 2000s, as was mentioned in earlier chapters, the HIV/AIDS epidemic further increased the uncertainty associated with projections for many African countries. In the *2010 Revision* the medium-variant projection for Malawi's population in 2050 was adjusted downwards by 8 million to 50 million to take account of rising mortality associated with the virus. However, this revision coincided, at least in part, with the onset of a quite rapid fertility transition which has seen the TFR fall from six to four births since 2000. As a result, Malawi's projected population in 2050 is now 38 million – 20 million less than it was just over a decade ago. The projection for the end of the century has been almost halved, from 130 million to 67 million. Malawi's population may still be growing at 2.5% a year, but the significance of the lower projections cannot be overstated for a country in which, like Burundi, 90% of the population depends on smallholder farming for a living and the population density is among the highest in Africa at 500 people per km² of arable land.

The most striking change to a country projection in the *2019 Revision* was the reduction of the medium variant for Uganda in

2050 from 105.7 million to 89.4 million. This may have undermined President Museveni's celebration in 2018 of potentially breaking the 100 million mark, although the US Census Bureau projection is closer to that 'target', at 97 million. The revision was largely caused by a reduction of about 0.5 births in the current TFR following publication of the 2016 DHS report.[5] That showed a fall of 1.3 births since the 2006 DHS, clearly indicating the start of a fertility transition that, if sustained, would be classed as rapid.

Substantial revisions of country projections are frequently cited by UNPD's detractors as 'proof' that the agency habitually overestimates. The downward revision of projections for Malawi and Uganda are thus 'evidence' that the across-the-board upward revisions since 2010 were misguided and that there is a clear trend emerging of faster fertility decline in Eastern Africa than anticipated by UNPD, with implications for continental population growth and projections. Such accusations are selective, and premature. Furthermore, less attention is paid to the fact that in Egypt, for example, one of Africa's population giants, the TFR has *risen* of late from a level still above three births, confounding the assumption in most projections that it would fall to replacement level by 2050. This is just as significant a development as the onset of a fertility transition in two high-fertility countries, and it has underpinned an increase in the medium-variant projection for Egypt from 123 million to 160 million. In 2020, the prime minister described population growth as 'the single largest challenge facing the state'.[6]

Alleged 'errors' by UNPD are also highlighted by critics as readily as downward revisions of country projections. A recent example in the *2019 Revision* was the inclusion of a figure of 53 million for Kenya's current population. The preliminary results of the census conducted just after publication of the *2019 Revision* recorded a population of 48 million, about 10% less than the UNPD figure. It was suggested that this undermines the medium-variant projection for a population of 92 million in 2050, a possibility welcomed by some Kenyans (but not, presumably, by Jimi Wanjigi). It is possible that Kenya's baseline population will be reset in the *2022 Revision*, but a downward revision to the 2050 projection will not follow automatically. The latest data on fertility will be equally if not more important, as Kenya's fertility decline has been a stop-start affair.

Again, apparent 'errors' cause upward as well as downward revisions. In an illustrative analysis of fertility in Mozambique carried out after the *2012 Revision*, the Russian demographers Julia Zinkina and Andrey Korotayev found that UNPD's TFR data differed from that of the DHS Program, its core source for fertility data. UNPD projections did not appear to take account of a stall in fertility decline evident in surveys since the late 1990s and seemingly confirmed by the 2007 census. In the 2011 DHS Mozambique's TFR of 5.9 births was in fact *higher* than in the 1997 and 2003 surveys. Despite this significant data, UNPD used an average TFR for 2010–15 of 4.7 births in the *2012 Revision*, and projected that Mozambique's fertility would fall faster than that of any neighbouring countries over the next six decades. Using a model 'essentially identical' to UNPD's, but inputting the higher TFR from the surveys, Zinkina and Korotayev produced a medium-variant projection for 2050 of almost 60 million compared to UNPD's 50 million. Their 2100 projection produced a population of 95 million compared to UNPD's 77 million. Zinkina and Korotayev added a caveat that if, in fact, Mozambique's fertility transition proceeded at the same (slower) rate projected for neighbouring Tanzania – a possibility on the basis of current data – their 2100 projection would be 140 million.[7]

Two subsequent large-scale health surveys in 2015 and 2018 by the same institutions that carry out the DHS confirmed that Mozambique's TFR remained above five births. No fertility transition was under way, the fertility rate having remained between five and six births for almost three decades. The detail shows why. In rural areas of the country, where most of the population lives, the TFR exceeds six births and is higher now than in the late 1990s. There is simply no evidence at present to justify any assumptions about when a fertility decline will even occur. In its *2019 Revision* UNPD adjusted the Mozambique projections upwards to 65 million by 2050 and 123 million by 2100.

Anyone expecting a pattern to emerge in sub-Saharan countries, or even within Eastern, Western and Middle Africa, over the next three decades is likely to be disappointed. 'In a few [sub-Saharan] countries, fertility has not started to decline, and may not change in the coming years,' explains the demographer Bruno Schoumaker. 'In many others, changes have been limited and hesitant, whereas some countries that were well advanced in their fertility transitions have also followed unexpected paths with slowing or stalling fertility transitions.'[8] Expectations in some quarters that fertility will fall faster than UNPD anticipates are also, on current trends, misplaced. A look at the facts in high-growth, high-fertility countries is revealing. The trajectories of these countries will not only significantly impact Africa's total population in the second half of the century but also determine whether the global population will stabilise – or continue upwards.

10

The Doubling Dozen

Multiple key indicators for 12 of Africa's fastest-growing, high-fertility populations confirm that current projections to 2050 are justified. Only in three of them is there unequivocal evidence of a fertility transition being under way. These 12 countries will alone add almost 650 million people to Africa's headcount over the next three decades.

There are 11 African countries with a population above 10 million that recorded average annual population growth of about 3% or higher between 2015 and 2020 (see Table 11). In the case of Niger, the growth rate is closer to 4%. Nigeria is added to the group: although its growth is not quite as rapid, its fertility rate and population size warrant inclusion. All 12 countries have a TFR of about five births or more; seven are among the 20 countries worldwide generating the biggest additions of people by 2050. Collectively they account for 43% of Africa's current population and 53% of sub-Saharan Africa's population.

The populations of all 12 countries will at least double by 2050, according to UNPD's medium-variant projections. Niger's will almost triple. Between 44% and 50% of the population of each country are below the age of 15. In none of them does the number of people above the age of 65 comprise more than 2–3% of the total population. These are very young countries. Between 2019 and 2050 they will add around 650 million to the total population of Africa, generating

Table 11: Africa's high-growth, high-fertility dozen to watch

Country*	Pop. 2019 (million)	TFR 2015–20 (births)	Annual growth 2015–20 (%)	Pop. 2050 (million)	TFR 2045–50 (births)	Annual growth 2019–50 (%)	Growth factor 1950–2050
Niger	23	7.0	3.8	66	4.3	3.5	25x
Uganda	44	5.0	3.6	89	2.7	2.2	17x
Angola	32	5.6	3.3	77	3.9	2.9	11x
DRC	87	6.0	3.2	194	3.4	2.6	16x
Burundi	12	5.5	3.2	25	3.5	2.4	11x
Tanzania	58	4.9	3.0	129	3.5	2.6	17x
Mali	20	5.9	3.0	44	3.5	2.5	9x
Burkina Faso	20	5.2	3.0	43	3.4	2.5	11x
Chad	16	5.8	3.0	34	3.5	2.5	14x
Mozambique	30	4.9	2.9	65	3.1	2.5	11x
Zambia	18	4.7	2.9	39	3.4	2.5	17x
Nigeria	201	5.4	2.6	401	3.6	2.3	11x
Total	561			1,206			13.1x
Average		5.5	3.1		3.5	2.6	
World	7,713	2.5	1.1	9,735	2.2	0.7	3.8x
Africa	1,308	4.4	2.5	2,489	3.1	2.1	10.9x
Sub-Saharan Africa	1,066	4.7	2.7	2,117	3.2	2.2	11.8x
Northern Africa	242	2.9	1.9	372	2.3	1.4	7.6x

*Countries are listed in descending order of average annual population growth rate, 2015–20. Population figures have been rounded to the nearest million. Population figures and TFRs for 2019 are UNPD estimates; those for 2050 are UNPD medium-variant projections.
Source: UNPD, *World Population Prospects: The 2019 Revision.*

about 55% of Africa's population growth (and 62% of sub-Saharan Africa's). Between 1950 and 2050 their populations will have expanded by between nine times (Mali) and 25 times (Niger). The demographic trajectories in these countries are of signal importance to Africa and to the trajectory of the global population.

UNPD's five-year average TFRs for each of the countries from the early 1990s to 2050 – actual and projected – are shown in Table 12. The third column from the right (in bold) shows the cumulative change over the past three decades. The TFR has eased in all 12 countries, but only in half of them has it fallen by 1.5 births or more since 1990–95 – the average fertility decline for sub-Saharan Africa. In Niger, DRC and Nigeria fertility has fallen by one birth or less during the period. Rapid fertility transitions around the world have involved a reduction in the TFR of one birth or more in a decade, with the fastest declines usually occurring in the first decades of the transition.

The extreme right-hand column (also in bold) shows the change in TFR anticipated by UNPD over the three decades from 2020 to 2050. The most rapid projected declines are in countries where there is no evidence of a fertility transition* having started (Niger, DRC and Mali), and those where a transition is definitely or possibly under way (Uganda, Burundi, Chad and Zambia). If a transition did not commence within three decades in Niger, DRC and Mali the duration of high fertility against a backdrop of improving mortality would be globally unprecedented.

Table 13 shows the TFR of the 12 countries recorded by the last three surveys in the DHS Program, for comparison. It suggests a more mixed picture regarding fertility decline than that conveyed by UNPD fertility data in Table 12. More than half the countries (highlighted in bold) have registered negligible declines – or even a slight rise – in their TFR. On the face of it, this is an anomalous impression, given that DHS is the main source of fertility data

---

* The TFR in all 12 has fallen more than 10% since its peak, which some demographers count as the start of a fertility transition. Others prefer to use a fall of 10% in the TFR since the previous DHS, the approach employed here.

Table 12: Africa's high-growth, high-fertility dozen: progression of TFR, 1990-2050 (UNPD estimates and projections)

	TFR 1990-95	TFR 1995-2000	TFR 2000-05	TFR 2005-10	TFR 2010-15	TFR 2015-20	TFR +/- 1990-2020	TFR 2045-50	TFR +/- 2020-2050
Niger	7.8	7.7	7.7	7.6	7.4	7.0	**-0.8**	4.3	**-2.7**
Uganda	7.1	7.0	6.8	6.4	5.8	5.0	**-2.1**	2.7	**-2.3**
Angola	7.1	6.8	6.6	6.4	6.0	5.6	**-1.5**	3.9	**-1.7**
DRC	6.8	6.8	6.7	6.6	6.4	6.0	**-0.8**	3.4	**-2.6**
Burundi	7.3	7.1	6.8	6.4	6.0	5.5	**-1.8**	3.5	**-2.0**
Tanzania	6.1	5.8	5.7	5.6	5.2	4.9	**-1.2**	3.5	**-1.4**
Mali	7.2	7.0	6.9	6.7	6.4	5.9	**-1.3**	3.5	**-2.4**
Burkina Faso	6.9	6.7	6.4	6.1	5.7	5.2	**-1.7**	3.4	**-1.8**
Chad	7.4	7.4	7.2	6.9	6.3	5.8	**-1.6**	3.5	**-2.3**
Mozambique	6.1	5.9	5.8	5.5	5.2	4.9	**-1.2**	3.1	**-1.8**
Zambia	6.3	6.1	6.0	5.6	5.2	4.7	**-1.6**	2.7	**-2.0**
Nigeria	6.4	6.2	6.1	5.9	5.7	5.4	**-1.0**	3.6	**-1.8**
Africa	5.7	5.4	5.1	4.9	4.7	4.4	**-1.3**	3.1	**-1.3**
Sub-Saharan Africa	6.2	5.9	5.6	5.4	5.1	4.7	**-1.5**	3.2	**-1.5**

Source: UNPD, *World Population Prospects: The 2019 Revision.*

for UNPD. The discrepancy can be explained by the shorter time frame, the smaller number of data points, and the averaging of the TFR over five-year periods by UNPD. For some countries, the latest DHS is now some time ago and the next is needed for clarification. However, it does serve to emphasise that fertility transitions are seldom smooth processes, and to caution against assuming an ongoing downward trend in the 12 countries suggested by Table 12. Not all countries are really in a fertility transition, even of the slowest variety.

Table 13: Africa's high-growth, high-fertility countries: TFR data from last three DHS (if available), 1990s to 2018

	DHS 1	DHS 2	DHS 3	Trend*
Niger**	7.2 (1998)	7.0 (2006)	7.6 (2012)	No decline
Uganda	6.7 (2006)	6.2 (2011)	5.4 (2016)	Decline
Angola	n/a	n/a	6.2 (2015/16)	n/a
DRC	n/a	6.3 (2007)	6.6 (2013/14)	No decline
Burundi	6.9 (1987)	6.4 (2010)	5.5 (2016/17)	Decline
Tanzania	5.7 (2004/5)	5.4 (2010)	5.2 (2015/16)	Decline
Mali	6.6 (2006)	6.1 (2012/13)	6.3 (2018)	No decline
Burkina Faso	6.4 (1998/9)	5.9 (2003)	6.0 (2010)	No decline
Chad	6.4 (1996/7)	6.3 (2004)	6.4 (2014/15)	No decline
Mozambique	5.5 (2003)	5.9 (2011)	5.3 (2015)***	No decline
Zambia	6.2 (2007)	5.3 (2013/14)	4.7 (2018)	Decline
Nigeria	5.7 (2008)	5.5 (2013)	5.3 (2018)	No decline

* Reduction of TFR by 0.5 births = decline. **The 2017 Niger DHS was invalidated as the data did not meet quality standards. Improbable durations for women's interviews were among the shortcomings cited. See 'Data Quality Evaluation of the Niger 2017 Demographic and Health Survey' www.dhsprogram.com/pubs/pdf/OD73/OD73.pdf. ***HIV/AIDS Indicator Survey (AIS), also conducted under the auspices of the DHS Program *Source:* Demographic and Health Surveys (various, dates shown in brackets), ICF International Inc.

Mali is an example of the different impression given by UNPD and DHS fertility trends. In Table 12 it can be seen that the TFR fell from 6.7 births in 2005–10 to 5.9 in 2015–20, a decline of almost one birth in a decade and suggestive of a reasonably fast transition. Table 13 presents no such impression. Mali's TFR is largely unchanged over the past three surveys, the most recent of which was conducted in 2018. Furthermore, the detail in the latest DHS report is instructive. For example, women respondents stated that their ideal number of children was six whereas for men it was eight – numbers that have declined by less than one child in 30 years. The TFR is higher than 5.8 in all regions of the country except that of the capital, Bamako, where

Table 14: Africa's high-growth, high-fertility dozen: infant and child mortality, 1990-2020

Country	Infant mortality* (average annual deaths per 1,000) 1990-95	Infant mortality* (average annual deaths per 1,000) 2015-20	Under-5 mortality (average annual deaths per 1,000) 1990-95	Under-5 mortality (average annual deaths per 1,000) 2015-20
Niger	126	62	293	85
Uganda	105	46	171	63
Angola	145	61	223	81
DRC	110	65	182	100
Burundi	111	42	182	63
Tanzania	105	41	164	57
Mali	127	66	246	105
Burkina Faso	104	54	204	84
Chad	119	75	198	123
Mozambique	138	54	229	73
Zambia	117	46	185	61
Nigeria	126	62	213	102

it is a little under five, and Kidal, where it is below four. Polygamy remains common, with more than 40% of women who have received no formal education having co-spouses, and even 20% of women who have had secondary or tertiary education. Almost 60% of women say they have no desire for family planning. A fertility transition is self-evidently not under way in Mali, nor in Chad at the time of its last survey in 2014–15. In Niger there was a clear upward trend in fertility in 2011. Regrettably, the 2017 survey did not meet the standards required by the DHS Program, so comprehensive, up-to-date fertility data is lacking.

Tables 14 and 15 present various measures which conventional demographic transition theory closely associates with fertility transitions: infant and child mortality, GDP per capita and the level

Table 14: Continued

Country	Infant mortality* (average annual deaths per 1,000) 1990–95	Infant mortality* (average annual deaths per 1,000) 2015–20	Under-5 mortality (average annual deaths per 1,000) 1990–95	Under-5 mortality (average annual deaths per 1,000) 2015–20
Comparators				
Africa	101	47	166	71
Sub-Saharan Africa	109	51	183	78
Ethiopia	114	37	190	55
Ghana	72	36	114	52
Kenya	74	36	108	47
South Africa	41	27	57	35
Zimbabwe	62	39	87	51
Eastern/ Southeastern Asia	41	13	53	16
Southern Asia	83	36	116	44
Asia	62	25	84	31
Latin America/ Caribbean	38	15	48	19
All low-income countries	107	48	178	71

*Infant denotes the first year of life. *Source:* UNPD Data Download Centre.

of urbanisation. High infant mortality is indicative of low spending on health and basic sanitation. Improvements in infant and child mortality always precede fertility declines, although there is often a lag during which populations grow rapidly. Higher GDP per capita and increasingly urban populations are widely treated as indicators (albeit flawed and of limited applicability to low-income, non-industrialised economies) of socio-economic improvements, modernisation and industrialisation, which are also associated with lower fertility.

Sustained and substantial declines in infant and child mortality are evident in all 12 countries. Uganda, Burundi and Zambia the three countries where there is a clear downward trend in fertility, now have infant mortality rates below 50 per 1,000 live births, although they still have some way to go before matching Ethiopia, Ghana, South Africa and Zimbabwe. Conversely, in DRC, Mali, Chad and Nigeria more than one in 10 children still die before their fifth birthday. Much-improved infant and child mortality rates alone are not always indicative of the imminent start of a fertility transition: Tanzania's are the best of any of the 12 countries and its TFR is falling, but at a very slow pace indeed.

With the exception of DRC (where GDP per capita is only one-third of its level in 1960) and Burundi, all the countries have recorded substantial increases in GDP per capita since 1990. Mozambique heads the list, this measure having expanded by a multiple of five, albeit from by far the lowest base of any of the countries. Seven countries – Uganda, Tanzania, Mali, Burkina Faso, Mozambique, Zambia and Nigeria – have exceeded the 2.6x average growth of low-income countries globally during the period. Positive though this turnaround is after the economic shocks of the 1970s and the 'lost decade' in the 1980s, even the best-performing African economies are still being considerably outpaced by many of their Asian peers. In Vietnam, for example, GDP per capita has multiplied almost tenfold since 1990 from much the same starting point as Tanzania.

Urbanisation levels have increased considerably everywhere except in Niger, Chad and Zambia. In Uganda, Tanzania, Angola, Mali, Burkina Faso and Nigeria the proportion of the population living in towns and cities roughly doubled. This indicator, even when taken alongside GDP per capita, provides more anomalies than helpful pointers. Most Angolans live in urban locations, and the country has by far the highest GDP per capita of all the countries – yet its TFR remains around six births. Burundi has an almost exclusively rural population and easily the lowest GDP per capita of the countries – yet a fertility transition is under way.

Mali is now almost half urban, half rural, but its TFR remains above six births and is showing no signs of decline. In many respects, DHS data provides far greater insights than indicators relying on GDP and urbanisation levels.

World Bank Human Capital Index scores are also shown in Table 15. Ten of the 12 countries rank in the lowest 30 positions worldwide. The index, which was launched in 2018, has three components:

- Survival component: the probability of survival to the age of five
- Education component: expected years of schooling and test scores provide a quality-adjusted years at school indicator
- Health component based in prevalence of stunting among children and the adult survival rate.

It is designed to measure 'the productivity of the next generation of workers relative to the benchmark of complete education and full health'. The three countries with the highest scores worldwide are Singapore, South Korea and Japan. Among Africa's mainland states, the top-ranking countries are Algeria and Kenya, narrowly ahead of Tunisia, Morocco and Egypt. The scores of these countries are 25% higher than that of Tanzania, the highest-ranking country among the 12 high-growth, high-fertility countries – a material difference.

Table 16 again shows the DHS TFR data from the two most recent surveys for the high-growth countries. Alongside it are some of the social indicators demographers expect to display positive association/inverse correlation with falling fertility. Individually they are not infallible, and others are also used; but collectively they make a basic judgement possible regarding fertility decline, and whether medium-variant projections to 2050 are 'obviously' too high, as some commentators claim (or too low).

Table 15: Africa's high-growth, high-fertility dozen: selected socio-economic indicators

Country	GDP per capita, purchasing power parity (current US$) 1990	GDP per capita, purchasing power parity (current US$) 2019	Urban population as % of total 1990	Urban population as % of total 2019	Human Capital Index 2020
Niger	757	1,270	15	16	0.32
Uganda	669	2,271	11	24	0.38
Angola	3,267	6,930	37	66	0.36
DRC	883	1,143	31	45	0.37
Burundi	615	783	6	13	0.39
Tanzania	960	2,771	19	35	0.39
Mali	804	2,423	23	43	0.32
Burkina Faso	590	2,280	14	30	0.38
Chad	698	1,645	21	23	0.30
Mozambique	291	1,333	25	37	0.36
Zambia	1,476	3,624	39	44	0.40
Nigeria	2,059	5,348	30	51	0.36

Use of modern contraceptive methods by married women aged 15–49

Although the extent to which the use of modern contraceptive methods drives fertility transition is still disputed – some experts say it is *the* deciding factor, while others consider desired fertility (see below) to be key – there is strong correlation between rising usage and falling fertility. The projected TFRs in 2050 would generally be associated with 55–60% usage rates.[1]

Table 15: Continued

Country	GDP per capita, purchasing power parity (current US$) 1990	GDP per capita, purchasing power parity (current US$) 2019	Urban population as % of total 1990	Urban population as % of total 2019	Human Capital Index 2020
Comparators					
Ethiopia	415	2,312	13	21	0.38
Ghana	1,237	5,637	36	57	0.45
Kenya	1,476	4,509	17	28	0.55
South Africa	6,421	12,999	52	67	0.43
Zimbabwe	1,773	2,953	29	32	0.47
Bangladesh	851	4,964	5	37	0.46
India	1,202	8,397	18	35	0.49
Peru	3,361	13,416	46	78	0.61
Vietnam	918	8,397	15	36	0.69

Sources: GDP/cap in US$ purchasing power parity from World Bank Open Data (accessed October 2020). Urbanisation data from World Bank Open Data (accessed October 2020). The Human Capital Index was launched by the World Bank in 2018. It is designed 'to capture the amount of human capital a child born today could expect to attain by age 18', given the provision of health and education in the country.

On average, about 25% of married women in sub-Saharan Africa use modern contraceptive methods, although the figure varies enormously by region and country (and in some countries contraception is used as much to space births as prevent them). The average for Northern Africa is about 30% and in Eastern Africa it is above 40%. In Western and Middle Africa the average is about 15%. In Europe, North America, Latin America/Caribbean and East and Southeast Asia prevalence rates above 60% are typical. In Africa,

usage exceeds 50% only in Egypt, Kenya, Malawi, Zimbabwe and all
the Southern Africa countries.[2]

Median age at first marriage

In high-fertility countries, childbirth usually follows soon after
marriage. The younger women (or girls) are when first married, the
more children they tend to have during their reproductive lifetime
and the less likely they are to be able to pursue educational and
employment opportunities.

In all of the 12 countries except Burundi, the median age at first
marriage is in adolescence (defined by the United Nations as between
the ages of 15 and 19) and the adolescent birth rate is at or above the
African average of 100 adolescent births per 1,000 births. Seven of
the countries have adolescent birth rates among the 10 highest in the
world: Niger, Uganda, Angola, DRC, Mali, Chad and Mozambique.[3]
Three of the countries – Nigeria, Angola and Mozambique – have the
highest rates of early adolescent childbirth globally, with more than
10 births per 1,000 to mothers aged between 10 and 14.[4]

The adolescent birth rate in Africa has declined by about 20 births
per 1,000 since 2000,but remains far higher than the 65 births per
1,000 in Latin America/Caribbean, the next-highest region. The rate
in Asia is 40 births per 1,000.

Later childbearing can be a sign of improving reproductive
health, education outcomes and 'empowerment'. High median
age at first marriage correlates with having fewer children. For
example, in countries like China, Hong Kong, Italy, Luxembourg
and Spain the mean age of childbearing is almost 32 years and the
TFR range is between 1.3 and 1.7 births. According to Professor
Alex Ezeh, if Africa's median age at first marriage were raised by
two years it would reduce UNPD's medium-variant projection to
2100 by about 10%.[5]

In contrast to the median age at first marriage, the mean age of
childbearing in sub-Saharan Africa is quite high at 29 years, compared

to 27 years in Latin America and the Caribbean. This can be explained by the fact that as well as having children earlier than in other regions of the world, women in Africa continue to reproduce for longer.[6]

Ideal (or 'desired') family size among married women (aged 15–49) and married men (aged 15–54 or 15–59, depending on country)

DHS interviewees are asked: 'If you could go back to a time when you had no children to choose exactly how many to have in your life, how many would you like to have?' Non-numeric responses such as 'as many as God will give me' are recorded, but account for low single-digit percentages. Even though the ideal number of children chosen by interviewees cannot be taken literally, high desired family size correlates with high fertility, especially when modern contraceptive usage is low.

According to John Bongaarts at the Population Council, 'transition in [sub-Saharan Africa] cannot proceed to replacement unless large declines in desired family size occur'.[7]

Wanted fertility rate

This is the theoretical average number of children a woman would have by the end of her childbearing years if she bore children at the current age-specific fertility rates and all unwanted births were prevented. For example, in Uganda women are having about one child more than they want (5.4 – 4.3 = 1.1). The particular significance of this measure is that if all women were able to have the number of children they say they want, which for Africa as a whole is 0.7 fewer than they actually have, Africa's population in 2100 would be 30% less than projected, according to Professor Alex Ezeh.[8]

Table 16: Africa's high-growth, high-fertility dozen: selected DHS data

	DHS 1	DHS 2	mCPR* DHS 1	mCPR* DHS 2	Median age at first marriage	Ideal or desired fertility (♀/♂), number of children	Total wanted fertility (♀), number of children
Niger	7.0 (2006)	7.6 (2012)	5.0	12.2	15.1	9.5/13.0	6.8
Uganda	6.2 (2011)	5.4 (2016)	26.0	34.8	17.6	5.1/6.0	4.3
Angola	n/a	6.2 (2015/16)	n/a	12.5	20.5	5.5/6.8	5.2
DRC	6.3 (2007)	6.6 (2013/14)	5.8	7.8	18.6	6.6/8.1	5.7
Burundi	6.4 (2010)	5.5 (2016/17)	17.7	22.9	19.5	4.0/3.9	3.6
Tanzania	5.4 (2010)	5.2 (2015/16)	27.4	32.0	18.6	5.2/5.6	4.5
Mali	6.1 (2012/13)	6.3 (2018)	9.9	16.4	16.6	6.2/8.7	5.5
Burkina Faso	5.9 (2003)	6.0 (2010)	8.8	15.0	17.6	5.8/7.0	5.2
Chad	6.3 (2004)	6.4 (2014/15)	1.6	5.0	15.8	8.6/11.8	6.1
Mozambique	5.9 (2011)	5.3 (2015+)	11.3	25.3	18.2	5.3/6.1 (DHS 2011)	5.1 (DHS 2011)
Zambia	5.3 (2013/14)	4.7 (2018)	44.8	47.5	18.2	5.1/5.5	4.0
Nigeria	5.5 (2013)	5.3 (2018)	9.8	12.0	19.1	6.6/7.7	4.8

*mCPR – Contraceptive Prevalence Rate (modern methods) among women aged 15–49.   +HIV/AIDS Indicator Survey (AIS).   Source: Demographic and Health Surveys, ICF International Inc.

The 12 countries can be divided into five categories.

No change, no sign of change: Niger, DRC, Mali and Chad

In four of the high-growth countries DHSs provide no signs of any significant change in fertility so far in the twenty-first century.

In addition to having the highest TFR of all the countries, **Niger** is unusual in that the ideal number of children wanted by men and women alike is *higher* than the number they have. The ideal family size for women is nine to 10 children, and among men it is 13 children – the highest figures in Africa (and the world). Even the wanted fertility among women is less than one birth below the TFR: Nigérienne women say they want about the number of children that they have. Almost 40% of girls are married by the age of 15 and the use of modern contraceptive methods is very low.[9]

In **DRC** the ideal number of children for men and women is also close to or above actual fertility. In both countries usage of modern contraception by women is negligible, at 12% in Niger and 8% in DRC, and virtually non-existent among the poorest quintile, where fertility is highest. In Niger, the median age at first marriage is about 15 years. It has risen by less than one year since the 1990s.

In **Mali**, usage of modern contraceptive methods by married women has increased very gradually since 2000, but remains well under 20%. The median age at first marriage is below 17 years and static – more than 10% of girls are married by the age of 15. The ideal family size cited by married women and men is 6.2 and 8.7 children respectively.

In **Chad**, at 5% the proportion of married women using modern methods of contraception is the lowest among the high-growth countries (and any country in Africa). The median age at first marriage – 16 years – is largely unchanged since the mid-1990s. Almost 40% of women are in polygamous unions. Desired family size is eight to nine children among married women and almost 12 among married men.

In all four countries, men's desired number of children exceeds women's by at least 1.5, implying little support for smaller families in patriarchal societies. In Niger and Chad the difference exceeds three children. Having many children is generally considered a source of prestige and pride, a divine gift and an economic asset.

The medium-variant projections for Niger, DRC, Mali and Chad assume fertility declines of 2.3 to 2.7 births by 2050. At present there are no signs of incipient decline in any of them. The latest DHSs for Mali and DRC showed slight rises in fertility. Furthermore, in another five years the projected fertility transitions would, at one birth or more per decade, be classified as rapid. The projected TFRs are modelled on trajectories of other countries that had the same fertility rate rather than the specific indicators of the specific country.[10]

If the TFR in Niger, DRC, Mali and Chad were 0.5 births higher than anticipated in mid-century, conforming to UNPD's high-variant projection rather than the medium-variant, it would imply a combined population of about 375 million, about 10% higher than envisaged by the medium-variant projection.

Little change, possible signs of change: Mozambique

The DHS data for **Mozambique** is inconclusive regarding the onset of a fertility transition. The results of the next DHS will be significant in this regard. Between the late 1990s and 2011 the country's TFR rose from 5.2 births to 5.9 births, a development which may have been associated in part with the end of a 15-year civil war in 1992. In 2015, another large-scale health survey indicated that the TFR had declined again to 5.3. If sustained, this rate of reduction – 0.6 births in just four years – would signal that a transition was certainly under way. This possibility is supported by a doubling between 2011 and 2015 of the percentage of married women using modern contraceptive methods to over 25%, a trend that has continued. More recent data confirms that Mozambique was among the 10 countries worldwide showing the largest increases in modern contraceptive usage, averaging more than 1% a year during the 2010s.[11]

On the other hand, the fact that the TFR has only returned to its 1997 level suggests caution until the next DHS results are published. So too does the fact that more than 10% of girls are married by the age of 15, and there has been a marked increase in the percentage of women having their first child between the ages of 15 and 19 – from an average of about 40% in the 2000s to more than 45% in 2015. As mentioned earlier, the 2017 census also showed that 80% of the population live in areas where the TFR is above five births (and more than 40% in provinces with a TFR above six births).

Slow fertility decline: Angola, Tanzania and Nigeria

In Angola, Tanzania and Nigeria fertility is trending downwards, but very slowly. In **Angola** the TFR fell by about one birth between the early 1990s and the mid-2010s and the median age at first marriage is the highest of all the countries at about 20. But it is unlikely that the rate will accelerate while usage of modern contraception remains at very low levels. Among married women the desired number of children is less than one below actual fertility. In **Tanzania** the use of modern contraceptive methods by married women has increased by more than 50% since 2004/5 and now exceeds 30%, but further increases may have been delayed by the antipathy of President Magufuli to family planning and contraception. At more than five children, desired family size is largely unaltered since the early 2000s.

The decline in **Nigeria**'s TFR is equally slow – about 0.7 births during the past three decades (and 0.4 births in the past two decades). The medium-variant projection of a decline of almost two births by 2050 therefore implies a marked acceleration. At present there is no evidence of this being about to start. More than 10% of girls are married by the age of 15; usage of modern methods of contraception by Nigerian women remains negligible (and non-existent among the poorest quintile); one in three women are in a polygynous union; and unmet need* is not only one of the lowest in Africa but unchanged

---

* The WHO defines unmet need as referring to women who 'are fecund and sexually active but are not using any method of contraception, and report not wanting any more children or wanting to delay the next child. The concept of unmet need points to the gap between women's reproductive intentions and their contraceptive behaviour.'

since the 1990s. DHS data attests to the strong preference among Nigerian women of all wealth and education levels not to use modern contraceptive methods. Furthermore, desired family size among women remains above six children and among men is almost eight children, levels nearly as high as in the Sahel countries to the north. More than 80% of Nigerian women consider four or more children to be ideal. Among women from the poorest households, the median age at first marriage is less than 16 years and over 40% of Nigerian women are married by the age of 18.

Nigeria has drawn up a number of progressive population policies, but they have remained largely unimplemented. The 1998 Nigerian National Population Policy is an example. It was eventually launched in 2004 and targeted a reduction in the TFR of 0.6 births every five years and a 2% increase annually in usage of modern contraceptive methods.

Outlook unclear: Burkina Faso

Like Mozambique, **Burkina Faso** was among the 10 countries worldwide showing the fastest increases in usage of modern contraception in the 2010s. It now exceeds 30%, double the level a decade earlier. While the most recent DHS was conducted in 2010, fertility data collected during a Malaria Indicators Survey (MIS) in 2017/18 suggest that the TFR has declined by almost one birth since 2010. No census has been undertaken since 2006, so the next DHS will be all the more important.

Rapid transitions under way: Zambia, Burundi and Uganda

In three of the high-growth countries, rapid fertility transitions appear to have commenced.

In **Zambia** the TFR fell by 1.5 births between the 2007 and 2018 DHS, a very rapid decline by any standards. It was one of five countries in 2015 to fulfil its undertaking in the 2001 Abuja Declaration to spend at least 15% of the budget on health (the others were Rwanda, Madagascar, Botswana and Togo). Although age at marriage is largely unchanged in three decades, usage of modern contraceptive methods by married women rose substantially between the 2007 and 2018 DHSs to almost 50% – one of the highest rates in Africa. The ideal number of children has declined since the early 1990s from an average of 6.2 to 5.1 among married women and from 6.3 to 5.5 among married men. The wanted fertility rate fell by more than one birth to four births between the 2007 and 2018 DHSs.

Burundi is the only country among the high-growth countries where the desired family size among married men is below that of married women. This can be an indicator of changing attitudes and norms conducive to a sustained fertility transition. Similarly, it is the only one of the high-growth countries where women's wanted fertility is now below four children – almost two children less than actual fertility. To close this gap, higher usage of modern methods of contraception would be required. Historically, the very influential Catholic Church has stood firm against contraception, preventing faster progress towards an official target of reducing the TFR to three births by 2025. The speed of Burundi's transition will depend significantly on whether political will starts to trump deep-seated religious attitudes.

Alongside Burkina Faso and Mozambique, **Uganda** was also among the 10 countries worldwide showing the fastest increase in uptake of modern contraceptive methods in the 2010s. More than one in three married women in Uganda now use modern contraceptive methods, the proportion having doubled since the mid-2000s. The median age at first marriage is rising. The TFR among rural women fell from 7.1 births to 5.9 between the 2006 and 2016 DHSs, a faster rate of decline than among women in urban areas, where the TFR fell from 4.4 births to four (and actually rose slightly between 2011 and 2016). This is evidence that the transition is widespread, although the TFR among women in the two poorest quintiles is still high, at 7.1 and 7.9 births respectively, and 70% of the population still live in regions with a TFR above five births.

In sum, the fertility decline of about two births projected by UNPD for Zambia, Burundi and Uganda will be realised if current trends continue. The projections for these three countries are much the most defensible. As fertility transitions are clearly under way, trends have been established. The combined contribution of these countries to Africa's population growth by mid-century is about 80 million, about 12% only of the 650 million people being added by all 12 high-growth countries.

As for the other nine high-growth, high-fertility countries, projected to account for more than 550 million additional people by 2050, the picture remains uncertain. For a few, projections may well have to be raised. In none is there any evidence yet to suggest the possibility of the opposite. These nine countries matter a great deal to global trends: they are currently expected to account for almost one-third of projected global population growth between 2020 and 2050. Any assertion that population growth will fall more swiftly than demographers expect rests on one of two things: wishful thinking, or an assumption of a very severe check to improving mortality. Whether Africa's women want to or can drive faster change is the subject of the next chapter.

11

Women's World

In the 12 high-growth, high-fertility countries of Africa examined in the last chapter, women are subjugated by husbands, religious leaders, traditional norms, other women, rumour and suspicion. 'Enforced motherhood'[1] is common, and family planning advice and modern contraception are often inaccessible when desired. This has adverse consequences for women's health and well-being, and that of their children. It prevents women from bearing the number of children they want, when they want to have them.

'The scourge is still largely unaddressed in many African countries,' says Professor Clifford Odimegwu, head of the demography and population studies programme at Wits University in South Africa. 'Violence against women is culturally accepted in many societies, and until now, women have been largely perceived as being subordinate to men, and are treated as such.'[2] The prevalence of wife-beating is one of many markers of the extent to which women throughout Africa are daily, in all facets of their lives, at an acute and frequently dangerous disadvantage. Improvement in women's social and economic situation is usually associated with declining fertility.

Wife-beating is not a distinctively African phenomenon: it is one of the most common forms of gender-based violence worldwide. It signals inequality and female disempowerment and, according to the 2018 report of the Guttmacher-Lancet Commission, entails 'severe consequences for physical and mental health and well-being, hindering the achievement of... social and economic goals'.[3] Within the African continent, the practice is particularly – but not exclusively – prevalent in Western and Middle Africa. But according to the OECD's Social Institutions & Gender (SIGI) Index, Northern Africa has a higher level of gender discrimination than all other African regions.[4]

In DHS interviews there are multiple questions relating to female empowerment and status. Women are asked about their employment and earnings; control over earnings; ownership of land, housing and other assets; decision-making power; access to healthcare; and about their experience of domestic violence. Survey results are always informative and fascinating, even more so as they are broken down to show responses by region, age group, educational background and wealth. No single indicator can provide a definitive measure of female empowerment, and composite indices constructed from DHS (or any other) data for African countries, and for other regions of the world, have never quite attained their intended objective. The process of amalgamating different indicators itself creates deficiencies, often producing results which tell us less than the individual indicators. However, three most frequently analysed empowerment indicators for the 12 high-growth countries give a reasonable impression of how able women are to have the number of children they want, and to have those children when they want them. In most of the countries women have more children than they would choose to.

Wife-beating

A woman subjected to frequent violence at the hands of her spouse is unlikely to have control over her reproductive health and behaviour. Significant reductions in fertility in sub-Saharan countries have usually been associated with rapidly diminishing justification for wife-beating by women and their husbands. A 2018 study found that 'women's attitudes toward violence emerged as the first and most persistent factor of women's empowerment across all four regions [of sub-Saharan Africa]'.[5] The authors of another study asserted that among female empowerment measures, 'not condoning wife-beating was the most consistently linked to a smaller ideal number of children'. Professor Odimegwu considers that domestic violence should be regarded as a 'new proximate determinant' of fertility.[6]

In DHS interviews women and their husbands are asked whether beating is justified if the wife:

- burns the food
- argues with her husband
- goes out without telling her husband
- neglects the children
- refuses to have sexual intercourse.

Table 17 shows how respondents in the high-growth countries replied to each question. The overall indicator in the right-hand column is the average of the individual answers.

The data for Tanzania, for example, shows that 58% of women and 40% of men consider wife-beating justified for at least one of the specified reasons. The lowest percentages among both sexes (20% among women, 6% among men) said it was justified for burning the food. A woman going out without telling her husband, neglecting children or arguing with her husband were the most justified reasons according to both sexes. In Angola and Mozambique, the results in each category are similar, and relatively low; wife-beating is not common. In all the countries, men regard a wife's refusal to have sex as one of the least justifiable reasons to beat her, ranking it much the same as burning the food (women agree on the latter). Neglecting children and arguing with the husband are the most justifiable reasons. Much lower support for the justifiability of wife-beating by males than females can indicate potential for the practice to become less common; and fertility transition is usually associated with a marked diminution in the proportion of both sexes regarding wife-beating as justified.

The association holds true for the three countries where a fertility transition is under way – Burundi, Uganda and Zambia. In Burundi,

Table 17: The doubling dozen: percentage of women (F) and men (M) who agree that a husband is justified in hitting or beating his wife for the specified reasons

Country (most recent DHS or AIS)	Burns the food (%)		Argues with husband (%)		Goes out without telling husband (%)		Neglects the children (%)		Refuses to have sex with husband (%)		At least one of these reasons (%)	
	F	M	F	M	F	M	F	M	F	M	F	M
Niger	35	9	50	19	43	15	42	15	50	13	60	26
Uganda	14	7	26	23	30	22	39	28	18	12	49	41
Angola	11	6	15	11	15	8	16	11	12	6	25	20
DRC	24	15	58	41	49	32	51	39	44	23	75	60
Burundi	22	5	30	10	39	17	52	25	42	13	62	34
Tanzania	20	6	42	25	41	23	48	31	31	14	58	40
Mali	23	11	69	37	54	22	52	24	63	23	79	46
Burkina Faso	10	7	31	20	30	17	30	19	20	11	44	33
Chad	49	27	50	22	59	28	60	36	41	23	74	49
Mozambique	2	5	7	8	8	8	4	7	6	7	14	17
Zambia	21	6	32	14	26	12	31	15	30	10	46	25
Nigeria	15	7	20	12	21	11	21	11	20	11	28	21

Interviewees are aged 15-49 (women) or 15-59 (men) and provide an answer to each question. Percentages are averages of the combined responses. *Source:* Demographic and Health Surveys Program (most recent survey reports), ICF International Inc.

where the TFR is poised to fall from above seven births in the early 1990s to less than four births, wife-beating is still endorsed by a higher percentage of women than in Uganda or Zambia, but the trend has been unmistakably downwards. In Uganda, the 2000/01 DHS report remarked that the very high level of acceptance of wife-beating by women and men was 'not surprising because traditional norms teach women to accept, tolerate, and even rationalise battery'.[7] Since then, the percentage of women regarding beating as potentially justified has declined from 77% to less than 50% as the TFR has fallen by almost two births, from 6.9 to five. Among Ugandan men the decline was less striking – from 64% to 41%, with improvement stalling between the 2011 and 2016 DHSs.[8] The overall improvement has been partly attributed to public programmes raising awareness of the unacceptability of wife-beating and other forms of spousal violence; and public declarations by President Museveni that wife-beating is 'cowardly'. In Zambia, 85% of women considered beating justified for one or more of the given reasons in the 2000/01 DHS. That has fallen to under half today. Among Zambian men the percentage has declined even more, from 69% to 25%. Attitudinal change is not as widespread as in Uganda: justification for beating remains far higher among less-educated women and those from poorer backgrounds.

As ever, it is important to acknowledge substantial variations within countries as well as between them. For example, in the Busoga and Bukedi regions of Uganda, 'only' one in five men find any justification for wife-beating; and in the Kampala, Bunyoro and Kigezi regions fewer than one in three women now consider beating to be justifiable under any circumstance. On the other hand, in Karamoja, Teso and West Nile, where the TFR is between six and eight births, two-thirds or more of women agree it is sometimes justifiable. Almost half of Ugandan women live in the seven regions (out of 15) where a majority of women and men find wife-beating justifiable for some reason, and in those regions the TFR is between five and eight births. It is also revealing that about 40% of Ugandan women with secondary education consider wife-beating justifiable for at least one reason; and that even in the richest wealth quintile between one and three and one in four women in Uganda, Burundi and Zambia – all countries where the practice is declining – regard beating as justified for one or more reasons. Averages mask the complexity of data comprising national trends.

Corroboration of the impression conveyed by the DHS data for wife-beating is provided by the pan-African research institute Afrobarometer. In its most recent survey round, carried out in 2016–18, almost 49,000 people were interviewed in 34 countries that account for 80% of the continent's population. The summary report found that acceptance of domestic violence was more than twice as common in Western Africa (40%) and Middle, or Central, Africa (46%) as in Northern (17%), Eastern (16%) and Southern Africa (14%). Furthermore, from the responses it would appear that the practice of wife-beating is 'no mere vestige of a dying norm: young adults are slightly more likely than their elders to consider it justified'.[9] This is a further counter-intuitive finding.

Participation in decision-making

A second example of the most-analysed DHS female empowerment indicators relates to participation in major household decisions. Women are asked three specific questions about whether they make decisions alone or jointly with their husband regarding:

- their own healthcare
- major household purchases
- visiting friends or relatives.

The responses are shown in Table 18. According to the DHS Program, 'only women who assert that they make their own decisions in all three key areas of life are considered to have autonomy in reproductive health decision-making'.

Once again, Mozambique and Angola are exceptions, in that about two-thirds of women have a high degree of participation in decision-making – the greatest proportion of any of the 12 countries – yet fertility remains elevated in both countries, with no compelling sign of a downward trend developing. Among the other countries there is a clear association between decision-making and fertility. In Uganda, Burundi and Zambia, the countries in fertility transition, more than half of women participate in all three decisions. Conversely, most women in Niger and Mali, and substantial percentages of women in Burkina Faso, Chad and Nigeria, have no say in any of the three decisions.

Table 18: The doubling dozen: percentage of women who participate in three types of decision-making

Country (most recent DHS or AIS)	Own healthcare (%)	Major household purchases (%)	Visits to friends or relatives (%)	All three decisions (%)	None of the three decisions (%)
Niger	21	20	39	12	56
Uganda	74	64	72	51	13
Angola	75	81	88	65	7
DRC	46	60	54	34	26
Burundi	72	69	81	60	13
Tanzania	72	46	58	35	18
Mali	20	20	28	10	63
Burkina Faso	24	20	52	12	41
Chad	25	40	47	17	39
Mozambique	79	76	81	65	11
Zambia	81	68	77	57	6
Nigeria	44	40	60	33	37

Source: Demographic and Health Surveys Program (most recent survey reports), ICF International Inc.

Various factors influence a woman's participation in decision-making. In Chad and DRC, educational attainment is more influential than wealth. In Niger, Uganda, Angola, Mali and Mozambique levels of participation do not vary greatly by educational level or wealth quintile. In Burundi, Tanzania, Burkina Faso, Zambia and Nigeria participation percentages improve noticeably by both educational level and wealth quintile.

As in any survey, some interviewees may not tell the truth when answering questions about spousal violence and decision-making. Some may not fully understand the question, and some will give what they consider to be the expected answer, as opposed to the real answer.

However, in countries where wife-beating is deemed justifiable in certain circumstances by well over half of both women and men, and where more than one in four women do not participate in any of the three specified household decisions, an imminent onset of a fertility transition is singularly unlikely.

In South Africa, where the fertility transition is almost complete, less than 10% of women or men consider wife-beating to be justifiable for any of the five reasons, despite the ubiquity of violence in society. Even where approval is higher than average – in certain provinces and among women with little education – the figure is barely in double figures. Similarly, almost 90% of South African women make the three specified household decisions alone or jointly, and only 3% are not involved in any of the decisions. In Egypt, also well advanced in its fertility transition, 60% of women participate in all three decisions and only 10% in none of them.

Of course, 'empowerment' is a multifaceted concept that makes concise definition difficult. It also raises a question regarding whether 'modern values' are or should be universal: some people object strongly to judging different societies and belief systems. What constitutes empowerment for a woman in Mali may differ in certain key respects for a woman in South Korea, or in Belarus. If she says that the more children she has, the more empowered she will be, that people will look up to her and respect her more, she is defying conventional perceptions in the West and other parts of the world. Similarly, does the fact that the wealthiest Ugandan women want four or five children denote a lack of empowerment and rejection of modern values? 'Women's empowerment may take on different meanings in Africa, where polygamy, HIV prevalence, ideal family size and the social importance of fertility are known to be greater than in the Asian context,' say the authors of one of the relatively few studies of empowerment and ideal family size in Africa.[10] This needs to be borne in mind when considering in what realm empowerment is most essential in order to catalyse fertility transition – social, economic, educational or political. There can be no set answer because there is never a single driver of fertility decline, as was discussed in Chapter 7. Everywhere, fertility transitions are triggered by a different 'cocktail' of factors.

Nevertheless, the selected indicators do attest to gender inequality and discrimination, and the authors of the Afrobarometer report conclude:

> Africans broadly support gender equality in principle and applaud government performance in promoting it... but fewer than half assert that the equality agenda has actually advanced in recent years, and attitudes point to persistent – and in some cases increasing – gender gaps with regard to education, land rights, the labour market, asset owner-ship, new technologies, and decision-making power in the household.[11]

Globally, more empowered mothers want fewer than four or five children, and they are better equipped to look after them. In most of the high-growth African countries DHS data shows few detectible improvements in the conditions under which women live.

Knowledge of the fertile period

A third insightful DHS measure concerns a different type of female empowerment – through basic knowledge of biology and the reproductive cycle. In surveys women are asked: 'From one menstrual period to the next are there certain days when a woman is more likely to become pregnant?' Almost 100% of women in all the high-growth countries answered in the affirmative. They were then asked if these days were:

- just before the menstrual period begins
- during the menstrual period
- right after the menstrual period has ended, or
- halfway between two menstrual periods.

Table 19: Africa's high-growth countries: % of women with correct knowledge of fertile period

Country	Women aged 15-49 with correct knowledge of fertile period (%)
Niger	20
Uganda	22
Angola	15
DRC	47
Burundi	21
Tanzania	21
Mali	27
Burkina Faso	39
Chad	29
Mozambique	n/a
Zambia	21
Nigeria	24

Source: Demographic and Health Surveys Program
(most recent survey report), ICF International Inc.

Table 19 shows that the lowest percentage of women giving the correct answer was in Angola, where only 15% of women knew when they are most fertile. At the opposite end of the scale, almost 40% of women in Burkina Faso gave the right answer. Despite the country being in a fertility transition and having a relatively high percentage of girls enrolled in education, Uganda's results are almost unchanged in two decades.

With the sole exception of Burkina Faso, the highest percentage of women in all countries answered, 'right after the menstrual period'. There is no significant difference according to age. In Uganda, for example, the lowest percentage answering correctly was the 15–19 age group (14%) and the highest the 25–29 age group (26%). Even in Zambia, where modern contraceptive use by women is highest of all, the percentage who answered correctly is strikingly low.

There is no apparent correlation between women's knowledge of the fertile period and literacy. Even in Uganda, Tanzania and Zambia, countries where more than two-thirds of women are literate, knowledge of the fertile period is lacking. It has been suggested that Internet access is a factor. In the 12 high-growth countries, fewer women regularly access the Internet than the African average of 28%; in Uganda, Burkina Faso, Niger and Mali the figure is less than 10%. This raises questions about the education of women and girls, considered by many experts to be the most influential factor in triggering and sustaining a decline in fertility, and in empowerment. This is considered in the next chapter.

12

The X Factor

Female education is frequently cited as the factor that will bring about faster fertility decline in Africa than is anticipated by UNPD population projections. The outlook for the 12 high-growth countries is not encouraging in this regard.

There are numerous studies attesting to an 'education effect' on population growth. Wolfgang Lutz and his colleagues at WIC have demonstrated such a strong relationship between education and fertility that they label it 'functional causality'.[1] The association between female education and fertility decline is considered particularly 'robust',[2] even more so when combined with lower infant mortality and higher usage of modern contraception by married women. According to the political demographer Jack Goldstone and colleagues, 'female education is the single most important factor in reducing fertility in tropical Africa', and is more significant than it has been in other developing regions.[3]

A 2017 study of 31 sub-Saharan countries accounting for 86% of the region's population attempted to quantify the effect that educating women has had on fertility, concluding that: 'on average increased women's schooling [accounted] for 54% of observed decline in fertility' in urban locations and 30% of the decline in rural areas.[4] Globally, when young women are in school for nine years or more the TFR is between two and four births, and usually below three births.[5] This 'rule' holds good for the only two mainland African countries where the education criteria is met – South Africa and Botswana – although there are several countries where the female education criteria are not met and the TFR is below four.

The logic underpinning the relationship between female education and lower fertility is straightforward. If young women are educated, more of their children survive and the health of the whole family improves. With more of their children surviving, aspirations for them rise. A 'quality/quantity' trade-off comes into play, where more is spent on the health and education of fewer children. The more a girl is educated, the more likely she will also be to marry (and first give birth) later, question or challenge societal norms, learn about and choose modern contraception to assist with family planning, and wish to join the labour force or start a small business. Fertility transitions elsewhere in the world have been associated with this sequence of developments.

Female secondary education is regarded as particularly influential in reducing fertility. Demographers have shown that women in developing countries who complete secondary education have at least one child less than those who only finish primary school. Kenya, where education for girls is a policy priority, is frequently held up as the exemplar in sub-Saharan Africa, indicative of the future for all other countries. About three-quarters of girls there now complete primary school, a similar percentage to boys, and almost half have some secondary education. It is also the case that Kenya's TFR declined from eight births to less than four between 1980 and 2015, and that usage of modern contraception by married women more than doubled in that time frame to about 60%, one of the highest rates in Africa. There is little sign yet of similar trends emerging and impacting fertility rates in most of the 12 high-growth countries. After the 2019 budget, the civic tech organisation BudgIT tweeted: 'without education, esp girls education Nigeria cannot escape the demographic doom that lays ahead with uncontrolled population growth'.[6]

Sub-Saharan governments inherited education systems from the colonial powers that were described by the World Bank in the 1980s as 'quite inadequate to meet the needs of self-governance and rapid economic growth'.[7] Colonial education systems across the region produced fewer than 10,000 secondary-school graduates in the 1950s, mostly in Nigeria and Ghana, and only a small minority of children received primary schooling. Education was therefore a priority after independence. In the 1960s, Ghana spent more on education as a proportion of GDP than any other country in the world.[8] In the 1970s, expenditure on education in sub-Saharan countries more than doubled to US$10 billion. Many succeeded in Africanising their curricula, the use of local languages in school grew, and investment in tertiary education was cranked up from a standing start to provide personnel with the required skills to implement national development plans. School enrolment increased at twice the rate of Asia and triple that of Latin America during the decade.

By the early 1980s, primary-school enrolment had reached about 75% in sub-Saharan countries, short of the universal target that many countries had aimed for by then, but a remarkable achievement nonetheless. Secondary-school enrolment was still only about 15% on average, and adult literacy around 20%, but both were rising. By 1987, Kenya was spending 33% of its total recurrent budget on education. Secondary-school enrolment had mushroomed from 30,000 in 1963 to 520,000, and the number of secondary schools had increased from 151 to 2,592.[9] Across the continent, more than 300,000 young men and women were enrolled in universities. The World Bank called the development of education systems across the region 'spectacular', 'impressive both absolutely and in relation to other sectors and other countries at other times', and 'a tribute to the determination demonstrated by African leaders and the sacrifices endured by African parents in their quest to provide a better standard of living for their children's generation'.[10]

Then the cumulative effect of the multiple crises of the 1970s and 1980s started to bite. No African country was immune from a combination of disasters that included the global recession and oil-price spikes, collapse in commodity prices, political turmoil and drought. By the end of the 1980s, social spending had been slashed due to ruinous levels of debt and the adoption of austerity measures required by World Bank/IMF SAPs. On average, spending on education halved during the decade.

At a crucial juncture in the development of their education systems (and much else besides), most countries were forced to abandon further progress for about 15 years. It seemed to many that all that had been achieved over two decades was to increase 'the mass of the educated unemployed'.[11] Funding shortfalls were not always solely down to external factors: in the early 1990s, 90% of budget funding for primary schools in Uganda was 'diverted'.[12] Only in the late 1990s could spending on education start to increase again, with debt relief in the early 2000s providing further headroom for governments. Some countries are only now regaining the enrolment rates of the 1980s. The fertility stalls that occurred in the 1990s and early 2000s have been partly attributed to the hiatus in education in the final decades of the twentieth century.[13]

On average, sub-Saharan governments now spend 17% of their budget on education, equivalent to about 5% of GDP. This is only just short of the 20% base target recommended by the Global Partnership for Education and the 2015 'Education for All' Incheon Declaration. It is a comparable level of expenditure to those of Latin America/ Caribbean and East Asia, although a much lower sum because of the relatively small size of most economies. According to UNESCO, average spend per pupil on primary education in sub-Saharan Africa is only about one-tenth that of East Asian countries and a quarter that of Latin American and Caribbean ones.

The regional average also masks considerable variation. Among the 12 high-growth countries, Nigeria spends the least on education – just 7% of the federal budget in 2017 and 2018 – despite having the continent's largest economy. Uganda budgeted 9% of its total expenditure for education in 2018–19. Even though this was not the 'huge allocation'[14] that the local press claimed, teachers make up half of the total civil service headcount and more than 40% of its wage bill.[15] At the other end of the scale Burundi, Tanzania and Burkina Faso are among continental leaders, fewer than 10 in number, that allocate 20%

or more of their budgets to education.[16] Despite rising expenditure, however, demographic pressure – the weight of numbers – means that per capita amounts have been declining throughout Africa.

Figure 15: Primary education net enrollment rate (top) - % of primary school age group; and secondary education net enrollment rate (bottom) - % of secondary school age group

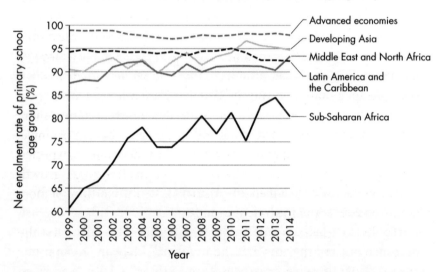

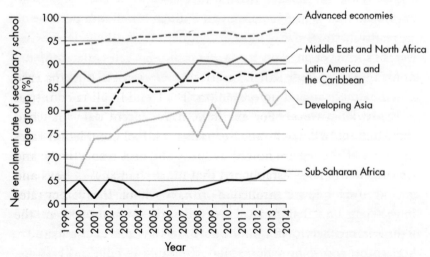

Source: IMF (2018), *The Future of Work in Sub-Saharan Africa*/World Bank, *World Development Indicators.*

Expenditure has been targeted mainly at primary education. Between 1990 and 2015, net primary enrolment increased from 52% to 80% in sub-Saharan Africa, with the number of children in primary school swelling from around 60 million to 150 million.[17] In most countries there is now universal primary education, and about a third of children attend pre-school. On average, girls complete about five years of schooling and boys around six years; however, in seven of the 12 high-growth countries – Niger, Burundi, Angola, Mali, Burkina Faso, Chad and Mozambique – the average is less than three years.[18] In DRC, Tanzania and Nigeria the average is four to five years; in Uganda and Zambia children complete seven to eight years. Among mainland countries, only in Botswana, South Africa, Gabon, Zimbabwe, Egypt and Tunisia do they complete eight or more years.[19] Average years of schooling will continue to rise. For example, in Mozambique a child enrolling at primary school now is expected to complete almost 10 years of schooling. But in all the high-growth countries the early enrolment of girls still lags, and one-third or more of those aged six to nine have no education.[20]

Table 20 presents DHS data for female education in the high-growth countries, with the equivalent figures for men for comparison. It reveals considerable variation. The left-hand column shows that only in Uganda and Zambia – where a fertility transition is under way – have less than 10% of women had no formal education. At the other end of the scale, two-thirds or more of women in the four Sahel countries – Niger, Mali, Burkina Faso and Chad – have had no education. The trend in all 12 countries is upwards, however. For example, more recent data for Chad indicates that primary- and secondary-school completion rates among all children are now above 40% and 20% respectively; and Uganda's 2016 DHS established that more than 80% of boys and girls aged six to 12 are enrolled in primary school. The literacy rates in the right-hand column are also indicative of improvement: the figures in brackets are for girls aged 15–19 and in all 12 countries are higher than those for women. In Uganda, Burundi and Tanzania literacy among girls has reached 80%–90%.

While about 80% of girls are now enrolled in primary school, and female literacy is rising, it is the figures for 'some secondary' and 'completed secondary/more than secondary' (highlighted in bold in Table 20) that are considered to have the greatest impact on fertility. About 30% of girls in sub-Saharan Africa receive some secondary education, compared to about 40% of boys.[21] Enrolment rates are higher in Northern Africa and in countries with a TFR below three births. In the high-growth Sahel countries and Mozambique, however, fewer than one in four women have some secondary education. In Niger and Burkina Faso the proportion is about one in 10.

Only in Nigeria have more than 50% of women received at least some secondary education, although in DRC and Zambia the figure is close to that level; and only in Nigeria and Zambia have more than one in eight women completed secondary education. Of these two countries, Zambia is alone in showing signs of a fertility transition. In all the others, secondary education of girls has either been too rare to have any perceptible downward impact on national fertility levels or is simply not having the expected effect.

Put another way, in Nigeria, where secondary education of girls is most extensive, the TFR is almost 4.5 births even among women who have had secondary education, most of whom live in the South East, South South and South West zones of the country where fertility is the lowest. In the more populous northern and eastern states, at least one-third of children under the age of 14 are not in school; in Gombe and Bauchi the proportion is more than half – and rates will be higher among girls.[22] In DRC, the TFR among women with secondary education is almost six births – and less than half of women with secondary education who already have five children want no more. In Ghana, widely considered a continental leader in the secondary education of girls, and where 80% of girls now complete lower-secondary education, the national TFR remains close to four births – just one birth lower than in the 1993 DHS. Anomalies abound. In a recent comparison of 24 sub-Saharan countries LSHTM's John Cleland concluded that 'the achievement of secondary schooling does not automatically translate into low fertility' in about one-third of them.[23]

Some experts assert that there is a threshold below which the effects of female secondary education on fertility are likely to be limited. One analysis, by the Russian demographers Julia Zinkina and Andrey Korotayev, asserts that if 70% or more of women have at least some secondary education, this 'is likely to secure replacement level [fertility]', although it will obviously take time.[24] They suggest that the quickest way to achieve such a goal would be the immediate introduction of compulsory secondary education for all children. Using Tanzania as an example, Zinkina and Korotayev estimate that if net female secondary-school enrolment rose by 3% a year, it would have the effect of halving UNPD's medium-variant projected population for the end of the century, which currently stands at more than 300 million. 'This', the authors conclude, 'means that making secondary education its top development priority is an indispensable, but insufficient, condition for Tanzania to avoid the risks of major sociopolitical destabilisation and violent conflicts caused by rocketing demographic pressure.'[25]

Universal secondary education is an aspiration of the African Union (AU)'s Agenda 2063, a 50-year blueprint for transforming the continent into 'the global powerhouse'. However, in none of the high-growth countries is such an initiative affordable even if the government were not required to subsidise fees. The funding shortfall for education across Africa is estimated at US$40 billion for the period 2015–30.[26] While more than 30 sub-Saharan governments provide free primary education, which in practice often means no more than supplying a teacher, only half that number endow some form of fee-free lower-secondary schooling. For many of the poorest in the populations of the high-growth countries, who comprise a substantial minority or even a majority of school children and among whose communities fertility is particularly high, paying any educational costs at all – uniforms, equipment, transport – can be impossible. For example, in Zambia about 20% of men and women from the

Table 20: Africa's high-growth countries: education by highest level of attainment (women aged 15–49, with male comparison)

	No formal education (%)	Some primary (%)	Completed primary* (%)	Some secondary (%)	Completed secondary/ more than secondary (%)	Literacy all respondents / literacy among 15–19-year-olds**
Niger (f)	80	10	2	8	<1	14/27
Niger (m)	63	17	3	15	3	42/50
Uganda (f)	10	45	13	24	10	68/80
Uganda (m)	4	42	14	25	16	79/83
Angola (f)	22	29	6	31	12	58/71
Angola (m)	8	22	8	42	21	84/84
DRC (f)	15	29	8	36	12	64/78
DRC (m)	4	16	6	49	25	88/90
Burundi (f)	36	26	14	23	2	68/88
Burundi (m)	24	31	16	26	4	76/88
Tanzania (f)	15	12	50	23***	n/a	77/84
Tanzania (m)	8	16	48	28***	n/a	83/82
Mali (f)	66	9	4	19	2	28/44
Mali (m)	55	10	5	25	6	45/56
Burkina Faso (f)	74	10	3	11	2	23/38
Burkina Faso (m)	59	15	5	15	4	38/47
Chad (f)	62	18	5	12	3	22/40
Chad (m)	36	20	7	28	9	54/64
Mozambique (w)	26	44	8	17	5	51/62
Mozambique (m)	10	42	12	27	9	n/a
Zambia (f)	8	29	15	32	16	66/76
Zambia (m)	4	24	15	34	23	82/81
Nigeria (f)	35	4	10	16	34	53/64
Nigeria (m)	22	3	11	16	49	90/70

wealthiest quintile completed secondary school, but less than 2% from the poorest quintile.

Across sub-Saharan Africa, about one in five children of primary-school age are not in school – as are a third of adolescents of lower-secondary-school age (12–14) and more than half of youth (15–17) of upper-secondary-school age. All told, this amounts to almost 100 million out-of-school children, a higher number even than that of far more populous Southern Asia and one that comprises 40% of the global total.[27] Furthermore, in some of the high-growth countries universal secondary education is deemed impractical, culturally undesirable or politically unwise.

There have been determined efforts by the governments of a number of the high-growth countries to continue broadening access to education in the face of rapidly rising numbers of children. Seven years of fee-free schooling is now available in Chad. In Burundi, where a fertility transition is under way, the proportion of women with no education has declined from four out of five in the early 1990s to one in three; the proportion of women with some secondary education doubled between the two most recent DHSs to about one in four; and literacy rates among girls aged 15–19 are almost 90%. In Mozambique, the proportion of women with no education fell from almost half in 2003 to less than one in three in 2015. In Zambia, the proportion of women with secondary education or higher has doubled to almost 50% since 1996. These countries, it needs emphasising, are among the poorest in the world but have been able to raise enrolment quite dramatically.

There are other good examples to follow. In Ethiopia, in the two decades after the Derg regime was overthrown in 1991, the proportion

---

* Completion of primary school and even of secondary school does not necessarily imply literacy and numeracy; and literacy is not dependent on school attendance. (See Emily Smith-Greenaway (2015), 'Educational attainment and adult literacy: A descriptive account of 31 Sub-Saharan Africa countries', *Demographic Research*, Vol. 33, Art. 35, p. 1015: 'in some countries, large proportions of African women who never went to school can read, even as some of their peers who have completed primary school cannot'.)   ** Literacy is measured in DHSs by the respondent's ability to read one of four short, simple sentences in a language of their choice. UNESCO defines the national literacy rate as the percentage of the population aged 15 and above 'who can both read and write with understanding a short simple sentence on his/her everyday life'.   *** For Tanzania, the figure in the 'some secondary' column denotes some secondary education or higher.   *Source:* Demographic and Health Surveys Program (most recent survey reports), ICF International Inc.

of government expenditure allocated to education rose to more than a quarter, the number of primary schools tripled to more than 30,000 and primary-school enrolment grew from about 20% to over 90%. Even in Nigeria, where it is almost universally thought that education has been allowed to sink into a state of total decay, in one state, in the space of four years, a primary-school feeding programme was implemented, 22,000 unqualified teachers were laid off and qualified ones hired with a 30% salary increase.[28]

There is another dimension to education which needs to be considered – quality. There may be some downward effect on fertility from girls simply attending school, in that this means they are less likely to marry and embark on motherhood straight away; but for attitudes to change, for girls to be empowered or equipped to join the skilled labour force, the quality of their education matters. In February 2020 the director-general of UNESCO and Sahle-Work Zewde, President of Ethiopia, wrote an open letter to AU heads of state in which they referred to the state of education as 'an emergency for Africa'. A year earlier, a World Bank publication, *The Future of Work in Africa*, also stated that '[the] education system is in crisis, with… students learning very little in the early grades, low secondary school completion rates, and weak learning outcomes'.[29] The quality of primary and lower-secondary education was said to be 'abysmally low'.[30] The 2018 Ibrahim Index of African Governance registered worsening education outcomes for more than 50% of Africa's population, and a diminution in quality over both five and 10 years.[31] The Programme d'analyse des systèmes educatifs de la CONFEMEN PASEC (Analysis Programme of CONFEMEN Education Systems PASEC), which assessed 40,000 students in more than 1,800 schools in 10 francophone African countries, also described the 'alarming picture of the state of primary education'; and UNESCO studies have found that only one in 10 primary-school children throughout sub-Saharan Africa achieve the minimum level of proficiency in reading and mathematics before they move on.[32]

The deficiencies of education systems are well documented, country by country. A decade ago, only one-third of women who had completed primary school in Ghana, Nigeria and Sierra Leone could read. In most Middle African countries – Cameroon, Chad, Congo Brazzaville and DRC – only about half of women who had completed primary school could do so.[33] In Nigeria, after four years of primary school one-third of children are unable to read at least one of three words and one in five cannot correctly add two single-digit numbers.[34] In 2018, 84% and 88% of children in sub-Saharan Africa did not meet minimum proficiency in reading and mathematics respectively, compared to 57% for both competencies in Northern Africa/Western Asia, levels almost exactly matching global averages.[35] In its *African Economic Outlook 2020* the AfDB showed that if average years of schooling are adjusted for test scores in the high-growth countries, children in DRC, Tanzania, Angola, Burundi, Mali, Burkina Faso and Niger in effect complete two years or less of schooling.[36]

The causes of deficiencies vary. Among the 12 high-growth countries, class sizes of 50 children or more are common and basic equipment and teaching materials are mostly non-existent. In Angola and Mali about half of primary-school teachers are untrained (whereas almost all are trained in DRC and Burundi).[37] Across sub-Saharan Africa the proportion of teachers in primary education with the minimum required training has declined since 2005 to about two-thirds; in secondary education the decline is dramatic – from around 80% to 50%.[38] Lack of political will is commonly cited, and ruling elites are frequently accused of deliberately keeping the public barely educated because that renders them more malleable and makes their votes cheaper to buy.[39]

There is something close to consensus on the issue of educational quality among experts within the high-growth countries. In Tanzania, for example, the country with the lowest teacher-to-population ratio in the world[40] and where it is commonly said that a teacher's licence can be bought in any market, Professor Mwesiga Baregu refers to the 'major crisis' resulting from 'the systematic reproduction of ignorance through the provision of low-quality education'. In his opinion this is less a question of money than standards: 'the stark reality is that, despite the enormous advances in education made possible by investing trillions of shillings each year, the vast majority of children in Tanzania are not learning... a rising number of young people [are] completing secondary schooling without mastering the 3Rs'.[41] In Nigeria, the open-data campaigner Oluseun Onigbinde writes: 'What is the fate of a country with spiraling population growth... and failed health and education systems?'[42] 'About thirty years ago, the Zambian education system was something to talk about... Today the picture is radically different,' laments blogger Michael Chishala.[43] This matters in many more ways than simply not being potentially conducive to lower fertility.

The education challenge is not a new one for Africa. It has existed for the best part of half a century. In the mid-1980s the World Bank issued almost identical warnings to those heard throughout the continent today. The 130 million school-age population in sub-Saharan Africa in 1983 was forecast to rise to 220 million children in 2000 – an increase of 70% in just 17 years. This 'massive explosion in the potential demand for educational services', the World Bank observed, was going to 'sharply constrain African planners' options'. In financial terms it would require a doubling of recurrent expenditure just to maintain enrolment rates.[44] Yet today, whatever the shortcomings of education systems, more boys and girls in Africa receive some education than ever before. That is no mean achievement given the headwinds.

Once again, the task of expanding and improving education systems is magnified by the sheer number of children, and therefore the costs. Between 2015 and 2030, attendance at primary school in sub-Saharan Africa will have risen by 30%, from about 190 million to 250 million.[45] While primary-school completion rates are now around 70%, 60% of all 15–17 year-olds were not in school in 2017.[46] By 2050 the number of primary- and secondary-school children in the sub-Saharan countries is set to increase from less than 400 million to more than 650 million. In the high-growth countries the expansion is more pronounced. An analysis of Mozambique by Julia Zinkina and Andrey Korotayev shows that the country's school-age population will triple between 2010 and 2050 if a fertility transition does not begin by 2025. As of 2018, the TFR remained above five births. Keeping up with demand for school enrolment will be exacting enough in high-fertility countries. At the same time, it is easy to portray raising standards as an unmanageable burden on human ingenuity and resources – and public and private finances.

Africa is also not the only continent where an education crisis has been declared: the same is said of Southern Asia as well. The rollout of mass education for a burgeoning number of children is not a straightforward endeavour anywhere. The difference between the high-growth African countries and Southern Asia is that most countries in the latter region have commenced a fertility transition. Nine of the 12 high-growth African countries have not, and it is hard to envisage education, particularly for girls, improving sufficiently in coverage and quality to make a material difference to population projections for 2050.

As explained earlier, educational attainment is a core component of the multidimensional population projections modelled by Wolfgang Lutz and his colleagues at WIC, a 'proxy indicator for skills and human capital'.[47] WIC projections are favoured by population optimists because the medium-development scenario envisages Africa's population (and the world's) peaking at a lower level, and earlier, than UNPD's medium-variant projections. Five alternative 'shared socio-economic pathways' (SSPs) – scenarios based on different assumptions about fertility, mortality, migration and educational attainment – are presented; alternative educational outcomes account for a difference of about 1 billion people between WIC's highest and lowest development scenarios for 2050.

WIC's medium scenario (SSP2) for Africa in 2100 is predicated on just 6% of women aged 20–39 in 2050 having had no education, 25% having had primary education only, 51% secondary education and 17% tertiary education. For comparison, these proportions are almost identical to those for women in Latin America/Caribbean, and quite similar to those for women in Asia, in 2010. Some, maybe many, countries will attain these enrolment targets, but to date a number of the African high-growth countries are tracking the SSP3 'stalled-development scenario'. This incorporates little change in educational enrolment rates in Africa between 2010 and 2050,[48] leading to an African population of 2.7 billion in 2050 and 4.9 billion in 2100 – figures very similar to UNPD's medium-variant projections. In other words, levels of education attainment will be a key determinant of which of WIC's forecasts proves most accurate. It must be added that WIC's education scenarios measure attainment only, not quality.[49]

Lutz himself notes, when observing the 'moderate progress in education expansion in sub-Saharan Africa', that 'continued progress is not guaranteed'. As a consequence, he is clear that fertility decline in Africa is 'far from being a certainty'. In the high-growth countries, a third of women in Nigeria aged 20–39 currently have no, or only incomplete, primary education. The SSP2 'target' is 7%; to achieve that would encounter considerable opposition in many states if it were pursued in earnest. In northern states, more than 80% of women are illiterate and half are married by the age of 15. Likewise, it will be equally difficult for one in seven Nigeriénnes to have completed upper-secondary or tertiary education by 2050. Other examples abound of the scale of the challenge confronting the high-growth countries, in particular, if they are to attain the requirements for the SSP2 scenario. If instead sub-Saharan Africa or any of its regions were to follow the 'stalled-development' forecast, according to Lutz the consequences would 'largely resemble a Malthusian reality'.[50]

13

Guessing Games

While there is near-consensus among experts regarding the size of Africa's total population at mid-century, the outcome at the end of the century is largely a matter for speculation. Quite small departures in the next few decades from what is anticipated for some of the larger 'moving parts' could have very substantial consequences for trends after 2050. In the meantime, generalisations and received wisdom about the impact of rapid urbanisation, education and other factors on fertility need to be handled with care. Many of them fail to acknowledge realities on the ground.

The 12 high-growth, high-fertility countries that were the focus of the previous chapters give no grounds for arguing that UNPD's projection for Africa's population in mid-century is an overestimate. Collectively these countries account for more than half of the population of sub-Saharan Africa. It is anticipated that their combined population will increase by 650 million by 2050, almost two-thirds of the region's growth. Even if the trajectory of the 23 sub-Saharan Africa countries with a TFR still above four births were suddenly to follow that of a basket of 21 countries worldwide that had demonstrated a slow start to fertility transition followed by acceleration, the region's population would still be 1.9 billion instead of 2.1 billion, a difference of 10%.[1] This would make for an Africa total of 2.3 billion, compared to the medium-variant projection of 2.5 billion.

An across-the-board shift of this type is implausible at present; more likely, given that in nine of the 12 high-growth countries there is no sign of a fertility transition, is that in some of them the projected decline by 2050 proves overambitious. Equally, some countries within and outside this group that have commenced a fertility transition may experience stalls of various durations, and some of the high-fertility countries may still have a TFR above four by 2050. The bunching of most African countries in a range of 2.5–3.5 births in mid-century (see Table 21) looks more a function of modelling than likely to occur in real life. Carl Haub is one of many demographers to suggest that it is 'far from a sure bet'[2] that all African countries will follow the path of industrialised and industrialising countries around the world to replacement-level fertility.

Table 21 broadens the perspective, adapting and updating a typology presented by the demographer Jean-Pierre Guengant in 2017.[3] Some observations may be helpful. The table shows the fertility trajectories of all 37 African countries with a population greater than 5 million, and the expected fertility rate in each by 2050. In the early 1980s, more than 90% of the population of sub-Saharan Africa lived in 40 countries with a TFR above six, and almost 40% in 18 countries with a TFR above seven.[4] By 2020, less than 30% of all Africans lived in countries with a TFR above five, of which there are only eight. Fertility transitions *are* occurring, but mostly at a modest pace. In Angola and Uganda, two relatively populous countries among the high-growth high-fertility 12, it took 40 years for fertility to decline by 10% from its peak. In Mozambique, Niger and Tanzania this transition took 30–35 years.[5]

Although high fertility is concentrated in the Eastern, Middle and Western regions, there are individual anomalies. Sudan has a TFR – 4.1 – more in keeping with Eastern Africa than Northern Africa, the region in which it is included by UNPD. Burundi, Tanzania and Mozambique have TFRs close to the average for Western Africa (4.8), while Liberia and Sierra Leone have lower TFRs than the Eastern Africa average (4.1). In Eastern Africa, the TFRs of Kenya and Zimbabwe have almost fallen to the same level as that of Egypt, a country generally presented as close to completing a fertility transition despite the fact that its TFR is still above three (and trending upwards). There are only three countries in Africa – Rwanda, Kenya and Ethiopia – where fertility transitions have been as rapid, or almost as rapid, as the fastest in the world in the modern era. In Rwanda, this commenced with a decline of two births in the 1980s as the government took decisive steps to curtail population growth. After a post-genocide hiatus, initiatives were resumed by the new government in the 2000s. In Kenya, partly due to a perceived shortage of agricultural land, alarm bells rang for the government when the TFR reached eight births in 1978. In Ethiopia, impetus was provided by the determination of the government to reduce poverty and address a dire shortage of land in highland areas. On the other side of the continent, it is worth noting that if a real and sustained fertility transition began in Nigeria, it would have a marked impact not only on the weighting of the 'transition-under-way' category but on the figures and longer-term outlook for Western Africa.

Table 21: Fertility transitions in Africa, 2020–50
(UNPD medium-variant TFR and population projections)

Country/ Region	Est. pop. (million) 2020	Africa weighting (%) 2020	TFR 1980–85	TFR 2000–05	TFR 2020–25	40-year decline 1980/85–2020/25	TFR 2045–50	Proj. pop. 2050
TFR above 6 in 2020-25: very slow/ incipient transition	40.1	3.0						
Niger	24.2	1.8	7.9	7.6	6.5	1.4	4.3	65.6
Somalia	15.9	1.2	7.1	7.5	5.7	1.4	3.9	34.9
TFR above 5 in 2020-25: slow and irregular transition	382.6	28.6						

Country/ Region	Est. pop. (million) 2020	Africa weighting (%) 2020	TFR 1980–85	TFR 2000–05	TFR 2020–25	40-year decline 1980/85–2020/25	TFR 2045–50	Proj. pop. 2050
Mali	20.2	1.5	7.1	6.8	5.5	1.6	3.5	43.6
DRC	89.6	6.7	6.6	6.7	5.5	1.1	3.4	194.5
Chad	16.4	1.2	7.0	7.2	5.3	1.7	3.5	34.0
Angola	32.9	2.4	7.5	6.5	5.2	2.3	3.9	77.4
Nigeria	206.1	15.4	6.7	6.0	5.1	1.6	3.6	401.3
Middle Africa	179.6	13.4	6.7	6.4	5.1	1.6	3.5	382.6
Burundi	11.9	0.9	7.4	6.8	5.0	2.4	3.5	25.3
TFR above 4 in 2020–25: transition initiated	339.0	25.2						
Burkina Faso	20.9	1.6	7.2	6.4	4.8	2.4	3.3	43.4
Western Africa	401.9	30.0	6.9	5.9	4.8	2.1	3.5	796.5
Tanzania	59.7	4.4	6.5	5.7	4.6	1.9	3.5	129.4
Benin	12.1	0.9	7.0	5.8	4.5	2.5	3.4	24.3
Mozambique	31.2	2.3	6.4	5.8	4.5	1.9	3.1	65.3
Côte d'Ivoire	26.4	2.0	7.3	5.7	4.4	2.9	3.4	51.3
Guinea	13.1	0.9	6.6	5.9	4.4	2.2	3.1	36.0
South Sudan	11.2	0.8	6.8	6.0	4.4	2.4	3	20.0
Uganda	45.7	3.4	7.1	6.7	4.4	2.7	2.7	89.4
Zambia	18.4	1.4	6.9	5.9	4.4	2.5	3.3	39.1
Senegal	16.7	1.2	7.2	5.2	4.3	2.9	3.3	33.2
Cameroon	26.5	2.0	6.7	5.4	4.3	2.4	3.2	50.6
Rep. of Congo	5.5	0.4	5.8	4.9	4.2	1.6	3.3	10.7
Togo	8.3	0.6	7.0	5.3	4.1	2.9	3.1	15.4
Sudan	43.8	3.3	6.6	5.3	4.1	2.5	3.1	81.2
Eastern Africa	445.4	33.2	7.0	5.8	4.1	-2.9	2.9	851.2
Liberia	5.0	0.4	7.0	5.6	4.0	-3.0	3.0	9.3

Country/ Region	Est. pop. (million) 2020	Africa weighting (%) 2020	TFR 1980-85	TFR 2000-05	TFR 2020-25	40-year decline 1980/85-2020/25	TFR 2045-50	Proj. pop. 2050
TFR above 3 in 2020-25: transition under way	384.8	28.7						
Sierra Leone	8.0	0.6	6.7	6.1	3.9	2.8	2.6	13.0
Malawi	19.1	1.4	7.6	6.0	3.9	3.7	2.8	38.1
Ethiopia	115.0	8.6	7.4	6.2	3.8	3.6	2.5	205.4
Madagascar	27.7	2.1	6.5	5.3	3.8	2.7	3.0	54.0
Rwanda	12.9	1.0	8.4	5.4	3.7	4.7	2.6	23.0
Ghana	31.1	2.3	6.3	4.6	3.6	2.7	2.8	52.0
Kenya	53.8	4.0	7.2	5.0	3.3	3.9	2.4	91.6
Zimbabwe	14.9	1.1	6.3	3.7	3.3	3.0	2.4	24.0
Egypt	102.3	7.6	5.5	3.1	3.1	2.4	2.5	160.0
N Africa	246.2	18.4	5.7	3.1	3.1	2.6	2.5	371.5
TFR of 2-3 in 2020-25: transition near completion	158.7	11.8						
Algeria	43.8	3.3	6.3	2.4	2.8	3.5	2.1	60.9
Southern Africa	67.5	5.0	5.0	2.7	2.4	2.6	2.0	87.4
South Africa	59.3	4.4	4.9	2.6	2.3	2.6	2.1	75.5
Morocco	36.9	2.7	5.4	2.7	2.3	3.1	1.9	46.2
Libya	6.9	0.5	6.7	2.6	2.1	4.6	1.8	8.5
Tunisia	11.8	0.9	4.8	2.0	2.1	2.7	1.8	13.8
Countries with population < 5 million	34.8	2.6						
TOTAL POPULATION	**1,340**	**100**						**2,489**

Source: UNPD, *World Population Prospects: The 2019 Revision.*

At the start of the 2020s, about 55% of Africans live in a country with a TFR of four or more births, and less than 15% in a country with a TFR below three, most of them in Algeria and South Africa. For at least the next two decades Africa will continue to dominate the rankings of the world's most fertile countries. Only the presence of Timor-Leste and Afghanistan prevents an African clean sweep of the 20 countries globally with the highest TFR. As mentioned above, by 2050 all but a handful of African countries are projected to have a TFR of between two and four births, signifying that a fertility transition will be under way or complete almost everywhere.

Despite the gradual narrowing of TFR differentials between the five African regions, diverse population trends over half a century have had a pronounced impact on the distribution of people. If Southern, Eastern, Western and Middle Africa had collectively experienced the same rate of growth as Northern Africa since the 1960s, their combined population in 2015 would have been a little above 500 million instead of almost 1 billion. Conversely, whereas Northern Africa accounted for about 20% of the continent's population from the 1960s to the 2010s, by 2050 this will only be 13%. Southern Africa's share will have halved from 7% to 3.5% between the 1950s and 2050s. By mid-century Northern and Southern Africa will be of marginal significance compared to the three other regions, which will represent 84% of the African total. Whether Northern and Southern Africa (principally South Africa) still generate as much as 45% of the continent's GDP[6] by then is anyone's guess, but the continent's changing population distribution is bound to have economic as well as political effects.

Although the medium-variant projection for Africa's population in 2050 is robust given current evidence, prognoses for the end of the century are, as UNPD puts it, 'subject to a high degree of uncertainty, especially at the country level'.[7] They rest on assumptions about the choices, behaviour and health of people who are not yet born. However, the importance to outcomes in the second half of the century of fertility rates at the close of the first half cannot be overstressed. For example, if the TFR for Africa in

2050 is half a birth higher than the medium variant assumes – 3.6 births as opposed to 3.1 – the population would be 300 million more than the 2.5 billion medium-variant projection. If it were still half a birth higher at the end of the century – 2.6 births as opposed to 2.1 – the population would be 2 billion greater than the 4.3 billion envisaged by the medium variant.

As mentioned in the opening paragraph, if the 23 sub-Saharan countries with a TFR above four now began to follow the trajectory of the basket of 21 countries worldwide that had slow starts to their fertility transitions followed by acceleration, it would only reduce the region's population in 2050 by about 10%. However, it would imply a figure of 3.2 billion instead of 3.8 billion at the end of the century;[8] if the projection for Northern Africa remained the same, the continental total would likely be 3.7 billion. A difference of that magnitude would potentially decide the contentious, even acrimonious, issue as to whether or not the world's population will peak this century. It is worth noting that the lower figure for sub-Saharan Africa is right at the very bottom of UNPD's 80% probability range of 3.2–4.4 billion.

The 80% probability projections for the 12 high-growth countries in Table 22 highlight the extent of this uncertainty, and the huge implications for the rest of the century of 2050 fertility rates in those countries yet to commence a fertility transition, or only in the early stages of one. The population of Niger, for example, is projected to be anywhere between 96 million and 256 million by 2100. The population of Nigeria could be anywhere between 423 million and 1,149 million, the difference between the two figures being equivalent to the combined current populations of the US, Indonesia and Pakistan, the world's third, fourth and fifth most populous countries. As transitions progress the degree of uncertainty diminishes, although stalls remain a possibility.

Table 22: Africa's high-growth countries: UNPD medium-variant and 80% probability range projections to 2050 and 2100

Country	UNPD estimated population 2019 (million)	UNPD medium-variant projection 2050 (million)	UNPD 80% probability range 2050 (million)	UNPD medium-variant projection 2100 (million)	UNPD 80% probability range 2100 (million)
Niger	23	66	58–72	165	96–256
Uganda	44	89	79–100	137	88–208
Angola	32	77	70–84	188	122–267
DRC	87	194	167–216	362	206–573
Burundi	12	25	23–28	51	33–74
Tanzania	58	129	117–41	286	182–409
Mali	20	44	38–48	80	46–131
Burkina Faso	20	43	39–48	83	53–124
Chad	16	34	31–37	62	41–91
Mozambique	30	65	57–72	124	75–194
Zambia	18	39	35–43	82	53–117
Nigeria	201	401	353–441	733	423–1,149
Total	**561**	**1,206**	**1,067–1,230**	**2,353**	**1,418–3,593**
Africa	1,308	2,489	2,404–572	4,280	3,706–4,950
Sub-Saharan Africa	1,066	2,118	2,038 –195	3,775	3,226–4,418

Source: UNPD, *World Population Prospects: The 2019 Revision.*

At country level, the long-run effect of different fertility rates and the impact of quite small changes to fertility assumptions frequently provide material for population optimists. In the *2019 Revision* Nigeria was one such case, when its medium-variant projection for 2100 was reduced from 793 million to 733 million, making Africa's most populous country one of the very few whose end-of-century projection had returned to a level close to that of the *2010 Revision*.

The new figure is 20% below the 914 million envisaged in the *2012 Revision*. That was a total singled out by Deutsche Bank's rogue demographer, who had guessed at 514 million (and would probably now say, 'I told you so'). However, the reason for the revision is not simply that Nigerians noticed 'how crowded it was getting', as the rogue demographer maintained they would: it is altogether less flippant and more thought-provoking.

UNPD confirmed that 'no substantive changes were made in the estimates and projections of total fertility'[9] for Nigeria. Instead, the reduction of 60 million is largely down to a lowering of projected life expectancy at the end of the century from 75 to 70 years.[10] This is a timely and hugely important reminder that although fertility will be the prime determinant of Africa's demographic trajectory for the rest of the century, mortality should not be overlooked. Where healthcare services are very poor, the substantial improvements in life expectancy that have become commonplace in Africa in recent decades are likely to stall. Furthermore, if life expectancy in any country were to fall to about 45 years, replacement-level fertility would necessarily increase to around three births – the higher the mortality, the higher the fertility required to maintain the size of the population. In the *2019 Revision* life expectancy in 2100 was revised downwards for 17 African countries, including five from the group of 12 high-growth countries in addition to Nigeria: Angola, Chad, DRC, Mali and Niger.[11] In no case was this attributable to war, a public health catastrophe or political turmoil. The ability of health systems that are already overwhelmed, underfunded and neglected to deal with the needs of rapidly rising populations may have a marked impact on population growth in the twenty-first century, albeit not such a significant one as fertility.

In this context, the statistics make for sobering reading. Nigeria's health system, for example, is ranked the fourth worst in the world by the WHO. About 550,000 infants die before their first birthday each year, more than 7% of all live births. This is a comparable rate to those of Somalia and South Sudan, countries afflicted by war for decades with minimal health infrastructure. More than half of the infants die in the first 28 days of life, a number that has shown no improvement since the early 2000s.[12] Maternal mortality is almost three times that of Kenya. The federal health budget in Africa's most populous country and largest economy is only a little above US\$1 billion a year, less than 10% of Egypt's. According to the World Bank, the country 'spends less on health than nearly every country in the world... exposing large shares of the population to catastrophic health expenditures'.[13] Put simply, this is a country where successive governments have not believed that the health of citizens is any of their concern or responsibility. The health system of DRC is ranked by the WHO alongside that of Nigeria.

Less attention is paid by population optimists to instances of countries that were assumed to be proceeding smoothly through a fertility transition and then reversed course. Egypt is a salutary example and, as Africa's third most populous country, one where the consequences are magnified. In the 1980s and 1990s the TFR fell from 5.2 births to three, a rapid decline. By 2008, in spite of a well-funded 'Two is Enough' campaign, there were signs that fertility was increasing again and the 2014 DHS confirmed that the TFR had reached 3.5 births. Fertility rose almost across the board – among rural and urban populations, rich and poor, well- and less-educated, young and older. All the while, rates of contraception usage remained fairly constant at about 60% (and above 70% for young women aged 15–24). Levels of education among young women continued to improve steadily. The causes of rising fertility are of course unclear. Some attribute this extraordinary phenomenon to economic disruption associated with the 'Arab Spring' uprisings, others to religiosity or to the dearth of employment opportunities for women, especially those with high levels of educational attainment.[14] There is no evidence yet for the resumption of a downward trend in fertility that is implicit in UNPD's projections. Meanwhile, a large population counter above the Central Agency for Public Mobilization and Statistics in Cairo clocked 100 million in February 2020.

Ethiopia, another population heavyweight, also needs mentioning. The rapid increase in usage of modern contraception is often cited:

since 2000 this has risen from less than 10% to about 35% among married women, and among unmarried sexually active women it is now approaching 60%. The country is assumed to be in the midst of quite a rapid fertility transition – hence its non-inclusion as one of the 12 high-growth countries in previous chapters. However, Ethiopia's TFR fell by less than one birth between 2000 and 2016, and in rural areas where 80% of the population live it remains above five births. This is no South Korean or Thai fertility transition, as it has sometimes been billed. In the *2019 Revision* 20% was added to UNPD's medium-variant projection for 2100, taking it to almost 300 million.

The combined populations of Egypt and Ethiopia account for more than 15% of Africa's current total. By 2050 that percentage will hardly have changed, and the figure will have risen from 214 million to 350 million. The point here is that these populous countries considered to be in transition are having negligible downward effect on projections for Africa. It is not only the 'sprinters' that need watching, but also the countries with large population bases whose growth is not slowing as fast as expected.

Despite the trends and data, some commentators remain adamant that fertility will fall faster than anticipated in Africa in the next three to four decades. They may be proved right, but only through luck or tragedy on an unimaginable scale. Their claim usually rests on received wisdom and generalisations. A number of stylised examples follow. In each case reality shines a light on important aspects of myriad population trends across the continent.

> **'Demographers are quite wrong. I met a young woman in Kampala/Nairobi/Lagos/Kinshasa last month and she made it completely obvious to me why UN projections for 2050 are wrong. She and all her friends have been to university – they're savvy, middle class and definitely want no more than two or three children.'**

There are an ever-increasing number of young women who fit the description above, but they will not constitute a majority within a generation even in Kenya,* as should be evident from the previous two chapters. The 'learning crisis' and some of its causes have been alluded to, and Wolfgang Lutz and his colleagues at WIC acknowledge that the educational progress required for Africa to conform to his medium scenario forecasts is not a given. As of 2020, Africa (and the world) are not on track to attain the education-related Sustainable Development Goals (SDGs) by the target date of 2030. Among the observations in the most recent SDG tracking report are that the proportion of trained teachers in sub-Saharan Africa has fallen substantially since 2000, both in primary and secondary education; that only one in 10 children in the region achieve the required standard of proficiency at the end of primary school, compared to a global average of between one in two and one in three; and that learning standards are expected to drop by almost a third in francophone African countries by 2030.[15] At present there is little evidence for optimism about education outcomes, although it is hypothetically possible to transform the outlook in any country in the space of a decade.

Another point needs to be highlighted regarding the effect of female education on fertility and family size. On average, educated women all over Africa are continuing to choose to have more children than those in Asia or Latin America. In a 2018 analysis of the most recent DHS data for 34 sub-Saharan countries, the TFR of women with nine to 10 years of schooling was only below three births in Côte d'Ivoire, Burkina Faso and Ethiopia. In 12 of the countries (eight of which are in the high-growth group discussed in previous chapters), the TFR among women with this high level of educational attainment was above four births. As of 2013–14, in DRC the TFR among such women was six births.[16] This is a potent reminder of the importance of disaggregated data, and of

---

* 13% of Kenyan men and 10% of women had completed secondary school, according to the 2014 DHS; among the wealthiest quintiles of each sex these figures rise to 25% and 21% respectively.

not assuming that population trends in every country in Africa will soon conform to average (or even disaggregated) figures for other regions of the world.

In similar vein, the received wisdom that middle class and richer women have fewer children needs to be treated carefully. It is generally true, but not always to the extent that is assumed by commentators citing it. In Angola, women in the richest quintile have four children on average; in DRC, almost six; in Mali, 4.5; and in Uganda and Nigeria, almost four. In all these countries modern contraceptive methods are readily available for the wealthiest, and in many of them usage by such women is above 50%. The desired number of children may decline in decades to come, but at the moment wealthier families often want more children than the stereotypical two or three of demographic transition theory.

Furthermore, the extent of the 'middle class' is not as great as is often portrayed. In 2011, an AfDB report categorised one-third of Africa's population as middle class as they earned between US$2 and US$20 a day. The report made waves in the press and among investors, but was later deconstructed on multiple grounds. Leaving aside the conflation of middle class (a socio-economic concept typically defined by many more indicators than income alone) with middle income, it clearly conveyed a distorted impression of the buoyancy of personal finances throughout Africa. Nigeria is one of the countries associated with a vibrant middle class, but half the population is classified as living in extreme poverty and about two-thirds of Nigerians have no money left after buying food.[17] In 2015, only 1% of the population were earning US$10–20 a day,[18] a more reasonable definition of middle income than the one used by the AfDB. A study by the Institute of Economic Affairs (Kenya), another country associated with a sizeable and expanding middle class, defined the middle-income bracket among wage earners in the same year as US$764–1,024 per month. About 272,569 individuals fell into this category, just 11% of all Kenyans in formal employment (compared to 86% whose earnings were below the middle-income category), and less than 2% of the 17 million Kenyans aged 25–64.[19]

A focus on what is happening among the large majority in any country, rather than quite small privileged elites whose reproductive desires are not always as different from those of the poor as might be imagined, is still necessary for the time being. To date, the late, celebrated Hans Rosling has been wide of the mark with his claim that 'a very fast [fertility] transformation... [is] already happening among the better-off in Africa'.[20]

'Everyone's missing a trick. Rapid urbanisation is bound to bring down fertility far faster than expected. Look at Ethiopia. Urbanisation works like magic.'

This claim derives in part from classical demographic transition theory, reiterated by demographers over many years: in 2002, for example, John Caldwell stated that 'continued urbanisation will help to drive the African fertility transition, and, indeed, is probably a more significant determinant in the region than anywhere else in the world'.[21] In 1970 only 32 million people out of a total population of about 220 million in sub-Saharan Africa lived in urban settlements with a population above 20,000. Johannesburg and Kinshasa were the only cities with a population above 1 million. Today, over 40% of a population of more than 1 billion is urban-dwelling and the region is often described as the most rapidly urbanising in history. Yet the TFR has fallen from 6.7 to 4.7 births, a decline of only two births in half a century; and outside Southern Africa, according to most recent DHSs, Ethiopia is the only sub-Saharan country to have an urban TFR below three births.

Urban areas usually lead the way in fertility transitions. Part of the theoretical explanation for this is that children are less economically productive in towns and cities than in rural areas, where they can provide labour; and that simultaneously it is more expensive to school children and keep them healthy, or to obtain assistance with childcare while the mother works. Contraception and health services also tend to be more accessible, even though they are an additional expense, and infant and maternal mortality rates are lower. There is greater information flow and diffusion of ideas between people. In every

African country, fertility is indeed lower in urban areas than rural locations, but in many cases the differential is quite small, declines have seldom been very rapid, and there are multiple examples of urban stalls. Uganda is one: the urban TFR has remained at four births since 2000, while lower fertility in some (but not all) rural areas has driven the recent decline in the national TFR. There has been no change this century in Nigeria's urban TFR of 4.5 births either. In Nairobi, desired fertility is for a higher number of children than in Kenya as a whole. Health services in many cities' slums are worse than in rural areas.

Ethiopia is always cited as the lead indicator of the path that all other African countries will soon follow. It is not a good example to choose: what occurred to fertility in its capital city, Addis Ababa, where the TFR fell to 1.4 births in the 2005 DHS, is exceptional. As the Ethiopian demographer and economist Yohannes Kinfu has explained, changes brought about by the 1974 revolution were key to the situation in Addis:[22] the ruling committee, known as the Derg, that headed the new government was committed to gender equality. Literacy among the city's women rose from less than 30% in the late 1960s to 85% in 1994, and many more women proceeded to higher education. Women's labour-force participation also rose dramatically, delayed marriage and non-marriage were increasingly prevalent, and laws regarding property ownership changed. The combination of these factors in revolutionary Addis is arguably unique in modern Africa and their effects on fertility were magnified by more commonly observed influences.

Rising aspirations deterred women from bearing the costs of raising many children – it was uncommon in Addis for women to rely on extended family for childcare – and a classic quantity-for-quality trade-off became commonplace. Less significant, but paradoxically also driving fertility lower in Kinfu's opinion, were the endemic insecurity and violence, political tension, frequent food shortages and economic precarity that accompanied the positive developments in the city in the Derg years.

Addis is untypical even within Ethiopia, but because it accounts for such a large percentage of Ethiopia's urban population it has a commensurate effect on the national urban TFR – the Ethiopian capital is 10 times as populous as its nearest rivals Adama (Nazret), Gondar and Mekelle. In the 2016 DHS the country's urban TFR was recorded as 2.3 births (compared to 5.2 in rural areas). This was much the same as in the 2005 DHS, but the TFR in Addis rose from 1.4 to 1.8 between the surveys. If this upward trend were to continue, the national urban TFR would rise with it. Most anomalous of all is that the decline to sub-replacement fertility in Addis took place despite high infant mortality, the absence of a government family planning programme and half the population living below the poverty line (a situation normally associated with high fertility levels).[23]

Addis was cited by Hans Rosling as evidence that 'Africa will repeat what Asia did' in terms of a fertility transition.[24] However the city's fertility transition was highly atypical, even unique, with multiple catalysts. It would be rash to argue either that its distinctive triggers, characteristics and development will be replicated elsewhere – or that Addis 'proves' that sub-replacement fertility is soon to be a feature of African cities and other urban settlements. While other African cities may also reach replacement fertility in the future, it will not be because they replicated what happened in Addis – or elsewhere in the world. Transitions will be distinctive, not conforming to convenient generalisations.

Another reason to be wary of the 'rapid urbanisation' narrative lies in the definitions of rural and urban settlements. In Uganda, for example, the National Bureau of Statistics states that 'the growth in urban population from 2.9 million in 2002 to 9.4 million in 2017 was mainly driven by creation of new districts, municipalities and town councils subsequently gazetting former rural areas as urban areas'.[25] This type of 'urbanisation' is happening all over the continent for different reasons, sometimes connected to the demarcation of voting constituencies; so too is urban sprawl. Neither of these developments are necessarily synonymous with 'slumification', but they tend not to be accompanied by the economic functions and advantages typically associated with classical definitions of

urbanisation – agglomeration, industrialisation, job creation, higher
productivity, more accessible and extensive public services and all
the other trappings of 'modernisation' envisaged by demographic
transition theory. This also explains in part why the rapid rise
in the level of urbanisation in Africa has not been accompanied
by a clearly discernible boost to GDP per capita: 'countries are
becoming more urban, but not simultaneously richer', as the IMF
has put it.[26]

The question of *how* African countries are urbanising is a
fascinating, complex and evolving field of study. In some, not only
conflict-afflicted ones, there are clear signs of 'redoubt' urbanisation –
population growth driven by deprivation or desperation. It is worth
noting that Cameroon and Angola, for example, have similar
urbanisation levels to China – about 60% – but at least three times the
fertility rate (with no discernible recent change). Nigeria has a similar
urbanisation level to Thailand and Indonesia – about 50% – making
it one of the most urbanised countries in Africa. This has increased
from about 35% since 2000, but there has been no material change in
Nigeria's TFR in the past two decades and it remains more than three
times higher than in Thailand and Indonesia.

Finally, there are African countries where rural fertility is
not changing at all, acting as a strong brake on any downward
effect of urbanisation on national fertility figures. Cameroon is
an example. The urban TFR has fallen from 5.2 births to 3.8 over
three decades, but the rural TFR is much the same as it was in
1991 – six births. As a result, the national TFR remains close to
five births even though the population is more than 50% urban.
Somalia's population is also about 50% urban, and the national TFR
is over six births. There are other countries where urbanisation
and fertility are both high. The World Bank lists the population
of Gabon as 90% urban, but the TFR is still above four and has
barely declined this century. Generalising about urbanisation
and fertility in Africa is risky, and in this respect the continent
is not unique. Michel Garenne has pointed out that 'a detailed
analysis of the European fertility transition... showed virtually

no relationship between fertility decline and urbanisation or socioeconomic factors'.[27]

> **'Demographers are wrong about Africa. They don't seem to take any notice of the fact that seven out of the 10 countries with the largest declines in fertility in the 2010s were in sub-Saharan Africa – Chad, Ethiopia, Kenya, Malawi, Somalia, Uganda and Sierra Leone.'**[28]

This final piece of 'proof' that UNPD projections will prove too high is as misleading as any. As African countries predominate among high-fertility nations worldwide, it is almost inevitably true – but changes nothing. If it were not so, it would mean that fertility was only falling in a few of Africa's high-fertility 'hotspots'; and that in turn would imply that Africa's total population was on course to record a population of several billions by the end of the century – almost the size of the global population today.

14

Demographic Alchemy

After the 1994 Cairo conference 'family planning' was sidelined and funding declined. It was reinvigorated by a thought-provoking but contested and controversial theory formulated by economists at the Harvard School of Public Health. Within a decade, amid a return of concerns in the West about population growth in Africa and the state of the environment, the 'demographic dividend' had become the essential instrument for renewed efforts to increase modern contraceptive use in Africa.

When the Harvard academics David Bloom and Jeffrey Williamson published two papers about the demographic transition in the journal *Emerging Asia* at the end of the 1990s, their focus on age cohorts or 'structures' was not entirely new.[1] The American demographers Ansley Coale and Edgar M. Hoover had posited in the late 1950s that age structures could have a production effect (more people of working age and fewer dependants meant more production per capita), a savings effect (from higher earnings due to increased production), a human capital effect (as savings were invested in health and education, raising the quality of the workforce) and a wage effect (relatively cheap labour due to its abundance provided a competitive advantage).[2] What was novel in Bloom and Williamson's papers was quantification of the sum total of the demographic 'gift', the boost to economic growth potentially provided by changing age structures. The concept of the 'demographic dividend' was born, and it would soon become as influential in the family planning industry – and other sectors – as the 'good governance' agenda, devised by the World Bank in the early 1990s, was in international development. Africa would be the prime arena for deployment of the theory.

In simple terms, the theory is as follows: when the proportion of children and old people in a population is high and that of working-age youth and adults is low, there is a high level of dependency which will have a dampening effect on the growth of per capita GDP. However, the ratio of dependants to workers diminishes as the demographic transition proceeds. A 'bulge' of children becomes a 'bulge' of productive workers. This can potentially boost GDP per capita for a number of decades, until the proportion of elderly people swells and the dependency ratio starts to rise again. As Bloom succinctly put it, 'when the working-age share [of the total population] is high, economic growth is potentiated – this effect is the demographic dividend'.[3]

Bloom and Williamson modelled the size of the demographic gift for 78 countries for which there was sufficient data. In the East Asian 'miracle' economies, so called after a 1993 World Bank report,* the results looked particularly eye-catching. It appeared that for China, Hong Kong, Japan, South Korea and Taiwan, between one-fifth and one-third of the 6% average increase in GDP per capita annually between 1965 and 1990 could be attributed to the growth of the working-age share of the population. If a 'steady state' or underlying growth rate of 2% was assumed for this region, then population dynamics had accounted for about half of the incremental growth – 2% of 4%.[4] The model therefore suggested a very substantial impact of demography on economic growth. In Southeast Asia, where, at about 4% a year, the average growth in GDP per capita over the same period was lower than in East Asia, and where a fertility transition started

---

* The World Bank publication *The East Asian Miracle: Economic Growth and Public Policy* focused on eight economies: Japan, Hong Kong, South Korea, Singapore and Taiwan in East Asia and Indonesia, Malaysia and Thailand in Southeast Asia. Demography was not cited as a significant contributor to the success of the Asian 'tigers'.

later and was not as rapid, population dynamics were estimated to have accounted for as much as half of the growth.[5]

These two Asian regions were, according to the model, the only ones in the developing world to display such a marked contribution of changing age structures to growth of national income. The results for Africa were rather different, although 'Africa' was something of a misnomer. Only 18 countries were included in the study, and the continent's three population 'heavyweights' – Nigeria, Egypt and Ethiopia – were not among them. As the dependant population had grown faster than the working-age population throughout the period, and GDP per capita had increased by less than 1% a year, changes in Africa's age structures were estimated to have made a negligible, or even negative, contribution in three out of four modelled scenarios. Forecasts for the future were brighter. Over the period 1990–2025, it was envisaged that the number of Africa's economically active people would grow faster than that of its dependants and population dynamics would boost GDP per capita growth by between 0.68% and 1.63% annually.

The disparity in dependency ratios* between world regions was the result of demographic transitions occurring at different times and speeds. In 2000, there were only 88 dependants per 100 people of working age in East Asia, fewer than one dependant for every person of working age; in Africa the corresponding figure was almost 200, two dependants for each working-age person. In sub-Saharan Africa and most of its constituent countries, the dependency ratio in 2000 was higher than it had been in 1980, whereas in East Asia it had fallen by more than a third. In Northern Africa, however, dependency had fallen from 200 to about 160 between 1980 and 2000, and in Southern Africa from 180 to 150, as a result of declining fertility. By 2050, dependency in

---

* The ratio will differ according to the age definitions for dependants and the working-age population. The figures in this paragraph are based on UNPD's definition of dependants as those aged 0–24 and 65+; and working age as 25–64. By this measure, all youth (aged 15–24) are classed as dependants. UNPD uses different definitions elsewhere. For example, in *World Population Ageing 2020* working age is defined as 20–65.

Africa will have dropped substantially to about 130, but that will only be a comparable level to East Asia's in 1980 – and still well above that region and Asia as a whole in 2050. Indeed, in mid-century Africa's dependency will remain higher than 'rapidly ageing' Europe and North America: children and youth under the age of 25 will continue to account for more than 50% of Africa's total population.

Bloom and Williamson did not present the boost to economic growth resulting from age-structure changes associated with the demographic transition as inevitable. 'Rather,' they stated, in East Asia 'it occurred because... countries had social, economic, and political institutions and policies that allowed them to realise the growth potential created by the transition'.[6] Among the 'other transitional forces' cited were 'productivity gains from "borrowing" Western technologies, and shifting labour from sectors with low productivity (agriculture) to sectors with higher productivity (industry and services)'.[7] They emphasised that 'the demographic "gift"... may or may not be realised. It represents a growth potential whose realisation depends on other features of the social, economic and political environment'.[8] In other words, it was conditional.

Bloom and Williamson also made it clear that population dynamics, the changing age structures, not the rate of population growth was 'the mechanism driving economic growth'.[9] This neatly sidestepped – or leapfrogged – the inconclusive and decades-old debate about whether population size and growth had an effect on economic growth. They added that what they proposed was a theory: their work '[did] not prove that population dynamics affect economic growth during transitions'.[10] Another academic to the fore in demographic dividend research, Andrew Mason of the University of Hawaii, echoed the caveat that the demographic bonus was 'policy dependent' and not automatic: 'favourable (or unfavourable) demographics do not automatically translate into strong (or weak) economic growth. This is clear on *a priori* grounds.'[11] Changing age structure simply provided a 'window of opportunity' to realise a demographic dividend.[12] But the seeds of confusion on both points were already sown and important caveats – the 'small print' of demographic dividend theory – would often be overlooked by its champions in future, deliberately and inadvertently.

It is certainly easy enough to assume that the dividend is automatic: all modelling of this type is deterministic, creating an impression that demographic transition leads inevitably to age-structural change that generates demographic dividends which are reflected in income per capita. It has been observed that 'the dividend is a complex concept often described in the public policy arena in optimistic and fairly general terms, without the specific recommendations or qualifying conditions that decision-makers need to take effective action'.[13] Matters are further complicated by the fact that a small percentage of a demographic dividend *can* be represented as arising automatically. If there are proportionally more workers and fewer dependants, then there will be a straightforward arithmetical increase in GDP per capita provided that everything else remains constant, including productivity and wages. Crucially, the supply of jobs must also expand to meet the needs of the growing working-age population. Too few jobs or falling productivity per worker could mean no dividend at all, even an arithmetic one.

About a tenth of the increase in GDP per capita in Asia between 1975 and 1990 was attributed to 'pure demographics' by Bloom and Williamson; and about 30–40% of the total demographic bonus in East Asia, i.e. 30–40% of the 2% annual growth in GDP per capita generated in total by the demographic dividend, or 0.6–0.8% of the 6% annual growth. In South Asia the effect was 'less striking'.[14] The arithmetic boost of 'pure demographics' to East Asia's GDP per capita is not insignificant, especially as it accrued annually over decades, but a sense of context and perspective is important. At the time their research was published the Asian financial crisis had just occurred, threatening to wipe out decades of economic gains and trigger a global meltdown.

By the mid-2000s, Bloom declared that he and colleagues at Harvard had moved forward the debate about the impact of population on economies.[15] Refinements to demographic dividend theory came thick and fast. For example, in 2004 UNPD suggested a tighter definition of dependency with the 'window of opportunity' to secure a demographic dividend opening when the proportion of the

Figure 16: Demographic dividend 'window of opportunity'* for African regions and countries, 1990–2100

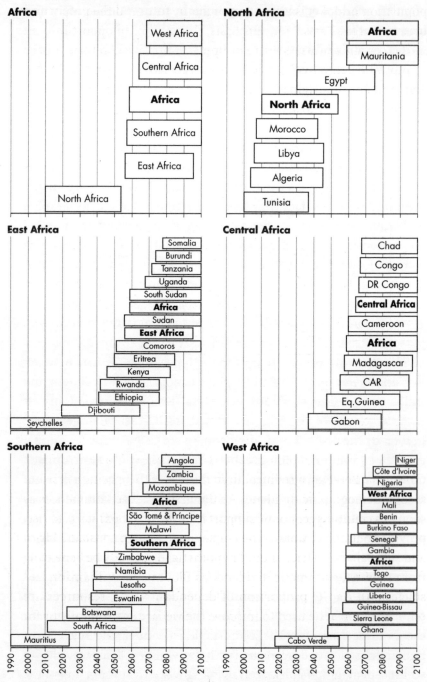

* The 'window of opportunity' for securing a demographic dividend is defined variously. Most commonly, it is assumed to open when the proportion of under-15s falls below 30% and the proportion of over-65s remains below 15% of the total population. *Source:* AfDB (2019), *Creating Decent Jobs: Strategies, Policies, and Instruments.*

population under 15 is less than 30% of the total and the proportion over 65 less than 15%.[16] On this basis, the window of opportunity in most African countries will not open until the second half of the century, a materially different proposition to suggesting, as Bloom and Williamson originally had, that the window opened as soon as the dependency ratio started to improve.

Figure 17: Working-age population (15-64 years) by selected world region as a proportion of total population, 1960-2050

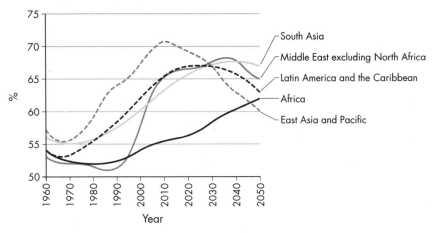

Source: Adapted from World Economic Forum, *The Africa Competitiveness Report 2017: Addressing Africa's Demographic Dividend.*

Andrew Mason and demographer Ronald Lee at the University of California, Berkeley, also introduced the idea of there being a first and second demographic dividend. As the first dividend commences as soon as a country's economic support ratio (see text box) starts to rise, provided output per worker and employment remain constant, Africa and sub-Saharan Africa should hypothetically already be benefiting from the first, arithmetic dividend (as Bloom and Williamson had suggested). As the proportion of dependants falls, resources are released that can be used to improve the welfare of the family or for economic development. The second dividend, potentially much larger than the first, can accrue many decades later if people save for old age and those savings are productively deployed.

National transfer accounts

Measuring dependency solely by the ratio of the working-age population to children and the elderly is quite simplistic or arbitrary. The experience and behaviour of people varies as they pass through working age, altering as a result of new policies, economic shocks, changes in family circumstances and choice. Workers reach their peak earning power at different ages in different countries.

Andrew Mason and Ronald Lee responded to the shortcomings of measuring dependency solely by age by focusing on the 'generational economy' and cyclical variations in an individual's earnings and expenditure, year by year.

Their main aims were to:

• improve the measurement of dependency

• isolate more precisely the extent to which age structures affected economic growth, independent of macro-economic fluctuations, political developments and government policies

• gather evidence of the relationship between lower fertility and increased spending on the health and education of young children.

Using labour income and consumption data – income and outgoings – Mason and Lee produced 'age-based accounting of economic flows'* and economic support ratios† (as opposed to dependency ratios) for 60 countries worldwide. The support ratio represents the proportion of 'net producers' to 'net consumers' in an economy. When the support ratio starts to increase as a result of the demographic transition, reflecting a higher proportion of producers to consumers, a first demographic dividend arises.

In 2011, Mason and Lee launched the National Transfer Accounts (NTA) project to 'estimate labour income and consumption profiles for African countries to enable them to put in place policies that would "reap" a demographic dividend'. The project was funded by the Bill & Melinda Gates Foundation through a grant to the Johns Hopkins Bloomberg School of Public Health. The researchers and think-tanks undertaking the research in the selected countries were mostly funded by the UNFPA. An early estimate for sub-Saharan Africa suggested a first demographic dividend of a contribution of 0.25%–0.5% a year to GDP per capita growth, lasting for half a century.

In 2010, in a separate initiative, 'How to secure the demographic dividend', papers were written for a dozen Western African countries by Jean-Pierre Guengant for Agence française de développement (AFD), the French development agency, for the 'Population, development and family planning conference' in Ouagadougou, Burkina Faso, in February 2011.

The demographic dividend had arrived in Africa. Kenya's 47-page 'Demographic Dividend Roadmap', published by the National Council for Population and Development, noted that the dividend was being 'fronted as a solution to the myriad of problems being experienced by developing countries'.

In a 2017 paper for UNPD, Mason, Lee and co-authors used the NTA approach to set out estimates showing that the first demographic dividend in Africa (based on data for 16 countries) would last the longest and be the largest of any world region. Accruing over 92 years, starting in the early 1990s, the cumulative increase in 'standards of living' – GDP per capita – was estimated at 35.1%, higher even than Asia's at 34.8% over 58 years.‡ All sub-regions of Africa except Northern Africa are forecast to show average annual increases of about 0.45% between 2015 and 2040.

---

* UNDESA (2019e), World Population Ageing 2019 – Highlights, p. 20.   † Andrew Mason et al. (2017), 'Support Ratios and Demographic Dividends: Estimates for the World', UNPD Technical Paper No. 2017/1, p. 5. The support ratio as calculated here is a refinement of many earlier approaches because it incorporates important variation across age in the amount that people contribute through their labour and in the amount of the resources that they claim through their consumption.'   ‡ Andrew Mason et al. (2017), 'Support Ratios and Demographic Dividends: Estimates for the World', p. 25.

Definitional issues aside, the essential catalyst for the change in age structures required to open a window of opportunity and potentially secure a demographic dividend is a fertility transition; and the more rapid the transition, the larger the dividend is likely to be. 'First and foremost focus on fertility decline,' Mason and Lee advised: a shift in high-fertility countries to the fertility trajectory of UNPD's low-variant projections was a prerequisite even to securing the first (arithmetic) dividend.[17] The dependence of demographic dividend theory on fertility decline was more explicit in the work of some interested individuals and institutions than others. Part of its appeal was that it could be used to address rapid population growth laterally or by stealth, focusing on the positives of a larger working-age population and lower dependency rate rather than the more controversial issue of the need to reduce fertility.

Whether explicit or not, demographers and other interested parties understood quite clearly the intended use of demographic dividend theory. In the mid-2000s, Martha Campbell at the Berkeley School of Public Health observed that 'reducing fertility has been framed as the sure way to achieve economic growth or development', even though fertility decline was 'not a solution by itself… merely a necessary but not sufficient factor'.[18] The '[demographic dividend] trend was set up by a group at Harvard School of Public Health… who wanted to promote family planning by highlighting its economic advantages', Michel Garenne later wrote, referring to the pioneering work of Bloom and his colleagues.[19] Before the end of the 2000s the demographic dividend had become a mainstream family planning advocacy tool. Anyone still in doubt only had to look at the sources of funding for demographic dividend research and its dissemination. To the fore were the US philanthropic institutions associated with promoting birth control in the 'Third World' in the 1970s – the William and Flora Hewlett Foundation, the David and Lucie Packard Foundation and the Rockefeller Foundation – and now backing its successor, family planning.[20] By the end of the 2000s they were joined by the Bill & Melinda Gates Foundation, which was soon to become the demographic dividend's biggest sponsor of all.

Figure 18: The effect of demographic transition on working-age population share (SWAP) in African countries

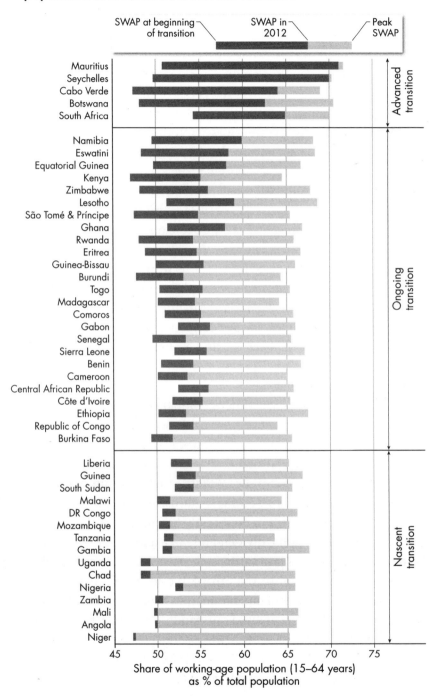

Source: IMF, *Finance & Development*, March 2016.

The theory was equally appealing to development practitioners, but a little slower to gain traction. A major World Bank report authored by the Tanzanian economist Benno Ndulu and published in 2007, *Challenges of African Growth*, contained plenty of analysis of the impact on African economies of a 'high level of age dependency' and the slow demographic transition, stating that 'demographic factors dominate in terms of Africa's contrast to the conditions for growth in the other [developing] regions'.[21] But the term 'demographic dividend' only appeared once in the report's 280 pages, and that was a quotation from one of Bloom and Williamson's papers.[22] The orthodox World Bank view was still that 'the rapid growth of the population, as manifested by a high dependency ratio, is inimical to rapid economic growth'.[23] However in 2008, the following year, the term appeared 10 times in a 328-page report, *Youth in Africa's Labour Market*. Inroads were being made. This was unsurprising given that securing a substantial dividend appeared to require most of the same essential ingredients as the World Bank's 'good governance' agenda, one of the most dominant international development paradigms since its invention in 1992.

Meanwhile, the shape-shifting of demographic dividend theory continued. With the benefit of hindsight, or even at the time, this did not always inspire confidence, especially among non-economists. Bloom and colleagues claimed that age-structure changes could even 'significantly'[24] improve the forecasting of 'long-run' economic growth. 'Slow' growth was predicted for the 23 sub-Saharan countries included in their investigation of the data for 90 countries worldwide over the period 2000–20. Only Ghana (0.2%), Togo (0.7%) and DRC (mysteriously listed as 'Congo, P.R.', 0.6%) were forecast by the model to achieve positive average annual GDP per capita growth over the two decades. Even if solely intended to be illustrative, this was treacherous territory: the predictions would collectively, and almost without exception individually, prove wildly wrong. There were subtler developments afoot too which were no less significant.

In another paper published the same year, 'Realizing the

Demographic Dividend: Is Africa Any Different?', Bloom and colleagues expounded on the institutional requirements for securing a demographic dividend. They asserted that 'only countries featuring high institutional quality are able to receive a demographic dividend'[25] and that 'efficiency losses due to poor institutional quality will outweigh any gains that a high proportion of working-age population will bring'.[26] On the other hand, there was 'a positive outlook for those countries *with the right set of institutions in place*'.[27] Although conceding that institutional quality was 'hard to define and even harder to measure',[28] this 'right set of institutions' and other preconditions included a stable and transparent political and economic environment, the rule of law, an efficient bureaucracy, control of corruption, political freedom and low risk of expropriation, openness (of the political system, and of trade) and freedom of political representation and of speech. More than that, a broader 'institutions measure' would include good-quality infrastructure for healthcare, schooling, roads and transport; and a 'formal labour market with unions protecting both employees and employers'.[29] To the lay reader or policymaker, the importance of changing age structures seemed to be rather swamped. Furthermore, it was a moot point whether South Korea and other East Asia countries had ticked all these required boxes on the way to securing their demographic dividend, not least because their economic miracles were not the product of the 'Washington Consensus' – World Bank and IMF – institutional and policy measures mentioned.

Africa was said to have a 'pronounced lag in institutional quality'.[30] The authors were 'most optimistic' on this score for Ghana, Côte d'Ivoire, Malawi, Mozambique and Namibia, 'who have done relatively well on the institutional side'.[31] They found that the most propitious age structures over the next two decades were those of Cameroon, Nigeria, Senegal, Tanzania and Togo, but added that these countries 'will likely have to significantly improve their institutional framework'. Much of this analysis was highly subjective, or wishful thinking. It was debatable, for example, whether institutions in Mozambique were all that was being assumed by the authors. Granted, President Guebuza (nicknamed 'Mr Gue-Business') had started appearing on the international conference circuit, GDP growth was strong and the IMF thought the country could be 'the next Vietnam'; but this did not inherently signify institutional quality or even improvement. In fact it was worsening, exemplified most prominently by a massive debt scandal uncovered in the following decade. The description of Nigeria's age structure as 'propitious' was equally puzzling to demographers familiar with the country's demographic profile: the country was certainly populous, but it was yet to show any real sign of commencing a fertility transition.

More seeds of confusion were sown in a 2011 article in the journal *Science* in which Bloom referred to the demographic dividend as 'the tendency for economic growth to be spurred by rapid growth of the working-age share of the population'.[32] A 'tendency' conveys greater certainty than a 'possibility', which is what most people understood a demographic dividend to be. When he subsequently wrote that 'the economic successes of Indonesia and East Asia are not coincidentally related to demographics. Rather they seem to be causally related to East Asia's and Indonesia's fertility transitions,' the mention of causality also implied that the demographic dividend was more than a hypothesis. Bloom continued: 'Of course the demographic dividend is not the sole explanation for the differing economic trajectories... But this explanation is intuitively plausible, theoretically sound and consistent with the data.'[33] Similarly, in an article citing his 2003 RAND paper, Bloom commented: 'the decrease in the youth dependency ratio comes with various economic benefits, leading to what has been called the demographic dividend'.[34] To anyone not steeped in the demographic dividend 'literature', this too implied a causal relationship between a 'decrease in the youth dependency ratio' and 'various economic benefits'. However, the messaging was mixed. The exact opposite was also implicit in the ever-growing list of conditions for gaining a demographic dividend.

By 2013, the prerequisites for securing a demographic dividend, mentioned in the space of four paragraphs of an article, included:

'the right mix of jobs that allow workers to contribute proactively to the economy', 'sustained investment in human capital', 'good governance', 'a carefully constructed trade policy', 'solid macroeconomic management', 'well-developed financial markets', 'good relationships with neighbouring countries' and 'absence of civil wars, conflict and foreign wars', labour-market reform and the rule of law. Bloom considered that 'the many challenges countries face in bringing about a demographic dividend are not insurmountable'.[35] In 2016, in a footnote, 'cultural attitudes, religion and technological progress' and 'global trade patterns' were added to the list.[36]

To borrow a phrase used recently by the Cameroonian economist Célestin Monga when referring to the World Bank's controversial 'Doing Business' project, securing a demographic dividend seemed to require 'an overwhelming and generic laundry list of reforms that no government has the capacity to achieve'.[37] This had profound implications for the way the demographic dividend was received in Africa. Not only was it being 'pushed' by influential family planning activists, practitioners and funders, but its policy conditions read like something that might have hailed from the World Bank or IMF during the structural adjustment era and the protracted trauma and indignity of negotiating mass debt relief.

As its profile grew, critiques of the demographic dividend methodology and its theoretical underpinnings emerged. The econometric estimation used in the modelling was controversial. 'These econometric findings... are based on strong assumptions and so cannot be accepted without question,'[38] remarked Robert Eastwood and Michael Lipton. These two eminent economists from the University of Sussex also pointed out that 'such research aims to give *causal* links from demography to development, but ultimately what is exhibited is *correlation*'.[39] This was a very important truth to speak as it had become increasingly obscured. Others also referred to 'causally ambiguous econometric analysis of cross-national data'.[40] Furthermore, in Eastwood and Lipton's view, assumptions about 'greater-than-arithmetical age-structure effects [because] reduced youth dependency raises savings' were not 'firmly established'. In

East Asia, they pointed out, 'most of the rise in savings cannot be attributed to the demographic transition'.[41]

There was also the thorny question of whether the apparent occurrence of a substantial demographic dividend in parts of Asia was of any direct relevance to Africa, in the past or future. 'Conditions in East Asia', Eastwood and Lipton observed, 'were very favourable to the exploitation of the opportunity presented by the demographic transition: high domestic savings, high investment in education, and an institutional and policy environment that both encouraged domestic entrepreneurs and stimulated large private capital flows from abroad all combined to the effect.' In other words, age structure should not be overplayed. Whether or not a dividend could be realised in Africa would 'rest on the availability of employment and on investment, the scale of which depends on many things, notably education and transportation'.[42]

The relevance of these critiques is not about what was 'wrong' or 'right'. Theories are debated. Such comments need highlighting simply because in many quarters the demographic dividend had become an empirically proved phenomenon, a scientific law, by 2012. It is little short of astonishing that an interesting, thought-provoking theory with many different interpretations could be used as the trump card in a revived campaign to lower fertility in Africa. But that is what happened next; and given that there was, for example, no certainty or consensus about the impact of population growth on economies, or what causes fertility to fall, or the extent to which family planning lowers fertility, it was not necessarily surprising.

In 2012, the UK government staged the London Summit on Family Planning, part-sponsored by the Bill & Melinda Gates Foundation and UNFPA. The aim of the conference was to resuscitate funding for family planning. Population growth had, in the words of Professor Alex Ezeh, been 'removed from the development vocabulary altogether'[43] since the 1994 International Conference on Population and Development in Cairo, and family planning had become *haram* – off-limits – since the shift of emphasis to promoting 'sexual and reproductive health and rights'. Funding had been further impacted by the reimposition of the 'global gag' rule by the George W. Bush administration in 2001, prohibiting US government funding for any organisation providing abortion advice, services or advocacy; and by the diversion of donor funds to tackle the HIV/AIDS crisis.

One reason for optimism among family planning advocates was that in Africa, real commitment to family planning programmes had been shown by the governments of Rwanda, Ethiopia and Malawi. What's more, these had produced some remarkable results in the first decade of the century. In Rwanda, the TFR fell from 6.1 to 4.6 births between 2005 and 2010 as the use of modern contraception by women soared from 10% to 45%, an almost unprecedented rate. On the other hand, in Malawi a similar rise in the contraceptive prevalence rate between 1998 and 2010 only produced a decline in the TFR from 6.3 to 5.7 births. Since then, despite a further fall in the TFR to 4.4 births by 2015 and an increase in modern contraceptive usage to 60%, the 2018 census showed that the population had grown by 35% in a decade, an annual growth rate of 2.9%. This is a robust reminder that modern contraception is not the only, or even the key, determinant of fertility decline.

In Rwanda and Ethiopia, the initiatives being undertaken were largely the result of conviction on the part of their respective governments, rather than external activism and the promise of funding. Additionally, UNPD's 2009 *World Population Policies* study had found that Africa had 'the highest percentage of countries who consider their population growth as too high'; and that the percentage of governments that did not intervene to influence population growth had fallen from 60% in 1976 to 21%. Such findings were precisely what generated suspicion in some quarters of the degree of objectivity underpinning UNPD's projections, but a record of policies and declarations of intent does not denote implementation. Finally, Africa was increasingly portrayed as the 'final frontier' of extreme poverty. If these were the justifications, the demographic dividend seemingly provided the ideal tool of persuasion. The 'you will starve unless you do what we say' narrative familiar to African leaders and governments in the 1980s could be replaced by 'it's in your economic interests to do as we suggest'.

The London Summit was hailed as 'a global historic breakthrough' and 'all about the power of partnership'[44] by UK government press releases. Pledges worth US$2.6 billion, including US$1 billion from the Bill & Melinda Gates Foundation, were announced to restore family planning as a 'global development priority'. Specifically, the main goal was 'empowering 120 million additional women and girls' by 2020 through providing access to contraception. This would increase usage by almost 50% in the 69 countries targeted, about half of which were African. The prime focus was women with unmet need, those who say they want to stop having children or delay their next birth for at least two years. It was estimated that in Africa as many as one in four women were in this category. Either side of the summit a splurge of demographic dividend articles appeared in journals and on the websites of family planning organisations, with titles like 'Family planning promotes the demographic dividend'.[45]

Despite the talk of a 'global movement' being galvanised, African participants were thin on the ground. Three presidents attended, but there were no religious and cultural leaders declaring their endorsement or tacit acceptance of the planned initiatives, let alone leaders of grass-roots African women's groups. There was no mistaking that the 'partnership' was principally between Western – or 'Global North' – individuals and concerns. No matter how good the intentions, the few representatives of low-income countries were essentially window-dressing.

President Museveni was a keynote speaker at this event six years before he made the speeches described in Chapter 2. He emphasised that population growth was not the problem, but agreed that the health of mothers and babies was an important issue that could be improved by spacing births better. He promised to increase his government's annual budget allocation for family planning supplies from US$3.3 million to US$5 million. Nigeria committed to achieving a contraceptive prevalence rate of 36% by 2018, by which date it was still only just in double figures. Niger expressed 'a high level of political commitment' to family planning.[46] At the time, the country's TFR was rising and there are no good grounds for believing that it may have fallen much below seven births since. By the time of a follow-up London Summit in 2017, none of the objectives set out in 2012 were within sight, as we shall see.

The fundraising success at the London Summit could partly be attributed to publication the previous year of *World Population Prospects: The 2010 Revision*, with its upward revision of projections for Africa and the world. 'How to manage Africa's population explosion', a brief produced by the Economist Intelligence Unit before the summit, reflected the reappearance of the dominant pre-Cairo population narrative, stating that 'with Africa's population spiraling, concerted effort is needed to head off a Malthusian nightmare'.[47] It also coincided with publication of *People and the Planet* by The Royal Society, intended to warn ahead of the Rio Earth Summit about the impact on the environment of the global population reaching 8–11 billion by 2050 amid 'unprecedented and rising levels of consumption'. The need to 'slow and stabilize' population growth 'by non-coercive means' was one of three major global challenges listed in the opening summary.[48] There was no repeat of the call for 'zero population growth in the life of our children' made by The Royal Society and other scientific academies in the run-up to the Cairo conference – the recommendation rejected by African science academies – but in the main text of the report it was stated that 'the consequences of inadequate family planning programmes are of particular concern in West Africa and across the Sahel'.[49]

An equally influential report, *One Planet, How Many People? A Review of the Earth's Carrying Capacity*, also appeared in 2012, underscoring the fact that carrying capacity was again to the fore as a means of trying to establish that overpopulation was (or soon would be) an incontrovertible truth. Published by the United Nations Environment Programme (UNEP), the briefing cited a 1995 article by Joel E. Cohen, in which he analysed 65 different estimates of the world's carrying capacity. The UNEP publication stated that Cohen had found that 'the majority of studies put the Earth's limit at or below 8 billion people, *a number that we will exceed in about 15 years*'.[50] This was a misrepresentation. What Cohen actually said was that the median of all the upper bounds of the 65 estimates was 12 billion and that of the lower bounds was 7.7 billion; he had then remarked that the range was very similar to the 7.8–12.5 billion range between UNPD's low-variant and high-variant projections for 2050.[51] Cohen also stated that '[such] estimates deserve the same profound skepticism as population projections' over that long a time frame, as they depended 'sensitively on assumptions about future natural constraints and human choices'.[52]

The year after the London Summit and the appearance of the UNEP and Royal Society reports, *World Population Prospects: The 2012 Revision* brought further upward revisions to population projections for Africa and the world. Population growth – and high fertility in parts of Africa – was firmly back on the agenda in the West, but family planning advocates were already finding that the key new tool in their armoury, the demographic dividend, had also been appropriated by another, very different constituency.

15

'Africa Rising'

The resurgence of Western family planning activism coincided with renewed optimism about Africa's economic performance and investment potential. Demographic dividend theory was reinterpreted by 'Africa Rising' cheerleaders and adherents of the 'just add people' school of economics. Within a few years the term was rendered meaningless by overuse and multiple definitions.

Interest in demographic dividend theory was not confined to family planning organisations, demographers and development wonks. The 2010s witnessed the sudden emergence of an influential new Africa narrative among investors and in the business world. In 2010 McKinsey, an international consultancy, published a report titled 'Lions on the Move', calling attention to the continent's economic resurgence and enormous potential. Soon afterwards *The Economist* highlighted 'Africa's impressive growth':[1] the GDP of sub-Saharan Africa had increased by an average of 6% a year since the turn of the century and the region had seven of the world's 10 fastest-expanding economies of the decade. This fact was quoted in so many Africa-focused events and media reports that it became a leitmotif. By the end of 2011, *The Economist*, the paper that had notoriously dubbed Africa 'the hopeless continent' on its May 2000 cover, presented 'The Hopeful Continent: Africa Rising'. 'Lions on the Move' was the canon for the new-found optimism fast becoming a phenomenon; now it had a catchy name to boot. Blood swiftly rushed to heads. Rather in the manner of the rogue demographer predicting that the global TFR would fall to replacement level by 2025, one investment bank boldly state that it *'expected'* (my italics) economic growth in sub-Saharan Africa to accelerate to 7–8% annually for the next four decades, and as a result 'by 2050 Africa will produce more GDP than the US and Eurozone combined do today'.[2]

Alongside world-beating economic growth, rising consumption, a growing middle class and rapid urbanisation, demography was a key component of the 'Africa Rising' narrative. Investment banks and consultancies sprinkled references to Africa's 'superb' and 'surging' demographics through their reports. At the Ibrahim Forum in 2012, held in Dakar with the theme of 'African Youth: Fulfilling the Potential', an audience including African presidents and senior policymakers was told that 'by 2035, Africa's labour force will be larger than China's' and asked, 'How do we ensure that Africa benefits from this imminent demographic dividend?'[3] Any participant who did not read the 'small print' of the forum report, which explained the theory in greater detail, could be forgiven for taking this to mean that a large workforce was synonymous with a demographic dividend. Furthermore, attendees were told that 'even though Africa's demographic transition has been delayed… it could yield the largest total demographic dividend over the long run'.[4] If Jimi Wanjigi had made his speech in front of them, it would not have seemed out of place.

Elsewhere, a leading private-equity investor in Africa equated a demographic dividend with a significant increase in consumers;[5] and a youthful population was, like a large workforce, also taken to be synonymous with a demographic dividend. By the end of 2012, in the world of investment and business in particular the dividend meant pretty much whatever the user wanted it to mean to buttress his or her argument. Any acknowledgement that a demographic dividend was substantially conditional rather than completely automatic was buried. The crucial ingredients originally cited by David Bloom and colleagues – higher savings, investment in human capital, appropriate policy and enough jobs to absorb a growing workforce – let alone his 'overwhelming and generic laundry list' of 'good governance' and institutional requirements were airbrushed out by this constituency.

Above all, fertility rates were deemed an irrelevance to this new school of demographic dividend theory, an extraordinary divergence from its parallel development as an advocacy tool for family planning. The World Bank's chief economist, Justin Yifu Lin, was called out for omitting, in a blog titled 'Youth bulge: A demographic dividend or a demographic bomb in developing countries?', to make any mention of the fact that fertility decline was one of the necessary preconditions for age structures to generate a demographic dividend; for implying that economic benefits were automatic when the necessary changes in age structures had occurred; and for referring to Africa's 'youth bulge' when in most countries the base of the population pyramid was growing ever larger – a point with important ramifications for dependency ratios.[6] As the Africa editor of the *Financial Times* would later wryly remark, the 'Africa Rising' narrative, and its proponents' understanding of a demographic dividend, seemed to be 'largely predicated on a theory of economic growth known informally as "just add people"'.[7]

African leaders and governments embraced 'Africa Rising' with conspicuously greater zeal than they did events like the London Summit on Family Planning. It was four decades since their continent had last been depicted so positively, and the first time ever that fast-growing, youthful populations had been portrayed as an unalloyed advantage, as opposed to an existential liability, by anyone in the West. The timing was also fortuitous. The 'Arab Spring' uprisings in Northern Africa in 2011 had resulted in the overthrow of a number of entrenched, authoritarian governments and there were fears that the unrest would spread southwards through the continent. Four years earlier, many governments further south had been more shaken by serious food riots following a spike in global prices than by the global financial crisis. This demographic dividend narrative seemingly converted the 'ticking time bomb', as it was frequently described, of legions of young unemployed people prominent in the uprisings neatly into a precious and valuable resource, one to be fulsomely praised and that would give Africa a competitive advantage in an ageing world.

The euphoria was short-lived. Commodity prices, which had been driven higher for many years by ever-greater demand from China, peaked just as 'Africa Rising' hype rose to fever pitch, and in 2014–15 the oil price slumped. Many African economies not dependent on natural resources for revenue and forex continued to perform well, but the largest – South Africa, Nigeria, Egypt and Angola – were all hit hard. This impacted aggregate figures for the continent – it could no longer boast seven of the 10 fastest-growing economies in the world – and perceptions. By 2016 growth in sub-Saharan Africa was at its lowest level since the mid-1990s.

In the context of a worsening economic outlook, the demographic dividend was still sprinkled liberally through the reports of Western investment banks, consultancies and businesses to remind potential investors that Africa's demographics remained superb and that part of the investment case, at least, remained intact. However, The Economist had spotted a hitch: how big would this dividend be and how could it even be measured if economies suffered a prolonged downturn? In March 2014 the paper carried an article focusing on a study by Jean-Pierre Guengant and John F. May. It was titled 'The dividend is delayed', and reported that 'hopes that Africa's dramatic population bulge may create prosperity seem to have been overdone'.[8]

As the 'Africa Rising' narrative waned, the 'other' demographic dividend theory consolidated its position. In a 2013 paper[9] Bloom and colleagues estimated the potential uplift to GDP per capita for Kenya, Senegal and Nigeria, with different levels of fulfilment of the unmet need for modern contraception among women. If there had ever been any doubt about the original purpose of demographic dividend theory, it was now dispelled: a contraceptive revolution would confer economic benefits. Wolfgang Lutz referred to the theory unequivocally as the 'dominant paradigm in the field of population and development, and an advocacy tool for highlighting the benefits of family planning and fertility decline'.[10] Demographer John Casterline at Ohio State University also noticed that 'rather suddenly during the past decade, the opportunity to realize a demographic dividend became the principal rationale for policies and programs to accelerate fertility decline in sub-Saharan Africa'.[11] Similarly, Gilles Pison, research director at France's Institut national d'études démographiques, observed that 'to persuade African governments that birth control is important, international organisations use the argument of the "demographic dividend"'.[12]

A sense of urgency (and binary hyperbole) accompanied the growing use of the demographic dividend as a family planning and 'good governance' advocacy tool, and in the 2010s the World Bank and IMF moved decisively behind it. An IMF report extolling the benefits of 'harnessing the demographic dividend' in sub-Saharan Africa warned that if no 'meaningful progress' was made, it 'could translate into an army of unemployed youth and significantly increase social risks and tensions'.[13] The following year a report co-published by AFD, the French development agency, and the World Bank was titled *Africa's Demographic Transition: Dividend or Disaster?*[14] The 2017 Africa Competitiveness Report warned that while a demographic dividend was attainable, '[if] the low GDP growth and low employment expectations are confirmed, African economies could face the risk that a larger unemployed young population could become a source of instability in already fragile societies'.[15] Some messaging was even more explicit. The first recommendation of a report by the Institute for Security Studies, a South African think-tank, called for the 'accelerated roll-out of modern contraception'[16] in low- and lower-middle-income African countries.

However, the leverage of the 'dividend-as-family-planning and "good governance" tool' advocates had been weakened by the intrusion of the 'just add numbers' school of economics. The term was now defined, deployed and interpreted in so many different ways that it had become largely meaningless. Lutz drew attention to the 'contradictory use' of the concept by family planning and development practitioners on the one hand, and politicians and policymakers in Africa on the other (to which group he might have added Western promoters of the 'Africa Rising' narrative). This, he continued, 'further adds to an already complex discussion about the effects of demographic trends on economic growth'.[17] The shared 'ownership' of the demographic dividend had come at a cost. A small sample of the multitude of available definitions illustrates the problem. The dividend was variously regarded as:

'an economic boom, led by the working-age population'[18]

'simply the relationship of your working-age population to your dependants'[19]

'the temporary "window [of opportunity]" in which working-age proportion is unusually high'[20]

'an economic surplus triggered by an increase of the employed working-age population relatively to the dependant population'[21]

'the increase in the ratio of producers to consumers generated by a shift of the population age structure during the demographic transition'[22]

'a verifiable, independent effect of age structure on economic growth.'

The last two even came from the same institution, the United Nations Department of Social Affairs; and it will be noticed that most of these definitions do not even refer to the same type of thing. Vincent Turbat, an associate professor at Georgetown University and consultant to the Population Reference Bureau, summed up the problem: 'Looking at the literature about the demographic dividend, one cannot help but notice that, in most cases, the concept is not fully explained and, when it is, there are large discrepancies among the definitions provided.'[23]

There were also multiple choices for when the demographic dividend occurred or, more specifically, when the 'window of opportunity' opens:

- UNPD usually defines the opening of the window of opportunity as occurring when the proportion of children and youth under 15 falls below 30% and the over-65s are still less than 15% of the population. By this yardstick, the window will not open in most countries in Africa until almost the middle of the century.
- A World Bank typology based on fertility rates has the window opening for 14 African countries between 2015 and 2030 because the share of the working-age population is increasing, and closing for Morocco, Tunisia, Mauritius and Seychelles. For the remaining two-thirds of African countries the window opens after 2030, but not until mid-century for many of them.[24]
- For Lee and Mason, originators of one of the branches of demographic dividend theory, the window opened in African countries as soon as the support ratio started to improve in the 1990s.
- Demographer Richard Cincotta proposes that the window opens when the median age of a population is about 26–7 years and closes after about 40 years.[25]
- The IMF considers the window to have opened in sub-Saharan Africa in the mid-1980s, when the working-age (defined as 15–64 years) share of the population, as opposed to the support ratio, started to increase and the dependency ratio started to improve. It noted in its 2015 *Regional Economic Outlook* that GDP per capita in sub-Saharan Africa had shown no increase in the first 25 years after that point, whereas in East Asia it had doubled in the first 25 years.[26]
- A 2018 report from the Institute of Security Studies in South Africa stated that low-income and lower-middle-income African states – the majority – were 'several decades away from achieving a demographic dividend' unless contraceptive use soared.[27]

There was a similar lack of alignment over end dates. World Bank economist S. Amer Ahmed, lead author of *How Significant Is Africa's Demographic Dividend for its Future Growth and Poverty Reduction?*, suggests that Africa's window of opportunity will only be open for another couple of decades;[28] it therefore closes before UNPD envisages the window opening. His blog also refers to the work of a colleague who posits that 'the Sahel's best window of opportunity lies in the next 15 to 20 years, and many in the region are optimistic',[29] an anomalous observation given that at the time the average TFR in Sahel countries was over six births and nowhere showing any sign of decline, that GDP per capita was plummeting and the region was increasingly beset by Islamist terrorist groups.

'It is easy to understand the confusion among African experts who are in charge of developing their country's roadmaps for harnessing the demographic dividend,'[30] two such experts, from Senegal, remarked. In their study of when the window of opportunity would open in 16 francophone countries – *Africa's Demographic Dividend – An Elusive Window of Opportunity?* – the date for Benin was variously 1993, 2032 or 2068 depending on which of the three most common definitions was used. For Mauritania, the window either opened in 1998 or will do so in 2023 or 2068.

Finally, the putative size of demographic dividends for any country ranges from the possible to the plausible to the patently absurd. In no corresponding order, in its 2015 *Regional Economic Outlook* the IMF estimated that the increasing share of the working-age population – the 'first' demographic dividend – could alone add 25% to its forecast for GDP per capita in 2050 and 55% to its forecast for 2100, provided current employment levels and labour productivity were maintained.[31] The OECD reported that Africa's 'burgeoning supply of workers' could boost Africa's annual growth of GDP per capita by up to half a percentage point, and noted estimates that by 2030 'the demographic dividend could contribute 10–15% of Africa's gross GDP volume growth'.[32] Representatives of UNFPA have frequently cited a figure 'based on the Asian experience' of a dividend of US$500 billion a year – about one-third of sub-Saharan Africa's current

GDP – lasting for at least 30 years.[33] The open-source DemDiv tool developed by the Health Policy Project for the Futures Group, funded by USAID, was used by UNICEF to estimate that 'with appropriate investments in human capital and policies to stimulate job creation', a demographic dividend could cause Africa's average GDP per capita to as much as quadruple by 2050, as opposed to merely double in a business-as-usual scenario.[34]

By the mid-2010s the demographic dividend was a classic example of 'the emperor has no clothes'. It was fervently invoked at investment conferences, family planning conferences, 'good governance' conferences, business conferences – almost any type of conference focusing on Africa; but scepticism, even cynicism, was increasingly prevalent among the audiences, who usually kept their reservations to themselves. With multiple definitions, expert opinions on timing, prerequisites and estimates of gains, the term had simply become jargon. Furthermore, despite that fact that Northern and Southern Africa were close to the end of their fertility transitions and dependency ratios had fallen sharply, no one was trumpeting a demographic dividend in either region despite the irrepressible Professor Bloom's reiteration that 'Africa has *a priori* large potential to enjoy a demographic dividend'.[35] Amber and red flags were raised. The limitations of demographic dividend theory were seemingly even alluded to by one of its originators: in 2013, Jeffrey Williamson wrote that 'it seems to me that there are many unanswered questions involving the impact of the demographic transition on country economic performance. Estimates of the first and second demographic dividends seem only to scratch the surface. We need to learn much more about schooling, emigration, and inequality connections as well as rural-urban dynamics.'[36] In other words, in addition to being complex, at another level the theory was overly simplistic.

In 2017, LSHTM's John Cleland and Kazuyo Machiyama reiterated earlier warnings that 'given the limited understanding of the mix of factors that drive economic growth and the unpredictability of global trends and policy directions, the results of all economic models of this type must be regarded as illustrative possibilities rather than predictions'; and observed that 'naively optimistic expectations' had been raised 'about the prospect of accelerated economic growth in Africa that may arise from falling fertility and declining dependency ratios, though such growth is contingent on other factors, notably appropriate policies'.[37] The first remark arguably exposes a deception at the heart of demographic dividend theory: it fuses demographic trends that can be forecast quite accurately over a few decades with a plethora of other elements – economic growth, quality of institutions etc. – that cannot, or are immeasurable.

In 2016, Bloom's suggestion of a causal effect of demography on economic growth was again challenged, as it had been by economists Eastwood and Lipton. Michel Garenne described the demographic dividend as a 'fashionable but controversial' concept lacking a 'proper analytical framework', and demonstrated that there was no relationship between economic growth and dependency ratios in a longitudinal analysis of African countries. Garenne succinctly explained:

> empirical evidence of the dependency ratio brought by [Bloom and] the Harvard group is only cross-sectional: it establishes a correlation between the dependency ratio and the economic growth of countries at a given point in time, which is different from the longitudinal perspective. Cross-sectional evidence from Asia invariably shows the expected correlation between a favourable dependency ratio and economic growth because countries which controlled fertility early, and therefore have a lower dependency ratio, were also those which followed favourable economic policies, and therefore have higher economic growth. This is above all a temporal correlation due to concomitant events, and not a functional relationship.

Longitudinal analysis showed that between 1950 and 2010, the correlation between dependency ratios and economic growth was 'mildly negative' in African countries: in other words, most of the growth was due to exogenous factors. Since the turn of the century, however, the correlation had turned positive, i.e. countries with the fastest growth also had higher dependency ratios. Garenne concluded that 'empirical evidence [for a demographic dividend] in Africa poses even more problems [than in Asia]', in part because – age structures and dependency ratios aside – there were so many factors that had caused extreme volatility in the growth rates of most African countries, conflict and global commodity prices among them.[38] Elizabeth Leahy Madsen at the Population Reference Bureau in Washington DC referred to the concept as 'much-ballyhooed'.[39] On the ground, Uche Charlie Isiugo-Abanihe, Professor of Demography at Nigeria's University of Ibadan, referred recently to 'the demographic dividend myth'.[40] However, for Museveni and many other African leaders aware of the rekindled zeal for fertility reduction in Africa, the 'myth' had its uses.

16

From Buzzword to Cliché: The End of 'DD'

Almost all African leaders chose to regard rapidly expanding and youthful populations as their demographic dividend. There were good reasons. For many, the reappearance on the international agenda of the 'population issue' was a threat requiring careful handling. But it provided an opportunity to express commitment to embattled and potentially destabilising young citizens.

The campaigning efforts over many years of a group of Western economists, public health advisers, demographers, family planning organisations and donors seemed to receive the ultimate rubber stamp in 2017: the AU incorporated the demographic dividend concept in its theme for the year. Eunice Mueni, a Kenyan demographer at a think-tank in Nairobi that had received funding for demographic dividend research, could write without exaggeration that 'the demographic dividend paradigm has taken African policymakers by storm, with many leaders eager to harness the opportunity presented by their countries' youthful populations to increase economic growth and employment'.[1] The question was, which demographic dividend: the one embraced by the 'just add people' school of economics, the one pushed by the 'good governance' advisers, or the one promoted by the 'have fewer children' campaigners?

The AU's 44-page *Roadmap on Harnessing the Demographic Dividend Through Investments in Youth*, adopted by member states in

January 2017, acknowledged that the dividend is not automatic. Rather, that it 'can arise when a country has a relatively large proportion of working-age population due to declining fertility, and effectively invests in their health, empowerment, education and employment through public action and private sector employment'.[2] In July the same year, delegates at the second London Summit on Family Planning were also reminded by the UN deputy secretary-general that 'the window for a demographic dividend is opening' and that the 'countries with the greatest potential to harness the demographic dividend are those undergoing fertility reduction'.[3] The fact that only 30 million of the 120 million women with unmet need for modern contraception targeted in the previous summit in 2012 had so far been reached was viewed as disappointing, but attributed to poor data, logistical complications and other technocratic shortcomings. Of the 38 'partner countries' which re-committed to 'build upon and strengthen existing commitments' from 2012, 26 were African, 10 of them among the 12 high-growth, high-fertility countries discussed in earlier chapters. This was viewed by insiders as a good sign that momentum would pick up.

At the end of the AU *Roadmap*, the leaders of 43 African countries made a brief comment. There are many references to the need for improved youth development, youth unemployment, investing in youth, the importance of youth and 'unleashing potential'. Cameroon's Paul Biya, Africa's longest-serving president, a near-nonagenarian heading a gerontocracy and largely resident in Geneva, produced the most grandiloquent contribution, calling his country's youth 'full of potential, dynamic and ambitious, inventive and conquering'. Only two presidents made any mention of population growth or fertility. President Nkurunziza of Burundi expressed an intention to ensure 'the control of population growth through family planning'; and President Idriss Déby of Chad remarked that 'we need to put in place bold interventions to manage fertility and population growth to be able to accelerate demographic transition, economic growth and job creation'.[4] All other leaders, and the *Roadmap* itself, simply ignored the essential prerequisite for a meaningful dividend

– the rapid fertility decline that generates more favourable dependency or support ratios. The approach was generally no different to that of the AU's Agenda 2063, drawn up a few years earlier: the pages of both were full of references to the demographic dividend, but there was silence regarding the issue of how high fertility and population growth might be reduced to bring it about.

The 2017 'World Population Data Sheet' from the Washington-based Population Reference Bureau suggested that the demographic dividend is 'particularly misunderstood by leaders and decision-makers in developing countries who, based on their large populations, are optimistic about the prospects of such a dividend'. In similar vein, the editors of *Africa's Population: In Search of a Demographic Dividend*, a seminal volume published the same year to which many leading Africa-focused demographers contributed, remarked that 'too many African policymakers, scholars, opinion leaders and business planners still believe that education and economic growth alone will trigger a fertility decline'.[5] In public most leaders speak from the same script: a youthful and growing population is a demographic dividend. The one, in the words of the Senegalese population statistician Cheikh Mbacké, 'seems to be seen as an unavoidable consequence' of the other.[6] This take was exemplified by Tanzania's President Magufuli in a speech in March 2020: 'In Africa, Nigeria has the largest population. It has about 202 million people and it benefits from the demographic dividends, a big population is a huge capital.'[7]

It is a moot point just where the misunderstanding lies, given political and social realities on the ground. In some – perhaps many – cases, 'misunderstanding' is quite deliberate. Many African leaders are sticking to the 'development is the best contraceptive' mantra embraced by their predecessors at the World Population Conference in Bucharest in 1974, and proclaiming that fast-expanding populations – and youthfulness – are Africa's greatest asset in an ageing world.[8] Given that conviction, why should leaders get hung up on a distinction between a larger workforce and a growing working-age share of the population? After all, for decades Western economists had proclaimed that a swelling labour force was a source of economic growth – more workers equalled more output.[9] Was there any reason to change tack just because some of their successors had now built a Trojan horse from which to press for smaller families with renewed vigour and urgency? Never mind what the small print says about lower fertility, if these people loudly declare that your country 'has a substantial demographic opportunity on the horizon', as Bloom had of Nigeria, or that its demographic dividend 'could raise per capita incomes by more than 30% by 2030, increase the economy to 2.7 times that of its current size, and lift 27 million additional people out of poverty'.[10] Embracing such a narrative was pragmatic politics in the face of sky-high youth unemployment rates, inadequate job creation and, in Nigeria's case, GDP per capita that collapsed by *one-third* in the five years following the prognosis cited above, back to the level recorded in 1980. It does not require abandonment of 'just add people' – or 'greatness is in numbers', as Jimi Wanjigi put it – economics, even if that has self-evidently not paid off yet.

'What we do with that population of youth today will determine the future of work in the world,' declared Akinwumi Adesina, president of the AfDB, in 2019, 'Africa must become the brimming workshop of the world.'[11] In the same publication – *Creating Decent Jobs* – the term 'demographic dividend' appears 85 times. It was interpreted simultaneously as 'an unprecedented opportunity to generate inclusive growth and reduce poverty' and an opportunity for the continent to be 'the main supplier of the world's workforce'.[12] In the publicity material promoting the 2018 Africa Investment Forum in Johannesburg, the continent's number one advantage was listed as its 'growing demographic'.

Another compelling reason to 'misunderstand' is to block the implicit bossiness and patronising with which this latest Western policy prescription, based on 'evidence' from the past in other parts of the world, is often thrust upon them. References by leading proponents of demographic dividend theory to 'governments that have historically had difficulty in promoting economic growth… [and] improving the lives of Africans'[13] in their countries, and admonitions that 'Africans need to get serious about eliminating gender inequality',[14] are unlikely to go down well. Even if presidents are not aware of all such slights, their essence imbues the dialogue, the conferences and the tacitly – or overtly – conditional offers of funding for health initiatives that incorporate family planning in the guise of 'sexual and reproductive health and rights'.

Ample encouragement for a partial understanding of demographic dividends can be plucked even from World Bank and IMF publications. In a 2016 article entitled 'Surfing the demographic wave' in the IMF's *Finance and Development* magazine, the authors state that sub-Saharan Africa 'will be the world's key demographic player this century', and that 'if policies support productive jobs for [the] new workers, the increase in the workforce will lead to higher growth and rising income per person – *voilà*: the demographic dividend'.[15] *Voilà* indeed – to the lay reader, the 'just add people' economic theory is modified only by the need to provide them with employment. Even if it was only the 'first' demographic dividend being referred to – the 'automatic' and much smaller one – distinctions between different definitions of the theory have long since blurred. This is even truer for media and business in Africa, who have neither the time nor inclination to research the origins of what is now a catch-all concept to be defined by the user. Phrases like 'the demographic dividend from population growth'[16] (in a South African business news publication) and 'clearly the boom of [Africa's] youth is a demographic dividend'[17] (from a leading African banker) are now the norm.

There are, of course, countries in Northern and Southern Africa and among Africa's island nations where the demographic transition is almost complete; and leaders and governments in Kenya, Ghana, Ethiopia, Rwanda and Malawi have at different times decided that their development objectives are best served by lower fertility and slowing population growth and have acted accordingly. But they are still a minority. Many of the other governments have rewritten population policies or drawn up a 'Demographic Dividend Roadmap' funded by donors, and have plenty of skilled ministers and civil servants well versed in demographic dividend speak. There is funding readily available for backing adoption of appropriate policies. The

Ouagadougou Partnership of nine francophone countries in Western Africa has secured more than US$100 million, and the World Bank has promised more than US$200 million to the Sahel Women's Empowerment and Demographic Dividend initiative. The Ouagadougou Partnership governments even committed to spend 5% of their national budgets annually on family planning to drive the TFR below three births by 2030. It was remarked at the time that 'the idea that Europeans may again be setting the African agenda rather than the Africans doing so is a feeling many people can not shake'.[18] In most of Western, Eastern and Middle Africa, as we have seen in earlier chapters, there is no great enthusiasm at the highest level for implementing or even adopting policies that might support one of the essential catalysts for a demographic dividend – namely, lower fertility.

Jean-Pierre Guengant has reviewed the development plans of a dozen, mostly francophone, countries and found that 'generally no attention is paid to the demographic dimensions of development, and most plans do not even include demographic projections'. All are 'striving to become emerging economies', he continues, '[but] there is no mention in the corresponding documents that all emerging economies have already achieved their fertility transition or are near in doing so'.[19] Meanwhile, with the possible exception of one or two island states, none of the countries approaching the end of fertility transition can realistically point to an economic miracle having been unleashed, or even supported, by lower fertility. If a dividend has been received by any of them, it is best not mentioned because it would make underlying economic performance in recent years appear even weaker.

Much has been made of President Museveni's 'conversion' and the inclusion of family planning in Uganda's national development plan. 'Museveni, historically an opponent of family planning promotion, has been convinced and other leaders are showing similar signs,' remarked John Cleland in 2017.[20] The president is by common consent one of the canniest political operators of the post-independence era; and Uganda has a patchy record on policy implementation. It is true that Museveni endorsed the 'Uganda Family Planning Costed Implementation Plan' in 2014, targeting a 50% modern contraceptive prevalence rate among women by 2020. That year he also hosted a conference in Uganda, at which he said that family planning should not be equated with population control and also that population size per se was not the problem: the biggest issue was the inadequacy of economic growth and transformation. The president has expressed his support for measures that improve the health of women and children. He has also said that having 'too many children is not good for development', and that if there were conservative religious leaders who could demonstrate that they can adequately take care of 15 children, he would be happy to meet them. But *pole pole* – steady progress – is the name of the game. The contraceptive target was missed by a country mile, the prevalence rate in 2020 being estimated at 30%; and Museveni's speeches in 2018 (see Chapter 2) were a reminder to *wazungus* that fertility, family size and population growth remain strictly sovereign or personal matters. It was a message of enduring, widespread appeal across much of Africa, as was his assertion that the continent remains underpopulated.

Eunice Mueni reflected that 'without localised ownership and financial commitment, the demographic dividend will, like other commitments in the past, end up being a mere development buzz-word, with no tangible action and benefits for most countries'. She noted that where studies had been made of the demographic dividend, these had all been entirely funded by UNFPA or other Western donors; and where countries had incorporated the research into national development plans, it was with no consideration of how the 'roadmaps' – implementation – would be funded. 'Is the demographic dividend an African driven agenda, or is it one of the many global population initiatives that developing countries, and in particular African countries, align themselves [with] to tap into the international funding boom?' she asked.[21]

In Mueni's view, Africa's leaders understood exactly how the 'Global North' was thinking about population growth after Cairo in 1994, and played along. The family planning and sexual and reproductive health and rights programmes in every country in Africa were substantially donor-funded; and the underwhelming results of the UN's Family Planning 2020 initiative, which monitored progress with the fulfilment of pledges made at the two London Summits, showed how weak the commitment to change was in most high-fertility countries. In similar vein, Chimaraoke Izugbara, professor-at-large at the School of Public Health at Wits University in South Africa, has noted that

> for many reasons... African political leaders are yet to go beyond rhetoric and work earnestly to create an enabling environment for harnessing the demographic dividend... economic models and other fiscal projections of how much wealthier and well-off the region will be in a few years – if the right investments are made today – do not appear to resonate well with African political leaders or inspire them sufficiently.[22]

If there is frustration or outrage on the part of outsiders about the implications for women, a historical perspective on the handling of population issues in and with Africa should at least temper any sense of surprise.

Outside government, where it has even been heard of, the mention of a demographic dividend mostly arouses suspicion or a weary sense of *déja vu*. Some regard it as the latest tool being deployed to enforce birth control in African countries; others as the latest guise of neocolonial domination, a direct successor to SAPs in a continent deemed a 'perpetual testing ground for unsubstantiated economic theories'.[23] More prosaically, Carlos Lopes, one of Africa's most prominent and respected public figures, simply reckons that 'the demographic dividend is not happening', that concepts like this and 'sustainable development' are 'not cutting it' in Africa.[24] He remains profoundly optimistic that spectacular development is attainable, but not by following manuals drawn up almost exclusively by non-Africans.

Beyond Africa, the demographic dividend narrative is now a cliché. Aside from the technical criticisms of methodology and a sense that the theory is too contrived, too ivory-tower, there is the plain fact that it appears increasingly irrelevant as far as Africa is concerned. By its own criteria, there is no discernible prospect of a demographic dividend of any meaningful size. UNPD's medium-variant projection for 2050 shows that the dependency ratio across sub-Saharan Africa will only improve quite slowly over the next three decades – far slower than it did in Asian regions. GDP growth would also have to be higher and far more consistent in future than over the past 50 years to 'tick the boxes', a requirement few African economists would consider plausible in present circumstances.

According to Kate Meagher at the LSE, the population profiles of most African countries '[look] more like a demographic liability than a demographic dividend'.[25] In inter-tropical Africa, the current pace of the demographic transition and dearth of jobs that might maintain, or ideally raise, productivity means, in the words of former World Bank economist Louise Fox, that any dividend 'will be realized in pennies at a time, rather than in a major boost to growth'.[26] One of the less fanciful studies quantifying potential dividends shows that if Nigeria's TFR follows the path of UNPD's low-variant projection, an unlikely supposition at the moment, the age-structure dividend – the 'first' or automatic demographic dividend – could amount to an annual increment to GDP per capita of 0.225% over 50 years.[27] While this is a positive rather than negative sum, and statistically significant, a dividend of this magnitude would at best be a minor curiosity, no matter what occurs in the Nigerian economy and society over the next half-century. For low- and lower-middle-income African countries the acknowledged objective is sustained annual GDP growth of at least 6–7% to achieve middle-income status, which translates into annual growth in GDP per capita of about 4–5%.

Finally, to increase productivity and boost savings to the degree needed to generate a meaningful demographic dividend would require acceleration in the structural transformation of economies.

Figure 19: Total dependency ratio (ratio of children (0–14 years) and the elderly (65+ years) to working-age population (15–64 years)), in selected world regions and China, 1950–2050

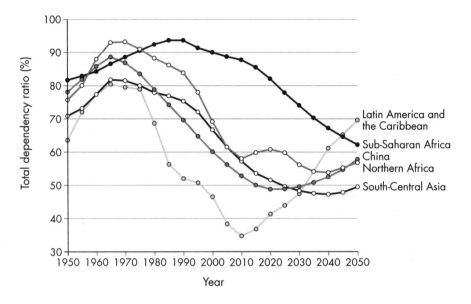

Source: UNPD, *World Population Prospects: The 2015 Revision.*

For countries where two-thirds of the workforce remain in agriculture and small family or household businesses, where education and health costs inflate relentlessly at a faster rate than incomes, a demographic dividend is simply a chimera. As Robert Eastwood and Michael Lipton pointed out when the dividend bandwagon started to roll, the issue for the time being in most sub-Saharan countries is whether current consumption can even be maintained, given the low savings rate after the ravages of the 1970s and 1980s and low productivity.[28] Echoing Lopes, scepticism does not mean that the outlook is necessarily bleak, simply that 'Africa' is not 'co-operating' with this particular econometric model.

Africa is not alone in 'failing' to meet the extreme requirements demanded by a theory, the poster child of which is a single, now industrialised sub-region – East Asia, and some countries in South and Southeast Asia. An IMF paper published in 2011 claimed that India was the recipient of a 'substantial' demographic dividend, age-structure changes having annually generated 40–50% of the improvement in GDP per capita during the 1980s and 1990s. These ongoing changes were forecast to add 2% a year to GDP per capita over the next 20 years.[29] On the other hand, Latin America, the Middle East and Northern Africa and the emerging economies of Eastern Europe had all 'failed'. In Latin America, this was the case despite a more rapid improvement in the dependency ratio than in any other developing region – it declined to a level in 2010 that was about half that of India (36% vs 66%) (see Figure 19). The absence of a dividend in Latin America is attributed by some to 'institutional failings' and insufficient job creation.[30] Presumably, then, India did not suffer from 'institutional failings', and its job creation was superior to that of Latin America? Like Iran, which according to Bloomberg is also apparently in 'full demographic-dividend mode'?[31]

India, like Africa, needs to generate 12 million decent jobs a year to absorb new entrants to the labour market, but created fewer than 1 million of them a year between 2012 and 2018. Furthermore, the biggest rises in India's working-age population between the beginning of the century and the mid-2020s are in the poorest states with the worst employment outlook. Uttar Pradesh alone will account for 25% of the increase. The result is that by the mid-2020s nearly half of India's working-age population will reside in its eight most impoverished states.[32] A further anomaly in the narrative of India, the recipient of a 'substantial' demographic dividend, and Latin America, which failed to capitalise on its changing age structures, is that two-thirds of the Indian population live in extreme poverty, a far higher percentage than in most African countries and a completely different order of magnitude from Latin America, where the prevalence of extreme poverty has fallen to just 10%. In contrast to the claims of the IMF paper, an article in the *Financial Times* the following year highlighted the fact that a young population only represented a demographic dividend 'if there are enough jobs for them – and that is not the case for India'. The article was titled 'The sad illusion of

India's demographic dividend'.[33] Perhaps Africa's 'failure' will not be as discernible or significant as some suggest.

The final nail in the coffin of the demographic dividend concept has been hammered by scholars questioning whether the dividend is a demographic one after all. Wolfgang Lutz and colleagues have plausibly argued that the 'demographic' dividend is actually the product of increasing human capital, specifically improved education, more than changing age structures. As we have seen, they argue that it is the education of girls and young women which triggers the fertility decline that drives the fall in dependency ratios which in turn produces a 'dividend'. Uptake of modern contraceptive methods is a subsidiary factor. Their analysis of the impact of changes in age structure and human capital on the economic growth of 165 countries during 1980–2015 showed a 'clear dominance of improving education over age structure'.[34] Jane O'Sullivan, honorary senior research fellow at the University of Queensland, has argued that the demographic dividend is in fact an infrastructure dividend, concluding in a 2017 paper that high expenditure on the development of infrastructure 'explains [the] economic stimulus [during rapid fertility transitions] to an extent that changes in age structure do not'.[35]

In 2019, a World Bank publication stated that 'fertility has remained stubbornly high in Africa'. Apart from being a generalisation, the choice of adverb was revealing; the dictionary definition of 'stubborn' is usually along these lines – 'having or showing dogged determination not to change one's attitude or position on something, especially in spite of good arguments or reasons to do so'. This really does not read well, no matter how compelling the 'arguments' may be.[36] Four areas of policy action were identified 'to accelerate Africa's poverty reduction'; the first was 'accelerate the fertility transition'. For many observers, this is an example of 'back to the future'/groundhog day, redolent as it is of the World Bank publications of the 1970s and 1980s. For *fifty years* the World Bank, the family planning industry, environmental campaigners and others have been telling African governments to curtail the fertility of their people. This is nothing if not persistent. However, the attempt to show that fertility decline can potentially assist poverty reduction and raise economic growth is simply not convincing, possibly because, for all the econometric modelling, the 'proof' is really no more watertight than 50 years ago.

The demographic dividend era is probably all but over. The appearance of successor – or usurper – narratives is among the indications. One of these has already been heavily pushed in Southern Africa: the 'Fourth Industrial Revolution' driven by 'big tech'. Devised by the World Economic Forum, '4IR' technologies are collectively packaged 'with futurist conviction and fantastical economic forecasts of exponential growth and job creation', according to Professor Alison Gillwald, director of Research ICT Africa, headquartered in Cape Town. They, like the demographic dividend, promise 'unprecedented economic prosperity' if skilfully deployed.

The 4IR concept has gained traction with multinational corporations, regional economic bodies, development banks and international consultancies. Before the Covid-19 pandemic, according to Tefo Mohapi in his *iAfrikan* 'Daily Brief', 'there was one buzzword that was rolling off the tongues of almost every single African policymaker, the 4th Industrial Revolution… It reached such heights that it became clear that most who garnished their speeches with "4IR" clearly did not even understand what they were talking about. It was like the parsley sitting randomly on your main course dish.'[37]

Among African leaders, President Ramaphosa is to the fore among those eager to embrace the latest 'development tool'. The South African government has been advised by an international consultancy that it can look forward to 5 trillion rand (US$340 billion) in economic benefits if it gets the 4IR 'right', and could create as many as 4 million new jobs. Professor Gillwald counsels caution regarding the global hype generated by what she judges to be 'one of the most successful lobbying and policy influence instruments of our time'. In her view, the 4IR narrative is 'reductionist' and 'utilitarian', but it 'fills a vacuum for many countries that haven't publicly invested in what they want their own futures to look like'. All the goals are 'objectives of current policy that South Africa has failed to achieve to different degrees over the past 25 years'; and Gillwald concludes that 'there is nothing inherent in so-called 4IR technologies that will necessarily result in economic growth, job creation or empowerment of the marginalised'.[38] For his part, Mohapi is concerned about the apparent confusion among African policymakers of automation processes and artificial intelligence. More important, however, is 'that certain things need to be available before we can even talk about 4IR. Some things you can't just "leapfrog".'[39] This all sounds rather familiar.

17

'A Challenge of Mammoth Proportions'[1]

Alongside a rapid fertility transition, adequate creation of jobs is an essential pillar of demographic dividend theory. Its leading theorists and exponents appear to gloss over the realities of labour markets in Africa. During the 2020s, 250 million young African men and women will reach working age. For decades, demand for employment has far outstripped supply. How rising unemployment, underemployment and vulnerable employment are addressed as the numbers get ever larger is of immense importance to every country, and to the world.

Each year during the 2020s, almost 30 million young Africans will reach the age of 15 and be defined as 'working age'.[2] Not all will want (or need) jobs immediately. An increasing number will continue in education, at least until the end of secondary school (although all but students from the wealthiest families will simultaneously be working to pay for education). In some countries, many girls will marry and have children instead. There are other reasons to delay or reject searching for employment, but by the age of 18 or 19 a vast majority of young men, in particular, need work. Between 2020 and 2030, Africa's working-age population – everyone between the ages of 15 and 64 – will swell by about one-third, from 750 million to almost 1 billion.

By 2035, Africa will have a larger workforce than China or India. They are countries, of course, whereas Africa is a continent; but as they have the largest labour forces in the world the comparison is instructive. By 2050, Africa's working-age population will have more than doubled from its current size to 1.5 billion. By the end point of the AU's Agenda 2063, it will have tripled in half a century to reach almost 2 billion.

Growth will be concentrated in the African regions with less developed economies. In Western and Eastern Africa the working-age population will more than triple by 2063, while in Middle Africa it will quadruple. Five countries will alone account for almost half of the total growth in labour supply: Nigeria, DRC, Ethiopia, Tanzania and Uganda.[3] In the 2060s Asia will still be home to about half of the global working-age population, but by then Africa's share will have increased from less than 10% to more than 30% in a century.

Since the mid-1990s the growth rate of many African economies, assisted by a boom in the prices of various commodities, has surpassed those of their East and South Asian counterparts, averaging about 5% a year (and even more in low-income countries). This is a significant turnaround from the previous quarter-century, and it was not derailed by the global financial crisis in 2007–8. However, it is a recovery that has not been accompanied by a commensurate improvement in the supply, quality and productivity of jobs. 'Jobless growth' in Africa is being cast with increasing frequency as a 'global challenge'.[4]

In Asian 'success stories', the substantial expansion of labour-intensive manufacturing, particularly for export markets, provided many more waged jobs in the second half of the twentieth century; and the relative importance of agriculture in the economy and as a livelihood declined. Most African economies have also undergone a degree of structural transformation, but of a different type – mostly expanding 'services' – and extent. As far as jobs are concerned, 'street hawkers typify city employment, and subsistence farmers typify agriculture', concluded a recent AfDB study.[5]

With the mind-boggling expansion of the working-age population, the IMF estimates that African economies need to create 18 million additional jobs every year for 20 years from 2015 to 2035.[6] It has described this as an 'extremely rapid and possibly unprecedented'[7] rate of job creation, but one that is necessary if most of those seeking work are to find the means to earn something. In common with the AfDB and the ILO, the IMF specifies that these jobs need to be 'decent' and 'high-productivity'. The World Bank presents an estimate of 15 million new jobs being needed each year until at least 2030;[8] the AfDB has a lower estimate of 10–12 million annually during the 2020s. According to one estimate, by 2050 the annual requirement in sub-Saharan Africa countries alone will have reached 30 million – and the working-age population will still be growing.[9]

Since 2000, sub-Saharan countries have added an average of about 9 million jobs a year. At least two-thirds have been in subsistence or smallholder agriculture, self-employment or providing low value-added services – activities that tend to be poorly remunerated and precarious. Less than a third of the jobs – 2.6 million – have been in waged employment, with only about 200,000–300,000 provided by the industrials sector. Opportunities for decent employment for young women are even scarcer than for young men.[10] Only 12% of working-age women were in waged employment in the whole region in 2016.[11]

Waged employment is prized, but no panacea: it does not always offer better pay or conditions than self-employment or 'informal' work. Almost 40% of waged employees in sub-Saharan Africa subsist on less than US$1.90 a day, the international poverty line. The proportion is higher still among working youth,[12] who are in the most precarious position of all. When launching its 'Jobs for Youth in Africa' strategy in 2015, the AfDB estimated that one-third of the 420 million Africans aged 15–35 – the AU's definition of youth – were unemployed or discouraged from looking for work. A further one-third were 'vulnerably' employed, and only one in six were in waged employment of some kind.[13] About 40% of all youth are 'food insecure'.[14] The AfDB has warned that if youth unemployment rates remain unchanged, more than 250 million young Africans – almost half of all those not still in education – will 'lack an economic stake in the system by 2025'.[15]

According to the AfDB, Africa has the lowest percentage of wage earners in the labour force of any region in the world.[16] In most of its economies, smallholder and subsistence agriculture remains the bedrock of employment, providing, on average, more than half of all employment and a quarter of GDP – much as it did at the start of the century. For everyone else, young or old, the informal economy is now the default economy. Almost two-thirds of global employment is provided by informal work. In Africa, the proportion is closer to 90%, about 20% higher than any other world region. If agriculture is excluded, the proportion is around 70%.[17] There is considerable variation between countries, ranging from 95% in Benin and Burkina Faso to 34% in South Africa.[18] Among African youth aged 15–24, 95% of those in work are informally employed.

Informal work covers a multitude of jobs, from motorbike taxiing to street-vending to waste-picking to domestic work to casual labour. Many formal enterprises – factories, transport companies and even government offices – hire people informally. But there are prevalent common characteristics of this type of work. Jobs tend to be insecure, of limited duration, badly paid, with low productivity and without decent working conditions or social protection. About 80% of informal workers fall within the category of 'working poor'. Few people operate in the sector by choice.

Africa's present and future requirement for additional (and better) jobs is seldom presented in a global context. The IMF's estimate of 18 million high-productivity jobs a year means a total of 180 million jobs during the 2020s, equivalent to 80% of the size of Europe's current labour force,[19] or more than double the total number of manufacturing jobs in all 37 OECD countries.[20] It is roughly equivalent to the total employed, formally and informally, in the manufacturing sectors of all sub-Saharan countries at present;[21] and roughly six times the number of formal jobs in all sectors currently being created each year in the whole of Africa.[22] To generate 360 million decent jobs between 2015 and 2035 would be equivalent to about 80% of all manufacturing jobs, formal and informal, in the world at present.[23]

Table 23: Africa's youth (15-24) and working-age (15-64) populations, 2000-50 (UNPD medium-variant projections)

Year	Population 15-24 (million)/ percentage of total Africa population (%)	Population 15-64 (million)/ percentage of total Africa population (%)
2000	164/20	437/54
2010	206/20	574/55
2020	258/19	753/56
2030	334/20	988/59
2040	398/19	1,260/61
2050	456/18	1,549/62

Source: UNPD, *World Population Prospects: The 2019 Revision.*

Even the AfDB's lower figure of 10–12 million new jobs a year suggests a total requirement of 200–240 million between 2015 and 2035. That is the same order of magnitude as the 200 million China created during its astonishing – and largely unrecognised at the time – economic 'take-off' between the late 1970s and mid-1990s.[24] It shows that such a formidable endeavour is not impossible; but China is a single, autocratic country whereas Africa comprises more than 50 sovereign nations with limited economic and political co-operation between regions and countries. Even if Africa as a whole were able to replicate over the next two to three decades the economic growth record, job-creation and transformational changes in economic structure achieved by the 'tiger' economies of Southeast Asia (Hong Kong, Singapore, South Korea and Taiwan) towards the end of the twentieth century, and their 'cubs' (Malaysia, Indonesia, Thailand, Vietnam and the Philippines) in this century, the continent would be hard-pressed to absorb a labour force of these dimensions in productive employment.

Western economists are mostly cautious or fatalistic in their prognoses on the employment issue. A report by the World Economic Forum estimated that only about a quarter of those seeking jobs by

2035 will find 'stable' wage-paying employment.[25] Former World Bank economist Louise Fox has pointed out that 'all other regions made it through this period of peak youth share of the labour force without facing a crisis. Africa should be able to as well.'[26] Where some even continue to talk of demographic dividends, LSE's Kate Meagher anticipates 'catastrophic youth unemployment, expanding informality and a rising tide of vulnerable and increasingly disaffected labour'.[27]

At the opposite end of the spectrum, Justin Yifu Lin, then chief economist of the World Bank, declared at the height of 'Africa Rising' fever that if China were to maintain its double-digit annual rate of economic growth, 85 million manufacturing jobs would 'migrate' as the sector moved up the value chain and wage costs of unskilled workers rose. For regions seeking to industrialise rapidly, Africa included, he regarded this as akin to China, the global hub of light manufacturing, leaving a 'huge pile of so many US$100 bills on the sidewalks'.[28]

If a manufacturing jobs 'bonanza' of the magnitude envisaged by Lin materialised, there would be fierce competition for them globally. Africa is only one of many locations touted as 'the next factory of the world',[29] and few of its economies have labour unit costs lower than leading Asian and Latin American competitors, or infrastructure and a business environment to match. The World Economic Forum report estimated that at the end of the 2000s unskilled labour costs in African Special Economic Zones (SEZs) were significantly higher than in SEZs in Asia. In Kenya and Ghana they were about double the prevailing costs in Bangladesh, and higher than those of an SEZ in Vietnam; in Nigeria wages were higher still – double those of Vietnam's SEZ and four times Bangladesh's.[30] A more recent study by the OECD and the AU estimated that the Africa–Asia labour productivity ratio has worsened since 2000, from 67% to 50%.[31]

Although the populations of some East Asian countries – China, Japan, South Korea – are stabilising or declining, they still need to create many new jobs each year. In China's case there are about 20 million new entrants to the labour market annually. Other parts of Asia will continue to add huge numbers to the global working-age population. In India the number of potential workers aged between 15 and 34 now exceeds the total populations of Japan, Indonesia and South Korea; as mentioned earlier, India, like Africa, needs to create at least 12 million decent new jobs a year indefinitely. Closer to, and overlapping with, Africa, the Middle East and Northern Africa region also needs to create 300 million jobs by 2050 according to the World Bank.[32] The Harvard economist Dani Rodrik is one of many to highlight a 'chronic state of shortage of goods jobs' globally.[33]

If Western economists are mostly restrained in their views about the prospects for job creation, the same cannot be said of respected politicians, economists and experts in Africa. Their opinions are the real bellwether, relating as they do to individual countries rather than generalising about the continent. On Africa Day 2018 Jay Naidoo, founding general secretary of the Congress of South African Trade Unions (COSATU) and a minister in Nelson Mandela's first cabinet, wrote in a newspaper column that 'Africa's greatest challenge is that its dynamic and ever-growing youth population is mostly devoid of prospects'. He continued:

> Today we have a rising tide of anger of a younger generation that is alienated from the political and economic narrative of the day. A system that more often than not leaves them behind. I hear them. I see them. They say 'we are exhausted by the talk, talk and talk. Our lives are littered with the broken promises of leaders. Our current leaders are out of touch. We are the richest continent under the ground but we are the poorest in the world. It's time for leadership and governance. It's time the older generation moved out of the way.'[34]

Among South Africans aged between 15 and 34, the country's definition of youth, the unemployment rate is over 50%.[35] For 15–24 year-olds it is higher still – the highest in the world according to the ILO, just ahead of the Occupied Palestinian Territory.[36] In 2019, the ruling African National Congress declared unemployment 'the single biggest challenge' facing South Africa.

Africa's two other largest economies are equally afflicted by unemployment, especially among the youth. In May 2019, the chief economist at a leading consulting firm in Nigeria asked very publicly, 'When will Nigeria declare youth unemployment a national emergency and take action?'[37] In Egypt, where 60% of the population are under 30, about one in three young people are unemployed. The political economist Adel Abdel Ghafar warns that joblessness is a 'ticking time bomb' and that 'if the Egyptian government does not deal with the specific problems of unemployment soon, it will likely face instability – and perhaps another uprising – in the years to come'.[38]

Together, the economies of Nigeria, South Africa and Egypt account for almost half Africa's GDP and more than a quarter of its population. What happens in these countries has a marked effect on the economies of Western Africa, Southern Africa and Northern Africa respectively, and on external perceptions of the entire content. They all remain substantially dependent on natural-resource extraction – oil or minerals – which bolsters government revenue but does not generate large numbers of jobs. The same is true of Algeria, the fourth-largest economy, and Angola, the fifth-largest until global oil prices plummeted in 2014.

Africa's small and medium-sized economies, even those with creditable growth records over the past two decades, are in the same boat as the continent's economic giants with respect to jobs. In August 2018, the Kenyan MP Anthony Oluoch called on parliament to declare youth unemployment a national disaster. His claim that it had reached 55% was challenged, with official statistics showing that the 3.5 million unemployed and underemployed young Kenyans constituted 'only' about one-third of those in their age bracket.[39] The difference is one of precise extent, but not of degree.

On the other side of the continent, in the Sahel countries of Burkina Faso, Chad, Mali, Mauritania and Niger, the number of people aged between 15 and 35 is set to increase by 46 million by 2050. This increase is equivalent to the total population of the two most populous of the

Figure 20: Informal employment rate by gender, 2018

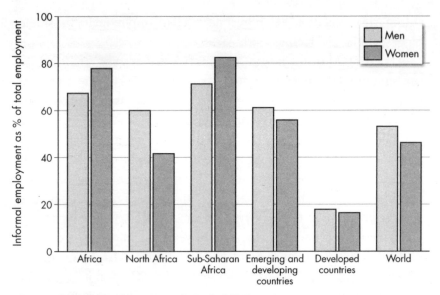

Source: AfDB (2019b), African Economic Outlook 2019.

Figure 21: Agriculture remains a larger employer in Africa than in other world regions, 1990–2010

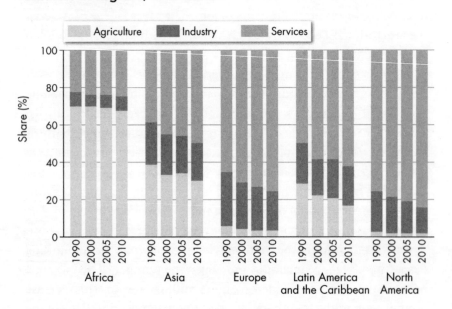

Source: AfDB (2019a), Creating Decent Jobs: Strategies, Policies, and Instruments.

Figure 22: Employment by sector in Africa, 2018

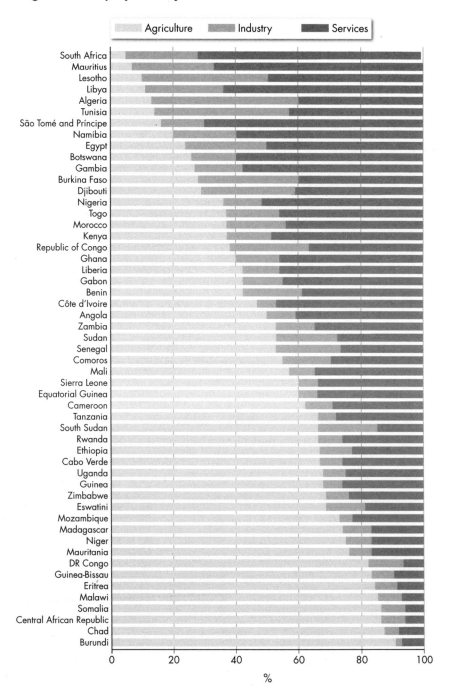

Source: AfDB (2019a), *Creating Decent Jobs: Strategies, Policies, and Instruments* (using data from ILO).

five in 2019, Niger and Burkina Faso.[40] For most young people, the chances of finding decent waged employment – in the formal or traditional economies – are slim.[41] In Mali, 300,000 reach working age every year but the economy is creating fewer than 50,000 jobs annually, few of which are either waged or decent.[42]

Headline unemployment figures in single figures (or even those in double digits) are almost always misleading. The AfDB concedes that governments have had 'difficulties convincing their national constituencies that the demand for labour… is so buoyant'.[43] Data is sometimes scarce, although availability has improved considerably in recent years; it may also not be easily comparable between countries. But the principal reason why figures are misleading is that in the strictest sense, as defined by the ILO,[44] unemployment is a luxury few can afford in countries with minimal or non-existent social safety nets. A better indication of lived reality is the rate of *under*employment. In Africa this is the highest anywhere in the world, affecting two-thirds of its active workforce.[45] Africa also has the highest proportion of workers in 'vulnerable' employment, defined as family and own-account workers and characterised by low earnings, low productivity and difficult – or atrocious – working conditions.[46]

A 2018 Afrobarometer public opinion survey carried out in 34 countries found that unemployment was cited as the single biggest problem – by far – that citizens would like their government to address. Almost three-quarters of 46,000 respondents rated their governments most poorly for their record in creating jobs.[47] Another survey in the same number of countries showed that two-thirds of business leaders cited youth unemployment and underemployment as the top risk to operating in their country within the next 10 years, rating these higher than 'failure of national governance', 'energy price shock', 'failure of critical infrastructure', 'fiscal crises' and runaway inflation.[48] The next chapter will set out the detail behind the sobering headline figures in some of Africa's largest economies.

The jobs 'emergency' is nothing new. When predicting at the end of the 1980s – quite accurately, as it turned out – that the labour force in sub-Saharan Africa would swell from 230 million to 610 million by 2020, the World Bank envisaged that 'only a fraction of the new workers who come on the job market will be able to find employment in the modern sector, even under the most optimistic of scenarios'.[49] The problem was exacerbated by the enormous job losses that accompanied the implementation, with varying degrees of vigour, of World Bank and IMF SAPs.[50] Formal job creation had virtually ceased in most of Africa's economies due to massive cuts in the civil service and state-owned enterprises, the backbone of nascent 'formal' sectors. State-sponsored and -planned industrial policy, including the protection of infant industries, was considered anathema by the World Bank. 'With SAPs, Africans were told by their betters to stop supporting industry because doing so was "wasteful",' says the Malawian economist Grieve Chelwa. 'Subsidies to industry were reduced. Protective trade barriers were removed. Planning for industry was done away with.'[51]

Whereas the rise in employment and population remained broadly in equilibrium in Latin America and Asia in the 1980s, in Africa annual population growth of 3% materially exceeded the 1% annual increase in jobs.[52] In the words of the Senegalese economist Ndongo Samba Sylla, a 'descent into hell'[53] was under way for many African economies and all jobseekers. He continues:

> Instead of making economies grow fast, the structural adjust-ment policy actually had a contractive impact. Fast-growing populations made matters worse. Formal employment was in ever shorter supply. Impoverished peasants looked for livelihoods in the cities. Factory workers lost jobs. Housewives wanted to earn money to supplement the dwindling incomes of households' main breadwinners, and so did youngsters who dropped out of school. Ever more families could no longer afford school fees or educational materials. Cohorts of young girls in disadvantaged neighbourhoods resorted to prostitution to earn the money they needed for eating once a day or obtaining sanitary napkins.[54]

The answer to the jobs conundrum, according to Western experts, lay in self-reliance, self-employment and the informal sector transforming itself into 'a seedbed for entrepreneurs, not a hotbed of racketeers'.[55] A chapter in the World Bank report *Sub-Saharan Africa: From Crisis to Sustainable Growth* was titled 'Fostering African entrepreneurship'. According to its detractors, this 'solution' to the dearth of jobs was the 'wishful thinking of bootstrap ideologues'. The new reality for most was 'informal survivalism' and 'forced entrepreneurialism' entailing, among other indignities, the 'extreme abuse of women'[56] and the absence of any opportunity, or even hope, for youth.*

Fast-forward two decades to the mid-2000s and many African countries were in the midst of a commodity-fuelled economic boom. However, the cumulative effect and continuing rate of population growth meant that even in those countries where GDP performance since the 1960s looked quite good, in per capita terms there was no improvement, or even a decline. For example, a rise in GDP averaging 7% a year over five decades in Burkina Faso, the star performer in francophone Africa, was reduced to a mere doubling in per capita terms. Few francophone countries showed any advance by this measure,[57] whereas South Korea, Singapore and other Southeast Asian economies had sustained annual increases in GDP per capita almost in double digits. Sheer weight of numbers also continued to impact employment: the extent to which African economies and labour markets had informalised caused considerable alarm inside and outside the continent. In language redolent of *The Population Bomb*, some in the West referred to a 'plague of informality'.[58] Decent work opportunities were as scarce for the best educated as for the unskilled.

In the face of a 'tide of young jobseekers', the AU launched its 'Youth Decade' Plan of Action 2009–18 – just as demographic

---

* In 1991 Tiyambe Zeleza offered a wry and interesting perspective on the 'discovery' of the informal sector in Kenya: 'The 1972 ILO Report of Employment in Kenya elevated the informal sector from an invisible backwater of the labour market into a locomotive to pull the country out of its deepening crisis.' Tiyambe Zeleza (1991), 'Economic policy and performance in Kenya since Independence', *Transafrican Journal of History*, Vol. 20.

dividend theory went mainstream. 'There is full recognition of the dire challenges and great opportunities of youth and most African countries are making efforts to involve young people in political and decision-making processes,' the plan announced on its opening page. In Northern Africa, uprisings in Tunisia, Libya and Egypt emphasised that those efforts were insignificant. In the wake of the 'Arab Spring', there was speculation and acute fear that the unrest would spread to sub-Saharan countries. In 2012, the ECA chose 'Promoting Youth Employment' as the special theme for its 2012 *African Economic Outlook*; and the AfDB launched its 'Jobs for Youth in Africa' strategy. This aspires to facilitate, through a 'suite of flexible financial tools', the creation of 25 million decent jobs and 'positively impact' 50 million young Africans by 2025. In 2019, the bank's president, Akinwumi Adesina, boldly asserted that if the 'unemployment crisis' for African youth were solved, Africa's GDP would grow by an incremental US$500 billion – one-fifth of current GDP – each year for the next 30 years. As we have seen, this 'pivot to youth' chimed perfectly with a pared-down version of the demographic dividend.

Well-intended initiatives, 'development strategies' calling for a 'holistic approach', #youthengagement and bold promises made at gatherings of African presidents abound. Workshops and conferences to discuss youth and youth unemployment are two-a-*naira*. A few years ago it was common for there to be no young speakers at such events, and certainly no young female speakers. 'Youth representatives' were sometimes grey-haired men in their fifties. That has changed for the better, and some leaders are demonstrably taking the plight of 15–35-year-olds – a majority of most national populations – more seriously. Others are less alarmed by mass youth unemployment than donor governments and international financial institutions like to believe.

The difficulty is making headway. The verdict from the South Africa-based Institute for Security Studies was that the achievements of the AU's 'Youth Decade' were 'on the whole, underwhelming', as the AU lacks 'an effective way to mobilise national governments around youth issues'.[59] A plethora of 'tiny youth projects with tiny results'[60] will not prove sufficient, and with many of them governments have no 'skin in the game'. The ILO regularly produces a *Success Africa* publication with details of initiatives in various countries that are said to have delivered 'excellent decent work results'. Of the 42 described in the 2019 edition, the reader is informed how this project in Algeria was funded by the UK Foreign & Commonwealth Office and that project in South Africa by the government of Flanders – not one is paid for by the host government and most involve an investment of less than US$1m. Government-backed initiatives typically focus on vocational training and education, with little consideration for providing jobs at the end or the economy's specific skills needs; or they are wildly unrealistic and tend to be launched at election time.

In 2017, President Kenyatta promised 6.5 million 'quality' jobs in five years if he was re-elected. Kenya's entire formal sector only comprises about 2.5 million jobs, and even in Kenya's 'Big Bang' employment boom of the mid-1990s the economy was only creating 400,000 jobs a year. A 'Youth Livelihood Programme' in Museveni's Uganda which doled out loans to entrepreneurial schemes was little more than a voting inducement ahead of elections, akin to hurling banknotes out of a limousine window.[61] In February 2019 the Burkinabé government announced its intention to implement a 'rapid industrialisation programme'. 'Many governments lack a basic understanding of their labour market and youth employment challenge,' says Louise Fox. 'Agriculture is often left completely out of the picture... Rather than developing expensive enclave youth projects in capital cities, countries need national strategies focusing on youth and all employment segments.'[62]

Young Africans are vocal in their criticism of tokenistic gestures, of the focus on 'youth' without differentiation even by sex, of being depersonalised by collectivisation as part of a 'youth bulge' or a 'youth dividend'. Jackie Chimhanzi, chief executive of the African Leadership Institute, laments that 'young Africans continue to be marginalised'.[63] There are no easy solutions for African countries – or any other developing region – as the world of work changes globally at what is arguably its most rapid pace in history. But progress is

Figure 23: Unemployment and vulnerable employment rates by country, 2018

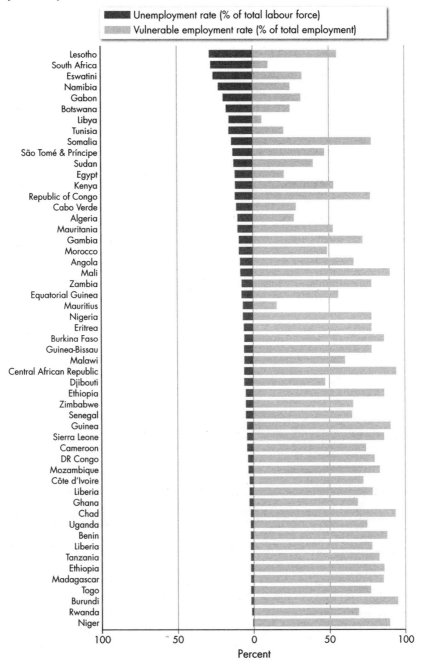

Source: AfDB (2019a), *Creating Decent Jobs: Strategies, Policies, and Instruments.*

not impossible: in Vietnam and Peru informal employment was as prevalent as in Africa at the start of the 2010s, but in the space of five years its share of the labour market declined by about 30%.[64] In Africa, however, the rhetoric has not changed since the 1980s. Informal enterprises are rebranded by global consultancy firms as 'SMEs' – small and medium-sized enterprises – and the continent is billed as a 'hotbed of entrepreneurial energy'.[65]

The Kenyan activist, lawyer and former Google policy manager for Africa, Ory Okolloh, is one of many to skewer such jargon and warn that people shouldn't 'fetishise entrepreneurship'. 'You can't "entrepreneur" around bad leadership, we can't "entrepreneur" around bad policy,' Okolloh stated flatly.[66] A Nigerian business intelligence firm speaks of 'necessity entrepreneurship'.[67] 'Much of today's growth that politicians and some economists celebrate is jobless, ruthless, futureless and voiceless,' says Makerere University lecturer Ramathan Ggoobi.[68] There is no shortage of successful entrepreneurs, but only a tiny fraction employ even one or two people. Vital as their economic contribution is, their enterprises are not the solution to the decent jobs crisis.

18

'Teetering on the Edge of a Cliff'

Closer inspection of employment data in some of Africa's largest economies exposes the full extent of the difficulty confronting young men and women seeking decent jobs.

The precise causes, characteristics and extent of unemployment, underemployment and vulnerable employment vary country by country. Nigeria and South Africa have completely different histories, economic structures and demography, yet the jobs predicament – especially among the youth – is of similar magnitude and gravity. The state of their labour markets highlights the scale of the task confronting their governments now and in coming decades.

Nigeria's economy was Africa's biggest at the end of 2019, the twenty-eighth-largest in the world and a similar size to those of Thailand, Venezuela, Austria and Iran. The country's oil and gas reserves place it in the global top 10 and it has Western Africa's most sizeable manufacturing base. While oil provides two-thirds of government revenue and 90% of foreign exchange, services like trade, real estate, telecoms and finance account for about 60% of GDP. Agriculture is the largest source of employment, however, providing around two-thirds of all Nigeria's jobs and a quarter of its GDP.

Nigeria's 'Vision 20:2020' development plan, launched in 2009, sought to secure a place among the world's 20-largest economies by 2020 through industrialisation and other strategies. Between 2000 and 2014, annual GDP growth averaged an impressive 7%. Measured by GDP per capita, the economies of six of Nigeria's 36 states rank among those of the top 10 countries in Africa. The economy of Lagos State is larger than those of Ghana and Tanzania, and almost as large as those of Kenya and Ethiopia. 'Nigeria with its shit together would be something to behold,'[1] tweeted one Nigerian in December 2019. Instead, wrote another, reflecting most local opinion, 'Vision 20:2020' was 'a beautiful architectural drawing that signalled the possibilities of utopia bereft, however, of precise or significant steps towards laying a foundation, much less building the proposed edifice'.[2]

In addition to being Africa's largest economy, Nigeria has the largest working-age population on the continent. This is set to expand by about two-thirds to 150 million between 2010 and 2030. In relative terms, the magnitude of this increase will be double that of 1990–2010, the previous 20 years, and equivalent to the addition of the entire population of France or Thailand. Between 2030 and 2050 the working-age population will expand by a further 100 million to 250 million.[3] By mid-century the labour force will have quadrupled in little more than a generation and will include a youth contingent aged 15–24 as large as the total labour force in 2020.

Between 2014 and 2018, almost 20 million young Nigerians sought to join the workforce, but only 3.5 million new jobs were created; in 2018 there were just 450,000. By the end of that year, the number of Nigerians unemployed but actively looking for work had almost quadrupled over five years to 21 million, an official unemployment rate of 23%. Among Nigerians with post-secondary-school education, the rate had almost tripled to 30%, meaning that an educated Nigerian was more likely to be unemployed than Nigerians in general. Unemployment of youth also tripled to 13.1 million in the same period, a rate of 30%.[4] If *under*employment among youth is added, the combined rate reached 55%. Young Nigerians are, in the words of Misan Rewane, chief executive of West Africa Vocational Education, 'teetering on the edge of a cliff'.[5]

Nigeria's unemployed total surpasses that of all EU member states combined. This may seem an inapt comparison, but given that the EU's population is more than three times the size, and that unemployment in Nigeria is a circumstance of last resort for all but the rich – there is little by way of a state welfare system – it serves to underscore the seriousness of the country's dilemma.[6]

Nigeria's National Bureau of Statistics estimates that about three-quarters of all new jobs are created by the traditional or informal sector. This accounts for more than half of GDP and the total workforce – about 55 million Nigerians in all.[7] Only one in 10 have formal waged employment, well below the level of two decades ago, and more than half of these prized jobs are in the public sector.[8] This compares with levels in Asian emerging markets like Indonesia, Philippines and Vietnam of 35% to almost 60%.[9] Even in the most commercial region of Nigeria, South West, only one in five people in work are waged. In towns and cities, street vending provides as much as 70% of employment, with domestic and home-based work two of the other most common types of occupation. Youth in northern states, where population growth is fastest, are increasingly marginalised by their lack of 'Western' education, by diverse security crises across the region as dire as at any time since the civil war in the 1960s, and by multiple other factors.

The chasm between job creation and demand in Nigeria has existed since the 1980s, if not earlier. Multiple surveys showed that unemployment was by some margin the single greatest concern among the working-age population even when GDP was growing vigorously in the 2000s: the most jobs created in a single year then was 2 million, of which two-thirds were part-time.[10] In northern states, home to four-fifths of Nigeria's poorest households, unemployment was at 'catastrophic levels' even before the textile industry based on Kano and Kaduna succumbed to the advent of cheaper imports from China and other factors.[11] In 2007, the Manufacturers Association of Nigeria reported that 60% of graduates in northern states were unemployed.[12]

With 45% of its population under the age of 15, the ranks of Nigerians seeking work – and the unemployed – will continue to swell far faster than the capacity of the economy to create sufficient and improving employment. According to Professor Kate Meagher at the LSE, 'faltering jobs markets' are facing a 'demographic tsunami'.[13] For the official unemployment rate simply to stabilise at its current level of 20–25% during the decade to 2030 will require the creation of 30–35 million jobs.[14] This is a tall order, even more so if economic growth remains negligible and GDP per capita continues to slide: it is almost 10 times the number of jobs created in the five years from 2014 to 2018, and whereas most new jobs were full-time in 2014, most are now part-time.[15] BudgIT, the country's leading civic tech organisation, projects that unemployment could triple to 60 million in the next five years 'if no drastic measures are taken'.[16]

One of the unwelcome consequences of the lack of decent jobs is that in 2018 Nigeria – Africa's largest economy, with a reputation for enterprise – was declared 'poverty capital of the world'. The number of Nigerian citizens living in extreme poverty overtook that of India, a country with a population almost seven times greater. In February 2019, approaching 100 million Nigerians were in 'multidimensional' poverty, which incorporates health, education and standard-of-living measures, as opposed to just income – about half the total population. In a speech in May 2019, Dr Joe Abah, former director-general of the Bureau of Public Service Reforms, articulated a national sense of frustration: 'Nigerians are tired of potential that never seems to translate into tangible improvements in the lives of citizens. They are tired of the "sleeping giant" epithet.'[17] The proliferation of serious or intensifying internal conflicts is also associated with joblessness and, as the Lagos-based consultancy SBM Intelligence briefed its clients in early 2020, 'until Nigeria's economy starts to generate jobs for its growing population it is unlikely that insecurity will reduce'.[18]

South Africa has the continent's most industrialised, formalised and diversified economy, and the most developed private sector; the latter provides almost 9 million formal jobs – more than in any other country.[19] If the national oil companies of Algeria and

Angola are excluded, South Africa can boast of having all but one of the top 30 African companies by turnover. The demographic transition is well advanced, with a TFR and the rate of population growth about half that of Nigeria. Yet the working-age population is still increasing at 2–3% a year and the dearth of jobs is no less critical than in Nigeria.

South Africa's world-leading rate of youth unemployment has been mentioned. The situation exists despite the fact that the 20 million South Africans aged between 15 and 34 only comprise about a third of the total population, a lower proportion than in any other country in Africa with over 50 million inhabitants. Furthermore, someone is considered officially 'employed' in South Africa even if they only worked one hour in the week in which they were surveyed, in line with the ILO definition of employment.[20] The official jobless rate among all ages – those not working, but available for work and actively seeking it – is almost as alarming as that for youth, reaching 28% of the workforce in mid-2019. Applying the national statistics agency's expanded definition of unemployment, which includes discouraged jobseekers, more than 10 million South Africans were out of work – almost 40% of the workforce, compared to about 30% a decade earlier.[21] People are 'discouraged' for a variety of reasons, including repeated failure to find a job, geographical distance from opportunities or the lack of money to look.

Although population growth is likely to slow to less than 1% annually by 2030, there are still 700,000 young South Africans entering the job market each year. They have to compete with those already unable to find employment as well as people categorised as 'not in employment, education or training' (NEET). There can be some overlap between unemployment and NEET – discouraged jobseekers in South Africa are included in NEET statistics and also the expanded unemployment figures – but headline statistics usually exclude NEETs from the calculation of the unemployment rate: to count as unemployed, a person has to have worked, however little, in the week of the survey, be available for work and be actively seeking. Among the NEETs there are millions who are not only discouraged jobseekers but who have not sought work at all. For some, like home-makers, this may be a matter of choice; for most it is not.

More than 8 million young South African men and women aged 15–34 are counted as NEET (and a further 6 million or so aged 35–64). A Department of Higher Education and Training brief notes that 'it is generally acknowledged, both nationally as well as internationally, that NEETs constitute one of the greatest threats to social stability'[22] due to their marginalisation or exclusion from employment, training or educational opportunity. The Centre for Economic Development and Transformation, based in Johannesburg, estimates that to absorb the annual number of potential new labour-market entrants alone, before making a dent in the unemployment and NEET rates, would require sustained annual GDP growth of somewhere between 6% and 10%.[23] While other economists have posited slightly lower estimates, even these are well above the 2.5% average annual rate of GDP growth since 2000 and, as is the case in Nigeria, GDP per capita has been negative every year since 2014. Also like Nigeria, South Africa's unemployment is not temporary or caused by economic recession. Since 2000 economic expansion has consistently outpaced that of total employment, including part-time and informal jobs. The official unemployment rate has not been below 20% this century.

Given the scale of unemployment and swelling ranks of people attempting to find work, it is sobering that the number of new jobs created between 2001 and 2012 was 2.5 million, an average of about 200,000 a year. Even in 2004–8, the strongest years for employment possibilities since the democratic transition to majority rule in 1994, the figure was only an average of 400,000 a year; most recently, in 2018, it was around 360,000. This was more than the five-year average of a little below 300,000, but nowhere near what is needed to commence a sustainable reduction in unemployment. In October 2019, 530,000 young South Africans applied for 14,000 positions advertised by the South African Police Service.

Private sector firms in South Africa have become increasingly capital- and skills-intensive. The same is true of agriculture. This does not address the urgent requirement for low- and medium-skilled jobs: half the youth in the labour force have no secondary education. The fastest-growing sector of the economy, now accounting for more than 20% of GDP, is financial and business services. This too is not a source of low-skilled jobs. Meanwhile, the weighting of labour-intensive manufacturing has declined.

Access to social services and housing, and the provision of welfare safety nets, widened dramatically in South Africa after the end of apartheid rule. No country in Africa has a welfare system to match. But with rising joblessness, poverty rates have remained static at best. Between 1994 and 2017 GDP per capita grew 1% a year in real terms, implying that standards of living should have risen modestly. On the contrary: Stats SA's 'lower-bound' poverty rate, the most quoted indicator, rose from 37% to 40% between 2011 and 2015.

Vimal Ranchhod, Professor of Economics at the University of Cape Town, sees 'no clear and immediate solutions to the unemployment problem'.[24] The same can be said of all of South Africa's neighbours. In Namibia, for example, unemployment among the under-35s is about 50%, and in Afrobarometer surveys in 2018 it was rated a greater worry for Namibians than drought, poverty or corruption.

The difference between headline statistics and broader, more realistic depictions of unemployment is greater in some countries than in others. In Museveni's Uganda, for example, the official unemployment rate in the 2018 Statistical Abstract was 9%, with youth unemployment at 13%[25] – considerably lower than in South Africa or Nigeria. The Uganda Bureau of Statistics (UBoS) categorises people in three ways: employed, unemployed or 'outside the labour force'. People whose occupation is subsistence agriculture – some 6 million, or 40% of the working population – are counted as being outside the labour force and are therefore not included in the calculation of unemployment.

As we have seen, Uganda is one of the youngest countries in the world, with 47% of its population under the age of 15 and annual

Figure 24: Job creation in Nigeria is falling well short of the growing number of jobseekers

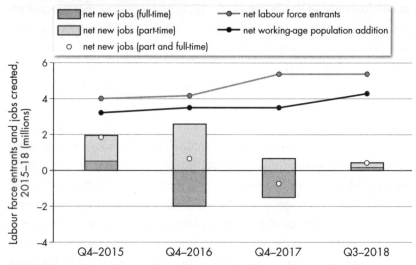

Source: World Bank, *Nigeria Economic Update, Fall 2019: Jumpstarting Economic Growth – Unlocking the Productive Potential of Nigeria's People and Resource Endowments.*

growth still above 3% a year. Among the 7.75 million youth, defined in Uganda as being between 18 and 30, 3.3 million are outside the labour force, of which 2.2 million are categorised as NEET and 1.1 million as 'potential labour force'. By simply adding the 'potential labour force' number to the 0.6 million young people who are officially unemployed, youth unemployment rises from the headline rate of 13% to 38%. Officially, this is euphemistically called the 'youth labour under-utilisation rate'.[26] UBoS is following international guidelines, not deliberately indulging in sleight of hand, but it is an example of how there is always 'hidden' unemployment in NEET and 'outside labour force' statistics.[27]

The full extent of joblessness among under-30s is even worse. The term 'in employment' as applied to 3.9 million young Ugandans is open to misinterpretation. Only about 2.1 million of them have 'transited' to a job deemed 'stable' or 'satisfactory', whether working for someone else or self-employment; the remaining 1.7 million are among 5 million Ugandans classified as 'in transition', meaning they are employed in temporary or unsatisfactory work, or in effect unemployed. By exactly how many those 'in transition' would further swell the ranks of the jobless is not discernible from official statistics, but the true extent of youth unemployment is certainly more than 50%. In recent years both the AfDB and Ugandan research institute Advocates Coalition for Development and Environment have asserted that the real figure is higher than 60%.[28] This implies that it is even greater than South Africa's – and therefore possibly the highest in the world.

About 800,000 young Ugandans will reach working age every year in the 2020s, a figure that is double the annual average in the 1990s and 2000s; in the 2030s, it will be 1 million.[29] The number of decent, waged job opportunities available each year is estimated at about 75,000. The consequence is that nine out of 10 of the youth counted as being 'in employment' (excluding subsistence agriculture) are working in the informal sector, and for seven out of 10 the work is irregular.[30] The median monthly wage of those fortunate enough to have found a waged job is less than 170,000 Ugandan shillings (US$50), a level that sees them officially classified as 'working poor'.[31]

A look at employment trends and job creation in Ethiopia, the African country associated more than any other with rapid economic growth and a determined attempt at industrialisation – at least until the so-called 'third revolution' in 2018 – shows little difference from the situations in Nigeria, South Africa and Uganda. After experiencing decades of turmoil, Ethiopia's income per capita was lower in the early 1990s than it had been in the 1960s, in common with many African nations. However, with improved political stability, heavy government expenditure, and the determined implementation of a number of clearly defined and targeted policies, Ethiopia reported average GDP growth of 9% a year between 2000 and 2010; in the most recent decade it was the fastest in the world, averaging about 10% a year. The architect of Ethiopia's industrialisation strategy remarked that the country's record had 'inspired the whole of Africa' and symbolised 'the continent's bright future'.[32] As agricultural productivity improved, the proportion of the population living in extreme poverty fell from over 50% to about 30%. This sustained growth is comparable to that achieved by the Asian 'tiger' economies during economic lift-off.

At 22%, Ethiopia has the highest proportion of youth aged 15–24 of any country in the world. Almost two-thirds of the population are under the age of 25, and 40% under 14. By 2020, Ethiopia's working-age population (15–64) had reached about 65 million.[33] It will grow by 2 million a year for at least the next decade.[34] At first sight, its record of tackling unemployment looks as impressive as its economic growth. Between 1999 and 2013, the date of the last comprehensive labour survey, the headline unemployment rate almost halved to 4.5%.[35] In rural areas, unemployment is (officially) virtually non-existent.[36] In urban areas it fell from 26% to 17%, although remained over 20% in Addis Ababa, the capital city, and in other major towns. Among youth aged 15–29, unemployment also declined, although it exceeds 20% in urban areas.[37]

The statistics for 1999–2013 imply that during those years Ethiopia succeeded, by and large, in absorbing more than 20 million young people into the workforce. However, a vast majority of new jobs were in smallholder and subsistence agriculture – not the high-growth sectors the government has strived to establish. Despite ever-increasing fragmentation and scarcity of land, this activity continues to provide almost three-quarters of total employment in Ethiopia, only a few percentage points less than at the turn of the century. Self-employment accounts for about 20% of those in work, including millions of women who collect wood and water for a living. Only 10% of those in work are in waged employment outside agriculture, a proportion that is barely increasing.[38]

Most of the 'jobs' in agriculture are unpaid. For many young people this is tantamount to being jobless. A survey in a large village in North Shoa Zone of Amhara Region highlighted by the French researcher René Lefort showed that for 75% of young people, 'their income was too meagre, too occasional, or too unpredictable to allow them to marry and establish a family'.[39] While it would be an exaggeration to say that this situation was ubiquitous, it is certainly common. Furthermore, countrywide almost two-thirds of children aged 10–14 work. Education curtailed of necessity makes seeking regular, waged employment well-nigh impossible for most young Ethiopians – even if such jobs were available in adequate numbers. Waged employment is almost exclusively confined to Ethiopia's cities and larger towns and the public sector has been the main provider. Including state-owned enterprises, the state has created more than a million new waged jobs since 2000 – well over half the total (and far exceeding the number generated by manufacturing, commerce or construction).

Manufacturing was identified by the government as potentially a major employment provider, and between 2005 and 2013 the number of jobs in the sector rose from 1.4 million to 1.7 million.[40] The total is now higher still, but remains small relative to the total working-age population, and will continue to be for the foreseeable future. It is services – not the industrial sector, including manufacturing – that has generated three-quarters of the growth in non-agricultural jobs. Between 1999 and 2013, employment in services and industry rose from 15% to 20% and 5% to 7% respectively of the total; that in agriculture declined by 8% to 72%.[41]

As the spearhead of Ethiopia's industrialisation strategy, manufacturing has attracted domestic and foreign investment, and the development of a dozen industrial parks is proceeding apace. In 2010, the Growth and Transformation Plan II included the promotion of industry as the leading sector of the economy by 2020. 'Vision 2025' envisaged manufacturing generating 20% of GDP by 2025. To date, Ethiopia is still a long way from achieving either objective. Despite strong recent growth, manufacturing accounted for about 6–7% of GDP in 2017, although the wider industrial sector had reached more than 25%.[42] Hawassa, one of the largest of the industrial parks, involving an investment of US$250 million, employs more than 15,000 people. The total number of jobs created by the parks had reached about 70,000 by mid-2019. These new jobs are but a tiny drop in an ocean of available labour,[43] a fact the government has readily acknowledged.

In Ethiopia, hidden un- and underemployment is again to be found among those classified as NEET and 'in transition'. While being a student or home-maker – the two most common NEET categories – may legitimately exclude someone from being counted as part of the workforce, a great many of these people are in effect also unemployed. Fewer than 2 million working-age Ethiopians were defined as unemployed in 2013,[44] but more than 5 million were NEET. They include one in 10 of the rural working-age population and more than one in five in town and cities. Four million of them never completed primary school.[45]

Among the youth – those aged between 15 and 29 who make up more than half of the working-age population – one in five are NEET. In the main towns and cities, where 20% of young Ethiopians are officially unemployed, a further one in three were categorised as NEET in a 2016 survey.[46] As is true elsewhere, real unemployment is substantially higher than the official headline rates. Furthermore, one-third of young workers earned wages below the extreme poverty line, a rate three times more than for older workers.[47] Female unemployment is two and a half times that of men; for young women, unemployment, underemployment and NEET rates are about twice as high as for their male counterparts.

Ethiopia has sought to emulate East Asian economic 'success stories' in its own way. It is a moot point whether its economy is transforming as fast as it is growing. In 1990, on the eve of the end of civil war in Ethiopia and the ejection of the Marxist Derg regime, the country's GDP per capita was about half Vietnam's; by the end of 2018, it was about 30%. Only in 2016 did its GDP per capita nudge ahead of that of Malawi, a country not usually cited as having one of Africa's most dynamic economies. Between 2014 and 2016, Vietnam created more *new* jobs in manufacturing than Ethiopia's manufacturing sector employs in total.[48] In the first half of 2019 Hanoi, Vietnam's capital, alone attracted one-third more foreign direct investment than Ethiopia did in the whole of

Figure 25: Expansion of Ethiopia's working-age population (15-64 years), 2008-37

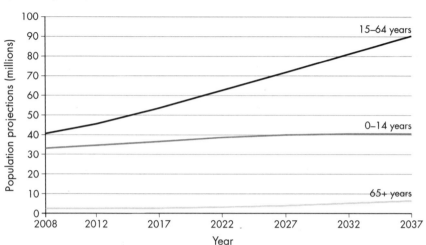

Source: Government of Ethiopia, *Ethiopia National Human Development Report 2018*.

2017, its best year ever. Similarly, Ethiopia's textile exports – one of the priorities in its manufacturing strategy – were US$235 million in 2017; from virtually a standing start in the early 1990s, Bangladesh's textile and apparel exports were US$37 billion.[49]

To some, these facts illustrate Ethiopia's huge potential. But employment trends are a leading indicator of structural transformation – the process undergone by all developed economies by which they moved from being primarily agrarian and rural to industrialised and urban, absorbing large numbers of young workers from the countryside, substantially raising productivity and improving the welfare of citizens along the way. By this measure, the realisation of Ethiopia's potential is still some way off.

Not only are more productive forms of employment unattainable for all but a fortunate few who are now joining the workforce, and an ever-growing number of young Ethiopians find themselves unwillingly NEET, but the extent of formal education severely limits options. Despite concerted efforts by the government over two decades to improve the accessibility and quality of education, in 2016

almost half of the labour force had never been to school and 80% had
not completed primary education.[50] This is not simply a historical
legacy that is now rapidly diminishing. While tertiary education is
increasingly common among the young in cities and towns, about
three-quarters of rural workers aged between 15 and 29 have had
incomplete primary education or no education at all.[51] Meanwhile,
although the TFR has fallen in Ethiopia's towns and cities, decline in
rural areas has stalled above five births. This means that two-thirds
of the population will still be rural in 2050, and at least half of the
working-age population below the age of 35.

Jimi Wanjigi's Kenya has not pursued rapid industrialisation through
manufacturing, although its formal manufacturing sector employs
a considerably greater number of people than Ethiopia's – about
300,000 all told, mostly in food production and textiles. The country
has, however, acquired a reputation for having one of the most vibrant
private sectors on the continent. In marked contrast to Ethiopia, the
number of waged jobs in the private sector – over 2 million – is more
than double those in the public sector.

The breathless blurb from international consultancies and
investment firms tells us that Kenya's middle class already accounts
for 45% of the population and is 'expected to continue expanding
by an average annual growth rate of 5%, giving rise to a thriving
shopping-mall lifestyle, a booming housing market, [and] growing
automobile industry'.[52] The mobile-money sector is the most
developed in Africa and in M-Pesa – the pioneering mobile-phone-
based money transfer, financing and microfinancing service – Kenya
has a brand of global repute. Used by 18 million people – almost 70%
of the adult population – mobile money is said to have 'chang[ed]
Kenya's economic paradigm'.[53]

According to the 2019 Knight Frank *Wealth Report* there are
almost 9,500 Kenyan dollar millionaires, a figure growing faster
than anywhere else in Africa and forecast to increase by a quarter by

2023.[54] Real-estate developments offering stupendous returns have been springing up all over Nairobi and elsewhere in the country during the 2010s. There are world-class hotels and tourist facilities. The horticulture sector, one of Kenya's largest foreign-currency earners, was a pioneer in growing vegetables and flowers for export to Europe by air. It has even been suggested that the rapid increase in the number of *boda bodas* – motorcycle taxis – from 130,000 in 2008 to over a million in 2017 to 1.4 million by early 2019 is evidence that Kenya is one of the most entrepreneurial countries in Africa.

Kenya's private sector can justifiably boast many successes. This makes its labour market an instructive case study: if any country in Africa were managing to keep up with demand for jobs, many commentators would instinctively say it would be Kenya. This is not the case, as any Kenyan economist and almost any young Kenyan could tell them. A cursory look at employment and wage trends confirms as much. Furthermore, with a TFR still around four births (or more than six births among the poorest quintile, women in the north-east and women with no education) and population growth above 2%, job-creation and wage rates remain under intense pressure.

Kenya's headline unemployment rate, using the ILO's strict definition, is in single figures. The 2015–16 Labour Force Survey enumerated an economically active population between the ages of 15 and 54 of 19.3 million Kenyans, of whom 1.4 million were classified as unemployed. If the underemployed are added, this figure rises to 5 million, or about a quarter of the active labour force. As is true everywhere in the continent, the difficulty in finding work is most severe for the young. About 85% of the unemployed were under 35, and among the youth underemployment is the norm.[55] Even the best-educated struggle, another common – and revealing – feature of labour markets throughout Africa: among Kenyans with tertiary education, more than a quarter were 'economically inactive'.[56] At the same time as the Labour Force Survey, in a countrywide survey of 2,000 Kenyans aged between 18 and 35 unemployment was unsurprisingly ranked by 63% of respondents as their biggest concern, a result that varied little by level of education.[57] Furthermore, the 'decent' jobs crisis is worsening and therefore the number of unemployed youth is forecast to double by 2035, with a commensurate rise in underemployment likely as well.[58]

More than 750,000 young Kenyans are entering the labour market annually, a number that will not start to ease until mid-century. In 2017 and 2018, the economy created between 850,000 and 900,000 new jobs.[59] As in Ethiopia, the headline figures suggest that the ever-growing ranks of new jobseekers are being absorbed. However, it is self-employment in the *Jua kali*, 'hustla' and other urban and rural informal sectors, or firms with a couple of 'employees', that generate almost 90% of new jobs – and account for over 80% of total employment in Kenya.[60] The category 'wholesale and retail trade, hotels and restaurants' includes 60% of all informal workers, with manufacturing the next-highest sector with 20%.[61] Whereas salaried 'modern' employment reached a total of 2.76 million in 2018, an increase of more than one-third in a decade,[62] in the same period the number of Kenyans in informal employment grew by 70% to 14.1 million, two-thirds of them in rural areas.[63] Only about one in 10 of eligible workers succeed in finding waged employment,[64] and over a quarter of these waged jobs are classified as 'casual' – not employed for longer than 24 hours at a time.[65]

The livelihood of most of Kenya's informal workers consists of subsistence and precarity, a daily struggle for survival. James Gatungu, director of production statistics at Kenya's National Bureau of Statistics, describes their work as 'indecent jobs' undertaken 'to eke out a living'.[66] Among them are also an increasing number of well-educated young men and women who aspire to be doctors, nurses, engineers, accountants and lawyers, not to be selling phone time on street corners, waiting on passers-by in a roadside café or pulling *mkokoteni* – handcarts – in an attempt to make ends meet.

For all Kenyans, the costs of living rise inexorably: the CPI increased 134% in the decade to 2017, with food prices up by 219%.[67] The 2019 *FinAccess Household Survey* attests to a hand-to-mouth existence for all but the wealthiest. Two-thirds of Kenyans are unable to meet day-to-day needs in each income cycle. There is then a knock-on effect on others, since help from friends and family or borrowing informally is the most common way of dealing with shortfalls and shocks. Overall, more than half of almost 9,000 households questioned in rural and urban areas in the final quarter of 2018 reported their financial status to have worsened during the year. Only 21.7% regarded themselves as 'financially healthy', a steep decline since the previous survey in 2016 when the figure was 39.4%.[68] This partly explains why the domestic savings rate declined from 17.3% of GDP in 2007 to 12.7% a decade later, the lowest in Eastern Africa.[69]

In 2017, average monthly earnings among employees in the 'modern' economy – the waged and formally self-employed – were US$316 after deductions, largely unchanged for three years.[70] Three-quarters of wage earners make less than US$500 a month.[71] Among formal wage earners in the agricultural sector, the situation is no better. The average monthly basic minimum wage was US$86 in 2017. For unskilled employees, the lowest-paid category of workers, the figure was US$64. For the highest-paid, including farm foremen and farm clerks, the average was US$115. While agricultural wages have risen every year since 2013, it is by less than inflation. Furthermore, a credible recent estimate of a monthly 'living wage' in rural Kenya – the ability 'to afford a basic lifestyle [for a family of 5.5] considered decent by society at its current state of development' – was US$139.[72] Even the best-paid rural employees are below this level, which is also close to the World Bank's US$3.20 per day 'minimum basic needs' poverty line for low-income countries.

In her column in Kenya's *Business Daily,* the development economist Anzetse Were echoed the call from MP Anthony Oluoch for youth unemployment to be declared a national emergency – 'because it is just that… a daily emergency'. She eloquently and forcefully summed up the predicament of the young in Kenya and throughout Africa:

> It seems this country views young people as a nuisance who 'need to find a job'.
> For the millions of unemployed Kenyans, unemployment means a brutal and harsh life, where every day is a gamble

and basic needs an insurmountable challenge to address. And the sad reality is that education does not change much. Many young people have either been financed or have incurred significant debt getting an education and yet find themselves unable to secure a decent job the way generations before them did.

As a result, most Kenyans find themselves running informal businesses, working a sector that has been long neglected by both public and private sectors.

Young people are expected to entrepreneur themselves out of poverty with absolutely no supportive structures in place, relegating most to subsistence living. And why are young people being told that they all have to be business people? Not everyone is an entrepreneur.

It is a travesty that young Kenyans are being left so abandoned and desperate... it says a lot about us when we leave our young to fend for themselves in an unforgiving environment.[73]

'If climate change is the most important matter of common concern around the world, what comes second?', the author and former foreign correspondent Howard French asked rhetorically in a 2019 article headed 'Why Africa's future will determine the rest of the world's' in *World Politics Review*. His answer? 'The future of employment in Africa, where unprecedented demographic transitions are under way.' Professor Emmanuel Nnadozie, executive secretary of the African Capacity Building Foundation, reverses the order: 'youth unemployment in Africa is a much more serious problem than climate change'.[74]

19

Grand Designs

The worst imaginings of Western agencies in the 1970s about population growth and the consequent likelihood of Malthusian reckonings did not come to pass. Today a second population 'explosion' is said to be under way, with rhetoric reminiscent of the 1970s and an accompanying set of crisis narratives. Every African country has its own challenges, some severe, some manageable. Depictions of the whole continent as a 'catastrophe-in-waiting' – or the opposite – are misguided, uninformative and often self-serving. Demographic detail is one antidote to generalisation and conjecture.

The mind-boggling growth of working-age populations in Africa and dearth of decent job creation recall warnings by the World Bank in the 1980s. In the 1986 report mentioned in Chapter 2, the working-age population of the sub-Saharan region was estimated at about 200 million in 1980. This was forecast to rise to almost 400 million by the year 2000, and to 700 million by 2020. How were these people going to find productive jobs? The authors of the report reckoned that agriculture could absorb about 70 million additional workers by 2000, and industry around 50 million. That still left tens of millions with not the slightest prospect of decent employment even before the 300 million more young Africans reaching working age between 2000 and 2020 were taken into consideration. 'The situation,' the bank had concluded, 'although not hopeless, is thus grim.'[1]

The rate of population growth in the sub-Saharan region was deemed by the World Bank 'neither desirable nor necessary'.[2] Amid the multiple vicissitudes of Africa's 'lost decade', it was perceived as having materially increased the threat of mass starvation and compromised the economics of sustaining substantial expenditure on education and health for the burgeoning number of children. The youth population was set to double again in two decades, implying that universal primary education and 'rudimentary' health services would alone absorb as much as half of government revenue in many countries over the same time frame. There was 'great concern about the region's ability to maintain even living standards already attained since independence':[3] in almost all countries, GDP per capita was lower than at the start of the 1970s. As for *raising* incomes, that was a pipe dream. Meanwhile, to the consternation of the authors of the World Bank report, 'most poor parents in Africa believe it pays to have many children'.[4]

Three years later, the bank again highlighted 'explosive population growth and accelerating environmental degradation' and reiterated that 'the difficulties facing Africa are formidable. The margin for maneuver is slim indeed. The risks are devastating in human terms.'[5] The main source of hope was a conviction that sub-Saharan countries were 'probably not' demographically exceptional and that high fertility would fall 'as development proceeds'.[6] There were signs that this process was already under way in Northern Africa, and the bank predicted a TFR for sub-Saharan Africa in 2020 of 3.4 births.

The FAO added to the alarm by claiming that 14 countries – including Nigeria, Kenya, Rwanda, Uganda and Ethiopia – that accounted for half of the population of the region had already exceeded their carrying capacity. A further seven, Ghana and Zimbabwe among them, would do so by the year 2000. Several countries, it was argued, would be unable to feed themselves even if they adopted equivalent technology and agricultural inputs to Latin America and Southeast Asia. If treated as a single agricultural unit, the maximum sustainable number of people in sub-Saharan Africa at minimum nutritional standards was estimated at 1.6 times the projection for 2000, or 1.2 billion.[7] The 'nightmare scenario' envisaged by the ECA in the early 1980s assumed that the total population of the continent would hit the high-variant figure projected by UNPD – 1.1 billion people – by 2008.

The Africa total duly reached the dreaded 1.1 billion mark just four years later than the ECA predicted – at the height of 'Africa Rising' fever in 2012. That of sub-Saharan Africa is poised to exceed its putative carrying capacity – 1.2 billion people – in 2025. The region's TFR in 2015–20 was 4.7 births compared to the 3.4 births envisaged by the World Bank in the mid-1980s, but its working-age population will reach 700 million by the middle of the current decade, just a few years later than envisaged. Calorie supply per person has improved by about a quarter since the mid-1980s, all nutritional indicators are better, and income per capita has more than doubled since 1990. On the face of it, the basic building blocks of the doomsday scenarios of the 1980s would appear to have crumbled. Many have accused the aforementioned institutions of 'crying wolf' and neo-Malthusian scaremongering. President Museveni would say that the *real* narrative was one of 'steady progress'.

The response from anyone accused of scaremongering in the 1980s would be that their only error was in the timing – and who could be expected to be accurate with that, even to the nearest decade, when trying to assess population and food-supply trends? They would marshal counter-data, pointing out, for example, that due to prolonged high population growth the doubling of sub-Saharan Africa's income per capita since 1990 was less than the improvement in all other developing regions: in the Middle East/Northern Africa, Latin America/Caribbean, South Asia and East Asia/Pacific incomes multiplied by 2.5 times, three times, five times and six times respectively. They might add that, partly due to slower growth, the populations of other developing regions had improved their calorie intake and nutritional indicators by much more; that the worldwide decline in the incidence of extreme poverty from 38% to just under 10% far exceeded that of sub-Saharan Africa, from 56% to 42%, making extreme poverty more and more of an 'Africa problem'; and that a jobs crisis had self-evidently turned into a jobs catastrophe. The data and development indicators can be made to 'show' many things about Africa and its countries. However, the precise extent to which high fertility and population growth have impacted on them is, as we have seen, still as contentious a question as it was in the 1970s and 1980s.

With the re-emergence in the past decade of a 'big debate' about the size and trajectory of the global population – a debate with Africa centre-stage – some of the key individual, as opposed to institutional, protagonists from the population explosion era have again attracted attention. Most notably, in 2018, the 50th anniversary of the publication of *The Population Bomb*, 'permabear' Paul Ehrlich repeated that the collapse of civilisation is a 'near-certainty within decades' due to the destruction of the natural world. Ehrlich considers a global population of 1.5–2 billion to be sustainable,[8] a level that could only be achieved this century through a catastrophe of unimaginable proportions – one that would dwarf the impact of the Black Death in the fourteenth century. Ehrlich's estimate is generous compared to that of the independent scientist and originator of the Gaia hypothesis, James Lovelock. In *The Revenge of Gaia*, published in 2006, Lovelock argued that only when the size of the human population had fallen to 0.5–1 billion would it be in equilibrium with the environment.

Many of the most prominent contemporary doomsters are household names. Like Ehrlich, Stephen Hawking concluded in the final years of his brilliant life that 'our earth is becoming too small for us, global population is increasing at an alarming rate and we are in danger of self-destructing'.[9] Humanity, in his estimation, had just a century left due to climate change and environmental destruction. David Attenborough is equally convinced that 'the world's population is increasing out of control',[10] and has declared, 'we must act now on population'. Natural systems are on the verge of collapse, he says: 'we have perhaps 10, 20 years', he told an IMF meeting in April 2019.[11] There is an increasingly widespread perception, as Massimo Livi Bacci observes, that 'certain limits have been reached, or are being approached, or have become visible'.[12]

In early 2020, the 11,000-member Alliance of World Scientists listed 'gradual' stabilisation of the global headcount 'within a framework that ensures social integrity' as one of the key measures required to tackle the climate 'emergency'.[13] The concept of 'overpopulation' is featuring more prominently in popular culture: the blockbuster movies *Inferno* (2016) and *Avengers: Infinity War* (2018) can be seen as successors to the grisly *Soylent Green* and the previous generation of dystopian films catching the population-explosion zeitgeist of the 1970s. All in all, it would appear that the population-bomb narrative is being well and truly reprimed.

The idea of population 'stabilisation' resounds widely, although many of its adherents seem to have no conception of the effect of population momentum (upwards or downwards), and their objective attracts as much controversy as ever. *Whose* population needs stabilising? And how should this be done? There is suspicion of racist undertones, and a danger of coercive or harmful implementation reminiscent of 'birth control' initiatives. Family planning advocates counter, as they always have, that significant headway could be made simply by facilitating universal access to contraception and legal, safe abortion. There is also opposition to using the impact of climate change to justify the need for stabilisation. Population growth is concentrated in regions and countries that contribute the least to carbon emissions and have the lowest consumption, so stopping growth of their populations – even if such a thing were possible, which in the short term it is not – would arguably make little difference over the next few decades to climate change:[14] Africa contributes just 3% of global emissions, although the impact of deforestation must also be taken into consideration. Disagreement about the interplay of continuing population growth and climate change (man-made or otherwise) will become increasingly prominent and vexed.

Some are fatalistic – or, as they would see it, realistic – about overpopulation. For Ugo Bardi, Professor of Physical Chemistry at the University of Florence, the solution is already well known to the human race. There is 'no need for evil elites plotting extermination, nor of well-intentioned activists teaching the poor how to use condoms'. Instead, 'the system itself will cause the population to collapse', just as it has done before. 'Think how interesting are the 400 plus million tons of human flesh existing today for predators such as viruses, bacteria, and assorted parasites,' Bardi mused towards the end of 2019; 'we are their prey, and we are rapidly becoming an abundant and easy prey.'[15] The magnitude of collapse he envisages may be within the bounds of our historical knowledge, but probably not within our ability to comprehend. A pandemic causing the same percentage of global deaths as the 'Spanish' flu after the First World War would kill a mere 280 million or so people today – a number that would be replaced within just four years at the current rate of global growth.[16]

At the opposite end of a spectrum are the standard-bearers of what Frank Götmark, Professor of Animal Ecology and Conservation Biology at the University of Gothenburg, pointedly describes in a review of Hans Rosling's bestseller *Factfulness* as 'selecting facts to make you happy'.[17] 'Possibilism' and 'Pinkerism' – after the Harvard University cognitive psychologist and author of popular-science books – are labels commonly associated with such thinking. The central, sunny proposition is that *data shows* that the world – developing countries included – has never had it better in terms of wealth, health, education and opportunity; and that there is no reason to think that this cannot continue, or even that the least-developed and war-torn countries – South Sudan or Yemen or Somalia, say – cannot emulate developed countries from Finland to Uruguay via the US. This highly influential world view is applauded and vilified in equal measure. Some of the biggest critics of such narratives charge that they completely ignore the cost to the environment and biodiversity of the ceaseless progress they celebrate; others that they rest on the manipulation or selective use of data and projection of past trends; and others still that their optimism is Panglossian at best, and at worst deeply patronising or offensive to large swathes of the human race. In many respects, the old battle between doomster Ehrlich and cornucopian Julian Simon is resurgent.

The opinions of population Jeremiahs are also vigorously countered by the architects and adherents of the 'Africa Rising' narrative who so successfully retooled demographic dividend theory to delete any mention of the prerequisite of rapid fertility decline and replace it with 'just add people'; and, as we have seen, by African leaders. Many Western investment firms and consultancies routinely refer to Africa, in quasi-science-fictional terms, as 'the final frontier' for an above-average and sustained increase in GDP (and investment returns), one that is 'on the cusp of transformative growth'. The supporting vocabulary is distinctive. Adherents talk of 'leapfrogging', of 'burgeoning' middle classes who will supposedly account for more than 40% of the population by 2030,[18] of how entrepreneurs will 'kick-start industrial revolution', of 'smart' and 'techno' cities. Ehrlich's term for this is 'faith-based economics'. Mention of poverty rates, of the shortcomings of health and education systems, or of real (as opposed to official) unemployment and underemployment is generally skirted over. Just as for Jimi Wanjigi in the Introduction to this book, 'superb' demographics are one of – if not *the* – the essential components of a glittering future for Africa. More people simply means more consumers, bigger markets and limitless low-cost labour. It is a trend without hazard, an unalloyed good. 'I think the demographic story is powerful enough to render this Africa's century,' a napster commented in the *Financial Times*'s 'beyondbrics' column.[19] 'Sub-Saharan Africa is the one bright spot when analyzing global demographic trends,' two of that paper's writers also observed.[20]

For devotees to this point of view, just as the phenomenally rapid proliferation of mobile phones and successful development of mobile money exemplifies 'progress' in Africa in recent decades, so the African Continental Free Trade Area, urbanisation and sundry other excitements are projected as symbols of the huge potential of the future. The head of Hilton Hotels says his development team are 'crapping their pants' at the prospect of building 1,000 more hotels in Africa.[21] Current and future success is invariably quantified by one metric above all others – GDP growth. This is an irrelevant measure for most Africans and one that is generally not fit for purpose in predominantly informal economies. Its main significance in Africa is as a barometer of the section of economies that preoccupies international investors and 'big business' – one could call it the super-economy. Donald Kaberuka, former president of the African Development Bank, likes to tell the story of the taxi driver in Senegal who, when he told him how well his country's economy was doing, replied, 'Well, I can't eat GDP.'

Figure 26: Global distribution of extreme poverty by population number (millions), 1990–2030

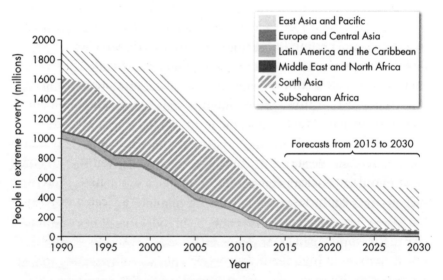

Source: World Bank Open Data.

Caution is merited with overarching narratives incorporating population, globally and within Africa. Like all grand designs, some are intended to assist understanding and make sense of the world succinctly, or for constructive advocacy; others are crafted with altogether less objective or entirely self-serving intent. In whatever form they come, positive or negative, nuance is often absent. News media, in particular, appreciate the clarity as it makes for bold, binary headlines. 'Roar or die – how Africa's booming population could make it richer and stronger – or kill it' ran a particularly eye-catching example in South Africa's *Mail & Guardian* in April 2015.[22] 'Miracle or Malthus?', asked an article in *The Economist* in December 2011, at the height of 'Africa Rising' frenzy. Reality is more complicated, more in-between, more *messy* than natty narratives or trite headlines usually allow, as we have seen by revisiting the warnings of the 1980s.

Leading Africa-focused demographers deal ultimately in detail – changes in fertility in Central Kenya compared to South West Nigeria, mortality trends in the Great Lakes region, the minutiae of a new census or DHS report. Some have spent their careers more interested in the causes of certain developments than the numerical outcomes. So it is conspicuous that none are sanguine about the demographic trajectory of high-fertility African countries and the potential impact of their population growth on regional neighbours and the continent. 'The African demographic question is undoubtedly the most acute,'[23] states Massimo Livi Bacci. John Cleland and Kazuyo Machiyama emphasise that 'the stakes are undoubtedly high', given that 30 out of 42 mainland African states (and 10 out of 12 of the high-growth, high-fertility countries profiled in earlier chapters) are categorised by the UN as 'least developed countries', compared to just 14 anywhere else in the world.[24] Michel Garenne considers that 'the consequences of this persistent high fertility are incalculable and will lead some countries to situations very difficult to manage'.[25] If not moderated, Garenne adds, the growth will '[create] unsustainable situations of overpopulation in many cases'.[26]

In a 2015 blog 'Africa's challenging demographic future', John Bongaarts declared that if 3 billion people are added to the population by the end of the century, it 'may lead to a continent in chaos'.[27] Carl Haub considers that Africa's population is more likely to match the UNPD's high-variant projection for 2100 than the medium-variant, and warns that 'the dire consequences of such an increase are difficult to ponder... But we must face facts.'[28] Jean-Pierre Guengant and John F. May have written of a 'second demographic explosion' generated by Africa,[29] and Jack Goldstone has warned of 'a new population bomb'.[30] At the height of 'Africa Rising' fever, John Weeks remarked that it was 'important and useful for the world to periodically be reminded that things are not alright in Africa'.[31] Their profession may stand accused of being as 'dismal' a science as economics,[32] but no respected foreign or African demographers are unequivocally trumpeting the benefits of the population growth currently projected for Africa in the second half of the century.

Some see a classic Malthusian threat to certain countries. After the publication of *World Population Prospects: The 2012 Revision*, Julia Zinkina and Andrey Korotayev warned that projected growth rates in Niger, Zambia, Malawi, Tanzania, Somalia, Burkina Faso, Uganda, Mali and Madagascar put them to the fore among those nations facing a 'looming demographic catastrophe'[33] caused by inadequate or failing food supply. John Cleland emphasises that 'the implications [of high population growth] for human welfare and the environment are far-reaching but also complex, contested and uncertain',[34] but concurs that 'for some countries, a Malthusian future, where continued rapid population growth outstrips [food] production, is probable'.[35]

The Sahel is the territory most frequently cited by demographers as likely to succumb. Populations three times their current size are universally considered utterly unsustainable, or simply impossible. 'This is the region where the fabric of civilisation, weakened by rapid population growth and stretched by climate change driven by bloated northern consumption, is likely to fail first... It would be satisfying to prove Malthus wrong once again, but the portents are not good,' wrote Malcolm Potts and co-authors in 2013.[36] According to some climatologists, food production may decline by as much as 50% this century in the worst-hit Sahelian countries.[37] John Cleland regards Niger's predicament as 'only an extreme example of a Malthusian crisis that will affect the whole of the Sahel'.[38] 'Boundaries are being reached in the Sahel,' wrote Malcolm Potts of the Bixby Center for Population, Health & Sustainability in 2013.

Political demographers examine age structures country by country, urbanisation data and other factors to draw inferences about the association between substantial and growing youth populations and the likelihood of political violence or conflict. In a 2014 paper,

Andrey Korotayev identified Malawi, Burkina Faso, Uganda, Eritrea, Tanzania and Kenya as countries at high 'structural-demographic' risk, and Niger at very high risk in the late 2010s or 2020s, on account of their urban-youth growth rates exceeding 30% within a five-year period.[39] Serge Michailof, former operations director at AFD and the author of *Africanistan*, believes that 'the demography of Niger and the Sahel Zone has the potential to destabilise all of western Africa'.[40]

Here, too, there is a need to handle with care narratives that meld the relative certainty over a few decades of demographic projections for Africa with catastrophic predictions and demographic determinism. Henrik Urdal, who has long studied the relationship between youth 'bulges' and violence, emphasises that 'a young youth structure does not make countries destined for violence; in fact, most countries with large youth bulges avoid armed conflict most of the time'.[41] However, received wisdom and standard news-media depictions in the West mostly perpetuate a view that all Africa is in a state of permanent crisis, more prey than any other world region to the vicissitudes of climate change, mired in conflict and confronted by dwindling water resources and renewed danger of mass starvation (among other afflictions). This is a very partial narrative, in both senses of the word – both biased and incomplete.

Reputable organisations underpin the crisis narratives. Analytics firm Verisk Maplecroft's Climate Change Vulnerability Index estimates that about half of Africa's GDP is at 'extreme risk' from climate change.[42] In a BBC article, 'Is Africa overtaking the Middle East as the new jihadist battleground?', a French expert tells us that 'Africa is going to be the battleground of jihad for the next 20 years and it's going to replace the Middle East.'[43] Acute water shortages and even 'water wars' are foreseen by numerous experts. Concerning the Malthusian challenge cited so firmly in the population explosion era, 'food wars' have also been predicted due to the combination of climate change, water scarcity and soil and biodiversity loss.[44]

There may be good grounds for envisaging new crises or the intensification of existing ones. As far as food supply is concerned, for example, imports and prices rise relentlessly year by year in much of Africa.[45] The Global Hunger Index places almost all countries in Eastern, Western and Middle Africa in the 'serious' or 'alarming' categories. In the Sahel, Zimbabwe, South Sudan, Somalia and elsewhere 'emergency' food assistance is now simply an integral part of annual supply. In many, two-thirds of arable land is said to be degraded and land scarcity acute; and growing populations are endeavouring to feed themselves and the nation off half a hectare of arable land per head of population or less. However, expert warnings on soil degradation, land scarcity and most other agricultural topics often bear a striking similarity to those heard in the 1980s – and the 1950s. In this context, it is worth pondering that Burundi (a country where a Malthusian disaster is widely considered almost a certainty) has the same area of arable land per head of population as Kenya (about which no such fears are voiced); and that Niger's population per square kilometre of arable land is one of the lowest in Africa.

Climate change is bringing improved conditions to some parts of Africa. Satellite data showed extensive regreening of the Sahel in the final decades of the twentieth century and greenification on the margins of the Sahara in recent years, developments largely attributable to increased rainfall. Accounts of relentless desertification in the Sahel or the 'disappearance' of Lake Chad are oversimplifications of complex changes (or, some would say, myths – see text box). Less than 10% of the area affected by rising sea levels around the world will be in Africa; about two and a half times as much land and a higher proportion of the population will be affected in Europe.[46] A sense of perspective is needed with regard to conflict. In 2019, just one year, 31,000 people were murdered in Mexico, mostly in connection with a long-running drugs war; that is a comparable number of deaths to that attributed to the Boko Haram insurgency in North East Nigeria in more than a decade. Over 60,000 Mexicans have also disappeared since the start of the drugs war in 2006, a comparable number to *all* conflict-related fatalities in Nigeria since 1997.[47] According to the Global Terrorism Index produced by the Institute for Economics and Peace in Australia, there were 982 ISIS-related deaths in the Sahel – often depicted as a global 'hotspot' being engulfed by terrorism – in

Further reading

On regreening see L. Olsson, L. Eklundh and J. Ard. (2005), 'A recent greening of the Sahel - Trends, patterns and potential causes', *Journal of Arid Environments*, Vol. 63, pp. 556-66; James Owen, 'Sahara desert greening due to climate change?', *National Geographic*, 31 July 2009; Francesco S.R. Pausata et al. (2020), 'The greening of the Sahara: Past changes and future implications', *One Earth 2*, pp. 235-50.

On desertification see Ian Scoones's review of Roy H. Behnke and Michael Mortimore (eds) (2016), *The End of Desertification: Disputing Environmental Change in the Drylands*, in *Pastoralism*, Vol. 8, Art. 26 (2018). 'It is quite a shock to be presented with an abundance of evidence that desertification doesn't happen, at least not in the way it has been explained. Scientifically, it is a meaningless and indefinable concept,' wrote John Magrath in another review of the same book ('Desertification: An ecological reality or a dangerous myth?', *The Guardian*, 14 July 2016). See also Tor A. Benjaminsen and Pierre Hiernaux (2019), 'From dessication to global climate change: A history of the desertification narrative in the West African Sahel, 1900-2018', *Global Environment*, Vol. 12, No. 1, pp. 206-36.

On the true state of Lake Chad see Frederi G. Viens (2019), 'Scientists say we can't be certain why Lake Chad is shrinking', *Quartz Africa*, 24 April; Jacques Lemoalle and Géraud Magrin (2014), *Le développement du lac Tchad: Situation actuelle et futurs possibles*, IRD Éditions, Marseilles; Géraud Magrin (2016), 'The disappearance of Lake Chad: History of a myth', *Journal of Political Ecology*, Vol. 23, No. 1, pp. 204-22; Janani Vivekanada et al. (2019), *Shoring Up Stability: Addressing Climate and Fragility Risks in the Lake Chad Region*, Adelphi Research, Berlin, p. 10.

2019. This was a terrible toll, but less than 4% of the worldwide total. By any measure, the State of Rio de Janeiro in Brazil is a far more dangerous environ than the Great Lakes region of Central Africa. This is not to make light of conflicts in a number of African countries and the suffering they entail, merely to highlight the prevalent bias of singling them out and the absurdity of portraying Africa as a 'war-torn' continent.

As for the received wisdom that climate change exacerbates armed conflict in Africa (and elsewhere), this is an area that has attracted enormous sums of research funding. However, there is no consensus on the links between the two.[48] A panel of 11 experts from different disciplines convened by Stanford University scholars to brainstorm the question and review existing research concluded that 'intensifying climate change is estimated to increase future risks of conflict'; but it also found that 'the effect [of climate change on organised armed conflict within countries] is small relative to those of other factors such as low socio-economic development, weak state capacity, unexpected economic shocks, and social polarisation'.[49] The OECD's Sahel and West Africa Club has similarly concluded that in the Sahel, 'environmental variables are of secondary importance at best compared to political, historical and economic variables'.[50]

Authoritative sources relate how 'surprisingly little is known about how groundwater in sub-Saharan Africa is replenished and how resilient it is to climate change', and that global warming and climate change 'could actually be good for increasing groundwater recharge overall' in Africa.[51] Colossal water resources exist like the Nubian Sandstone Aquifer System, containing as much water as the Nile will discharge in 500 years.[52] Furthermore, for most people in Africa, lack of water is not always to do with water scarcity – many other factors conspire to limit access, including cost.[53]

Again, the point is not to suggest, Pollyanna-like, that everything about the future is rosy. Nor is it to encourage fatalism or complacency. It is simply to underscore the need for caution when faced with grand narratives about Africa (or regions of Africa); and to acknowledge that the bleakest prophecies for Africa by expert outsiders from the 1970s onwards have all proved wayward. Africa should not be depicted as a 'catastrophe-in-waiting',[54] as Professor Simukai Chigudu at Oxford University's Department of International Development reminded the world when the Covid-19 pandemic developed. Catastrophes – like miracles – are only ever discerned after the event. Furthermore, the worst crises in Africa today – think, for example, of Libya, South Sudan, 'Anglophone' Cameroon, Central African Republic, Ethiopia, Somalia, Eastern DRC – have mostly been caused by conflicts in which it would be surprising to see any credible expert cite rapid population growth as a key, or even minor, catalyst.

In the Sahel, where it is commonly said that 'states have been pushed to the brink of collapse', and where huge tracts 'will remain ungovernable for the foreseeable future',[55] population growth may contribute to a worsening situation, but it cannot be said to have been a leading cause of the multiple conflicts and almost ubiquitous insecurity. Indeed, Daniel Eizenga, himself an acknowledged expert on the Sahel, cautions that 'experts of the region have… so far failed to offer a fully satisfactory explanation for the current state of affairs'.[56] A – if not *the* – leading trigger of today's instability was the NATO-led invasion of Libya in 2011, and subsequent military escapades by foreign powers, a fact frequently omitted from analyses and press coverage. In similar vein, Madagascar, with a population of about 25 million, is the only African country not affected by serious conflict that is poorer now – a lot poorer – than it was in 1960. Here, too, blaming the tribulations of the world's second-largest island country predominantly, or even partly, on population pressure would be decidedly eccentric.

Detail is the antidote to generalisation, and demography has a vital role to play in this regard. Local population facts, figures and trends can focus the mind in a manner that national, regional and continental totals do not. They influence politics, societies and economies in myriad important ways. For anyone interested in Nigeria, and most of all for Nigerians, it is informative to know what the country's fertility 'map' looks like, region by region; contrary to received wisdom, there are a good number of states across the three (predominantly Christian) southern zones where the fertility rate is higher than ones in the (predominantly Muslim) north. Burkinabés should surely know that if their capital city, Ouagadougou, continues at its present rate of growth it will be home to 13 million people by 2050, six times its size in 2010. Will Uganda's President Museveni really be delighted to learn that Kampala is on track to grow from less than 2 million people to more than 10 million by 2050, and that his country's population density will then surpass that of India? And why exactly did the TFR in Karamoja region rise from 6.4 to 7.9 births between the last two DHSs? Does it not matter – because it is politically marginal – that in Kenya's Samburu County 20% of the population are under the age of five and that three-quarters of adults have no formal education?[57] Was the late President Magufuli really delighted that Dar es Salaam could be heading for a population of 20 million? Perhaps so.

Such details are more than curiosities. As well as being the essential foundation stones of competent planning, they provide relief to the map of Africa, highlighting complexity and diversity that is often overlooked. Most important of all, they are a reminder that headline figures refer to *people* and the way they live their lives – they are not just numbers. Yet it is notable how often basic demographic details are ignored. In this context, the inclusion of demographic data and a population pyramid in the 'Africa at 60' country-by-country infosheets produced by the African Studies Centre at the Universiteit Leiden in 2020 was a commendable innovation.

Generalised disaster warnings about Africa's future do not only hail from the West. Within Africa, the role in the early 1980s of the ECA in depicting a potential 'nightmare scenario' in 2008 has been assumed by the African Capacity Building Foundation (ACBF), based in Harare, Zimbabwe. The ACBF is the AU's 'specialised agency for capacity development' and was commissioned to assess the 'internal and external risks associated with the implementation of the AU's Agenda 2063'. Its 2015 publication contrasts strikingly with the upbeat, aspirational text of Agenda 2063, which targeted aggregate GDP 'proportionate to [Africa's] share of the world's population and natural resource endowments',* but was otherwise silent on the issue of population growth.

The assessment contains passages as downbeat – and in places as broad-brush – as anything produced outside the continent. It noted: 'many of Africa's 1.1 billion people continue to struggle with access to basic healthcare, nutrition, primary education, and employment', an unfavourable situation 'exacerbated by disease pandemics, militarised and gender violence, politicised ethnicity and sectarianism, fundamentalist radicalism, destructive conflicts, rising levels of poverty, and environmental degradation'. It also warned that after the collapse of oil and commodity prices in the first half of the 2010s, 'many of the continent's 35 least developed countries face the prospect of stagnating economic expansion, with profound effects on social welfare, political stability, and livelihoods'.[58]

This was the expansive backdrop to the presentation by the ACBF of an equally generalised but simultaneously quite specific and tangible threat: 'the dramatic increase in the population of youth and the risk that they will face bleak futures of poverty, homelessness, and unemployment at a time when African governments' welfare efficiency is being tested'.[59] The internal and external factors are set out that combine to 'subject growing numbers of African citizens – especially its youth – to a Hobbesian future where life tends to be "nasty, brutish and short"' (as Robert D. Kaplan had also predicted two decades earlier in his dystopian vision of Africa's future).

Various country, regional and global threats to the achievement of the Agenda 2063 objective of securing 'a peaceful and secured Africa, people-driven development, inclusive growth and development' are also assessed. They include the nature of the post-colonial state, political violence and slow social development. Each is given a score. The 'growing population of youth' is given the highest score – 20 – signifying an extreme risk. The assessment of the future for Africa's youth could not have been bleaker.

---

* In 2020, Africa's share of global GDP was about 3% compared to its 17% share of the global population; the latter is forecast to be almost 30% in the mid-2060s.

20

A Luta Continua!
('On with the Struggle!')*

Youth protests are becoming more frequent, better organised and effective across Africa. But there are many entrenched obstacles to achieving the enduring change in political norms required to accelerate development. What population growth will mean country by country rests ultimately on politics and the political settlements that the current generation of young Africans can secure by diverse means. The outcomes of their efforts are of immense importance first and foremost to themselves, but also to the future of a continent that, not least on account of its demography, is moving inexorably towards a position at the centre of global affairs. This fact needs to be clearly understood by non-Africans and responded to with more than crisis narratives.

'Leaders are very frightened of youth… their rent-seeking behaviour is under threat,' Carlos Lopes, Bissau-Guinean former executive secretary of the ECA, told the audience at the annual lecture of the Royal African Society in October 2017. They are well aware that 'the liberation of the continent was a youth phenomenon' – think Nasser, Lumumba, Nkrumah, Cabral, Fanon at their peaks, and the numerous women activists whose key role has been airbrushed out of

---

* Rallying cry of the Mozambique Liberation Front (FRELIMO), coined by Eduardo Mondlane in the late 1960s and subsequently adopted by other independence and protest movements across Africa. The second clause of the phrase is *vitória é certa* – 'victory is certain'.

liberation history. Yet 'leadership has not listened'. The 'number-one problem', according to Lopes, bigger than corruption or any of their most frequently cited shortcomings, is 'lack of respect for diversity' among political elites – the immense diversity of people, cultures, beliefs and needs within the boundaries of the countries they govern.[1]

The travails of youth are attested to by individuals quoted in the chapters focusing on the lack of employment and elsewhere in this book. A great deal is known about the attitudes and aspirations of young men and women across the continent due, in part, to the rise of social media and mass surveys. Young people feel marginalised, frustrated, disillusioned, robbed of hope and angry, sometimes to the point of violence. Away from international conferences, where they are referred to by their political leaders as 'the greatest resource', or, in the case of absentee President Biya of Cameroon, 'full of potential, dynamic and ambitious, inventive and conquering', at home they are largely ignored or dismissively referred to as 'lazy' and 'trouble-making'. Young women, in particular, are so marginalised by patriarchy they feel invisible. As Black Lives Matter protests spread around the world after the killing of George Floyd in July 2020, the Kenyan columnist Tee Ngugi highlighted that police brutality was a run-of-the-mill, everyday reality throughout Africa: 'African lives don't matter to their leaders and police.'[2]

Also in 2020, in the wake of mass protests in Nigeria and internationally to close down the infamous and brutal Specialist Anti-Robbery Squad, or 'specialist robbery squad' as it was more commonly known, the writer and designer Chukwudi Ukonne explained the significance of the #EndSARS movement:

> For powerless Nigerians, this has not just been a movement; it has been the movement. It is arguably Nigeria's most significant mass movement since the pro-democracy rallies of the mid- to late 90s. These protests might prove to be the political epiphany for a generation of younger Nigerians who have never been seen nor heard but have now made it clear that the government will no longer ignore them.[3]

With #EndSARS and widespread protests in the country about other issues, the editor-in-chief of the Lagos-based *Stears Business* similarly observed, 'Nigeria's youth, and its women specifically, have shown that they will not take the abuse of rights laying down.'[4] For Wale Lawal, editor of *The Republic: A Journal of Nigerian Affairs*, writing in the *Financial Times*, the #End SARS protests showed

> the extent to which the government reflects an older, out-of-touch minority: a generation that seems incapable of recognizing younger members of society as equal citizens. The problem is a societal one. Older Nigerians hate being held accountable, especially by the young. They prefer silence and unwavering respect and they weaponise 'tradition' to avoid having to earn or reciprocate such respect.[5]

Many Nigerian political leaders 'believe violence, not service, is the language of authority and that impunity is synonymous with leadership', Lawal concluded dismally.

Two years earlier, young people were the driving force behind events leading to a revolution in Ethiopia, the after-effects of which still convulse the country. In 2019, non-violent protests in Algeria forced the resignation of a military-backed president seeking a fifth term in power. In an extraordinary and unexpected turn of events in Sudan at the end of that year, another non-violent movement with women and social media playing prominent roles succeeded – after three astonishingly courageous months – in unseating another military-backed president of three decades' standing. There were also significant protests in Zimbabwe, South Africa and elsewhere, many of them intentionally leaderless and employing other innovative tactics. In Kenya and Malawi young people played a part in forcing the rerun of elections. Although coverage by Western news media of these events was ephemeral by comparison with its reporting of the occupation of Cairo's Tahrir Square in 2011 that eventually forced President Mubarak from power, there is a palpable sense within Africa that a tidal wave of discontent is building in cities across the continent.

'This generation is yearning for change and I am here to deliver it,' declared the 38-year-old musician Robert Kyagulanyi Ssentamu – aka 'Bobi Wine' or 'Ghetto President' – shortly before standing against President Museveni in Uganda's 2021 presidential election.[6] 'The Museveni regime is increasingly struggling to build legitimacy among [the youth], which wants public services and employment rather than distant stories about how the regime brought an end to war when it came to power in 1986,' observe Anna Reuss and Kristof Titeca. 'It risks losing its hold on the "Museveni babies" – the more than 80% of the population born after 1986.'[7] Despite intense intimidation during the campaign and the election, Bobi Wine secured 35% of the vote. Throughout Africa, household-name musicians are frequently to the fore in calling out injustice and encouraging mobilisation, as they have always been everywhere.

Some grievances are less tangible. 'Waithood' is a term* used to describe the limbo that most young men find themselves in even if they are fortunate enough to have completed secondary school. In 'traditional' and 'modern' worlds alike, gaining recognition as an adult, marriage and supporting a family become yearly more difficult in the absence of sufficient work and the continually rising costs of accommodation, food and other necessities. For young women who have not been subjected to early- or late-adolescent marriage, the issues of social acceptance, matrimony and securing decent work create a minefield. Youth everywhere regard themselves as being denied the independence and certainties that they perceive older generations to have had at the same age; and they are quite clear about the identity of those who have denied them: their political leaders.

There are countries where governments do not have the resources to spend more than a few tens of dollars a year per citizen; and there are ones recovering from war where funds are equally scarce. But protests have mostly been in richer countries (in relative terms), whose young (and older) citizens are all fully aware that their governments could have done more to protect personal safety, improve education and

---

* The term was coined by the Mozambican scholar Professor Alcinda Honwana.

health services, and provide *something* more by way of opportunity. The governments of all of them stand accused of being little more than criminal enterprises, the current winners in a continual game of gangster politics as corrupt as anything ever spawned in Europe, the US, Asia or Latin America. South African newspapers have estimated the cost of corruption in their country over the past decade to be equivalent to about one-third of GDP. Members of the dos Santos regime in Angola, one of Africa's richest countries, are accused of appropriating tens of billions of dollars of state resources over two decades – possibly more than US$100 billion. Oil and gas exports are estimated to have generated US$640 billion for their government since 2002,[8] yet half the population is classified as living in extreme poverty, less than US$2 billion is spent annually on health services and the defence budget exceeds the allocation to health services *and* education. Government revenue, as opposed to private revenue from state assets, in DRC, a huge country with a population of almost 100 million, is a paltry US$4 billion a year.[9] But no country can quite match Nigeria for having had the funds to transform the futures of all its citizens but choosing not to.

A Chatham House report quoted a figure of 'close to US$400 billion' as the sum misappropriated from public accounts in Nigeria between 1960 and 1999. This was equivalent to about two-thirds of all donor assistance – 'aid' – to all African countries since independence. Additionally, illicit financial flows from the country between 2005 and 2014 alone are estimated at US$180 billion.[10] A March 2020 analysis of the finances of the Nigeria National Petroleum Corporation by the reputable civic activist organisations #Fixouroil and BudgIT concluded that more than US$200 billion had been siphoned off through the state oil company since 1980. *The Sunday Times* put a figure of £540 billion on what has been 'stolen' from the public purse since independence.[11] These are colossal sums in a country where the federal budget for health and education for almost 200 million people in 2020 amounted to just US$2.6 billion – a mere US$13 a head. The state's 'abject failure to provide public goods such as healthcare, power supply, potable water, employment and education has been well documented', observes Chris Ngwodo in an article titled 'The great unravelling: The disintegration of the Nigerian state'[12] – as well documented as the torrent of funds 'leaking' from the economy by one means or another since independence. It is no surprise that indignation and anger are inexorably rising among the citizens of the 'Giant of Africa'.

Equatorial Guinea, a country with one of the smallest populations but until recently the highest GDP per capita on the Africa mainland – close to US$20,000 in 2014, thanks to its oil reserves – is in the lowest quartile of the United Nations Human Development Index. In 2019 the government was even forced to borrow hundreds of millions of dollars from the IMF. Meanwhile, Teodoro Obiang, in power for more than four decades, is accused of presiding over an 'oil kleptocracy'.[13] On the other side of the continent, in Djibouti, with its strategic position at the entrance to the Red Sea, through which 40% of the world's oil trade is shipped, and a population similar in size to Equatorial Guinea, substantial port revenues are siphoned off in their entirety while 80% of the population live in extreme poverty. In early 2021, President Ismail Omar Guelleh secured a fifth term in office with 97% of the vote. These are private enterprises, not progressive governments of nation-states.

Corruption, it is often said, is a symptom, not a cause. In Africa, many identify its roots in the colonial state or in the 'dog-eat-dog' economic turmoil of the late 1970s and 1980s, exacerbated by being strong-armed into swallowing the World Bank and IMF's structural adjustment 'medicine'. There is widespread conviction among older policymakers and academics – those educated in the 1960s and 1970s – that 'global power structures' have always made it impossible for African economies to realise their potential; and that external parties – foreign governments, investors and businesses – have encouraged rapacity and been equally rapacious. Some or all of these explanations for the current state of affairs may be believed by some youth protestors, and the precise causes and triggers for their actions differ from country to country. But in light of the needs of the present – education, security, food and, top of the wish-list in most surveys, a decent job – historical grievances and catalysts extensively catalogued and analysed in academia are remote explanations compared with the conduct of current political elites and their predecessors. Furthermore, the importance in the present of pride and shame should not be overlooked. Young Nigerians, for example, are acutely aware that in the 1970s their country was considered a land of milk and honey. Money flowed as freely as the oil exports, and education, health services and prospects were good. Now, the world around all but the privileged few is one in which more than half the population live in extreme poverty, the health and education sectors are broken, the shortage of jobs is catastrophic and anything a citizen needs has to be paid for. The lottery jackpot win was squandered. Worse still, politicians and other leaders who genuinely consider the situation to be unacceptable are seemingly too few and far between, or too disempowered, to make much difference.

Rapid population growth is viscerally well understood by young activists, intellectuals and commentators who live with the consequences in more and more countries where investment is not keeping pace. This is most obviously so in Nigeria. A Nigerian Twitter thread started by BudgIT began:

> A Ticking Time-Bomb? With 100% population growth, Nigeria is estimated to become the 3rd most populous country in the world by 2050. ALARM: It's currently filled with 24m unemployed youths. What then lies ahead of 2050?

Responses included:

> Without education, esp. girls' education, Nigeria cannot escape the demographic doom that lays ahead with uncontrolled population growth.

> Pop growth in Nigeria will only confer advantages in the long run if converted to human capital assets.

> The resources will just never be enough if people continue to birth at this rate.

Why do we still not have any properly publicised population strategy in Nigeria? Those who will explode our population by 2050 are already born.

In an article titled 'Youth in crisis', Wale Lawal depicts the regions of his country as being in danger of 'cracking under the weight of their own populations'.[14] Yomi Kazeem, a reporter at *Quartz Africa*, concurs: 'under some circumstances, a country's population could be cited as a strength but when, like in Nigeria's case, population growth outpaces infrastructure and development by far, then it's a huge red flag'.[15] Uche Charlie Isiugo-Abanihe, Professor of Demography at the University of Ibadan, alludes to the approach of 'demographic fatigue', a state where Nigeria 'cannot stabilize its population growth, and is unable to deal effectively with a range of threats [including] natural disasters as well as diseases and population induced crises such as land degradation, communal clashes, banditry, insurgency, irregular migration and insecurity'.[16]

The consequence of inadequate development expenditure over decades of rapid population growth was alluded to by Kwame Owino at the start of this book: the value of human capital declines in step with physical capital – a vicious cycle if ever there was one. Whereas 'population growth' is abstract, the needs of people are real. 'I think about the future of my continent in terms of three questions,' says Nigerian demographer Alex Ezeh. 'Are Africans healthy? Do they have access to a good education? And do they have opportunities to apply their skills?'[17] In similar vein, in its 2015 risk assessment the ACBF declared that 'in short, Africa can sustainably manage its demographic challenges only if it improves healthcare and education and, more broadly, all components of human and social capital'.[18] 'Contrary to popular belief,' Jean-Pierre Guengant wrote in 2012, 'the demographic future of sub-Saharan Africa has not been written... In a nutshell, it comes down to the capacity of a country to satisfy the basic needs of its population in terms of health and education'[19] – and, he might have added, jobs. The backdrop, one of inadequate inward and domestic investment, waning commitments from external donors, and capital dilution everywhere (the inevitable consequence of states not investing enough to maintain national wealth), is not on the face of it auspicious.[20]

The potential for transformation rests on one thing more than any other: politics. This is not to place unrealistic expectations on national leaders or electoral contests to bring about change, simply to emphasise that population trends in Africa's regions – and whether those trends ultimately prove advantageous or deleterious – will be determined by everyday politics and the conduct of political 'machines'. More robust social contracts between the governing and the governed and greater inclusion – not miracles – are the objective of every youth protest movement: 'better' politics, leading to better 'governance' or 'development' and opportunity rather than simply lumpen representation and cut-price bread and circuses.

If the lives of families having large numbers of children were improving, rates of population growth would diminish in importance, and probably also in extent over time. While there are countries where the status of women is so abysmal that childbirth is enforced, fertility in most involves choices by both parents – and where the future offers opportunity to 'get ahead', and a greater degree of certainty, most people globally choose to have fewer children. Preferences across Africa regarding the most desirable number of children are unlikely ever to be uniform and may not conform to other regions of the world, but it is inconceivable that across the 12 high-growth, high-fertility countries examined earlier the choice in this improving scenario would be to have *more* children. In this context, promoting modern contraception as a poverty reduction and female empowerment tool can appear to be a case of not seeing the wood for the trees.

This is not a reprise of the 'development is the best contraceptive' mantra embraced for decades by African leaders. Rather it is to emphasise the importance of the essential prerequisite: development depends almost entirely on politics, and the 'primacy of politics'[21] in Africa cannot be overstated. Yet development agencies, donors, global charities and international finance institutions like the World Bank and IMF tend to treat 'development' as a predominantly technocratic exercise. They steer clear of politics, considering it a purely domestic concern, while many foreign economists and investment advisers analysing Africa simply ignore politics and political dynamics altogether, as if economic trajectories occur in some kind of vacuum. On the other hand, less scrupulous foreigners understand 'the primacy of politics' all too well and know precisely how to exploit it. 'Vampire states', 'kleptocracies', 'spoils politics', 'politics of the belly', 'gangster politics', 'super-clientilism' – all exist with varying degrees of connivance or assistance from some party or parties from 'the international community'.[22] At grass-roots level, the reason why public services are non-existent in a certain town, that a conflict is left to spread, that there is no functioning borehole despite an abundance of accessible water, that land reform or agricultural policy is not implemented invariably comes down to politics, rather than a lack of money or capacity. All too often, politics quite deliberately stymies human capital development.

There are governments that are strategically 'anti-developmental',[23] including those of two of the most resource-rich and populous countries on the continent – Nigeria and DRC. It is no coincidence that they have among the highest rates of extreme poverty. Poverty is as political as the non-provision of services. The World Bank may state that extreme poverty is set to become a 'predominantly sub-Saharan phenomenon' by 2030, but this hides an important truth. Half of the continent's extreme poor live in just five countries – Nigeria, DRC, Ethiopia, Tanzania and Madagascar – and three-quarters in 10 countries.[24] This is not to deny that 'lived' poverty is on the rise almost everywhere on the continent,[25] that the measure of extreme poverty should rightly be three or even four times US$1.90 a day, that by 2030 half of the extreme poor globally will be African children – 305 million in number[26] – or that urban poverty is rising in every country. It is to highlight that about 80% of Africa's countries do not have an outsized extreme-poverty problem, that Africa and extreme poverty should not be treated as synonymous, and that the blight of extreme poverty is not intractable, as many countries have already demonstrated. Most of those that have not are what has been termed 'case studies in inertia', mostly for an obvious (political) reason.[27] Ethiopia is a conspicuous exception.

Any national of any African country can explain the geography of poverty in their country in political terms. In Uganda, President Museveni is always quick to highlight the country's 7% average GDP growth in the 1990s and 2000s and the reduction of extreme poverty from above 60% of the population to about 20%. These were substantial achievements. Less attention is drawn to the fact that in the same time frame, poverty levels soared in two of Uganda's four regions that are home to almost half the population – Eastern and Northern.[28] The Uganda Bureau of Statistics has also recorded an increase in national poverty, according to its own definition, from 20% in 2013–14 to 27% in 2016–17.

The obstacles to change in the basic character of politics of any country are formidable. In Africa, substantial youth protests are nothing new, and political elites have proved very adept at absorbing or diffusing threats to their hegemony through skilful use of much stick and a little carrot. Elections are often 'managed', to the extent that fewer and fewer young people bother to cast a vote, exacerbating their sense of marginalisation. In countries that lack much or most of the usual state machinery – DRC or Somalia, for example – there is difficulty identifying at national level with whom or what to try to force a political settlement; sometimes the only option is to seek to influence local power structures. In Nigeria, 'politics is a fraud', according to barrister Dr Joe Abah, former director-general of the Bureau of Public Service Reforms; 'it is not based on ideology, principles or manifestos [but] designed to empower a few to oppress and torment the majority.'[29]

So far, the potent force of inter-generational solidarity is too seldom deployed. Likewise, rural populations are almost everywhere a majority, often a significant one, but they tend to be more conservative than their urban contemporaries. Even when successful at toppling post-independence regimes, uprisings have never yet succeeded in altering the political landscape permanently or forcing the development of an enduring social contract. In Tunisia, Egypt,

Algeria, Zimbabwe and so many other countries there was little or no change for the better after victory.

Despite the many obstructions and disappointments, in time this generation of youth will gain real purchase or even prevail in some countries – perhaps many. All over the world it has sources of inspiration, and most importantly within Africa itself, in the shape of the struggles for independence. The proportion of 15–24s or 15–35s in many populations may not be substantially different from what it was in the 1970s, but the sheer number of the discontented and desperate is nowadays as formidable as their aspirations are bold. There is a palpable sense in many places that enough really is enough, that a T-shirt and a little something will no longer send people home contented, and that basic public services are a right, not an occasional personal favour. 'Youth do not want to *discuss* the future, they *are* the future,' Carlos Lopes points out; and that future 'will ultimately depend on the outcome of the battle between rent-seeking and the developmental state, and whether integration occurs' on the African continent.[30]

The young cannot succeed alone, but they are not exactly alone. 'Youth' is much more than an age cohort. It comprises members of feminist and other women's organisations, Pentecostal and other church congregations, organised informal worker societies, students, musicians and artists, people from the professional and middle classes – a plethora of groups which have older members as well and which can provide inter-generational bridges. Resistance is a long game, usually, and there is no knowing for certain what the 'new tide of people power'[31] will achieve. 'What is clear', a Kenyan businessman tweeted in February 2019, 'is that a very young, very informed and very connected African youth demographic is set to alter existing equilibrium between rulers & subjects, and a rebalancing has begun.'[32]

The stakes could not be higher. What happens in states where the quality of education deteriorates further, inadequately funded health systems collapse under the weight of demand for their services, and youth unemployment ratchets still higher? First and foremost, they will be even less able to overcome the specific and varying challenges

posed by the potential threats woven into the crisis narratives
mentioned in the previous chapter – including climate change,
internal conflicts, food production and access to water. As far as
European governments and commentators are concerned, although
most migration by young Africans in search of opportunity and the
means of survival is within their own countries, the possibility of a
'tsunami' of migration out of Africa – a latter-day equivalent of the
migration of about a quarter of Europe's mid-nineteenth-century
population across the Atlantic in the course of 100 years – is now a
fixation. In *The Scramble for Europe*, Stephen Smith, former Africa
editor of *Libération* and *Le Monde*, suggests that by 2050 there could
potentially be up to 200 million 'Afro-Europeans' living in Europe
– about a quarter of the total population. The demographer François
Héran counters that this conclusion is based on 'economic conjecture'
and 'does not stand up to scrutiny'; in his view, 'the most realistic
figure is five times less'.[33] Wherever the true figure lies, 'anticipation
of mass migration within the next 35 years is justified', according to
LSHTM's John Cleland and Kazuyo Machiyama.[34]

**A sense of perspective – and humility – is often lost in the analysis
of Africa's population trends.** Demographic transition theory, rooted
in the experience of Western populations, endeavoured to provide a
unifying narrative for global changes over a couple of centuries only.
The last 50 years of the twentieth century witnessed sustained rapid
growth, described by the United Nations in *The World Population in
1970* as 'an unprecedented situation of unforeseeable consequences'.[35]
But these are specks of time in the evolutionary history of the planet.

About 100,000 years ago, the global population numbered about
1 million, of whom 90% lived in Africa.[36] Ever since then, as John
Reader relates in his magisterial *Africa: A Biography of the Continent*,
'surges and lapses in population growth' have been part and parcel
of evolutionary history, usually regulated by the availability of
adequate food and water resources and 'highly unpredictable'

changes in climate. 'Cycles of "boom and bust" are a commonplace of human existence,' Reader reminds us, as are 'constant migration and colonization'.[37] By the end of the current century the dominant demographic theory, seeking to rationalise what has happened to world populations since 1900, or 1950 or 2000, will quite possibly bear little resemblance to what is proposed today: no matter how reliable the view to mid-century, the second half could well change everything. The UN publication mentioned above referred to 'our vast ignorance of the future'.[38]

'Vast ignorance' of the African past (and present) often precludes or obstructs contemplation of futures that are different from those most commonly envisaged by foreign institutions and commentators. Even the most rudimentary knowledge of pre-colonial history is a powerful counterbalance – or antidote – to a surfeit of Western imaginings. The histories (or even names) of great polities and empires – Aksum, Ghana, Kongo, Mali, Songhai, Zimbabwe, Ashanti, Zulu, Abyssinia – are too little known outside (and inside) the continent, but even basic familiarity broadens horizons and illuminates its immense diversity and dynamism in the past two millennia. Furthermore, the recent histories of Ghana and Somalia, Central African Republic and Kenya, Madagascar and Tunisia could scarcely be more different. There is no reason at all to suspect that this will ever not be so, no matter how successful efforts at regional and continental integration prove in the twenty-first century.

Fortunes and narratives can change very rapidly, and in a completely unforeseen way. To older Africans, the August 1976 cover of a special issue of *Ebony* magazine proclaiming 'Africa... Continent of the Future'[39] must have seemed like a cruel joke a decade later. In 1970 Nigeria's GDP per capita was roughly double that of China. By the end of the 1990s China had caught up, and by 2015 its GDP per capita was five times that of Nigeria. Neither trajectory was forecast by economists until clearly visible in the rear-view mirror. As we saw earlier, the East Asian economic 'miracle' was only so named by the World Bank when it had been under way for two decades or more.

Between 1980 and 2010, 29 emerging and developing Asian countries increased GDP per capita by an average of about 11 times.[40]

In the late 1970s, Kenya, with a TFR of eight births, was the country whose rate of population growth triggered the same degree of trepidation as Niger does today. Whatever challenges the former has to deal with now, they are certainly not considered comparable to those facing the latter. Conversely, in 1990 Kenya's GDP per capita was about three times higher than that of Vietnam. In 2000, Vietnam, Kenya and Tanzania were level-pegging. By 2017, Vietnam's GDP per capita was 50% higher than Kenya's and more than double Tanzania's. Vietnam gains more foreign direct investment in a year than all the countries of Northern Africa, the region that attracts the most in Africa.

Similarly, Bangladesh's GDP per capita has quadrupled since 2000 to exceed that of Kenya, partly because its garment industry expanded from a few hundred factories in the mid-1980s to more than 4,500 today. The country has earned the moniker 'South Asia's standout star'.[41] Ten years ago, Peru exported about US$300m of soft fruit a year; today that figure exceeds US$8 billion, almost three times Ethiopia's *total* exports. To emphasise the point with a 'rich-world' example of the vagaries of economic fortunes, for two centuries Glasgow was a world leader in shipbuilding and the second city of the British empire. The collapse of its shipbuilding industry, and with it the entire local economy, took just two decades.[42]

The identity of the narrator is always important. In the late 1990s, after structural adjustment and 'orthodox' economic policies had mostly failed to produce the results expected by the World Bank and IMF in Africa and Latin America, Western experts 'proved' with the use of econometrics that Africa's poor economic performance and 'slow development' could be attributed to the tropical climate, geography, the natural resource 'curse', low-quality institutions, 'bad neighbourhood effects', ethnic diversity and 'bad culture'. Ha-Joon Chang, Reader in the Political Economy of Development at Cambridge University, finds 'the implications of such thinking very disturbing'. While he agrees that 'meta-structural' factors do matter, he sees a clear confusion of cause and symptom and ably demonstrates that 'some of this stuff isn't even half true'. In sum, it creates the impression that some countries are *destined* for underdevelopment and that Africa has 'to be treated as if on permanent disability benefit'. Chang bemoans the fact that 'some Africans even agree with this stuff',[43] and reminds anyone willing to listen that there is no insult that has ever been levelled by Westerners at the politics, culture, economic management and people of African countries that was not earlier directed at his own country, South Korea, in the 1960s.

The centrality of Africa in global affairs in the twenty-first century is now certain. The sheer size and growth of its youth population alone is a prime reason why the continent's current affairs (and history) should be of greater interest beyond its shores. The consequences of youth endeavours to change politics will be of global importance. As the populations of Europe, China and other Asian countries age and contract, this is all the more true. Global economic growth and world trade patterns are likely to be materially influenced by African countries. Alongside India, Africa could well prove to be an immense bulwark of liberal democracy, however flawed in parts. It can be said with near-certainty that by mid-century about one-third of the world's working-age population will be African; so too will 85% of the world's French speakers (compared to less than half now).[44] Africa is arguably already the 'global centre' of Christianity.[45] The list of reasons why Africa matters is endless and needs to be carefully considered as an antidote to the current dominance of stale crisis narratives that could equally well (and equally erroneously) be deployed to depict any of the world's continents. Quite simply, as a blog in *The Washington Post* succinctly put it, 'Africa, for better or worse, is more important than ever.'[46]

In reality, often Africa is still absent altogether from global narratives. It remains common to read a blog analysing revolts and protests around the world that (paradoxically) makes no mention of any occurring in Africa; or to watch an event at which what will happen in the world in the coming year is discussed without Africa even being mentioned (or with Africa being evaluated solely by non-Africans). As the Kenyan writer and journalist Christine Mungai has observed, it is as if many foreign observers, analysts and commentators simply do 'not envision a place for the continent in the world's game of thrones'.[47] This is an increasingly foolish, even dangerous, oversight: again, the sheer size of Africa's population and its location alone will underpin its central importance in world affairs. In an article in *World Politics Review* titled 'Why Africa's future will determine the rest of the world's', Howard W. French put this perfectly: 'how Africa's population evolves, and how the continent's economies develop, will affect everything people near and far assume about their lives today'.[48]

Endnotes

Abbreviations

AfDB – African Development Bank
AU – African Union
N-IUSSP: online news magazine of the International Union for the Scientific Study of Population
OECD – The Organisation for Economic Co-operation and Development, Paris
UNDESA – United Nations Department of Economic and Social Affairs, New York
UNECA – United Nations Economic Commission for Africa
UNFPA – United Nations Population Fund (formerly United Nations Fund for Population Activities), New York
UNPD – United Nations Department of Economic and Social Affairs/Population Division, New York

INTRODUCTION: 'YOU START WITH THE NUMBERS'

1 James Mwangi, 'Wanjigi urges Kenyans to churn out more babies', *The Standard*, 12 December 2018.

2 'Make babies inside family and outside', *Daily Nation* YouTube channel, 12 December 2018 https://www.youtube.com/watch?v=v2IS1sSpoxs&ab_channel=Nation.

3 Kenya Demographic and Health Survey (DHS) Final Report 2014, Chapter 5 ('Fertility'), *passim*.

4 United Nations Department of Economic and Social Affairs, Population Division (hereafter UNPD), *World Population Prospects: The 2019 Revision*.

5 'Make babies inside family and outside', *Daily Nation* YouTube channel, 12 December 2018 https://www.youtube.com/watch?v=v2IS1sSpoxs&ab_channel=Nation.

6 'Magufuli advises against birth control', *The Citizen*, 10 September 2018.

7 'Tanzania suspends US-funded family planning ads on radio, television', *The Citizen*, 20 September 2018.

8 Fumbuka Ng'wanakilala, 'President urges Tanzania's women to "set ovaries free", have more babies to boost economy', Reuters, 10 July 2019; also 'President Magufuli again urges Tanzanians to bear more children to boost economy', *The Citizen*, 16 March 2020.

9 Alex Ezeh, 'Empowering women lies at the centre of controlling population growth in Africa', *The Conversation*, 20 September 2018.

10 Rashid Abdi (Horn of Africa analyst at International Crisis Group) tweet on 11 July 2019.

11 Kwame Owino, 'There's no economic advantage to a procreation race among nations', *Daily Nation*, 3 January 2019.

12 See Lauren A. Johnston (2019), *A Timely Economic Demography Lesson from China for the G20*, Institute for Global Dialogue/UNISA Occasional Paper 75, p. 6.

13 Ibid., *passim*. A 'rich' country is defined as 'high-income' by the World Bank. For 2019 the threshold was GDP per capita US$12,536.

14 Kwame Owino, op. cit.

15 Africa Check, 'Does Kenya have one of the worst maternal mortality rates in the world?', 12 June 2019. World Health Organization (WHO) World Health Statistics 2020 stated a maternal mortality rate of 342 deaths per 100,000 live births in 2018.

16 World Bank (2016), *Kenya Gender and Poverty Assessment 2015/16*, p. 64.

17 World Bank Open Data resource, data for 2019. In Kenya DHS Final Report 2014 (p. 114) the figures were one death in 39 and one death in 22 respectively.

18 World Bank (2016), *Kenya Gender and Poverty Assessment 2015/16*, p. 159.

19 Eliya Zulu, 'How to defuse sub-Saharan Africa's population bomb', *New Scientist*, 26 April 2012.

20 'High population growth complicates Vision 2030', *Business Daily*, 18 November 2010.

21 Ibid.

22 'In the next two decades, Somalis will have overtaken the top three largest communities in Kenya to be the most populous group if the current population trends remain', Paul Wafula, 'Population numbers: Somalis race to join big four', *The Standard*, 31 March 2018.

23 Carl Haub, 'What if experts are wrong on world population growth?', Yale E360, 19 September 2011.

24 Philip Aldrick, 'Ageing workforce will soon be global crisis, warns IMF', *The Times*, 10 April 2018.

25 UNPD (2015b), *World Fertility Patterns 2015 – Data Booklet*, p. 6. The global replacement level is about 2.3 births (due to higher average mortality).

26 UNPD (2019a), *World Population Prospects: The 2019 Revision*.

27 H.R. McKlveen (1895), 'The depopulation of civilized nations', *Journal of The American Medical Association*, Vol. XXV, No. 13, pp. 527–9. France's population at the end of the nineteenth century was less than 40 million; today it is more than 65 million.

28 See, for example, Jeremy Grantham, 'The severe cost of the world's baby bust', *Financial Times*, 13 March 2021. The opening sentence of the article reads: 'We are in a global baby bust of unprecedented proportions. It is far from over and its implications are gravely underestimated.' In fact, a 'bust' has not even begun.

29 John Weeks, 'The drop in child mortality helps explain the population explosion', Weeks Population blog, 8 September 2017.

30 Justin Fox, 'Where demographic dividends will pay out next', Bloomberg, 1 June 2018.

1: 'THINK AFRICA!'

1 David E. Bloom (2011), '7 billion and counting', *Science*, Vol. 333, Issue 6042, p. 562.

2 See, for example, John Bongaarts (2017b), 'Africa's unique fertility transition', Supplement to *Population and Development Review*, Vol. 43, p. 39.

3 Speech at World Economic Forum on Africa, Cape Town, September 2019.

4 Valentina Romei and John Reed, 'The Asian century is set to begin', *Financial Times*, 26 March 2019.

5 Robert Eastwood and Michael Lipton (2012), 'The demographic dividend: Retrospect and prospect', *Economic Affairs*, Vol. 32, Issue 1, p. 29.

6 See UNPD (2019a), *World Population Prospects: The 2019 Revision – Data Booklet*. Among countries with a population >5 million Burundi, Uganda, Tanzania, Angola, Chad, DRC, Mali and Niger had an average annual population growth rate in 2015–20 in excess of 3%.

7 Ibid. The countries are Uganda, Burundi, Somalia, DRC, Angola, Chad, Gambia, Burkina Faso, Mali, Niger and Nigeria.

8 Max Fisher, 'The amazing, surprising, Africa-driven demographic future of the Earth in 9 charts', *The Washington Post*, 16 July 2013.

9 Richard Cincotta (2011), 'Africa's reluctant fertility transition', *Current History*, Vol. 110, Issue 736, p. 186.

10 All future populations mentioned in the following two paragraphs are medium-variant projections from UNPD (2019a), *World Population Prospects: The 2019 Revision.*

11 Ibid.

12 See African Development Bank (hereafter AfDB) (2019a), *Creating Decent Jobs: Strategies, Policies, and Instruments*, p. 6; and AfDB (2019b), *African Economic Outlook 2019*, p. 46.

13 UNPD (2019a), *World Population Prospects: The 2019 Revision – Highlights*, p. 14.

14 See IMF (2015), *Regional Economic Outlook: Sub-Saharan Africa*. They include Malawi, Mozambique, Somalia, Zambia, Uganda, Angola, Chad, DRC, Gabon, Gambia, Guinea, Mali, Niger and Nigeria.

15 UNPD (2019a), *World Population Prospects: The 2019 Revision – Highlights*, p. 17.

16 'Africa's population – can it survive such speedy growth?', *The Economist*, 14 August 2014.

17 @voxdotcom tweet, 13 October 2018.

18 'Generation games', *The Economist*, 16 September 2017.

19 Akinwumi Adesina speech at African Development Bank annual meeting, Ahmedabad, May 2017.

20 Acha Leke, Mutsa Chironga and Georges Desvaux (2018), *Africa's Business Revolution*, Harvard Business Review Press, Boston MA.

21 IMF, World Economic Outlook Database (accessed 5 December 2020).

22 Jack Goldstone, 'The new population bomb', *Foreign Affairs*, January/February 2010.

2: MUSEVENI'S MIRACLE: AN AFRICAN PERSPECTIVE

1 'Address on National State of Affairs', 9 September 2018.

2 See UNPD (2019a), *World Population Prospects: The 2019 Revision* and Uganda Bureau of Statistics, 'Statistical Abstract' 2018, p. 12.

3 Ramathan Ggoobi, 'Here is how to make 2019/20 budget transformative', *Daily Monitor*, 24 May 2019.

4 Uganda Demographic and Health Survey 2016 Final Report (Chapter 5 – Fertility).

5 Uganda Bureau of Statistics, National Population and Housing Census reports 2002 and 2014.

6 US Census Bureau, Population Division, 'Population trends: Uganda', September 1994.

7 Paul Ehrlich (1968), *The Population Bomb: Population Control or Race to Oblivion?*, Sierra Club-Ballantine Books, New York, p. 12.

8 John C. Caldwell and Chukuka Okonjo (eds) (1968), *The Population of Tropical Africa*, Longmans, London, p. 12.

9 See UNDESA (1971), *The World Population Situation in 1970*, Population Studies No. 49, p. 3. The OECD projection was based on UNDESA (1966), *World Population Prospects as Assessed in 1963*, Population Studies No. 41.

10 Ehrlich cited *Born to Hunger* (Heinemann, London, 1968) as evidence, the journalist Arthur Hopcraft's account of a 45,000-mile global tour of malnutrition 'hotspots' for the UK Committee of the Freedom from Hunger campaign.

11 See Richard Grossman, 'The world in which the next 4 billion people will live', N-IUSSP, 13 November 2017.

12 https://www.nobelprize.org/prizes/peace/1970/borlaug/facts/ (accessed 1 August 2020).

13 See John Weeks, 'Population bomb's 50th anniversary', Weeks Population blog, 21 May 2018.

14 Frank Notestein, PAA annual meeting, Atlanta 1970.

15 See, for example, Fred Pearce (2011), *Peoplequake: Mass Migration, Ageing Nations and the Coming Population Crash*, Eden Project Books, London, Chapter 3 ('Saving the White Man').

16 UNDESA (1971), op. cit., p. 69.

17 Paul R. Ehrlich and John P. Holdren (1971), 'The impact of population growth', *Science*, Vol. 171, Issue 3977, p. 1212.

18 Charles C. Mann, 'The book that incited a worldwide fear of overpopulation', *Smithsonian Magazine*, January 2018.

19 UNECA (1990), *African Alternative Framework to Structural Adjustment Programmes for Socio-Economic Recovery and Transformation* (AAF-SAP), p. 5.

20 See UNECA (2001), *The State of the Demographic Transition in Africa*, p. 8: 'the main concern of African countries was to give priority to nation building'.

21 Rashid Faruqee and Ravi Gulhati (1983), 'Rapid Population Growth in Sub-Saharan Africa: Issues and Policies', World Bank Staff Working Papers No. 559.

22 David Holmes, 'Fred Sai: The godfather of family planning', *The Lancet*, 17 November 2012.

23 Fred T. Sai (1988), 'Changing perspectives of population in Africa and international responses', *African Affairs*, Vol. 87, No. 347, p. 270.

24 UNDESA (1971), op. cit., p. 71. The sale of contraceptives was illegal in France as well, the former colonial power, until legislation was passed in 1967 and 1969.

25 Diop cited in Mwesiga Baregu (1987), 'The African "population problem": Situational versus world historical perspectives', *Utafiti*, Vol. 9, No. 2, p. 22.

26 Speech on NBS Television, 14 March 2018.

27 See Dominique Tabutin and Bruno Schoumaker (2004), 'The demography of sub-Saharan Africa from the 1950s to the 2000s: A survey of changes and a statistical assessment', *Population*, Vol. 59, No. 3/4, p. 464 for the estimates of Jean-Noël Biraben.

28 Shane Doyle, 'Demography and Disease', in John Parker and Richard Reid (eds) (2003), *The Oxford Handbook of Modern African History*, Oxford University Press, p. 40.

29 Doyle op. cit. says 'perhaps 130 million' out of a global population of 1.6 billion. Tabutin and Schoumaker (2004) p. 464 suggest 100 million.

30 Joe Bish, 'Addressing population challenge is not impossible', YaleGlobal Online, 30 June 2020.

31 Population Reference Bureau, '2018 World Population Data Sheet', p. 8 and p. 10. PRB sources the arable land statistics from the FAO and uses its own mid-year population estimates.

32 FAOSTAT data for (total) 'agriculture' and 'arable' land (accessed 5 November 2019).

33 The World Bank's online 'Africa Development Indicators 2012/13'

dataset provided yet another density measurement – rural population per km^2 of arable land. See https://databank.worldbank.org/reports.aspx?source=1147&series=EN.RUR.DNST (accessed 4 November 2019).

34 UNPD (2004), *World Population to 2300*, p. 64.

35 Howard W. French, 'A history of denial', *The New York Review of Books*, 19 April 2018.

36 'Miracle or Malthus?', *The Economist*, 17 December 2011.

3: A MESSAGE FROM THE WEST

1 G.M. Higgins et al. (1982), *Potential Population Supporting Capacities of Lands in the Developing World*, FAO/IIASA/UNFPA.

2 Ibid.

3 See, for example, World Bank (1986), *Population Growth and Policies in Sub-Saharan Africa*, pp. 26–7.

4 World Bank (1983), *The Demographic Situation in Burundi*, p. 97.

5 FAO (1985), *The State of Food and Agriculture 1984*, p. v.

6 See Economic Commission for Africa (2001), *The State of the Demographic Transition in Africa*, p. 19.

7 World Bank (1986), *Population Growth and Policies in Sub-Saharan Africa*, p. v.

8 Ibid., p. 30.

9 UNECA/AU (2011), *Economic Report on Africa 2011 – Governing Development in Africa – the Role of the State in Economic Transformation*, p. 102.

10 World Bank (1986), *Population Growth and Policies in Sub-Saharan Africa*, p. 1.

11 John Iliffe (2017), *Africans: The History of a Continent*, Cambridge University Press, p. 293.

12 See Ramathan Ggoobi, 'How to make 2019/20 budget transformative', *Sunrise*, 8 May 2019.

13 Professor Michael Lipton points out that in East and South Asia governments 'typically allocated 20 per cent of public spending to agriculture'. In 'short Africa' – excluding Northern Africa and South Africa – allocations today are of the order of 5-10%. See Michael Lipton (2013), 'Income from work: The food-population-resource crisis in 'the short Africa', *British Academy Review*, Issue 22, pp. 37. It should be noted that most of the larger agricultural economies spend less than 5% of their budget on agriculture.

14 See Sharon Stanton Russell, 'International Migration', Chapter 8 in Karen A. Foote, Kenneth H. Hill and Linda G. Martin (eds) (1993), *Demographic Change in Sub-Saharan Africa*, The National Academies Press, Washington DC, p. 308.

15 World Bank (1986), *Population Growth and Policies in Sub-Saharan Africa*, p. 30.

16 See Aderanti Adepoju (1975), 'African population growth and politics', *African Affairs*, Vol. 74, No. 297, p. 468.

17 Diana Coole (2013), 'Too many bodies: The return and disavowal of the population question', *Environmental Politics*, Vol. 22, No. 2, p. 12.

18 UNECA (2001), *The State of the Demographic Transition in Africa*, p. 28.

19 D. Vlasblom (2013), 'The Richer Harvest: Economic Development in Africa and Southeast Asia Compared: The 'Tracking Development' Study 2006–2011, African Studies Centre Leiden Occasional Paper, p. 1.

20 Rashid Faruqee and Ravi Gulhati (1983), 'Rapid Population Growth in Sub-Saharan Africa: Issues and Policies', World Bank Staff Working Papers No. 559, p. 25.

21 Ibid., pp. 55–6.

22 See Jean-Paul Kimonyo (2016), *Rwanda's Popular Genocide: A Perfect Storm*, Lynne Rienner Publishers Inc., Boulder CO, p. 49: a memo in 1974 to President Habyarimana from the Rwandan delegation to Uganda to discuss refugees 'emphasizes the country's overpopulation, poverty and lack of resources' as reasons to oppose their repatriation.

23 UNECA (1983), *ECA and Africa's Development 1983–2008: A Preliminary Perspective Study*, *passim*.

24 Mwesiga Baregu (1987), 'The African "population problem": Situational versus world historical perspectives', *Utafiti*, Vol. 9, No. 2, *passim*.

25 Nelson P. Moyo (1986), 'Population policy: Do we need it? Prospects and problems', *Zimbabwe Journal of Economics*, Vol. 1, No. 3, *passim*.

26 Teresa J. Ho (1985), 'Population Growth and Agricultural Productivity in Sub-Saharan Africa', in *Proceedings of the Fifth Agriculture Sector Symposium: Population and Food* (ed. Ted J. Davis), World Bank, Washington DC, p. 92.

27 Gerhard K. Heilig (1996), 'World Population Prospects: Analyzing the 1996 UN Population Projections', Paper WP-96-146, International Institute for Applied Systems Analysis (IIASA), Laxenburg, p. 16.

28 Rashid Faruqee and Ravi Gulhati (1983), op. cit., p. 27.

29 Ibid., pp. 60–1.

30 Ibid., p. 62.

31 World Bank (1989), *Sub-Saharan Africa: From Crisis to Sustainable Growth*, p. 1.

32 Ibid., pp. xi–xii and p. 2.

33 Ibid., p. 40.

34 Ibid., p. 6.

35 Ibid., p. 6 and p. 4.

36 John and Pat Caldwell (1990), 'High fertility in sub-Saharan Africa', *Scientific American*, Vol. 262, No. 5, p. 125.

37 Thandika Mkandawire (1994), 'Social sciences in Africa: Some lessons for South Africa', *South African Sociological Review*, Vol. 6, No. 2, p. 6.

38 Norman Myers (1989), 'Population Growth, Environmental Decline and Security Issues in Sub-Saharan Africa', in A. Hjort af Ornäs and M.A. Salih (eds), *Ecology and Politics: Environmental Stress and Security in Africa*, Scandinavian Institute of African Studies, Uppsala, p. 214.

39 World Bank (1989), *Sub-Saharan Africa: From Crisis to Sustainable Growth*, p. 4.

4: REVOLUTION IN CAIRO

1 *The Annual Register: A Record of World Events 1990*, Vol. 232, p. 275, Longmans, London, 1991.

2 Mike Davis (2007), *Planet of Slums*, Verso Books, London, p. 191.

3 See UNECA (2001), *The State of the Demographic Transition in Africa*, p. 9 and *passim*.

4 Geoffrey Hawker (2005), 'Huntington's dog that didn't bark: Africa in the "Clash of Civilizations"', *Australian Quarterly*, May–June, p. 7.

5 Robert D. Kaplan, 'The coming anarchy', *Atlantic Monthly*, February 1994.

6 Richard Dowden (1994), 'Here is the news – of 1994: Africa', *The Independent*, 2 January.

7 OAU/UNECA (1994), *Population and Development in Africa*.

8 See Mary Tiffen, Michael Mortimore and Francis Gichuki (1994), *More People, Less Erosion: Environmental Recovery in Kenya*, John Wiley & Sons, Chichester.

9 John Cleland (2005), 'The continuing challenge of population growth', in *The ICPD Vision: How Far Has the 11-Year Journey Taken Us?* Report from a UNFPA Panel Discussion at IUSSP XXV International Population Conference, Tours, July 2005, p. 20.

10 Lant H. Pritchett (1994), 'Desired fertility and the impact of population policies', *Population and Development Review*, Vol. 20, No. 1, pp. 1–55.

11 See Jean M. Guilfoyle, 'The World Scientific Academies' Population Summit', Population Research Institute, 1 March 1994.

12 Martha Campbell (2007), 'Why the silence on population?', *Population and Environment*, Vol. 28, p. 241.

13 Ben Wattenberg, 'The population explosion is over', *The New York Times Magazine*, 23 November 1997.

14 Ibid.

15 Nicholas Eberstadt, 'The population implosion', *The Wall Street Journal*, 16 October 1997.

16 'A Joint Statement by Fifty-Eight of the World's Scientific Academies', The National Academies Press, Washington DC, 1993.

17 Alex Ezeh, 'Empowering women lies at the centre of controlling population growth in Africa', *The Conversation*, 20 September 2018.

18 Joel E. Cohen (1995), 'Population growth and Earth's human carrying capacity', *Science*, Vol. 269, p. 344.

19 Massimo Livi Bacci (2017), *Our Shrinking Planet*, Polity Press, Cambridge, p. 53.

20 See also World Bank (1989), *Sub-Saharan Africa: From Crisis to Sustainable Growth*: the Bank projected (p. 70) that the TFR in sub-Saharan Africa would fall to 3.4 births by 2020; according to UNPD data for 2015–20 the TFR for the region was 4.7 births.

21 UNECA (1983), *ECA and Africa's Development 1983–2008: A Preliminary Perspective Study*, p. 94.

22 'Africa has plenty of land. Why is it so hard to make a living from it?', *The Economist*, 28 April 2018.

23 Emi Suzuki, 'World's population will continue to grow and will reach nearly 10 billion by 2050', World Bank data blog, 8 July 2019.

24 Louis-Marie Nindorera, 'Burundi under Malthus' scrutiny', Africa at LSE blog, 8 January 2018.

25 Ibid.

26 Alex Ezeh, op. cit.

5: AFRICAN TRANSITIONS

1 Statement to the Commission on Population and Development by Joseph Chamie, director, United Nations Department of Economic and Social Affairs/Population Division (UNPD), 22 March 1999.

2 See UNPD (2001), *World Population Prospects: The 2000 Revision*.

3 John Cleland (2013), 'World population growth: Past, present and future', *Environmental and Resource Economics*, Vol. 55, Issue 4, p. 544.

4　Dudley Kirk (1996), 'Demographic transition theory', *Population Studies*, Vol. 50, No. 3, p. 361.

5　Frank Notestein (1945), 'Population: The Long View', in Theodore W. Schultz (ed.), *Food for the World*, University of Chicago Press, pp. 36–57.

6　Dudley Kirk (1996), op. cit., p. 361.

7　John Bongaarts (2017b), 'Africa's unique fertility transition', Supplement to *Population and Development Review*, Vol. 43, p. 40. On the other hand, John and Pat Caldwell (2002), 'The Fertility Transition in Sub-Saharan Africa', Paper presented at the Conference on Fertility and the Current South African Issues of Poverty, HIV/AIDS and Youth, Pretoria, 24 October 2002, stress the importance of sustained economic growth and government policy to further fertility decline in sub-Saharan Africa.

8　Michel Garenne (2017a), 'Family Planning and Fertility Decline in Africa: From 1950 to 2010', in Zouhair O. Amarin (ed.), *Family Planning*, IntechOpen, London, p. 120. See also Michel Garenne (2012), *Education and Fertility in Sub-Saharan Africa: A Longitudinal Perspective*, DHS Analytical Studies No. 33, ICF International, p. 1: van de Walle and Knodel in their 'classic' longitudinal (about dynamics/trends) study (as Garenne refers to van de Walle and Knodel (1980)) of the European fertility transition 'found virtually no correlation between onset and speed of the fertility transition and various socio-economic indicators, such as levels of education, urbanization, income, or industrialization'.

9　UNECA (2001), *The State of the Demographic Transition in Africa*, p. 2.

10　John C. Caldwell and Pat Caldwell (1995), 'The beginning of fertility decline in sub-Saharan Africa', *Populations du Sud*, p. 233.

11　See R. Lesthaeghe and C. Jolly (1995), 'The start of the sub-Saharan fertility transition: Some answers and many questions', *Journal of International Development*, Vol. 7, Issue 1, pp. 25–6.

12　Michel Garenne (2017c), 'Record high fertility in sub-Saharan Africa in a comparative perspective', *African Population Studies*, Vol. 31, No. 2, p. 3706.

13　See UNPD (2015b), *World Fertility Patterns – Data Booklet*.

14　See also Nelson C. Onuoha and Ian M. Timaeus (1995), 'Has a fertility transition begun in West Africa?', *Journal of International Development*, Vol. 7, No. 1, p. 95: 'Despite lively debate as to exactly how to interpret what is happening, there is some consensus that the stimulus for change has been increased effort by African family planning programmes combined with economic difficulties throughout the continent, situated against a longer term background of economic and social change and declining infant and child mortality.'

15　R. Lesthaeghe and C. Jolly (1995), op. cit., p. 42.

16　Data from Jean-Pierre Guengant and John May (2011b), 'Proximate Determinants of Fertility in Sub-Saharan Africa and Their Possible Use in Fertility Projections', UNPD Expert Paper No. 2011/13, p. 23, p. 28, p. 29.

17　Paulina Makinwa-Adebusoye (2001), 'Sociocultural Factors Affecting Fertility in Sub-Saharan Africa', Paper presented at UNDP Workshop on Prospects for Fertility Decline in High Fertility Countries, 9–11 July 2001, pp. 7–8.

18　Gail M. Gerhart, review of World Bank publication *Can Africa Claim the 21st Century?* (Oxford University Press), *Foreign Affairs*, November/December 2000.

19 See John Bongaarts (2006), 'The causes of stalling fertility transitions', *Studies in Family Planning*, Vol. 37, No. 1, pp. 1–16, and (2008) 'Fertility transitions in developing countries: Progress or stagnation?', *Studies in Family Planning*, Vol. 39, No. 2, pp. 105–10.

20 See Michel Garenne (2008), *Fertility Changes in Sub-Saharan Africa*, DHS Comparative Report No. 18, Macro International.

21 See David Shapiro and Tesfayi Gebreselassie (2007), 'Fertility Transition in Sub-Saharan Africa: Falling and Stalling', Paper presented at the annual meeting of the Population Association of America, New York, 29–31 March.

22 Bruno Schoumaker (2009), 'Stalls and Reversals in Fertility Transitions in Sub-Saharan Africa: Real or Spurious?', Document de travail No. 30, Université catholique de Louvain.

23 Kazuyo Machiyama (2010), 'A Re-examination of Recent Fertility Declines in Sub-Saharan Africa', DHS Working Paper No. 68, ICF Macro, Calverton MD, p. 1.

24 Michel Garenne (2011a), 'Testing for fertility stalls in demographic and health surveys', *Population Health Metrics*, Vol. 9, Art. 59, pp. 6–7.

25 John Cleland (2017a), 'Prospects for accelerated fertility decline in Africa', *The Journal of Population and Sustainability*, Vol. 1, No. 2, p. 49.

26 Ibid., p. 47.

27 John Bongaarts (2011), 'Can family planning programs reduce high desired family size in sub-Saharan Africa?', *International Perspectives on Sexual and Reproductive Health*, Vol. 37, No. 4, p. 210.

28 Clifford Odimegwu et al. (2018), 'Fertility, family size preference and contraceptive use in Sub-Saharan Africa: 1990–2014', *African Journal of Reproductive Health*, Vol. 22, No. 4, p. 49.

29 John Bongaarts (2011), op. cit., p. 210.

30 Ibid., p. 211.

31 Elizabeth Leahy Madsen (2013b), 'Why has the demographic transition stalled in sub-Saharan Africa?', New Security Beat blog, 7 August.

32 See Patrick Gerland, Ann Biddlecom and Vladimirá Kantorová (2017), 'Patterns of fertility decline and the impact of alternative scenarios of future fertility change in sub-Saharan Africa', Supplement to *Population and Development Review*, Vol. 43, Issue S1.

33 See AfDB, *African Development Report 2012*, Chapter 2 – 'Main Drivers of Africa's Economic Performance', p. 7.

34 Ibid., p. 9.

35 John Cleland (2010), 'Diversity of fertility levels and implications for the future', Selected Papers of Beijing Forum 2007, *Procedia – Social and Behavioural Sciences*, Vol. 2, Issue 5, pp. 6920–7.

36 UNPD (2009b), 'What Would It Take to Accelerate Fertility Decline in the Least Developed Countries?', Policy Brief No. 2009/1, p. 1.

6: INCONVENIENT TRUTHS

1 Philip M. Hauser (1968), 'The World's People Will Nearly Triple in Number', in Emmanuel G. Mesthene (ed.), *Toward the Year 2018*, Foreign Policy Association, New York, pp. 136–47.

2 Ibid., p. 143.

3 Gerhard K. Heilig (1996), 'World Population Prospects: Analyzing the 1996 UN Population Projections', Paper WP-96-146, International Institute for Applied Systems Analysis (IIASA), Laxenburg, p. 2.

4 Statement to the Commission on Population and Development by Joseph Chamie, director, Population Division UNDESA, 22 March 1999.

5 John Bongaarts and Rodolfo Bulatao (2000), *Beyond Six Billion: Forecasting the World's Population*, The National Academies Press, Washington DC, p. 38.

6 Ibid., p. 38.

7 Ronald Lee (2011), 'The outlook for population growth', *Science*, Vol. 333, Issue 6042, p. 573.

8 John Cleland (2017a), 'Prospects for accelerated fertility decline in Africa', *The Journal of Population and Sustainability*, Vol. 1, No. 2, p. 37.

9 'The UN revises down its population forecasts', *The Economist*, 22 June 2019.

10 UNPD (2002), *Completing the Fertility Transition*, p. xi.

11 Ibid., p. 7.

12 John Bongaarts and Rodolfo A. Bulatao (eds.) (2000), op. cit., pp. 43–4.

13 Ibid., p. 42.

14 Ron Duncan and Chris Wilson (2004), 'Global Population Projections: Is the UN Getting it Wrong?', Working Papers in Economics and Econometrics No. 438, Australian National University, Canberra, p. 2. The credibility of the paper was somewhat compromised by referring throughout to the total fertility rate (TFR) as being measured as a percentage, as in 'the TFR will stabilise at about 2.1 per cent' (p. 3), rather than being the number of live births per woman.

15 Jean-Pierre Guengant and John F. May (2001), 'Impact of the Proximate Determinants on the Future Course of Fertility in Sub-Saharan Africa', Paper presented at the UNPD Workshop on Prospects for Fertility Decline in High Fertility Countries, 9–11 July, p. 3.

16 'Africa's population: The baby bonanza', *The Economist*, 27 August 2009.

17 Gerhard K. Heilig et al. (2010), 'Future population trends found to be highly uncertain in least developed countries', UNDP unpublished manuscript, March, pp. 4–5.

18 UNPD (2013a), *World Population Prospects: The 2012 Revision – Highlights and Advance Tables*, p. 28.

19 See UNPD (2013b), *Explaining Differences in the Projected Populations Between the 2012 and 2010 Revisions of World Population Prospects: The Role of Fertility in Africa*, Population Facts No. 2013/10, p. 1.

20 UNPD (2004), *World Population to 2300*, p. 115.

21 'Population change and economic growth in Africa', *National Transfer Accounts Bulletin*, No. 6, August 2013, p. 1.

22 Fred Pearce (2011), *Peoplequake: Mass Migration, Ageing Nations and the Coming Population Crash*, Eden Project Books, London, p. 293.

23 Sanjeev Sanyal, 'The End of Population Growth', Project Syndicate, 30 October 2011.

24 Norma Cohen, 'The rogue demographer strikes back', *Financial Times*, 11 September 2013.

25 Sanjeev Sanyal, 'The Wide Angle: Predictions of a Rogue Demographer', Deutsche Bank Research, 9 September 2013, p. 2.

26 John Weeks, 'When Deutsche Bank talks about fertility rates, should we listen?', Weeks Population blog, 21 September 2013.

27 Markus Jaeger, 'Demography and the Global Economy – "Continental" Drift is Well Underway', Deutsche Bank Research, 25 September 2015.

28 James Pethokoukis, 'The end of global population growth may be almost here – and a lot sooner than the UN thinks', American Enterprise Institute blog post, 13 September 2013.

29 Floyd Norris, 'Population growth forecast from the UN may be too high', *The New York Times*, 20 September 2013.

30 Izabella Kaminska, 'Peak-population investing', *FT Alphaville*, 13 September 2013.

31 UNPD (2019a), *World Population Prospects: The 2019 Revision – Highlights*, p. 8. On population momentum, see also UNPD (2017d),

The Impact of Population Momentum on Future Population Growth, p. 1. 'The share of future growth or decline that is attributable to population momentum can be determined by projecting the population forward while assuming that in each country: a/ mortality rates remain constant at levels observed in 2010–15; b/ fertility instantly equals the replacement levels associated with the mortality level of 2015–20; and c/ net migration equals zero starting in 2015–20.'

32 Julia Zinkina and Andrey Korotayev (2014a), 'Projecting Mozambique's demographic futures', *Journal of Futures Studies*, Vol. 19, No. 2, p. 33.

7: IS AFRICA DIFFERENT?

1 Dalton Conley, Gordon C. McCord and Jeffrey D. Sachs (2007), 'Africa's Lagging Demographic Transition: Evidence from Exogenous Impacts of Malaria Ecology and Agricultural Technology', Working Paper 12892, National Bureau of Economic Research (NBER), Cambridge MA, p. 4.

2 John Bongaarts (2017b), 'Africa's unique fertility transition', Supplement to *Population and Development Review*, Vol. 43, p. 54.

3 Ibid., p. 55.

4 John Casterline (2017a), 'Prospects for fertility decline in Africa', Supplement to *Population and Development Review*, Vol. 43, p. 4.

5 See UNPD (2020a), *World Fertility and Family Planning 2020: Highlights – 'Ten Key Messages'*. It took 19 years for the TFR to fall from six to four births in Northern Africa and Western Asia (1974–93); in East and Southeast Asia it took 24 years (1950–74), in Oceania (excluding Australia and New Zealand), 35 years (1968–2003). The same decline is likely to be completed in 2029, 34 years after commencement in 1995.

In Latin America/Caribbean the decline was only slightly more rapid (between the 1950s and 1980s).

6 Michel Garenne (2008), *Fertility Changes in Sub-Saharan Africa*, DHS Comparative Report No. 18, Macro International, p. 29.

7 Ibid.

8 Lyman Stone, 'African Fertility is Right Where It Should Be', Institute for Family Studies, 29 October 2018.

9 Phrase attributed to John C. Caldwell and Pat Caldwell (1988), 'Is the Asian family planning program model suited to Africa?', *Studies in Family Planning*, Vol. 19, No. 1, pp. 19–28, in Etienne van de Walle and Andrew Foster (1990), 'Fertility Decline in Africa: Assessment and Prospects', World Bank Technical Paper 125, p. 17.

10 Cheikh Mbacké (2017), 'The persistence of high fertility in sub-Saharan Africa: A comment', Supplement to *Population and Development*, Vol. 43, p. 330 and p. 332.

11 John Bongaarts (2015), 'Modeling the fertility impact of the proximate determinants: Time for a tune-up',

Demographic Research, Vol. 33, Art. 19, p. 536.

12 See Endale Kebede, Anne Goujon and Wolfgang Lutz (2019), 'Stalls in Africa's fertility decline partly result from disruptions in female education', *Proceedings of the National Academy of Sciences of the United States of America (PNAS)*, Vol. 116, No. 8, pp. 2891–6.

13 See Alex Ezeh, Blessing Mberu and Jacques Emina (2009), 'Stall in fertility decline in Eastern African countries: Regional analysis of patterns, determinants and implications', *Philosophical Transactions B*, The Royal Society, Vol. 364, Issue 1532, pp. 2991–3007.

14 See World Bank (2010), *Determinants and Consequences of High Fertility: A Synopsis of the Evidence*, p. 11.

15 See World Bank (1972), *The World Bank Atlas: Population, Per Capita Product and Growth Rates*.

16 John Bongaarts (2017b), 'Africa's unique fertility transition', p. 40.

17 Etienne van de Walle and Andrew Foster (1990), 'Fertility Decline in Africa: Assessment and Prospects', World Bank Technical Paper No. 125, p. 28.

18 Ibid.

19 For example, Shane Doyle's research on three neighbouring societies within the Great Lakes region – the Nkole, Ganda and Haya ethnic groups – showed material (and changing) differences in fertility through the twentieth century despite sharing diverse cultural characteristics. Shane Doyle (2012), 'Sexual behavioural change in Ankole, western Uganda, *c*.1880–1980', *Journal of Eastern African Studies*, Vol. 6, Issue 3, pp. 490–506.

20 Andrey Korotayev et al. (2016), 'Explaining current fertility dynamics in tropical Africa from an anthropological perspective: A cross-cultural investigation', *Cross-Cultural Research*, Vol. 50, No. 3, p. 260. The influence of hoe-based production was also emphasised by Ester Boserup in *Women's Role in Economic Development*, Routledge, London, 1970.

21 Cheikh Mbacké (2017), 'The persistence of high fertility in sub-Saharan Africa', p. 332.

22 Jennifer Johnson-Hanks (2007), 'Natural intentions: Fertility decline in the African demographic and health surveys', *American Journal of Sociology*, Vol. 112, No. 4, p. 1036, quoted in Tom Moultrie and Ian Timæus (2014), 'Rethinking African Fertility: The State in, and of, the Future Sub-Saharan African Fertility Decline', Paper presented to Population Association of America Conference, Boston MA, 1–3 May, p. 2.

23 Jack Goldstone et al. (2018), 'Why Does High African Fertility Persist?', Center for the Study of Social Change, Institutions, and Policy (George Mason University, Fairfax VA), Working Paper No. 2–2018, p. 3.

24 Michel Garenne (2011b), 'Testing for fertility stalls in demographic and health surveys', *Population Health Metrics*, Vol. 9, Art. 59, p. 1.

25 'Cash for kids: South Korea seeks to raise falling birth rate', *Channel News Asia*, 7 December 2018.

26 Massimo Livi Bacci (2017), *Our Shrinking Planet*, Polity Press, Cambridge, p. 124.

8: AFRICA GALLOPING

1 See Patrick Gerland et al. (2014), 'World population stabilization unlikely this century', *Science*, Vol. 346, Issue 6206, pp. 234–7.

2 Robert Kunzig, 'A world with 11 billion people? New population projections shatter earlier estimates', *National Geographic*, 19 September 2014.

3 Brandon Keim, 'BOOM! Earth's population could hit 12 billion by 2100', Wired.com, 18 September 2014.

4 A probabilistic methodology had been developed over a number of years by UNPD demographers in partnership with the Center for Statistics and the Social Sciences at the University of Washington. It had first been used with the compilation of medium-variant fertility projections in *World Population Prospects: The 2010 Revision*. In the *2012 Revision* it was also used in mortality projections. The UNPD's publication of full probabilistic projections for countries, flagged in the *Science* article, looked very much like a consultative initiative with a view to publishing full probabilistic projections for all countries in future *World Population Prospects*.

5 Coincidentally, as some leading demographers noted, the figure of 13.4 billion was very close to the estimate of the maximum number of people the planet could support made by Antonie van Leeuwenhoek, the Dutch 'father of microbiology', in 1679. See Joel E. Cohen (1995), 'Population growth and Earth's human carrying capacity', *Science*, Vol. 269, p. 342.

6 Patrick Gerland et al. (2014), 'World population stabilization unlikely this century', p. 234.

7 The Burkina Faso example was used in Leontine Alkema (2015), 'The United Nations probabilistic population projections: An introduction to demographic forecasting with uncertainty', *Foresight*, Vol. 37, pp. 19–24.

8 Nicholas Eberstadt, 'The new population boom could easily be a dud', *The Wall Street Journal*, 22 September 2014.

9 Ibid.

10 John Weeks, 'When Deutsche Bank talks about fertility rates, should we listen?', Weeks Population blog, 21 September 2013.

11 UNPD (2019c), *Fertility Among Very Young Adolescents*, Population Facts No. 2019/1.

12 In Africa, excluding South Africa, very few countries officially record even half of deaths. See Bruno Masquelier and Gloria Mathenge, 'Counting who is dying in sub-Saharan Africa and what they are dying from: An imperative for the post-2015 agenda', N-IUSSP, 7 March 2016.

13 Mo Ibrahim Foundation (2019), *Agendas 2063 & 2030: Is Africa on Track?*, African Governance Report, p. 79 and p. 71.

14 UNPD (2017b), *World Fertility Report 2015*, pp. 11–12.

15 See Leontine Alkema et al. (2012), 'Estimating trends in the total fertility rate with uncertainty using imperfect data: Examples from West Africa', *Demographic Research*, Vol. 26, Art. 15, pp. 331–62.

16 UNPD (2017d), *The Impact of Population Momentum on Future Population Growth*, Population Facts No. 2017/4, p. 1.

17 Henri Leridon (2020), 'Population mondiale: Vers une explosion ou une implosion?', *Population & Sociétés*, No. 573, p. 4.

18 UNPD (2017d), *The Impact of Population Momentum on Future Population Growth*, p. 2 endnote 5.

19 Anthony Cilluffo and Neil G. Ruiz, 'World's population is projected to nearly stop growing by the end of the century', Pew Research Center, 17 June 2019.

20 The Wittgenstein Centre is a collaboration between the Department of Demography of the University of Vienna, the World Population Program of the International Institute for Applied Systems Analysis (IIASA), the Austrian Academy of Sciences and the Vienna Institute of Demography of the Austrian Academy of Sciences.

21 See letter from Wolfgang Lutz et al. to the journal *Science*, 31 October 2014.

22 See, for example, Wolfgang Lutz, Warren Sanderson and Sergei Scherbov (2001), 'The end of world population growth', *Nature*, Vol. 412, pp. 543–5. In 2008, IIASA estimated the probability of the global population peaking in the twenty-first century at 85%.

23 This was based on the assumption that countries would follow the average path of school expansion that other countries further advanced in the process had done.

24 The difference with UNPD projections is, according to IIASA, 'mostly due to different methods of deriving fertility assumptions for the different parts of the world, where the UN relies primarily on statistical extrapolation models and IIASA gives more weight to expert arguments and scientific reasoning'. See Wolfgang Lutz et al. (eds) (2018), *Demographic and Human Capital Scenarios for the Twenty-First Century,* Publications Office of the European Union, p. 117.

25 See letter from Wolfgang Lutz et al. to *Science*, 31 October 2014.

26 Stuart Basten, Wolfgang Lutz and Sergei Scherbov (2013), 'Very long range global population scenarios to 2300 and the implications of sustained low fertility', *Demographic Research*, Vol. 28, Art. 39, p. 1155. UNPD estimated that the scenario had no more than a 5% chance of proving to be correct.

27 Ibid., p. 1147.

28 Fred Pearce (2011), *Peoplequake: Mass Migration, Ageing Nations and the Coming Population Crash*, Eden Project Books, London, p. 293.

29 Wolfgang Lutz to Edward Paice, 9 October 2019. The only occasion in the preceding two decades where Lutz had included a figure commencing with a 5 was in Wolfgang Lutz et al. (2001), op. cit., pp. 543–5. In this letter to the editors of *Nature* a median projection for the world population in 2100 of 8.4 billion was presented, 'with the 80 per cent prediction interval bounded by 5.6 and 12.1 billion' (p. 543).

30 See Wolfgang Lutz et al. (eds) (2018), op. cit., p. 117. In December 2020 the WIC medium scenario projections remained largely unchanged. Its online Data Explorer: http://dataexplorer.wittgensteincentre.org/wcde-v2/showed a medium scenario projection for 2100 of 9.3 billion, with peak population at 9.7 billion in about 2075. The projection for 2050 has remained at 9.4 billion.

31 In Wolfgang Lutz, Warren Sanderson and Sergei Scherbov (2004), *The End of World Population Growth in the 21st Century* (Earthscan, London) p. 39, the 'median forecast' had been 8.98 billion by 2070 declining to 8.41 billion by the end of the century.

32 See WIC Data Explorer: the stalled development scenario for 2060 projects an African population of 2.7 billion.

33 In Jack Goldstone et al. (2018), 'Why Does High African Fertility Persist?' (Center for the Study of Social Change, Institutions, and Policy, George Mason University, Fairfax VA, Working Paper No. 2–2018), the chart on p. 4 shows that UNPD projected fertility declines in

sub-Saharan Africa for the period 1990–95 to 2010–15 were higher than those recorded in DHS reports by 0.5 – one child. For Ethiopia, UNPF projected a decline greater than two children when the actual outcome was less than 0.5. In no country in the DHS Program was the fertility decline greater than projected by UNPD.

34 Samir KC and Wolfgang Lutz (2017), 'The human core of the shared socioeconomic pathways: Population scenarios by age, sex and level of education for all countries to 2100', *Global Environmental Change*, No. 42, pp. 181–2.

35 For example, in his 2013 book *Population 10 Billion* Danny Dorling, Professor of Geography at Oxford University, predicted peak population at 9.27 billion in the 2060s. Five years later, in *Why Demography Matters*, Dorling and co-author Stuart Gietel-Basten added a new scenario a population peak occurring at much the same time but at a level about half a billion people higher.

36 Darrell Bricker and John Ibbitson (2019), *Empty Planet: The Shock of Global Population Decline*, Robinson, London, p. 32.

37 Ibid., p. 2.

38 Ibid., p. 42.

39 Jørgen Randers, '2052: A global forecast for the next forty years', University of Cambridge Programme for Sustainable Leadership, 2012 (adapted from a 2012 lecture).

40 It has now been argued that fertility might have declined even faster in China if the one-child policy had not been implemented. See John Weeks, 'Would China's population be even smaller had there been no one-child policy?', Weeks Population blog, 8 November 2019.

41 John McKeown, 'Part 1 of a review of Darrell Bricker and John Ibbitson, *Empty Planet*', The Overpopulation Project (www.overpopulation-project.com), 11 April 2019.

42 Paul Morland, review of *Empty Planet* in *The Globe and Mail*, 6 February 2019.

9: SWINGS AND ROUNDABOUTS

1 UNPD (2004), *World Population to 2300*, p. 27 (Table 3).

2 Ibid.

3 UNPD (2017b), *World Fertility Report 2015*, p. 1: 87% of increased population in Africa by 2050 from fertility (as opposed to mortality and migration).

4 Patrick Gerland, Ann Biddlecom and Vladimirá Kantorová (2017), 'Patterns of fertility decline and the impact of alternative scenarios of future fertility change in sub-Saharan Africa', Supplement to *Population and Development Review*, Vol. 43, Issue S1, p. 35.

5 The average TFR for 2015–20 was reduced from 5.46 to 5.01 births.

Other lesser factors included a population estimate for 2019 3.2% lower than in the *2017 Revision*. Edward Paice correspondence with Thomas Spoorenberg (UNPD), 23 September 2019.

6 'Egypt's booming population hits 100 million', *Al Jazeera*, 12 February 2020.

7 See Julia Zinkina and Andrey Korotayev (2014a), 'Projecting Mozambique's demographic futures', *Journal of Futures Studies*, Vol. 19, No. 2, *passim*.

8 Bruno Schoumaker (2017), 'African Fertility Changes', in Hans Groth and John F. May (eds), *Africa's Population: In Search of a Demographic Dividend*, Springer, Cham, p. 197.

10: THE DOUBLING DOZEN

1 See Jean-Pierre Guengant and John F. May (2011b), 'Proximate Determinants of Fertility in Sub-Saharan Africa and Their Possible Use in Fertility Projections', p. 32, UNPD Expert Paper No. 2011/13, using the FamPlan model.

2 See UNPD (2020a), *World Fertility and Family Planning 2020 – Highlights*, p. 16. All other countries in the top 10 were also in sub-Saharan Africa: Malawi, Lesotho, Kenya, Sierra Leone, Liberia, Burkina Faso, Senegal, Uganda and Madagascar.

3 Global top 10: Niger, Mali, Angola, Mozambique, Chad, Guinea, Malawi, Côte d'Ivoire, Uganda and DRC.

4 UNPD (2019c), *Fertility Among Very Young Adolescents*, Population Facts No. 2019/1.

5 Alex Ezeh, 'Empowering women lies at the centre of controlling population growth in Africa', *The Conversation*, 20 September 2018.

6 UNPD (2019d), *Potential Impact of Later Childbearing on Future Population*, Population Facts No. 2019/5.

7 John Bongaarts (2011), 'Can family planning programs reduce high desired family size in sub-Saharan Africa?', *International Perspectives on Sexual and Reproductive Health*, Vol. 37, No. 4, p. 211.

8 Alex Ezeh, op. cit.

9 UNPD (2019c), *Fertility Among Very Young Adolescents*.

10 See UNPD (2011), *World Population Prospects: The 2010 Revision – Volume I: Comprehensive Tables*, pp. 28–9: 'Especially for countries at the beginning of their fertility transition, limited information exists as to their speed of decline and future trajectories, so the future potential trajectories (and speed of decline) are mostly informed by the world's experience and the variability in trends experienced in other countries at similar fertility levels in the past.'

11 See UNPD (2020a), *World Fertility and Family Planning 2020 – Highlights*, p. 16. The other nine countries in the top 10 were also in sub-Saharan Africa: Malawi, Lesotho, Kenya, Sierra Leone, Liberia, Burkina Faso, Senegal, Uganda, Madagascar.

11: WOMEN'S WORLD

1 A term associated with Margaret Sanger, the controversial American birth-control pioneer and activist.

2 Clifford Odimegwu, Olusina S. Bamiwuye and Sunday A. Adedini (2015), 'Gender-based violence as a new proximate determinant of fertility in sub-Saharan Africa', *Southern African Journal of Demography*, Vol. 16, No. 1, p. 114.

3 Ann Starrs et al. (2018), 'Accelerated Progress – Sexual and Reproductive Health and Rights for All: Report of the Guttmacher-Lancet Commission', *The Lancet*, Vol. 391, p. 2652.

4 OECD, Social Institutions & Gender (SIGI) Index 2019. SIGI measures discrimination in the family, restricted physical integrity, restricted access to productive and financial resources, restricted civil liberties.

5 See Ibitola O. Asaolu et al. (2018), 'Measuring women's empowerment in sub-Saharan Africa: Exploratory and confirmatory factor analyses of the demographic and health surveys', *Frontiers in Psychology*, Vol. 9, Art. 994, p. 5: 'women's attitudes toward violence emerged as the first and most persistent factor of women's

empowerment across all four regions'. The regions are Eastern, Western, Middle and Southern Africa. This is one of the most recent peer-reviewed attempts to 'provide a validated measure of women's empowerment' for countries in sub-Saharan Africa.

6 Among the studies to have found a 'significant association' between domestic violence and higher levels of fertility in Africa, and to have proposed that domestic violence be regarded as a 'new proximate determinant' of fertility, see Clifford Odimegwu, Olusina S. Bamiwuye and Sunday A. Adedini (2015), 'Gender-based violence as a new proximate determinant of fertility in sub-Saharan Africa', *Southern African Journal of Demography*, Vol. 16, No. 1. Their study focused on Gabon, Nigeria and Zambia.

7 Uganda 2000–1 DHS Final Report, p. 36.

8 In Afrobarometer Round 7 'Summary of Results' (Hatchile Consulting, 2017), more than 80% of Ugandans said it was 'never justified' for men to beat their wives. The randomly

selected sample size was 1,200. The contrast with the 2016 DHS data (and previous DHS findings) is anomalous and unexplained. The questions posed by DHS are more specific, asking for responses about specific circumstances, whereas Afrobarometer asks a more general question: 'Is it sometimes/always/ never justified for men to beat their wives?' The sample size is also many times larger.

9 Carmen Alpin Lardies, Dominique Dryding and Carolyn Logan (2019), 'Perceptions and Experiences of Gender in Africa', Afrobarometer Policy Paper No. 61, p. 11.

10 See Ushma D. Upadhyay and Deborah Karasek (2012), 'Women's empowerment and ideal family size: An examination of DHS empowerment measures in sub-Saharan Africa', *International Perspectives on Sexual and Reproductive Health*, Vol. 38, No. 2.

11 Carmen Alpin Lardies, Dominique Dryding and Carolyn Logan (2019), op. cit., p. 34.

12: THE X FACTOR

1 Samir KC and Wolfgang Lutz (2017), 'The human core of the shared socioeconomic pathways: Population scenarios by age, sex and level of education for all countries to 2100', *Global Environmental Change*, No. 42, p. 182: 'functional causality' [indicated] that – while it is nearly impossible to prove causality for all times and all different cultural settings – there are good reasons to assume that the effect of education on lowering mortality and fertility can indeed be assumed to hold over the projection period covered here'. Michel Garenne (2012) presents an alternative view in *Education and Fertility in Sub-Saharan Africa:*

A Longitudinal Perspective, DHS Analytical Studies No. 33, ICF International, December 2012. This study found that 'the relationship between long-term trends in education and in fertility was weak and complex'. Garenne argues that 'numerous factors other than education operate to accelerate or to slow the fertility transition' and 'most of the fertility decline in Africa seems to be induced by the use of modern contraceptives, even though in some countries other factors such as increasing age at marriage contributed to lower fertility to a certain extent'.

2 See Patrick Gerland et al. (2014), 'World population stabilization unlikely this century', *Science*, Vol. 346, Issue 6206, p. 237: 'Among the most robust empirical findings in the literature on fertility transitions are that higher contraceptive use and higher female education are associated with faster fertility decline.'

3 Jack Goldstone et al. (2018), 'Why Does High African Fertility Persist?', Center for the Study of Social Change, Institutions, and Policy (George Mason University, Fairfax VA), Working Paper No. 2–2018, p. 12.

4 David Shapiro and Michel Tenikue (2017), 'Women's education, infant and child mortality, and fertility decline in urban and rural sub-Saharan Africa', *Demographic Research*, Vol. 37, Art. 21, p. 669.

5 Bruno Schoumaker (2017), 'African Fertility Changes', in Hans Groth and John F. May (eds), *Africa's Population: In Search of a Demographic Dividend*, Springer, Cham, p. 207.

6 @BudgITng tweet, 19 November 2019.

7 World Bank (1987), *Education Policies for Sub-Saharan Africa: Adjustment, Revitalization, and Expansion*, p. x.

8 John Caldwell, I.O. Orubuloye and Pat Caldwell (1992), 'Fertility decline in Africa: A new type of transition?', *Population and Development Review*, Vol. 18, No. 2, p. 227.

9 Tiyambe Zeleza (1991), 'Economic policy and performance in Kenya since Independence', *Transafrican Journal of History*, Vol. 20, p. 57.

10 World Bank (1987), *Education Policies for Sub-Saharan Africa: Adjustment, Revitalization, and Expansion*, pp. x, 1, 4, 10. Thirty-nine countries were included in the study.

11 UNECA (1983), *ECA and Africa's Development 1983–2008: A Preliminary Perspective Study*, p. 8.

12 See Matthew Lockwood (2012), 'Adaptation Policy, Governance and Politics in Sub-Saharan Africa', Paper presented at an International Symposium on the Governance of Adaptation, Amsterdam, 22–3 March, p. 9.

13 See Endale Kebede, Anne Goujon and Wolfgang Lutz (2019), 'Stalls in Africa's fertility decline partly result from disruptions in female education', *Proceedings of the National Academy of Sciences of the United States of America* (*PNAS*), Vol. 116, No. 8, pp. 2891–6.

14 'Uganda's priority sectors funded despite debt risk', *The Nation*, 25 June 2018.

15 Uganda Bureau of Statistics, Statistical Abstract 2018, p. 37.

16 UNESCO Institute for Statistics.

17 *The Millennium Development Goals Report 2015: Regional Backgrounder – Sub-Saharan Africa*.

18 AfDB (2020), *African Economic Outlook 2020: Developing Africa's Workforce for the Future*, pp. 55–7.

19 Ibid., Figure 2.7, p. 63.

20 DHS Final Reports, Tables 2.12.2.

21 United Nations Development Programme (UNDP) Human Development Index, 2018.

22 SB Morgen (SBM) Intelligence Nigeria, 'School's out', 9 October 2018 (data from National Bureau of Statistics and Nigerian Population Commission).

23 John Cleland (2017a), 'Prospects for accelerated fertility decline in Africa', *The Journal of Population and Sustainability*, Vol. 1, No. 2, p. 48. The statement was 'evidenced by 7 of these 24 countries'.

24 Julia Zinkina and Andrey Korotayev (2014b), 'Explosive population growth in Tropical Africa: Crucial omission in development forecasts – emerging risks and way out', *World Futures*, No. 70, p. 127.

25 Ibid., p. 132.
26 AfDB (2020), op. cit., p. 124.
27 UNESCO Institute for Statistics Fact Sheet No. 56, September 2019 (figures are for 2018).
28 Joe Abah, 'Taking Kaduna from Good to Great: The Challenge of Personal Example', the Kaduna Inauguration Lecture, www.joeabah.com (28 May 2019).
29 Jieun Choi, Mark Dutz and Zainab Usman (2019), *The Future of Work in Africa*, World Bank, p. 74.
30 Ibid., p. 77.
31 Mo Ibrahim Foundation (2019), *Africa's Youth: Jobs or Migration?*, Ibrahim Forum Report, p. 30.
32 UNESCO Institute for Statistics Global Education Monitoring Report (2019), 'Meeting Commitments: Are Countries on Track to Achieve SDG 4?', p. 10.
33 Emily Smith-Greenaway (2015), 'Educational attainment and adult literacy: A descriptive account of 31 sub-Saharan Africa countries', *Demographic Research*, Vol. 33, Art. 35, p. 1021.
34 World Bank (2019), *Nigeria Economic Update: Accelerating Economic Expansion, Creating New Job Opportunities*, p. 30.
35 United Nations, *The Sustainable Development Goals Report 2019*.
36 AfDB (2020), op. cit., p. 63.
37 UNDP Human Development Index, 2019.
38 UNESCO Institute for Statistics Global Education Monitoring Report (2019), op. cit., p. 10.
39 See, for example, Mwesiga Baregu, 'Worrying trends of education in Tanzania as illiteracy expands', *The Citizen*, 8 January 2017.
40 ILOSTAT (accessed October 2019).
41 Mwesiga Baregu, op. cit.
42 Oluseun Onigbinde, 'Nigeria remains stuck after 20 years of its Fourth Republic', *Stears Business*, 12 June 2019.
43 Michael Chishala, 'Zambia's falling education standards!', *Zambian Economist*, 29 July 2015.
44 World Bank (1987), op. cit., p. x.
45 UNICEF (2017), *Generation 2030 Africa 2.0*, p. 37.
46 UNESCO Institute for Statistics Global Education Monitoring Report (2018).
47 Samir KC and Wolfgang Lutz (2017), op. cit., p. 182.
48 Ibid., p. 190.
49 Ibid., p. 182: Educational attainment is 'a proxy indicator for skills and human capital... It does not include the quality dimension of education... nor does it cover informal education which also contributes to human capital'.
50 Wolfgang Lutz et al. (2018), *Demographic and Human Capital Scenarios for the 21st Century*, Publications Office of the European Union, p. 118.

13: GUESSING GAMES

1 Patrick Gerland, Ann Biddlecom and Vladimirá Kantorová (2017), 'Patterns of fertility decline and the impact of alternative scenarios of future fertility change in sub-Saharan Africa', Supplement to *Population and Development Review*, Vol. 43, Issue S1, pp. 31–5. The basket of 21 countries included Bangladesh, China, El Salvador, Morocco, Peru, South Africa, Sri Lanka, Thailand, Turkey and Uzbekistan.
2 Carl Haub, 'What if experts are wrong on world population growth?', Yale E360, 19 September 2011.
3 See Jean-Pierre Guengant (2017), 'Africa's population: History, Current Status, and Projections', in Hans Groth and John F. May (eds), *Africa's Population: In Search of a*

Demographic Dividend, Springer, Cham, pp. 11–31.

4 Ibid., pp. 18–20.

5 See Patrick Gerland, Ann Biddlecom and Vladimirá Kantorová (2017), op. cit.

6 Economic Commission for Africa/ African Development Bank/African Union Commission (2019), *African Statistical Yearbook 2019*.

7 UNPD (2019a), *World Population Prospects: The 2019 Revision – Vol. I: Comprehensive Tables*, p. iii.

8 Patrick Gerland, Ann Biddlecom and Vladimirá Kantorová (2017), op. cit., p. 35. At the time of publication of the article, UNPD's medium-variant projection for the population of sub-Saharan Africa in 2100 was 4 billion.

9 Edward Paice correspondence with Thomas Spoorenberg (UNPD), 23 September 2019.

10 Ibid. Higher projections for net migration also contributed.

11 See UNPD (2019b), *World Population Prospects 2019: Methodology of the United Nations Population Estimates and Projections*, *passim*.

12 World Bank Open Data. For comparison, Nigeria's population and GDP per capita are about 25% greater than those of Bangladesh, yet in Bangladesh the annual number of neonatal and infant deaths is 56,000 and 82,000 respectively.

13 World Bank (2018), *Nigeria Health Financing System Assessment*, p. viii.

14 See Anne Goujon and Zakarya Al Zalak (2018), 'Why has fertility been increasing in Egypt?', *Population & Societies*, No. 551, *passim*.

15 UNESCO Institute of Statistics, 'New Projections Show the World is Off Track in Meeting its Education Commitments by 2030', 9 July 2019; and 'Meeting Commitments: Are Countries on Track to Achieve SDG 4?'

16 See David Shapiro (2018), 'Frustrated Fertility Goals of Well-Educated Women in Sub-Saharan Africa' (n.b. South Africa was not included in the study), Paper presented at the annual meeting of the Population Association of America, Denver CO, 26–28 April.

17 See, for example, 'Discretionary income Nigeria', SB Morgen (SBM) Intelligence, August 2019 https:// www.sbmintel.com/wp-content/ uploads/2019/08/201908_Nigeria-discretionary-spending.pdf and Afrobarometer surveys.

18 Wale Lawal, 'Youth in crisis', *Stears Business*, 9 August 2015.

19 Kwame Owino, Noah Wamalwa and Ivory Ndekei (2017), *How Kenya Is Failing to Create Decent Jobs*, Africa Research Institute (Counterpoints series), June.

20 BBC News, 'How will a population boom change Africa?', 1 April 2018.

21 John C. Caldwell and Pat Caldwell (2002), 'The Fertility Transition in Sub-Saharan Africa', Paper presented at the Conference on Fertility and the Current South African Issues of Poverty, HIV/AIDS and Youth, Pretoria, 24 October, p. 4.

22 Yohannes Kinfu (2000), 'Below-replacement fertility in Tropical Africa? Some evidence from Addis Ababa', *Journal of Population Research*, Vol. 17, No. 1, pp. 63–82.

23 For an explanation of how poverty in Addis Ababa led to lower fertility, see Eshetu Gurmu and Ruth Mace (2008), 'Fertility decline driven by poverty: The case of Addis Ababa', *Journal of Biosocial Science*, Vol. 40, No. 3, pp. 339–58.

24 Hans Rosling quoted in BBC News, 'How will a population boom change Africa?', 1 April 2018.

25 Uganda Bureau of Statistics Statistical Abstract 2018, p. 13.

26 IMF (2018), 'The Future of Work in Sub-Saharan Africa', African Department Paper No. 18/18, p. 21.

27 Michel Garenne (2008), *Fertility Changes in Sub-Saharan Africa*, DHS Comparative Report No. 18, Macro International, p. 30, citing Etienne van de Walle and J. Knodel (1980),

'Europe's fertility transition: New evidence and lessons for today's developing world', *Population Bulletin*, Vol. 34, No. 6, pp. 3–44.

28 UNPD (2020a), *World Fertility and Family Planning 2020 – Highlights*, p. 1.

14: DEMOGRAPHIC ALCHEMY

1 David E. Bloom and Jeffrey G. Williamson (1997), 'Demographic Transitions, Human Resource Development and Economic Miracles in Emerging Asia', Working Paper 6268, National Bureau of Economic Research, Cambridge MA; and (1998), 'Demographic transitions and economic miracles in emerging Asia', *The World Bank Economic Review*, Vol. 12, No. 3, pp. 419–55.

2 Richard Cincotta (2011), 'Africa's reluctant fertility transition', *Current History*, Vol. 110, Issue 736, p. 186.

3 David E. Bloom et al. (2013), 'A Demographic Dividend for Sub-Saharan Africa: Source, Magnitude, and Realization, Working Paper No. 110, Programme on the Global Demography of Aging (PGDA), Harvard University, p. 4.

4 See Jeffrey G. Williamson (2013), 'Demographic dividends revisited', *Asian Development Review*, Vol. 30, No. 2, p. 7.

5 David E. Bloom and Jeffrey G. Williamson (1998), op. cit., p. 442.

6 Ibid., p. 419.

7 Ibid., p. 428.

8 Ibid., p. 422.

9 Ibid., p. 450.

10 Ibid.

11 Andrew Mason (2007), 'Demographic Transition and Demographic Dividends in Developed and Developing Countries', Paper for United Nations Expert Group Meeting on Social and Economic Implications of Changing

Population Age Structures, Mexico City, 31 August–2 September 2005, p. 97.

12 Ibid., p. 82.

13 Scott Moreland and Elizabeth Leahy Madsen (2017), 'Africa's Population: In Search of a Demographic Dividend', in Hans Groth and John F. May (eds), *Africa's Population: In Search of a Demographic Dividend*, Springer, Cham, p. 453.

14 David E. Bloom and Jeffrey G. Williamson (1998), op. cit., pp. 445–6. Robert Eastwood and Michael Lipton (2011), 'Demographic transition in Sub Saharan Africa: How big will the economic dividend be?', *Population Studies*, Vol. 65, No. 1, calculated that 'pure demographics' may have enhanced GDP per capita growth by 0.52% a year in East Asia between 1965 and 2005.

15 See David E. Bloom and David Canning (2006), 'Booms, busts, and echoes', *IMF Finance & Development*, Vol. 43, No. 3: 'Population neutralism is only recently giving way to a more fine-grained view of the effects of population dynamics in which demographic change does contribute or detract from economic development. To make their case, economists and demographers point to both the "arithmetic accounting" effects of age structure change and the effects of behavioural change caused by longer life spans.' Also, 'Several studies have estimated that this demographic shift was

responsible for one-third of East
Asia's economic growth during
the period [1965–1990], a welcome
demographic dividend.'

16 See UNPD (2004), *World Population to 2300.*

17 *National Transfer Accounts Bulletin,* August 2013, *passim.*

18 Martha Campbell (2007), 'Why the silence on population?', *Population and Environment,* Vol. 28, p. 238.

19 Michel Garenne, 'Demographic dividend in Africa: Macro- and micro-economic effects', N-IUSSP, 5 December 2016.

20 For example, these organisations funded the RAND Corporation 2003 study *The Demographic Dividend: A New Perspective on the Economic Consequences of Population Change* by David Bloom, David Canning and Jaypee Sevilla (Population Matters Monograph MR-1274, RAND, 2003).

21 Benno J. Ndulu (2007), *Challenges of African Growth: Opportunities, Constraints, and Strategic Directions,* World Bank, p. 90.

22 Ibid., p. 206. This is a passing reference in a section about Africa's dependency ratios to David E. Bloom and Jeffrey G. Williamson (1998) 'Demographic transitions and economic miracles in emerging Asia', who 'emphasize the demographic dividend that accrued to East Asian countries between 1960 and 2000 as a result of a falling ratio of dependents to workers'.

23 Benno J. Ndulu (2007), *Challenges of African Growth: Opportunities, Constraints, and Strategic Directions,* p. 106.

24 David E. Bloom et al. (2007b), 'Does Age Structure Forecast Economic Growth?', Working Paper 13221, National Bureau of Economic Research, Cambridge MA, p. 4.

25 David E. Bloom et al. (2007a), 'Realizing the Demographic

Dividend: Is Africa any Different?', Working Paper 2307, Program on the Global Demography of Aging (PGDA), Harvard University, p. 13.

26 Ibid., *passim.*

27 Ibid., p. 20

28 Ibid., p. 17.

29 Ibid., *passim.*

30 Ibid., p. 20.

31 Ibid., p. 21.

32 David E. Bloom (2011), '7 billion and counting', *Science,* Vol. 333, Issue 6042, p. 566.

33 David E. Bloom et al. (2013), op. cit., p. 7.

34 David E. Bloom, Michael Kuhn and Klaus Prettner (2016), 'Africa's Prospects for Enjoying a Demographic Dividend', IZA Discussion Paper No. 10161, Institute of Labour Economics, Bonn, p. 2.

35 David E. Bloom et al. (2013), 'A Demographic Dividend for Sub-Saharan Africa: Source, Magnitude, and Realization', pp. 14–15.

36 David E. Bloom, Michael Kuhn and Klaus Prettner (2016), op. cit., p. 5, fn. 2.

37 AfDB (2019a), *Creating Decent Jobs: Strategies, Policies, and Instruments,* Policy Research Document 2, p. 1.

38 Robert Eastwood and Michael Lipton (2012), 'The demographic dividend: Retrospect and prospect', *Economic Affairs,* Vol. 32, Issue 1, p. 28.

39 Robert Eastwood and Michael Lipton (2010), 'Demographic Transition in Sub-Saharan Africa: Accounting and Economics', Paper presented at the Fourth Annual Research Conference on Population, Reproductive Health and Economic Development, Cape Town, January, p. 15.

40 Scott Moreland and Elizabeth Leahy Madsen (2017), op. cit., p. 453.

41 Robert Eastwood and Michael Lipton (2010), 'Demographic Transition in Sub-Saharan Africa: Accounting and Economics', p. 19.

42 Robert Eastwood and Michael Lipton (2012), op. cit., pp. 28–9.

43 Alex Ezeh, 'Empowering women lies at the centre of controlling population growth in Africa', *The Conversation*, 20 September 2018.

44 Carolyn Lamere (2012), 'New support for international family planning: The significance of the London Summit', New Security Beat blog, 21 December.

45 'Family Planning Promotes the Demographic Dividend', Policy Brief 1, Aspen Institute, December 2011.

46 'Summaries of Commitments', UK Aid, London Summit on Family Planning, 7 September 2012, p. 11.

47 'How to manage Africa's population explosion', Economist Intelligence Unit Perspectives, 20 June 2012.

48 The Royal Society (2012), *People and the Planet*, p. 8.

49 Ibid., p. 93.

50 United Nations Environment Programme (UNEP), *One Planet, How Many People? A Review of Earth's Carrying Capacity*, June 2012, p. 3.

51 Joel E. Cohen (1995), 'Population growth and Earth's human carrying capacity', *Science*, Vol. 269, p. 342.

52 Ibid.

15: 'AFRICA RISING'

1 'Africa's impressive growth', *The Economist*, 6 January 2011.

2 Introduction to *The Fastest Billion*, Renaissance Capital, 2012.

3 *African Youth: Fulfilling the Potential*, Ibrahim Forum Report 2012, p. 1. On page 23 readers are told that 'to realise this potential [demographic dividend], expanded family planning programmes, sufficient opportunities for productive employment and effective means for the accumulation of human and physical capital during the dividend period will be required'.

4 Ibid.

5 'We are going to benefit from a demographic dividend. You are going to have this significant increase in consumers': John van Wyk of Actis LLP quoted in Reuters, 'Africa's demographics: Dividend or disaster?', 18 April 2012.

6 Elizabeth Leahy Madsen, 'The missing links in the demographic dividend', N-IUSSP, 9 March 2012.

7 David Pilling, 'Africa's population boom is both danger and opportunity', *Financial Times*, 7 July 2016.

8 'The dividend is delayed', *The Economist*, 8 March 2014. The article referred to Jean-Pierre Guengant and John F. May, 'Africa 2050: African Demography', Africa Emerging Markets Forum Briefing, June 2013.

9 David Bloom et al. (2013), 'A Demographic Dividend for Sub-Saharan Africa: Source, Magnitude, and Realization', Working Paper No. 110, Programme on the Global Demography of Aging (PGDA), Harvard University.

10 Wolfgang Lutz et al. (2019), 'Education rather than age structure brings demographic dividend', *Proceedings of the National Academy of the United States of America (PNAS)*, Vol. 116, No. 26, p. 12798.

11 John Casterline (2017a), 'Prospects for fertility decline in Africa', Supplement to *Population and Development Review*, Vol. 43, p. 11.

12 Gilles Pison (2017a), 'Why African families are larger than those of other continents', *The Conversation*, 11 October.

13 Paolo Drummond, Vimal Thakoor and Shue Yu (2014), 'Africa Rising: Harnessing the Demographic

Dividend', IMF Working Paper
WP/14/143, p. 4.

14 See for example Reuters, 'Africa's
    demographics: Dividend or disaster?,
    18 April 2012; David Canning,
    Sangeeta Raja and Abdo S. Yazbeck
    (2015), *Africa's Demographic
    Transition: Dividend or Disaster?*,
    World Bank/AFD; 'Demographic
    explosion: Dividend or disaster?',
    a 2018 PowerPoint presentation by
    Joseph Stiglitz.

15 World Economic Forum (2017), *The
    Africa Competitiveness Report 2017:
    Addressing Africa's Demographic
    Dividend*, p. 3.

16 Jakkie Cilliers (2018), *Getting to
    Africa's Demographic Dividend*,
    Institute for Security Studies,
    Pretoria, p. 2.

17 Wolfgang Lutz et al. (2019),
    'Education rather than age structure
    brings demographic dividend', *PNAS*,
    Vol. 116, No. 26, p. 12798.

18 Anuj Krishnamurthy, 'In Lesotho,
    population pressures have created a
    perfect storm of human insecurity',
    New Security Beat blog, 17 July 2017.

19 Jakkie Cilliers, 'How Africa's young
    population impacts development', ISS
    Africa webcast, 18 September 2018.

20 Jane O'Sullivan and Roger Martin,
    'The risk of misrepresenting the
    demographic dividend', N-IUSSP, 18
    April 2016.

21 Hans Groth, John F. May and Vincent
    Turbat (2017), 'Policies Needed to
    Capture a Demographic Dividend in
    Sub-Saharan Africa', IUSSP XXVIII
    International Population Conference,
    29 October–3 November 2017, p. 1.

22 UNPD (2017g), *Changing Population
    Age Structures and Sustainable
    Development: A Concise Report*, p. 19.

23 Vincent Turbat (2017), 'The
    Demographic Dividend: A
    Potential Surplus Generated by a
    Demographic Transition', in Hans
    Groth and John F. May (eds),

*Africa's Population: In Search of a
Demographic Dividend*, Springer,
Cham, p. 183. Turbat himself added
the economic dependency ratio
(EDR) as an alternative to the basic
dependency ratio and more complex
support ratio. This showed that
in the countries of sub-Saharan
Africa in 2016 the EDR was about
three times the DDR (and only 25%
higher in East Asia). The burden
of dependency was therefore much
higher in sub-Saharan Africa than
the DDR implied.

24 UNICEF (2017), *Generation Africa
    2.0*, p. 32.

25 Richard Cincotta, 'Opening the
    demographic window: Age structure
    in sub-Saharan Africa', New Security
    Beat blog, 26 October 2017.

26 IMF (2015), *Regional Economic
    Outlook: Sub-Saharan Africa*, p. 31.

27 Jakkie Cilliers (2018), op. cit., p. 1.

28 S. Amer Ahmed, 'How significant
    could Africa's demographic
    dividend be for growth and poverty
    reduction?', World Bank blogs, 2
    March 2015.

29 Meera Shekar, 'In the Sahel,
    accelerating the demographic
    dividend', World Bank blogs, 11 July
    2014.

30 Latif Dramani and Cheikh Mbacké
    (2017), 'Africa's Demographic
    Dividend – An Elusive Window
    of Opportunity?', Paper 6568,
    IUSSP XXVIII International
    Population Conference, Cape
    Town, 29 October–3 November,
    p. 1. Elsewhere, Latif Dramani and
    Jean-Baptiste Idossou Oga (2017),
    'Understanding demographic
    dividends in Africa: The NTA
    approach', *Journal of Demographic
    Economics*, Vol. 83, No. 1, p. 90,
    articulated the different definitions
    of the first demographic dividend:
    'The first demographic dividend
    has two possible interpretations: the

per capita income growth due to changes in population age structure OR the effect on consumption of the changing age structure while holding constant work effort, interest rate, assets, saving and net transfers from the rest of the world'.

31 IMF (2015), *Regional Economic Outlook: Sub-Saharan Africa*, April, p. 38. The existing forecast was for GDP per capita to grow by a factor of 3.6 times between 2010 and 2050, a little over 3% a year. In the IMF's most favourable scenario, requiring 'better policies and lower fertility', the demographic dividend could be as much as an incremental 50% and almost 120% by 2050 and 2100 respectively (see Chapter 2, p. 25).

32 AU/OECD (2018), *Africa's Development Dynamics 2018: Growth Jobs and Inequalities*, p. 77.

33 See UNFPA (2014), *The State of World Population 2014*, p. 21; and 2017 interview with Mabingué Ngom, UNFPA regional director for West and Central Africa, 'What to expect from Africa's demographic dividend', Ideas for Development (ID4D), 18 January 2017.

34 UNICEF (2017), *Generation Africa 2.0*, p. 12.

35 David E. Bloom Michael Kuhn and Klaus Prettner (2016), 'Africa's Prospects for Enjoying a Demographic Dividend', IZA Discussion Paper No. 10161, Institute of Labour Economics, Bonn, p. 5.

36 Jeffrey G. Williamson (2013), 'Demographic dividends revisited', *Asian Development Review*, Vol. 30, No. 2, p. 20.

37 John Cleland and Kazuyo Machiyama (2017), 'The challenges posed by demographic change in sub-Saharan Africa: A concise overview', *Population and Development Review*, Vol. 43, Issue S1, p. 5 and p. 6.

38 Michel Garenne, 'Demographic dividend in Africa: Macro- and micro-economic effects', N-IUSSP, 5 December 2016.

39 Elizabeth Leahy Madsen, 'What's behind West and Central Africa's youthful demographics? High desired family size', *New Security Beat* blog, 11 May 2015.

40 Uche Charlie Isiugo-Abanihe, 'Why Nigeria can't fix its development agenda: And where the solutions lie', *The Conversation*, 25 October 2020.

16: FROM BUZZWORD TO CLICHÉ: THE END OF 'DD'

1 Eunice Mueni, 'African governments should come of age and take charge of their development priorities', AFIDEP blog, 15 March 2018.

2 African Union (2016), *AU Roadmap on Harnessing the Demographic Dividend Through Investments in Youth*, p. 2.

3 The summit was co-hosted by the UK, UNFPA, the Bill & Melinda Gates Foundation and the Family Planning 2020 secretariat. US$2.5 billion was pledged to 'rights-based family planning'.

4 AU (2016), *AU Roadmap on Harnessing the Demographic Dividend Through Investments in Youth*, p. 35.

5 Hans Groth and John F. May, 'Failure to address Africa's rising population is not an option', *Financial Times*, 7 July 2017.

6 Cheikh Mbacké (2017), 'The persistence of high fertility in sub-Saharan Africa: A comment', Supplement to *Population and Development*, Vol. 43, p. 330.

7 'President Magufuli again urges Tanzanians to bear more children

to boost economy', *The Citizen*, 16 March 2020.

8 In AfDB (2011), *Africa in 50 Years' Time*, the lagging demographic transition is perceived as a positive factor. Some drawbacks to rapid population growth are noted, but there is no recognition of a need to accelerate fertility decline.

9 Louise Fox (2016), 'What Will it Take to Meet the Youth Employment Challenge in Sub-Saharan Africa?', Growth and Labour Markets in Low Income Countries Programme, GLM/LIC Synthesis Paper No. 2, IZA Institute of Labour Economics, Bonn p. 4: 'Western economists for years claimed that a growing labour force was a source of economic growth – "more people can produce more output".'

10 David E. Bloom et al. (2015), 'Prospects for Economic Growth in Nigeria: A Demographic Perspective', Working Paper No. 127, Program on the Global Demography of Aging (PGDA), Harvard University, p. 27.

11 AfDB (2019a), *Creating Decent Jobs: Strategies, Policies, and Instruments*, p. xi.

12 Ibid., p. 7.

13 David E. Bloom et al. (2013), 'A Demographic Dividend for Sub-Saharan Africa: Source, Magnitude, and Realization', Working Paper No. 110, Programme on the Global Demography of Aging (PGDA), Harvard University, p. 1.

14 Jakkie Cilliers (2018), *Getting to Africa's Demographic Dividend*, Institute for Security Studies, Pretoria, p. 2.

15 Vimal Thakoor and John Wakeman-Linn, 'Surf the demographic wave', *IMF Finance and Development*, March 2016, p. 22.

16 Crecey Kuyedzwa, 'Sub-Saharan Africa may miss out on demographic dividend – World Bank', Fin24 (South Africa), 29 February 2018.

17 Carl Manlan, 'Capitalising on Africa's demographic dividend', Project Syndicate, 20 November 2018.

18 Joe Penney, 'West African governments want to cut population growth in half, but for whose benefit?', *Quartz Africa*, 1 August 2017.

19 Jean-Pierre Guengant (2017), 'Africa's population: History, Current Status, and Projections', in Hans Groth and John F. May (eds), *Africa's Population: In Search of a Demographic Dividend*, Springer, Cham, p. 20.

20 John Cleland (2017a), 'Prospects for accelerated fertility decline in Africa', *The Journal of Population and Sustainability*, Vol. 1, No. 2, p. 51.

21 Eunice Mueni, op. cit.

22 Chimaraoke Izugbara et al. (2018), 'Fostering political leadership for the demographic dividend in Africa: Relevant cultural values', *Development in Practice*, Vol. 28, Issue 5, pp. 708–9.

23 Brenda K. Kombo, 'What are the alternatives to neoliberal trade?', Africa Is a Country (https://africasacountry.com), 5 February 2019.

24 Carlos Lopes, 'Too Young to Matter? How the Youth Will Shape Africa's Future', The Royal African Society Annual Lecture, 7 October 2017 https://www.mixcloud.com/royafrisoc/too-young-to-matter-how-the-youth-will-shape-africas-future-prof-carlos-lopes/

25 Kate Meagher (2016), 'The scramble for Africans: Demography, globalisation and Africa's informal labour markets', *The Journal of Development Studies*, Vol. 52, No. 4, p. 489.

26 Louise Fox (2016), op. cit., p. 4.

27 John Cleland and Kazuyo Machiyama (2017), 'The challenges

posed by demographic change in sub-Saharan Africa: A concise overview', *Population and Development Review*, Vol. 43, Issue S1, p. 267, citing Quamrul H. Ashraf, David N. Weil and Joshua Wilde (2013), 'The effect of fertility reduction on economic growth', *Population and Development Review*, Vol. 39, No. 1, p. 124.

28 Robert Eastwood and Michael Lipton (2010), 'Demographic Transition in Sub-Saharan Africa: Accounting and Economics', Paper presented at the Fourth Annual Research Conference on Population, Reproductive Health, and Economic Development, Cape Town, January, p. 25.

29 Ashoka Mody, 'The Demographic Dividend: Evidence from the Indian States', IMF Working Paper, February 2011.

30 See John Cleland (2012), 'Will Africa benefit from a demographic dividend?', Health & Education Advice & Resource Team (HEART) Briefing Note, p. 6.

31 Justin Fox, 'Where demographic dividends will pay out next', Bloomberg Opinion, 1 June 2018.

32 Ajit Jumar Singh (2016), 'India's demographic dividend: A sceptical look', *Indian Journal of Human Development*, Vol. 10, No. 1, pp. 16–17.

33 Henny Sender (2017), 'The sad illusion of India's demographic dividend', *Financial Times*, 17 October.

34 See Wolfgang Lutz et al. (2019), 'Education rather than age structure brings demographic dividend', *PNAS*, Vol. 116, No. 26, p. 12798.

35 Jane O'Sullivan (2017), 'The Contribution of Reduced Population Growth to Demographic Dividend', Paper presented at XXVIII International Population Conference, Cape Town, 29 October–4 November, p. 17.

36 The World Bank (2019), *Africa's Pulse*, Vol. 20, October, p. 48.

37 Tefo Mohapi, *iAfrikan* 'Daily Brief', Issue 94, 27 May 2020.

38 Alison Gillwald, 'South Africa is caught in the global hype of the fourth industrial revolution', *Mail & Guardian* (South Africa), 26 August 2019.

39 Tefo Mohapi (2020), op. cit.

17: 'A CHALLENGE OF MAMMOTH PROPORTIONS'

1 AfDB (2019a), *Creating Decent Jobs: Strategies, Policies, and Instruments*, p. 234.

2 AU/OECD (2019), *Africa's Development Dynamics 2019: Achieving Productive Transformation*.

3 AfDB (2019a), *Creating Decent Jobs: Strategies, Policies, and Instruments*, p. 237: the breakdown of the largest contributors to growth in the working-age population is Nigeria (18%), DRC (9%), Ethiopia (7%), Tanzania (6%) and Uganda (5%). Together with Egypt, Niger, Kenya and Angola these countries will account for 60% of Africa's growth in working-age population 2013–63.

4 See, for example, Valerie Mueller and James Thurlow (2019), *Youth and Jobs in Rural Africa: Beyond Stylized Facts*, International Food Policy Research Institute/Oxford University Press, p. 286: 'Addressing youth unemployment in Africa is a global challenge…'

5 AfDB (2019a), *Creating Decent Jobs*, p. 178.

6 IMF (2015), *Regional Economic Outlook: Sub-Saharan Africa*. The figure cited in IMF (2018), *The Future of Work in Sub-Saharan Africa*, p. 21, is for a requirement for '16 to 20 million new jobs on average each year' for sub-Saharan Africa.

7 IMF (2015), *Regional Economic Outlook: Sub-Saharan Africa*, p. 25.

8 Jieun Choi, Mark Dutz and Zainab Usman (2019), *The Future of Work in Africa*, World Bank, p. 74.

9 Valerie Mueller and James Thurlow (2019), op. cit., p. 278. The figure of 30 million refers to sub-Saharan Africa only.

10 IMF (2018), *The Future of Work in Sub-Saharan Africa*, p. 1.

11 ILO (2018), *Women and Men in the Informal Economy: A Statistical Picture*, p. 29.

12 United Nations (2019), *The Sustainable Development Goals Report 2019* (p. 22) states that almost 40% of employed workers in sub-Saharan Africa live on less than US$1.90 a day. According to ILO (2020), *Global Youth Employment Report 2020*, p. 46: 'approximately 42% of young workers in sub-Saharan Africa live in extreme poverty'.

13 AfDB (2016), *Jobs for Youth in Africa: Strategy for Creating 25 Million Jobs and Equipping 50 Million Youth, 2016–2025*, p. 6 (referring to AfDB (2015), *African Economic Outlook 2015*, p. 12). The AfDB defines youth as 15–35.

14 AfDB (2016), *Jobs for Youth in Africa*, p. 13.

15 Ibid., p. 8. Jobs are defined as 'a formal or informal set of tasks performed for an employer or for oneself that generate income and do not violate fundamental rights and principles at work'.

16 AfDB (2019a), *Creating Decent Jobs*, p. 5.

17 ILO (2018), *Women and Men in the Informal Economy*, p. 13, p. 14 and p. 29. Most recent data for Angola, Cameroon, Chad, Congo and DRC is from the 2000s.

18 Ibid., p. 30.

19 According to Eurostat Statistics, *Labour Market Including Labour Force Survey (LFS) 2017*, Europe's labour force numbered 227 million.

20 OECD data, 'Employment by activity' (accessed 21 December 2020).

21 IMF, *World Economic Outlook 2015*, pp. 25–6; and see Neil Balchin (2016), *Developing Export-Based Manufacturing in Sub-Saharan Africa*, Overseas Development Institute (ODI), p. 2: 'The share of manufacturing in total formal and informal employment (ILO data) fell from 6.4% in 1991 to 5.3% in 2013, but the total numbers of employees in SSA increased from 11.0 million to 17.7 million.'

22 AfDB (2016), *Jobs for Youth in Africa*, p. 6.

23 In 2014 the ILO estimated that all manufacturing employment worldwide – formal and informal – reached 466 million jobs.

24 UNDP (1996), *Human Development Report*, p. 94: the figure covers the period 1978–93. Many of the jobs were in labour-intensive export industries, but there was average annual growth of 2.5% in rural employment as well as 3.5% in urban employment.

25 World Economic Forum (2017), *The Africa Competitiveness Report 2017: Addressing Africa's Demographic Dividend*, p. 36.

26 Louise Fox (2019), 'Three Myths About Youth Employment in Africa and Strategies to Realize the Demographic Dividend', Chapter 3 of *Foresight Africa 2019* (pp. 56–8), Brookings Institution, Washington DC, p. 56.

27 Kate Meagher (2016), 'The scramble for Africans: Demography, globalisation and Africa's informal labour markets', *The Journal of*

Development Studies, Vol. 52, No. 4, p. 483.

28 Justin Yifu Lin, 'How to seize the 85 million jobs bonanza', World Bank blogs, 27 July 2011.

29 Irene Yuan Sun (2017), *The Next Factory of the World: How Chinese Investment Is Reshaping Africa*, Harvard Business Review Press. Also see Irene Yuan Sun, 'The world's next great manufacturing centre', *Harvard Business Review*, May–June.

30 World Economic Forum (2017), *The Africa Competitiveness Report 2017*, p. 65.

31 AU/OECD (2019), *Africa's Development Dynamics*, p. 5.

32 'Middle East's demographic earthquake: The generation fuelling protests', *Financial Times*, 10 February 2020.

33 Dani Rodrik, 'We are in a chronic state of shortage of good jobs', *Financial Times*, 14 February 2021.

34 Jay Naidoo, 'Most African migrants head for Africa, not Europe, and they support economic growth', *Daily Maverick*, 12 April 2019.

35 This figure utilises the 'expanded' definition of unemployment, as defined by StatsSA, the national statistics agency. See AfricaCheck, '"One South Africa for all!" Fact-checking the DA's 2019 election manifesto', 25 March 2019.

36 Ibid.

37 Andrew S. Nevin (chief economist, Pwc Nigeria), tweet posted on 14 May 2019.

38 Adel Abdel Ghafar, 'Youth unemployment in Egypt: A ticking time bomb', Brookings blog, 28 July 2016.

39 According to the Kenya National Bureau of Statistics 2015–16 Labour Force Report there were 1.2 million unemployed and 2.23 million underemployed Kenyans between the ages of 15 and 34, about a third of the population in that age bracket.

40 'G7 Framework on Decent Job Creation for Rural Youth in the Sahel', G7 meeting, Biarritz 2019, citing UNDESA statistics.

41 The ILO defines decent work as follows: 'decent work involves opportunities for work that are productive and deliver a fair income, security in the workplace and social protection for families, better prospects for personal development and social integration, freedom for people to express their concerns, organize and participate in the decisions that affect their lives and equality of opportunity and treatment for all women and men'.

42 AfDB (2019a), *Creating Decent Jobs*, p. 166.

43 Ibid., p. 4.

44 To be unemployed an individual cannot have worked a single hour in the week before the survey and must have been actively seeking a job for at least a month.

45 AfDB (2019a), *Creating Decent Jobs*, p. 5, citing ILO (2018), *World Employment and Social Outlook 2018*, p. 11. The underemployed are defined as 'those who are unable to find full-time work at a decent wage, or skilled workers forced to take low-skilled and low-productivity jobs'.

46 AfDB (2019a), *Creating Decent Jobs*, p. 3 and p. 4.

47 Afrobarometer, 'Taking Stock: Citizen Priorities and Assessments Three Years into the SDGs', Policy Paper No. 51, November 2018, pp. 5–6 and p. 22. The survey conducted 45,823 interviews in 34 countries between September 2016 and September 2018. 'Unemployment' was named by 40% of interviewees among the top three important problems they thought their government should address. The

second most frequently named
problem was 'Health', on 27%.

48 World Economic Forum (2019), 'The
Sub-Saharan Africa Risks Landscape',
White Paper, Geneva, September,
p. 5. The survey was conducted in 34
countries in sub-Saharan Africa.

49 World Bank (1989), *Sub-Saharan
Africa: From Crisis to Sustainable
Growth*, p. 41.

50 Abdul Raufu Mustapha, 'Structural
Adjustment and Multiple Modes of
Social Livelihood in Nigeria', United
Nations Research Institute for Social
Development Discussion Paper
26, June 1991, p. 7, quoting UNDP
(1996), *Human Development Report
1996*, p. 17: 'structural adjustment,
which in many cases meant trying to
balance the economy at the cost of
unbalancing people's lives'.

51 Grieve Chelwa, 'Is Africa really
rising? History and facts suggest it
isn't', Africa Is a Country https://
africasacountry.com/, 18 June 2015.

52 UNDP (1996), *Human Development
Report 1996*, p. 90.

53 Ndongo Samba Sylla, 'Descent into
hell', *Development and Cooperation
(D+C)*, 1 August 2018.

54 Ibid.

55 World Bank (1989), *Sub-Saharan
Africa*, p. 4.

56 Mike Davis (2007), *Planet of Slums*,
Verso Books, London, Chapter 8,
passim.

57 Jean-Pierre Guengant and Yarri
Kamara (2012), 'How can we
capitalize on the demographic
dividend?', *A Savoir 09*, AFD, p. 13.

58 Hans Groth, John F. May and Vincent
Turbat (2017), 'Policies Needed to
Capture a Demographic Dividend in
Sub-Saharan Africa', IUSSP XXVIII

International Population Conference,
29 October–3 November, p. 9.

59 Muneinazvo Kujeke, 'Can a new
network bring the AU to Africa's
youth?', *ISS Today*, 4 November 2019.

60 Louise Fox (2019), op. cit., p. 59.

61 Anna Reuss and Kristof Titeca
(2017), 'When revolutionaries grow
old: The Museveni babies and the
slow death of liberation', *Third World
Quarterly*, Vol. 38, Issue 10, p. 2.

62 Louise Fox (2016), 'What Will It
Take to Meet the Youth Employment
Challenge in Sub-Saharan Africa?',
Growth and Labour Markets in
Low Income Countries Programme,
GLM/LIC Synthesis Paper No. 2,
IZA Institute of Labour Economics,
Bonn, p. 2.

63 Jackie Chimhanzi, 'An Abundance
of Young Africans but No Seat at the
Table', African Leadership Institute,
August 2018.

64 ILO (2018), *Women and Men in
the Informal Economy: A Statistical
Picture*, p. 16.

65 See, for example, Acha Leke, Mutsa
Chironga and Georges Desvaux
(2018), 'Africa's overlooked business
revolution', *McKinsey Quarterly*, 15
November: 'The World Bank, for
example, estimates that SMEs are
responsible for 77% of all jobs in
Africa and as much as half of GDP in
some countries.'

66 Efosa Ojomo, 'How Africa can
"entrepreneur" its way out of
bad leadership and the vital role
of innovation', *Quartz Africa*, 12
December 2019.

67 'Nigerians are not real entrepreneurs',
Stears Business, 15 February 2018.

68 @rggoobi tweet, 20 June 2019.

18: 'TEETERING ON THE EDGE OF A CLIFF'

1 @seyitaylor tweet, 8 December 2019.

2 Ayo Olukotun quoted in Ebuka
Onyeji, 'Why Nigeria's Vision
20:2020 was bound to fail', *Premium
Times*, 19 January 2020.

3 World Bank (2015), *More, and More Productive, Jobs for Nigeria: A Profile of Work and Workers*, p. xx.

4 National Bureau of Statistics cited in World Bank (2019), *Nigeria Economic Update*: 'Jumpstarting Inclusive Growth: Unlocking the Productive Potential of Nigeria's People and Resource Endowments', Fall 2019, p. 8. In Nigeria unemployment denotes working less than 20 hours a week; anyone working more than 20 hours a week counts as employed, but those working 30–40 hours are classified as underemployed.

5 Misan Rewane, 'Teetering on the edge of a cliff', *The Republic*, 6 September 2019.

6 Eurostat Statistics, Labour Market including Labour Force Survey (LFS) 2017 registered 18 million unemployed.

7 World Bank (2019), *Nigeria Economic Update* (December), p. 10. Leandro Medina et al., 'The Informal Economy in Sub-Saharan Africa: Size and Determinants', IMF Working Paper No. 17/156 (July 2017), states 65% of GDP. This study used a 'light intensity approach' to estimating the size of informal economies.

8 World Bank (2019), *Nigeria Economic Update* (December), p. 10.

9 World Bank (2015), *More, and More Productive, Jobs for Nigeria*, p. 18.

10 National Bureau of Statistics cited in World Bank (2019), *Nigeria Economic Update* (December), p. 8.

11 Kate Meagher (2013), 'The jobs crisis behind Nigeria's unrest', *Current History*, Vol. 112, Issue 754, p. 171.

12 'Nigeria's elections: Big Men, big fraud and big trouble', *The Economist*, 26 April 2007.

13 Kate Meagher (2013), op. cit., pp. 169–70.

14 World Bank (2019), *Nigeria Economic Update* (December), p. 34.

15 Ibid. p. 10.

16 @BudgItng tweet, 19 November 2019.

17 Joe Abah (2019), 'Taking Kaduna From Good to Great: The Challenge of Personal Example', the Kaduna Inauguration Lecture, www.joeabah. com.

18 SBM Intelligence, 'Commentary', 30 January 2020.

19 Zaakhir Asmal, Haroon Bhorat and John Page (2020), 'Exploring new sources of large-scale job creation: The potential role of Industries Without Smokestacks', *Foresight Africa 2020*, Brookings Institution p. 37.

20 AfricaCheck Fact Sheet: 'Unemployment Statistics in South Africa Explained', December 2014.

21 AfricaCheck, '"One South Africa for all!" Fact-checking the DA's 2019 election manifesto', 25 March 2019.

22 'Fact sheet on "NEETs"', Department of Higher Education and Training, South Africa, p. 3.

23 Alison Gillwald, 'South Africa is caught in the global hype of the fourth industrial revolution', *Mail & Guardian*, 26 August 2019; Sipho Mabaso, 'Ramaphosa's big jobs headache as outlook remains bleak', *Sunday Independent*, 16 June 2019.

24 Vimal Ranchhod, 'Why is South Africa's unemployment rate so high?', *GroundUp*, 15 February 2019.

25 Uganda Bureau of Statistics, National Labour Force Survey 2016/17, p. 36.

26 On NEETs, see World Bank (2017), *Ethiopia: Employment and Jobs Study*, p. 8: 'NEET is particularly applicable to youth, as it measures a state of complete idleness (in the sense of not being employed nor investing in skills to improve future employability) at a crucial time when skills and work experiences should be accumulated. According to the ILO (2013), 'What does NEETs mean and why is the concept so easily misinterpreted?': 'Because they

are neither improving their future employability through investments in skills nor gaining experience through employment, NEETs are particularly at risk of both labor market and social exclusion.' Also: 'NEET may better capture the extent of vulnerability, marginalization and exclusion in little-developed labour markets... Unemployment and NEET are correlated.'

27 Uganda Bureau of Statistics, National Labour Force Survey 2016/17, June 2018, p. 88 and p. 102.

28 Advocates Coalition for Development and Environment (2014), 'Youth Unemployment and Job Creation in Uganda', Infosheet No. 26, pp. 64–70.

29 World Bank (2020), *Uganda: Jobs Strategy for Inclusive Growth – Factsheet.*

30 Uganda Bureau of Statistics, National Labour Force Survey 2016/17, June 2018, pp. 94–106.

31 Ibid., pp. 87–106, and Statistical Abstract 2018, pp. 34–6.

32 Arkebe Oqubay, 'Will the 2020s be the decade of Africa's economic transformation?', ODI Insight blog, 14 January 2020.

33 Population Reference Bureau, '2017 World Population Data Sheet', and UNPD (2019a), *World Population Prospects: The 2019 Revision – Vol. I: Comprehensive Tables.*

34 World Bank (2017), *Ethiopia: Employment and Jobs Study*, p. i.

35 Unemployment is computed using the ILO's 'relaxed' definition, which only includes those who are without work but available (Ethiopia Central Statistical Authority, Labour Force Survey 2013, Section 6.3).

36 Ethiopia Central Statistical Authority, Labour Force Survey 2013 (the most recent).

37 World Bank (2017), *Ethiopia: Employment and Jobs Study*, p. 1: 'The definitions employed in this study are based on the ILO international standards pre-2013 (13th ICLS). An individual is considered employed if he worked for at least 1 hour in any productive activity, including waged work, production of goods and services for sale, unpaid family work, etc. According to the ILO relaxed definition of unemployment and in line with the standards of the Ethiopian CSA, an individual is classified as unemployed if he did not work at least 1 hour in the reference week and he was available for work in the reference period. The third criterion "seeking work", i.e. someone actively looked for work in a specified recent period, identifies together with the first two the unemployed according to the ILO strict definition of unemployment. Following the practice in Ethiopia, we will not use this strict definition. Underemployment is defined as working less than 35 hours per week but wanting to work more.'

38 World Bank (2017), *Ethiopia: Employment and Jobs Study*, p. iv; also Ethiopia National Human Development Report 2018, 'Industrialisation With a Human Face', p. 48.

39 René Lefort, '"Leba! Leba!" Abiy inspires farmers' revolt in North Shoa village', *Ethiopia Insight*, 31 November 2018.

40 World Bank (2017), *Ethiopia: Employment and Jobs Study*, p. 10; AfDB (2019), *Creating Decent Jobs: Strategies, Policies, and Instruments*, p. 198.

41 Ethiopia Central Statistical Authority, Labour Force Survey 2013.

42 Arkebe Oqubay, 'Africa's economic transformation and the future of EU-Africa cooperation', CESifo Forum, Ifo Institute, Vol. 21, Issue 02, pp. 3–10.

43 World Bank (2017), *Ethiopia: Employment and Jobs Study.*
44 Ethiopia Central Statistical Authority, Labour Force Survey 2013, Section 6.4.
45 World Bank (2017), *Ethiopia: Employment and Jobs Study*, pp. 7–8.
46 Ibid., p. 48.
47 Ibid., p. 5.
48 Sebastian Eckardt, Deepak Mishra and Viet Tuan Dinh, 'Vietnam's manufacturing miracle: Lessons for developing countries', Brookings blog, 17 April 2018.
49 AU/OECD (2019), *Africa's Development Dynamics 2019: Achieving Productive Transformation*, p. 29.
50 World Bank (2017), *Ethiopia: Employment and Jobs Study*, p. 17.
51 Ibid., p. vii and p. 17.
52 Deloitte, 'Kenya: Grounding Africa's Economic Growth', October 2016, p. 7.
53 World Bank (2017), *Ethiopia: Employment and Jobs Study*, p. vii.
54 See *Business Daily*, 6 March 2019, '306 more Kenyans rise to millionaires rank in a year'.
55 See Kenya National Bureau of Statistics, 2015/16 Kenya Integrated Household Budget Survey: Labour Force Basic Report, p. 3.
56 Ibid., pp. xii–xiv.
57 The Aga Khan University/East African Institute, 'The Kenya Youth Survey Report 2015'. Survey size 1,854 from across the country.
58 OECD (2017), *Social Protection in East Africa: Harnessing the Future*, p. 46.
59 Kenya National Bureau of Statistics – Economic Survey 2019, p. 39.

60 Kenya National Bureau of Statistics – Economic Survey 2018, pp. 40–1.
61 Ibid., p. 50.
62 Kenya National Bureau of Statistics – Economic Survey 2019, p. 40.
63 Ibid., p. 39.
64 Kwame Owino, Noah Wamalwa and Ivory Ndekei (2017), *How Kenya Is Failing to Create Decent Jobs*, Africa Research Institute (Counterpoints series), June, p. 5.
65 Kenya National Bureau of Statistics – Economic Survey 2018, p. 44.
66 Alphonse Shiundu, 'Are 70% of Kenyans who can work jobless? Union chief mangles numbers', AfricaCheck, 26 May 2017.
67 Kenya National Bureau of Statistics – Economic Survey 2019, p. 54.
68 Central Bank of Kenya/Kenya National Bureau of Statistics/FSD Kenya, 2019 FinAccess Household Survey, April 2019.
69 IMF World Economic Outlook Database 2016.
70 Kenya National Bureau of Statistics – Economic Survey 2019, p. 39.
71 Kwame Owino et al. (2017), *How Kenya Is Failing to Create Decent Jobs*, p. 5.
72 Richard Anker and Martha Anker (2017), 'Living Wage Report – Kenya', Global Living Wage Coalition, Series 1, Report 10, p. 8.
73 Anzetse Were, 'Unemployed Kenyan youth sinking deeper into misery', *Business Daily*, 17 March 2019.
74 Quoted in Kesa Pharatlhatlhe, 'Time for leaders and youth to share the Africa they want, together', ECDPM blog, 20 April 2018.

19: GRAND DESIGNS

1 World Bank (1986), *Population Growth and Policies in Sub-Saharan Africa*, p. 30.
2 Ibid., p. v.
3 Ibid., p. vi.
4 Ibid., p. 19.

5 World Bank (1989), *Sub-Saharan Africa: From Crisis to Sustainable Growth*, p. 4 and p. xii.

6 Ibid., pp. 12–13.

7 World Bank (1986), *Population Growth and Policies in Sub-Saharan Africa*, p. 26, referring to J.M. Higgins et al. (1982), 'Potential Populations Supporting Capacities of Lands in the Developing World', FAO/IIASA/UNFPA.

8 Damian Carrington interview with Paul Ehrlich, *The Guardian*, 22 March 2018.

9 Patrick Caughill, 'Stephen Hawking believes humankind is in danger of self-destruction due to AI', *Futurism*, 25 November 2017.

10 BBC News, 'Is population growth out of control?', 29 September 2013.

11 Philip Aldrick, 'Climate change is driving mass migration, says Attenborough', *The Times*, 12 April 2019.

12 Massimo Livi Bacci (2017), *Our Shrinking Planet*, Polity Press, Cambridge, p. 127.

13 William J. Ripple et al. (2020), 'World scientists' warning of a climate emergency', *Bioscience*, Vol. 70, Issue 1, pp. 8–12.

14 See Mark Maslin, 'Stabilising the global population not a solution to the climate emergency – but we should do it anyway', *The Conversation*, 7 November 2019.

15 Ugo Bardi, 'Overpopulation problem? What overpopulation problem?', Cassandra's Legacy blog, 2 July 2018.

16 John Cleland (2017a), 'Prospects for accelerated fertility decline in Africa', *The Journal of Population and Sustainability*, Vol. 1, No. 2, p. 37.

17 Frank Götmark, '"Factfulness": A more accurate title for this new book would have been "Selecting Facts to Make You Happy"', The

Overpopulation Project, 28 August 2018.

18 Landry Signé, 'Capturing Africa's high returns', Brookings Opinions, 14 March 2018.

19 Paul Jackson, 'This will be Africa's century', *Financial Times* beyondbrics forum, 30 January 2020.

20 Jonathan Eley and Norma Cohen, 'Africa calling: Rewarding patient investors', *Financial Times*, 15 February 2013 (quoting a research report by Morgan Stanley's 'Sustainable + Responsible' research team).

21 John Arlidge, 'Hilton boss Chris Nassetta joins the scramble for Africa', *The Sunday Times*, 21 October 2018.

22 Lee Mwiti, 'Roar or die – how Africa's booming population could make it richer and stronger, or kill it', *Mail & Guardian*, 22 April 2015.

23 Massimo Livi Bacci (2017), op. cit., p. 21.

24 John Cleland and Kazuyo Machiyama (2017), 'The challenges posed by demographic change in sub-Saharan Africa: A concise overview', *Population and Development Review*, Vol. 43, Issue S1, p. 264.

25 Michel Garenne (2017a), 'Family Planning and Fertility Decline in Africa: From 1950 to 2010', in Zouhair O. Amarin (ed.), *Family Planning*, IntechOpen, London, p. 120.

26 Ibid., p. 145.

27 John Bongaarts, 'Africa's challenging demographic future', *Humanosphere*, 22 October 2015.

28 Carl Haub, 'What if experts are wrong on world population growth?' Yale E360, 19 September 2011.

29 Jean-Pierre Guengant and John F. May (2011a), 'Sub-Saharan Africa within global demography', *Études*, Vol. 415, Issue 10.

30 Jack Goldstone, 'The new population bomb', *Foreign Affairs*, January/February 2010.

31 John Weeks, 'A useful reminder about Africa's demography', Weeks Population blogspot, 20 December 2011.

32 See Derek Thompson, 'Why economics is really called 'the dismal science', *The Atlantic*, 17 December 2013.

33 Julia Zinkina and Andrey Korotayev (2014a), 'Projecting Mozambique's demographic futures', *Journal of Futures Studies*, Vol. 19, No. 2, p. 26.

34 John Cleland (2013), 'World population growth; Past, present and future', *Environmental and Resource Economics*, Vol. 55, Issue 4, p. 552.

35 John Cleland, 'The growing continent', *The World Today*, April/May 2013, p. 44.

36 Malcolm Potts, Cortney Henderson and Martha Campbell (2013), 'The Sahel: A Malthusian challenge?', *Environmental and Resource Economics*, Vol. 55, pp. 510–11.

37 Jean-Pierre Guengant and John F. May (2014), 'Les défis démographiques des pays sahéliens', *Études*, Vol. 6.

38 John Cleland (2017a), op. cit.

39 Andrey Korotayev, Sergey Malkov and Leonid Grinin (2014), 'A Trap at the Escape from the Trap? Some Demographic Structural Factors of Political Instability in Modernizing Social Systems', in *History & Mathematics: Trends and Cycles*, Uchitel Publishing House, Volgograd, p. 257.

40 Serge Michailof (2016), *Programmed Explosion? The Potential Consequences of the Rapid Population Growth in Sub-Saharan Africa*, Konrad Adenauer Stiftung International Reports, Issue 4, p. 48.

41 Henrik Urdal (2012), 'Youth Bulges and Violence', in Jack Goldstone,

Eric Kaufmann and Monica Duffy Toft, *Political Demography*, Paradigm Publishers, Boulder CO, p. 118.

42 Verisk Maplecroft, Climate Change Vulnerability Index 2018.

43 Frank Gardner, 'Is Africa overtaking the Middle East as the new jihadist battleground?', BBC News, 3 December 2020.

44 See, for example, Julian Cribb (2019), *Food or War*, Cambridge University Press.

45 On food price inflation, see Paul Adams and Edward Paice (2017), 'The "Silent Crisis" of Food Price Inflation in Africa', Africa Research Institute; various papers by Thomas Allen at the OECD/Sahel and West Africa Club and the SBMintel Jollof Rice Index.

46 Massimo Livi Bacci (2017), op. cit., p. 31, citing Gordon McGranahan, Deborah Balk and Bridget Anderson (2007), 'The rising tide: Assessing the risks of climate change and human settlements in low elevation coastal zones', *Environment & Urbanization*, Vol. 19, No. 1, pp. 17–37.

47 See OECD/Sahel and West Africa Club (2020b), *The Geography of Conflict in North and West Africa*, p. 67.

48 Cullen Hendrix and John O'Loughlin, 'In search of consensus on climate-conflict links', *New Security Beat* blog, 12 August 2019.

49 See Katharine J. Mach et al. (2019), 'Climate as a risk factor for armed conflict', *Nature*, Vol. 571, 12 June.

50 Philipp Heinrigs (2010), *Security Implications of Climate Change in the Sahel Region: Policy Considerations*, OECD/Sahel and West Africa Club, p. 6.

51 Mark Cuthbert and Richard Taylor, 'Groundwater reserves in Africa may be more resilient to climate change than first thought', *The Conversation*, 7 August 2019.

52 Mary Caperton Morton, 'Ancient water underlies arid Egypt', www.eos.org, 18 June 2019.
53 See Horman Chitonge, 'Water scarcity for most people in Africa is socially-induced', LSE blog, 11 December 2020.
54 'Global Health Security and Pandemics: Africa and COVID-19', seminar organised by Mile End Institute, Queen Mary (University of London), 28 April 2020.
55 Malte Lierl, 'Growing State Fragility in the Sahel: Rethinking International Involvement', GIGA Focus, No. 7, December 2020.
56 Daniel Eizenga (2019), 'Long term trends across security and development in the Sahel', *West African Papers*, No. 25, OECD Publishing, Paris, p. 22.
57 Samburu Country Smart Report 2018.
58 African Capacity Building Foundation (2015), *Assessment of Internal and External Risks Associated with the Implementation of the African Union's Agenda 2063*, p. 12.
59 Ibid., p. 3.

20: *A LUTA CONTINUA!*

1 Carlos Lopes, 'Too Young to Matter? How the Youth Will Shape Africa's Future', The Royal African Society Annual Lecture, 7 October 2017 https://www.mixcloud.com/royafrisoc/too-young-to-matter-how-the-youth-will-shape-africas-future-prof-carlos-lopes/
2 Tee Ngugi, 'African lives don't matter to their leaders and police', *The East African*, 3 December 2020.
3 Chukwudi Ukonne, 'The political awakening of the youth', *Stears Business Daily*, 20 October 2020.
4 Tokunbo Afikuyomi, *Stears Business Daily* editorial, 20 October 2020.
5 Wale Lawal, 'Nigeria's problems cannot be solved by young people alone', *Financial Times*, 29 October 2020.
6 Interview with Evelyn Lirri, *The Africa Report*, 12 January 2021.
7 Anna Reuss and Kristof Titeca (2019), 'Its own worst enemy? The Ugandan government is taking desperate measures to control rising dissent', Egmont Africa Policy Brief, No. 22, January 2019, p. 2 and p. 4.
8 'Augean Angola', *The Economist*, 5 May 2018.
9 Wim Marivoet, Tom de Herdt and John Ulimwengu (2019), 'Who benefitted from the peace dividend in the DRC?', *Review of African Political Economy*, 9 April.
10 See Leena Koni Hoffmann and Raj Navanit Patel (2017), *Collective Action on Corruption in Nigeria: A Social Norms Approach to Connecting Society and Institutions*, Chatham House (The Royal Institute of International Affairs).
11 Adrian Blomfield, 'Going, going gone: African dictators losing luxury lifestyle', *The Sunday Times*, 6 October 2019.
12 Chris Ngwodo, 'The great unravelling: The disintegration of the Nigerian State', *The Republic*, 6 December 2017.
13 Neil Munshi, 'Four decades of growth, but Equatorial Guinea still mired in poverty', *Financial Times*, 31 December 2019.
14 Wale Lawal, 'Youth in crisis', *Stears Business*, 9 August 2015.
15 Yomi Kazeem, 'Nigeria's population problem is the result of poor policy implementation – and it'll only get worse', *Quartz Africa*, 5 January 2018.

16 Uche Charlie Isiugo-Abanihe, 'Why Nigeria can't fix its development agenda: And where the solutions lie', *The Conversation*, 25 October 2020.

17 Alex Ezeh, 'Empowering women lies at the centre of controlling population growth in Africa', *The Conversation*, 20 September 2018.

18 African Capacity Building Foundation (2015), *Assessment of Internal and External Risks Associated with the Implementation of the African Union's Agenda 2063*, p. 34.

19 Jean-Pierre Guengant and Yarri Kamara (2012), 'How can we capitalize on the demographic dividend?', *A Savoir 09*, AFD, p. 3.

20 See, for example, Robert Eastwood and Michael Lipton (2012), 'The demographic dividend: Retrospect and prospect', *Economic Affairs*, Vol. 32, Issue 1, p. 29.

21 Matthew Lockwood (2005), 'Will a Marshall Plan for Africa make poverty history?', *Journal of International Development*, Vol. 17, p. 785.

22 Matthew Lockwood (2012), 'Adaptation Policy, Governance and Politics in Sub-Saharan Africa', Paper presented at an International Symposium on the Governance of Adaptation, Amsterdam, 22–3 March, p. 11.

23 Ibid., p. 10.

24 The World Bank (2019), *Africa's Pulse*, Vol. 20, October, pp. 37–8.

25 See Robert Mattes (2020), 'Lived Poverty on the Rise', Afrobarometer Policy Paper No. 62, March.

26 Maria Quattri and Kevin Watkins, 'Children in Africa Will Make Up More Than Half of Global Poverty by 2030', ODI/Save the Children UK press release, 27 August 2019.

27 Ibid.

28 Jamie Hitchen (2016), 'Steady Progress? 30 Years of Museveni and the NRM in Uganda', Africa Research Institute Briefing Note 1601, February, p. 2.

29 Joe Abah, 'When neutrality helps the victim', www.joeabah.com, 29 April 2018.

30 Carlos Lopes, op. cit.

31 Zoe Marks, Jide Okeke and Erica Chenoweth, 'People power is rising in Africa', *Foreign Affairs*, 25 April 2019.

32 @alykhansatchu tweet, 20 February 2019.

33 François Héran (2018), 'Europe and the spectre of sub-Saharan migration', *Population & Societies*, No. 558.

34 John Cleland and Kazuyo Machiyama (2017), 'The challenges posed by demographic change in sub-Saharan Africa: A concise overview', *Population and Development Review*, Vol. 43, Issue S1, p. 21.

35 UNDESA (1971), *The World Population in 1970*, p. 1.

36 John Reader (1998), *Africa: A Biography of the Continent*, Penguin Books, London, p. 126.

37 Ibid., p. 128 and p. 126.

38 UNDESA (1971), *The World Population in 1970*, p. 10.

39 I am grateful to Halimatou Hima for bringing this to my attention. She highlighted the fact that among those featured was Jeanne Martin Cissé, who in 1972 became the first female president of the UN Security Council.

40 AfDB (2016), *Jobs for Youth in Africa: Strategy for Creating 25 Million Jobs and Equipping 50 Million Youth, 2016–2025*, p. 11, n. 20.

41 Mihir Sharma, 'South Asia should pay attention to its standout star', Bloomberg Opinion, 1 June 2021.

42 Richard Davies, 'Glasgow's voyage from riches to ruin is a lesson for us all', *The Sunday Times*, 15 September 2019.

43 Ha-Joon Chang, 'Are Some Countries Destined for Under-development?', Global Development Institute, University of Manchester lecture, 6 February 2018 (available on YouTube).

44 BBC News, 'Why the future of French is African', 8 April 2019.

45 Yomi Kazeem, 'Africa is set to be the global center of Christianity for the next 50 years', *Quartz Africa*, 4 April 2019.

46 Max Fisher, 'The amazing, surprising, Africa-driven demographic future of the Earth in 9 charts', *The Washington Post*, 16 July 2013.

47 Christine Mungai, 'How will Africa change by 2030', World Economic Forum, 25 June 2015.

48 Howard W. French, 'Why Africa's future will determine the rest of the world's', *World Politics Review*, 6 November 2019.

Bibliography

Abbreviations

AFD – Agence française de développement, Paris
AfDB – African Development Bank, Tunis/Abidjan
AU – African Union, Addis Ababa
IIASA – Institute for Applied Systems Analysis, Laxenburg
ILO – International Labour Organization, Geneva
IMF – International Monetary Fund, Washington DC
N-IUSSP: online news magazine of the International Union for the Scientific Study of Population
OECD – The Organisation for Economic Co-operation and Development, Paris
UNDESA – United Nations Department of Economic and Social Affairs, New York
UNECA – United Nations Economic Commission for Africa, Addis Ababa
UNFPA – United Nations Population Fund (formerly United Nations Fund for Population Activities), New York
UNPD – United Nations Department of Economic and Social Affairs/Population Division, New York
UNU-WIDER – United Nations University World Institute for Development Economics Research, Helsinki

Abate, Yohannis (1978), 'African population growth and politics', *Issue: A Journal of Opinion*, Vol. 8, No. 4, pp. 14–19.

Adepoju, Aderanti (1975), 'Population policies in Africa: Problems and prospects', *African Affairs*, Vol. 74, No. 297, pp. 461–79.

AfDB (2011), *Africa in 50 Years' Time: The Road Towards Inclusive Growth*, Tunis.

AfDB (2012), *African Development Report 2012*, Addis Ababa.

AfDB (2016), *Jobs for Youth in Africa: Strategy for Creating 25 Million Jobs and Equipping 50 Million Youth, 2016–2025*, Abidjan.

AfDB (Célestin Monga, Abebe Shimeles and Andinet Woldemichael, eds) (2019a), *Creating Decent Jobs: Strategies, Policies, and Instruments*, Policy Research Document 2, Abidjan.

AfDB (2019b), *African Economic Outlook 2019*, Abidjan.

AfDB (2020), *African Economic Outlook 2020: Developing Africa's Workforce for the Future*, Abidjan.

African Capacity Building Foundation (2015), *Assessment of Internal and External Risks Associated with the Implementation of the African Union's Agenda 2063*, Harare.

Ahmed, S. Amer et al. (2015), 'How Significant Is Africa's Demographic Dividend for Its Future Growth and Poverty Reduction?', Policy Research Working Paper 7134, World Bank, Washington DC.

Alkema, Leontine et al. (2011), 'Probabilistic projections of the total fertility rate for all countries', *Demography*, Vol. 48, pp. 815–39.

Alkema, Leontine et al. (2012), 'Estimating trends in the total fertility rate with uncertainty using imperfect data: Examples from West Africa', *Demographic Research*, Vol. 26, Art. 15, pp. 331–62.

Alkema, Leontine et al. (2015), 'The United Nations probabilistic population projections: An introduction to demographic forecasting with uncertainty', *Foresight*, Vol. 37, pp. 19–24.

Anthony Rae Foundation (2013), *Global Population to 2050 and Beyond: Sources, Analysis and Discussion*, www.anthonyrae.com.

Asaolu, Ibitola O. et al. (2018), 'Measuring women's empowerment in sub-Saharan Africa: Exploratory and confirmatory factor analyses of the demographic and health surveys', *Frontiers in Psychology*, Vol. 9, Art. 994, pp. 1–10.

Askew, Ian, Maggwa, Ndugga and Onyango, Francis (2015), 'Fertility Transitions in Kenya and Ghana: Trends, Determinants and Implications for Policy and Programs', Paper presented at National Research Council Committee on Population Workshop on Recent Trends in Fertility in sub-Saharan Africa, Washington DC, 15–16 June.

Asmal, Zaakhir, Bhorat, Haroon and Page, John (2020), 'Exploring new sources of large-scale job creation: The potential role of industries without smokestacks, *Foresight Africa 2020*, Brookings Institution, Washington DC, pp. 35–47.

Asserate, Asfa-Wossen (2018), AU (2016), *African Exodus,* Haus Publishing, London.

AU (2016), *AU Roadmap on Harnessing the Demographic Dividend Through Investments in Youth*, Addis Ababa.

AU/OECD (2018), *Africa's Development Dynamics 2018: Growth, Jobs and Inequalities*, OECD Publishing/AU Commission, Paris/Addis Ababa.

AU/OECD (2019), *Africa's Development Dynamics 2019: Achieving Productive Transformation*, OECD Publishing/AU Commission, Paris/Addis Ababa.

Austin, Gareth, Frankema, Ewout and Jerven, Morten (2016), 'Patterns of Manufacturing Growth in Sub-Saharan Africa: From Colonization to the Present', EPR Discussion Paper 11609, Centre for Economic Policy Research, London.

Bacci, Massimo Livi (2017), *Our Shrinking Planet*, Polity Press, Cambridge.

Baregu, Mwesiga (1987), 'The African "population problem": Situational versus world historical perspectives', *Utafiti*, Vol. 9, No. 2, pp. 21–31.

Basten, Stuart, Lutz, Wolfgang and Scherbov, Sergei (2013), 'Very long range global population scenarios to 2300 and the implications of sustained low fertility', *Demographic Research*, Vol. 28, Art. 39, pp. 1145–66.

Basu, Alaka M. and Basu, Kaushik (2014), 'The Prospects for an Imminent Demographic Dividend in Africa: The Case for Cautious Optimism', UNU-WIDER Working Paper 2014/053.

Bill & Melinda Gates Foundation (2018), *Goalkeepers: The Stories Behind the Data 2018*, Seattle WA.

Blacker, John (1994), 'Some thoughts on the evidence of fertility decline in Eastern and Southern Africa', *Population and Development Review*, Vol. 20, No. 1, pp. 200–205.

Blacker, John et al. (2005), 'Fertility in Kenya and Uganda: A comparative study of trends and determinants', *Population Studies*, Vol. 59, No. 3, pp. 355–73.

Bloom, David E. (2011), '7 billion and counting', *Science*, Vol. 333, Issue 6042, pp. 562–4.

Bloom, David E. (2020), 'Population 2020', *IMF Finance & Development*, March 2020, pp. 6–9.

Bloom, David E. and Williamson, Jeffrey G. (1997), 'Demographic Transitions, Human Resource Development and Economic Miracles in Emerging Asia', Working Paper 6268, National Bureau of Economic Research, Cambridge MA.

Bloom, David E. and Williamson, Jeffrey G. (1998), 'Demographic transitions and economic miracles in emerging Asia', *The World Bank Economic Review*, Vol. 12, No. 3, pp. 419–55.

Bloom, David E. et al. (1998), 'Geography, demography, and economic growth in Africa', *Brookings Papers on Economic Activity*, Vol. 1998, No. 2, pp. 207–95.

Bloom, David E., Canning, David and Sevilla, Jaypee (2003), *The Demographic Dividend: A New Perspective on the Economic Consequences of Population Change*, Population Matters Monograph MR-1274, RAND Corporation, Santa Monica CA.

Bloom, David E. and Canning, David (2006), 'Booms, busts, and echoes', *IMF Finance & Development*, Vol. 43, No. 3.

Bloom, David E. et al. (2007a), 'Realizing the Demographic Dividend: Is Africa Any Different?', Working Paper 2307, Program on the Global Demography of Aging (PGDA), Harvard University.

Bloom, David E. et al. (2007b), 'Does Age Structure Forecast Economic Growth?', Working Paper 13221, National Bureau of Economic Research, Cambridge MA.

Bloom, David E., et al. (2012), 'Microeconomic Foundations of the Demographic Dividend', Working Paper No. 93, Program on the Global Demography of Aging (PGDA), Harvard University.

Bloom, David E. et al. (2013), 'A Demographic Dividend for Sub-Saharan Africa: Source, Magnitude, and Realization', Working Paper No. 110, Programme on the Global Demography of Aging (PGDA), Harvard University.

Bloom, David E. et al. (2015), 'Prospects for Economic Growth in Nigeria: A Demographic Perspective', Working Paper No.127, Program on the Global Demography of Aging (PGDA), Harvard University.

Bloom, David E., Kuhn, Michael and Prettner, Klaus (2016), 'Africa's Prospects for Enjoying a Demographic Dividend', IZA Discussion Paper No. 10161, Institute of Labour Economics (IZA), Bonn.

Bongaarts, John (2006), 'The causes of stalling fertility transitions', *Studies in Family Planning*, Vol. 37, No. 1, pp. 1–16.

Bongaarts, John (2008), 'Fertility transitions in developing countries: Progress or stagnation?', *Studies in Family Planning*, Vol. 39, No. 2, pp. 105–10.

Bongaarts, John (2011), 'Can family planning programs reduce high desired family size in sub-Saharan Africa?', *International Perspectives on Sexual and Reproductive Health*, Vol. 37, No. 4, pp. 209–16.

Bongaarts, John (2013), 'How Exceptional Is the Pattern of Fertility Decline in Sub-Saharan Africa?', UNPD Expert Paper No. 2013/4, New York.

Bongaarts, John (2015), 'Modeling the fertility impact of the proximate determinants: Time for a tune-up', *Demographic Research*, Vol. 33, Art. 19, pp. 535–60.

Bongaarts, John (2017a), 'The effect of contraception on fertility: Is sub-Saharan Africa different?',

Demographic Research, Vol. 37, Art. 6, pp. 129–46.

Bongaarts, John (2017b), 'Africa's unique fertility transition', Supplement to *Population and Development Review*, Vol. 43, pp. 39–58.

Bongaarts, John and Bulatao, Rodolfo A. (eds) (2000), *Beyond Six Billion: Forecasting the World's Population*, The National Academies Press, Washington DC.

Bongaarts, John and Casterline, John (2013), 'Fertility transition: Is sub-Saharan Africa different?', *Population and Development Review*, Vol. 38, Supplement 1, pp. 153–68.

Brass, William et al. (1968), *The Demography of Tropical Africa*, Princeton University Press.

Bricker, Darrell and Ibbitson, John (2019), *Empty Planet: The Shock of Global Population Decline*, Robinson, London.

Caldwell, John C. (1982), *Theory of Fertility Decline*, Academic Press, London.

Caldwell, John C. (1990), 'The soft underbelly of development: Demographic transition in conditions of limited economic change', *The World Bank Economic Review*, Vol. 4, Supplement 1, pp. 207–74.

Caldwell, John C. and Okonjo, Chukuka (eds) (1968), *The Population of Tropical Africa*, Longmans, London.

Caldwell, John C. and Caldwell, Pat (1986), *Limiting Population Growth and the Ford Foundation Contribution*, Continuum International Publishing, London.

Caldwell, John C. and Caldwell, Pat (1987), 'The cultural context of high fertility in sub-Saharan Africa', *Population and Development Review*, Vol. 13, No. 3, pp. 409–37.

Caldwell, John C. and Caldwell, Pat (1990), 'High fertility in sub-Saharan Africa', *Scientific American*, Vol. 262, No. 5, pp. 118–25.

Caldwell, John C., Orubuloye, I.O. and Caldwell, Pat (1992), 'Fertility decline in Africa: A new type of transition?', *Population and Development Review*, Vol. 18, No. 2, pp. 211–42.

Caldwell, John C. and Caldwell, Pat (1995), 'The beginning of fertility decline in sub-Saharan Africa', *Populations du Sud*, pp. 233–43.

Caldwell, John C. and Caldwell, Pat (2002), 'The Fertility Transition in Sub-Saharan Africa', Paper presented at the Conference on Fertility and the Current South African Issues of Poverty, HIV/AIDS and Youth, Pretoria, 24 October 2002.

Caldwell, John C. and Schindlmayr, Thomas (2002), 'Historical population estimates: Unraveling the consensus', *Population and Development Review*, Vol. 28, No. 2, pp. 183–204.

Campbell, Martha (2007), 'Why the silence on population?', *Population and Environment*, Vol. 28, pp. 237–46.

Campbell, Martha et al. (2007), 'Return of the population growth factor', *Science*, Vol. 315, pp. 1501–2.

Campbell, Martha et al. (2014), 'Population and climate change: Who will the grand convergence leave behind?', *The Lancet*, Global Health Vol. 2, pp. 253–4.

Canning, David, Raja, Sangeeta and Yazbeck, Abdo S. (2015), *Africa's Demographic Transition: Dividend or Disaster?*, World Bank/AFD, Washington DC/Paris.

Casterline, John (2001), 'The pace of fertility transition: National patterns in the second half of the twentieth century', *Population and Development Review*, Vol. 27, pp. 17–52.

Casterline, John (2017a), 'Prospects for fertility decline in Africa', Supplement to *Population and Development Review*, Vol. 43, pp. 3–18.

Casterline, John (2017b), 'Fertility Decline in Africa: Are the Determinants Different?', Paper presented at IUSSP XXVIII International Population Conference, Cape Town, 29 October–4 November.

Casterline, John and Bongaarts, John (eds) (2017), 'Fertility transitions in sub-Saharan Africa', Supplement to *Population and Development Review*, Vol. 43.

Casterline, John B. and Agyei-Mensah, Samuel (2017), 'Fertility desires and the course of fertility decline in sub-Saharan Africa', Supplement to *Population and Development Review*, Vol. 43, pp. 84–111.

Chang, Ha-Joon (2011), *23 things they don't tell you about capitalism*, Penguin, London.

Chen, Martha Alter (2012), 'The Informal Economy: Definitions, Theories and Policies', Working Paper No. 1, Women in Informal Employment: Globalizing and Organizing (WIEGO).

Choi, Jieun, Dutz, Mark and Usman, Zainab (2019), *The Future of Work in Africa* (Companion to the World Development Report 2019), World Bank, Washington DC.

Cilliers, Jakkie (2018), *Getting to Africa's Demographic Dividend*, Institute for Security Studies, Pretoria.

Cincotta, Richard (2010), 'The future of sub-Saharan Africa's tentative fertility decline', *New Security Beat* blog, 25 August.

Cincotta, Richard (2011), 'Africa's reluctant fertility transition', *Current History*, Vol. 110, Issue 736, pp. 184–90.

Cincotta, Richard (2017a), 'Opening the demographic window: Age structure in sub-Saharan Africa', *New Security Beat* blog, 26 October.

Cincotta, Richard (2017b), '8 rules of political demography that helped forecast tomorrow's world', *New Security Beat* blog, 12 June.

Cincotta, Richard and Engelman, Robert (2007), 'Economics and Rapid Change: The Influence of Population

Growth', Occasional Paper, Population Action International, Washington DC.

Cleaver, Kevin M. and Schreiber, Götz A. (1994), *Reversing the Spiral: The Population, Agriculture, and Environment Nexus in Sub-Saharan Africa*, World Bank, Washington DC.

Cleland, John (2005), 'The continuing challenge of population growth', in *The ICPD Vision: How Far Has the 11-Year Journey Taken Us?* Report from a UNFPA Panel Discussion at IUSSP XXV International Population Conference, Tours, July, pp. 19–23.

Cleland, John (2010), 'Diversity of fertility levels and implications for the future', Selected Papers of Beijing Forum 2007, *Procedia – Social and Behavioural Sciences*, Vol. 2, Issue 5, pp. 6920–7.

Cleland, John (2012), 'Will Africa benefit from a demographic dividend?', Health & Education Advice & Resource Team (HEART), Briefing Note, Oxford.

Cleland, John (2013), 'World population growth: Past, present and future', *Environmental and Resource Economics*, Vol. 55, Issue 4, pp. 543–54.

Cleland, John (2017a), 'Prospects for accelerated fertility decline in Africa', *The Journal of Population and Sustainability*, Vol. 1, No. 2, pp. 37–52.

Cleland, John (2017b), 'Population growth, employment, and livelihoods: The triple challenge', *Journal of Demographic Economics*, Vol. 83, pp. 51–61.

Cleland, John et al. (2006), 'Family planning: The unfinished agenda', *The Lancet*, Vol. 368, pp. 1810–27.

Cleland, John and Machiyama, Kazuyo (2017), 'The challenges posed by demographic change in sub-Saharan Africa: A concise overview', *Population and Development Review*, Vol. 43, Issue S1, pp. 264–86.

Cohen, Joel E. (1995), 'Population growth and Earth's human carrying capacity', *Science*, Vol. 269, pp. 341–6.

Coole, Diana (2013), 'Too many bodies: The return and disavowal of the population question', *Environmental Politics*, Vol. 22, No. 2, pp. 195–215.

Cuaresma, Jesús Crespo, Lutz, Wolfgang and Sanderson, Warren (2014), 'Is the demographic dividend an education dividend?', *Demography*, Vol. 51, pp. 299–315.

Dalton, Conley, McCord, Gordon C. and Sachs, Jeffrey D. (2007), 'Africa's Lagging Demographic Transition: Evidence from Exogenous Impacts of Malaria Ecology and Agricultural Technology', Working Paper 12892, National Bureau of Economic Research (NBER), Cambridge MA .

Davis, Mike (2007), *Planet of Slums*, Verso Books, London.

Donge, Jan Kees van, Henley, David and Lewis, Peter, 'Tracking development in South-East Asia and sub-Saharan Africa: The primacy of policy', *Development Policy Review*, No. 30, Special Issue 1, 2012, pp. 5–24.

Dramani, Latif and Oga, Idossou Jean-Baptiste (2017), 'Understanding demographic dividends in Africa: The NTA approach', *Journal of Demographic Economics*, Vol. 83, No. 1, pp. 85–101.

Dramani, Latif and Mbacké, Cheikh (2017), 'Africa's Demographic Dividend – An Elusive Window of Opportunity?', Paper 6568, IUSSP XXVIII International Population Conference, Cape Town, 29 October–3 November.

Drummond, Paolo, Thakoor, Vimal and Yu, Shue (2014), 'Africa Rising: Harnessing the Demographic Dividend', IMF Working Paper WP/14/143.

Duncan, Ron and Wilson, Chris (2004), 'Global Population Projections: Is the UN Getting it Wrong?',

Working Papers in Economics and Econometrics No. 438, Australian National University, Canberra.

Eastwood, Robert and Lipton, Michael (2010), 'Demographic Transition in Sub-Saharan Africa: Accounting and Economics', Paper presented at the Fourth Annual Research Conference on Population, Reproductive Health and Economic Development, Cape Town, January.

Eastwood, Robert and Lipton, Michael (2011), 'Demographic transition in sub-Saharan Africa: How big will the economic dividend be?', *Population Studies*, Vol. 65, No. 1, pp. 1–27.

Eastwood, Robert and Lipton, Michael (2012), 'The demographic dividend: Retrospect and prospect', *Economic Affairs*, Vol. 32, Issue 1, pp. 26–30.

Eberstadt, Nicholas (2017), 'Manpower, Education, Skills and Jobs in Sub-Saharan Africa: Past Trends and Future Outlook', in Hans Groth and John F. May (eds), *Africa's Population: In Search of a Demographic Dividend*, pp. 225–50.

Ehrlich, Paul R. (1968), *The Population Bomb: Population Control or Race to Oblivion?*, Sierra Club-Ballantine Books, New York.

Ehrlich, Paul R. and Holdren, John P. (1971), 'The impact of population growth', *Science*, Vol. 171, Issue 3977, pp. 1212–17.

Ehrlich, Paul R. and Ehrlich, Anne H. (2009), 'The population bomb revisited', *The Electronic Journal of Sustainable Development*, Vol. 1, No. 3, pp. 63–71.

Ehrlich, Paul R. and Ehrlich, Anne H. (2013), 'Can a collapse of global civilization be avoided?', *Proceedings of The Royal Society B*, Vol. 280, Issue 1754, Art. 20122845.

Ehrlich, Paul R. and Ehrlich, Anne H. (2016), 'Population resources, and the faith-based economy: The situation in

2016', *Biophysical Economics Resource Quality*, Vol. 1, Art. 3, pp. 1–9

Eizenga, Daniel (2019), *Long Term Trends Across Security and Development in the Sahel*, West African Papers, No. 25, OECD Publishing, Paris.

Engelman, Robert (2016), 'African population will soar dangerously unless women are more empowered', *Scientific American*, 1 February.

Ezeh, Alex (2018), 'Empowering women lies at the centre of controlling population growth in Africa', *The Conversation*, 20 September.

Ezeh, Alex, Mberu, Blessing and Emina, Jacques (2009), 'Stall in fertility decline in Eastern African countries: Regional analysis of patterns, determinants and implications', *Philosophical Transactions B*, The Royal Society, Vol. 364, Issue 1532, pp. 2991–3007.

Fadayomi, T.O. (2011), 'The demographic bonus: How prepared is Africa for the gains?', *African Population Studies Review*, Vol. 25, No. 2, pp. 226–49.

Faruqee, Rashid and Gulhati, Ravi (1983), 'Rapid Population Growth in Sub-Saharan Africa: Issues and Policies', World Bank Staff Working Papers No. 559.

Filmer, Deon and Fox, Louise (2014), *Youth Employment in Sub-Saharan Africa*, Africa Development Series, World Bank, Washington DC.

Food and Agriculture Organization of the United Nations (FAO) (1985), *The State of Food and Agriculture 1984*, Rome.

Foote, Karen A., Hill, Kenneth H. and Martin, Linda G. (eds) (1993), *Demographic Change in Sub-Saharan Africa*, The National Academies Press, Washington DC.

Fox, Louise (2016), 'What Will It Take to Meet the Youth Employment Challenge in Sub-Saharan Africa?', Growth and Labour Markets in Low Income Countries Programme, GLM/ LIC Synthesis Paper No. 2, Institute of Labour Economics (IZA), Bonn.

Fox, Louise (2019), 'Three Myths About Youth Employment in Africa and Strategies to Realize the Demographic Dividend', Chapter 3 of *Foresight Africa 2019* (pp. 56–8), Brookings Institution, Washington DC.

Fox, Louise et al. (2013), 'Africa's Got Work to Do: Employment Prospects in the New Century', IMF Working Paper 13/201.

Fox, Louise, Thomas, Alun and Haines, Cleary (2017), 'Structural Transformation in Employment and Productivity: What Can Africa Hope For?', Departmental Paper No. 17/02, IMF (African Department), Washington DC.

Frankema, Ewout and Jerven, Morten (2013), 'Writing history backwards or sideways: Towards a consensus on African population, 1850–2010', *The Economic History Review*, Vol. 67, Issue 4 (Special Issue: *The Renaissance of African Economic History*), pp. 907–31.

Frankema, Ewout and Waijenburg, Marlous van (2018), 'Africa rising? A historical perspective', *African Affairs*, Vol. 117, Issue 469, pp. 1–26.

Garenne, Michel (2008), *Fertility Changes in Sub-Saharan Africa*, DHS Comparative Report No. 18, Macro International, Calverton MD.

Garenne, Michel (2009), 'Situations of fertility stall in sub-Saharan Africa', *African Population Studies*, Vol. 23, No. 2, pp. 173–88.

Garenne, Michel (2011a), 'Fifty years of research in African demography: Progresses and challenges', *African Population Studies*, Vol. 25, No. 2, pp. 151–67.

Garenne, Michel (2011b), 'Testing for fertility stalls in demographic and health surveys', *Population Health Metrics*, Vol. 9, Art. 59.

Garenne, Michel, (2012), *Education and Fertility in Sub-Saharan Africa: A Longitudinal Perspective*, DHS Analytical Studies No. 33, ICF International, Calverton MD.

Garenne, Michel (2017a), 'Family Planning and Fertility Decline in Africa: From 1950 to 2010', in Zouhair O. Amarin (ed.), *Family Planning*, IntechOpen, pp. 119–150.

Garenne, Michel (2017b), 'Impacts démographiques des crises africaines: Une perspective historique', FERDI document de travail/HAL archives-ouvertes.

Garenne, Michel (2017c), 'Record high fertility in sub-Saharan Africa in a comparative perspective', *African Population Studies*, Vol. 31, No. 2, pp. 3706–23.

Gayawan, Ezra et al. (2010), 'Modelling fertility curves in Africa', *Demographic Research*, Vol. 22, Art. 10, pp. 211–36.

Gelb, Alan, Meyer, Christian and Ramachandran, Vijaya (2013), 'Does Poor Mean Cheap? A Comparative Look at Africa's Industrial Labor Costs', Center for Global Development Working Paper 325, Washington DC.

Gerland, Patrick et al. (2014), 'World population stabilization unlikely this century', *Science*, Vol. 346, Issue 6206, pp. 234–7.

Gerland, Patrick, Biddlecom, Ann and Kantorová, Vladimirá (2017), 'Patterns of fertility decline and the impact of alternative scenarios of future fertility change in sub-Saharan Africa', Supplement to *Population and Development Review*, Vol. 43, Issue S1, pp. 21–38.

Ghislandi, Simone, Scherbov, Sergei and Sanderson, Warren C. (2019), 'A simple measure of human development: The human life indicator', *Population and Development Review*, Vol. 45, No. 1, pp. 219–33.

Global Burden of Disease 2017 Population and Fertility Collaborators (2018), 'Population and fertility by age and sex for 195 countries and territories, 1950–2017: A systematic analysis for the Global Burden of Disease Study 2017', *The Lancet*, Vol. 392, No. 10159, pp. 1995–2051.

Goldstone, Jack (2010), 'The new population bomb: The four megatrends that will change the world', *Foreign Affairs*, January/February.

Goldstone, Jack (2019), 'Africa 2050: Demographic truth and consequences', *Governance in an Emerging New World*, Winter Series Issue 119, Hoover Institution, Stanford CA.

Goldstone, Jack, Kaufmann, Eric and Toft, Monica Duffy (2012), *Political Demography*, Paradigm Publishers, Boulder CO.

Goldstone, Jack, Marshall, Monty and Root, Hilton (2014), 'Demographic growth in dangerous places: Concentrating conflict risks', *International Area Studies Review*, Vol. 17, No. 2, pp. 120–33.

Goldstone, Jack et al. (2018), 'Why Does High African Fertility Persist?', Center for the Study of Social Change, Institutions, and Policy (George Mason University, Fairfax VA), Working Paper No. 2–2018.

Goujon, Anne and Zalak, Zakarya Al (2018), 'Why has fertility been increasing in Egypt?', *Population & Societies*, No. 551, pp. 1–4.

Groth, Hans and May, John F. (eds) (2017), *Africa's Population: In Search of a Demographic Dividend*, Springer, Cham.

Groth, Hans, May, John F. and Turbat, Vincent (2017), *Policies Needed to Capture a Demographic Dividend in Sub-Saharan Africa*, IUSSP XXVIII International Population Conference, 29 October–3 November.

Guengant, Jean-Pierre (2017), 'Africa's Population: History, Current Status, and Projections', in Hans Groth and

John F. May (eds), *Africa's Population: In Search of a Demographic Dividend*, Springer, Cham, pp. 11–31.

Guengant, Jean-Pierre and May, John F. (2001), 'Impact of the Proximate Determinants on the Future Course of Fertility in Sub-Saharan Africa', Paper presented at the UNPD Workshop on Prospects for Fertility Decline in High Fertility Countries, 9–11 July.

Guengant, Jean-Pierre and Rafalimanana, Hantamalala (2005), 'The Cairo Approach: Making Reproductive Health and Family Planning Programmes More Acceptable or Embracing Too Much?', Paper for IUSSP XXV International Population Conference, Tours, July.

Guengant, Jean-Pierre and May, John F. (2011a), 'Sub-Saharan Africa within global demography', *Études*, Vol. 415, Issue 10, pp. 305–16.

Guengant, Jean-Pierre and May, John F. (2011b), 'Proximate Determinants of Fertility in Sub-Saharan Africa and Their Possible Use in Fertility Projections', UNPD Expert Paper No. 2011/13, New York.

Guengant, Jean-Pierre and Kamara, Yarri (2012), 'How can we capitalize on the demographic dividend?', *A Savoir 09*, AFD, Paris.

Guengant, Jean-Pierre and May, John F. (2013a), 'African demography', *Global Journal of Emerging Market Economies*, Vol. 5, Issue 3, pp. 215–67.

Guengant, Jean-Pierre and May, John F. (2013b), 'Africa 2050: African Demography', Africa Emerging Markets Forum Briefing, Abidjan, June.

Guengant, Jean-Pierre and May, John F. (2014), 'Les Défis démographiques des pays sahéliens', *Études*, Vol. 6, pp. 19–30.

Gurmu, Eshetu and Mace, Ruth (2008), 'Fertility decline driven by poverty: The case of Addis Ababa', *Journal of Biosocial Science*, Vol. 40, No. 3, pp. 339–58.

Haub, Carl (2011), 'What if experts are wrong on world population growth?', Yale School of the Environment E360, New Haven CT, 19 September.

Heilig, Gerhard K. (1996), 'World Population Prospects: Analyzing the 1996 UN Population Projections', Paper WP-96-146, IIASA, Laxenburg.

Heilig, Gerhard K. et al. (2010), 'Future population trends found to be highly uncertain in least developed countries', UNPD unpublished manuscript, March, New York.

Hertrich, V. (2017), 'Trends in age at marriage and the onset of fertility transition in sub-Saharan Africa', Supplement to *Population and Development Review*, Vol. 43, pp. 112–37.

Ho, Teresa J. (1985), 'Population Growth and Agricultural Productivity in Sub-Saharan Africa', in *Proceedings of the Fifth Agriculture Sector Symposium: Population and Food* (ed. Ted J. Davis), World Bank, Washington DC, pp. 92–118.

Howse, Kenneth (2015), 'What is fertility stalling and why does it matter?', *Population Horizons*, Vol. 12, No. 1, pp. 13–23.

Iliffe, John (2017), *Africans: The History of a Continent*, Cambridge University Press.

ILO (2018), *Women and Men in the Informal Economy: A Statistical Picture* (third edition), Geneva.

ILO (2020), *Global Employment Trends for Youth 2020*, Geneva.

IMF (2015), *Regional Economic Outlook: Sub-Saharan Africa*, Washington DC.

IMF (2018), 'The Future of Work in Sub-Saharan Africa', African Department Paper No. 18/18, Washington DC.

Izugbara, Chimaraoke O., Tilahun, Tizta and Owii, Hilda (2018), 'Fostering political leadership for the demographic dividend in Africa:

Relevant cultural values', *Development in Practice*, Vol. 28, Issue 5, pp. 705–13.

Jerven, Morten (2016), 'Africa by numbers: Reviewing the database approach to studying African economies', *African Affairs*, Vol. 115, Issue 459, pp. 342–58.

Johnston, Lauren A. (2019), 'A Timely Economic Demography Lesson from China for the G20', Institute for Global Dialogue/University of South Africa (UNISA), Occasional Paper 75.

KC, Samir and Lutz, Wolfgang (2017), 'The human core of the shared socioeconomic pathways: Population scenarios by age, sex and level of education for all countries to 2100', *Global Environmental Change*, No. 42, pp. 181–92.

Kaplan, Robert D. (1994), 'The coming anarchy', *Atlantic Monthly*, February.

Kebede, Endale, Goujon, Anne and Lutz, Wolfgang (2019), 'Stalls in Africa's fertility decline partly result from disruptions in female education', *Proceedings of the National Academy of Sciences of the United States of America (PNAS)*, Vol. 116, No. 8, pp. 2891–6.

Keilman, Nico (1998), 'How accurate are the United Nations World Population Projections?', *Population and Development Review*, Vol. 24 (Supplement), pp. 15–41.

Keilman, Nico (2005), 'Data quality and accuracy of United Nations population projections, 1950–95', *Population Studies*, Vol. 55, pp. 149–64.

Kimonyo, Jean-Paul (2016), *Rwanda's Popular Genocide: A Perfect Storm*, Lynne Rienner Publishers Inc., Boulder CO.

Kinfu, Yohannes (2000), 'Below-replacement fertility in Tropical Africa? Some evidence from Addis Ababa', *Journal of Population Research*, Vol. 17, No. 1, pp. 63–82.

Kirk, Dudley (1996), 'Demographic transition theory', *Population Studies*, Vol. 50, No. 3, pp. 361–87.

Korotayev, Andrey, Malkov, Sergey and Grinin, Leonid (2014), 'A Trap at the Escape from the Trap? Some Demographic Structural Factors of Political Instability in Modernizing Social Systems', in *History & Mathematics: Trends and Cycles*, pp. 201–67, Uchitel Publishing House, Volgograd.

Korotayev, Andrey et al. (2016), 'Explaining current fertility dynamics in tropical Africa from an anthropological perspective: A cross-cultural investigation', *Cross-Cultural Research*, Vol. 50, No. 3, pp. 251–80.

Kulczycki, Andrej (2018), 'Overcoming family planning challenges in Africa: Toward meeting unmet need and scaling up service delivery', *African Journal of Reproductive Health*, Vol. 22, No. 1, pp. 9–13.

Lam, David (2011), 'How the world survived the population bomb: Lessons from fifty years of extraordinary demographic history', *Demography*, Vol. 48, No. 4, pp. 1231–62.

Lam, David (2017), 'The world's next 4 billion will differ from the previous 4 billion', N-IUSSP, 24 July.

Lee, Ronald (2011), 'The outlook for population growth', *Science*, Vol. 333, Issue 6042, pp. 569–73.

Lee, Ronald and Mason, Andrew (2006), 'What is the demographic dividend?', *IMF Finance and Development*, No. 43, Issue 3.

Lee, Ronald and Mason, Andrew (2010), 'Fertility, human capital, and economic growth over the demographic transition', *European Journal of Population*, Vol. 26, pp. 159–82.

Leridon, Henri (2020), 'Population mondiale: Vers une explosion ou une implosion?', *Population & Sociétés*, No. 573.

Lesthaeghe, R. (2014), *The Fertility Transition in Sub-Saharan Africa into the 21st Century*, Center for Population Studies, University of Michigan, PSC Research Report No. 14-823.

Lesthaeghe, R. and Jolly, C. (1995), 'The start of the sub-Saharan fertility transition: Some answers and many questions', *Journal of International Development*, Vol. 7, Issue 1, pp. 25–45.

Lipton, Michael (2013), 'Income from work: The food-population-resource crisis in "the short Africa"', *British Academy Review*, Issue 22, pp. 34–8.

Lockwood, Matthew (1995), 'Development policy and the African demographic transition: Issues and questions', *Journal of International Development*, Vol. 7, Issue 1, pp. 1–23.

Lockwood, Matthew (2005), 'Will a Marshall Plan for Africa make poverty history?', *Journal of International Development*, Vol. 17, pp. 775–89.

Lockwood, Matthew (2012), 'Adaptation Policy, Governance and Politics in Sub-Saharan Africa', Paper presented at an international symposium on the Governance of Adaptation, Amsterdam, 22–23 March.

Lopes, Carlos (2019), *Africa in Transformation: Economic Development in the Age of Doubt*, Palgrave Macmillan, Cham.

Lutz, Wolfgang, Sanderson, Warren and Scherbov, Sergei (2001), 'The end of world population growth', *Nature*, Vol. 412, pp. 543–5.

Lutz, Wolfgang, Sanderson, Warren and Scherbov, Sergei (2004), *The End of World Population Growth in the 21st Century: New Challenges for Human Capital Formation and Sustainable Development*, Earthscan, London.

Lutz, Wolfgang and KC, Samir (2010), 'Dimensions of global projections: What do we know about future population trends and structures?', *Philosophical Transactions of The Royal Society B*, No. 365, pp. 2779–91.

Lutz, Wolfgang, Butz, William P. and KC, Samir (eds) (2014), *World Population & Human Capital in the Twenty-First Century – Executive Summary*, Wittgenstein Centre/IIASA.

Lutz, Wolfgang et al. (eds) (2018), *Demographic and Human Capital Scenarios for the Twenty-First Century*, Publications Office of the European Union, Luxembourg.

Lutz, Wolfgang et al. (2019), 'Education rather than age structure brings demographic dividend', *Proceedings of the National Academy of the United States of America (PNAS)*, Vol. 116, No. 26, pp. 12798–803.

Machiyama, Kazuyo (2010), 'A Re-examination of Recent Fertility Declines in Sub-Saharan Africa', DHS Working Paper No. 68, ICF Macro, Calverton MD, September.

Madsen, Elizabeth Leahy (2012a), 'The missing links in the demographic dividend', N-IUSSP, 9 March.

Madsen, Elizabeth Leahy (2012b), 'Age Structure and Development through a Policy Lens', in Jack Goldstone et al. (eds), *Political Demography*, pp. 81–97.

Madsen, Elizabeth Leahy (2013a), 'New UN population projections released: Pockets of high fertility drive overall increase', *New Security Beat* blog, 26 June.

Madsen, Elizabeth Leahy (2013b), 'Why has the demographic transition stalled in sub-Saharan Africa?', *New Security Beat* blog, 7 August.

Madsen, Elizabeth Leahy (2014), 'UN further refines population projections: 80 percent probability of 1–12 billion people by 2100', *New Security Beat* blog, 16 October.

Madsen, Elizabeth Leahy (2015), 'What's behind West and Central Africa's youthful demographics? High desired family size', *New Security Beat* blog, 11 May.

Makinwa-Adebusoye, Paulina (2001), 'Sociocultural Factors Affecting

Fertility in Sub-Saharan Africa', Paper presented at UNDP Workshop on Prospects for Fertility Decline in High Fertility Countries, 9–11 July.

Malmberg, Bo (2008), *Demography and the Development Potential of Sub-Saharan Africa*, Current African Issues No. 38, Nordiska Afrikainstitutet/The Nordic Africa Institute, Uppsala.

Mason, Andrew (2007), 'Demographic Transition and Demographic Dividends in Developed and Developing Countries', Paper for United Nations Expert Group Meeting on Social and Economic Implications of Changing Population Age Structures, Mexico City, 31 August–2 September 2005, pp. 81–101.

Mason, Andrew, Lee, Ronald and Jiang, Jennifer Xue (2016), 'Demographic dividends, human capital, and saving', *The Journal of the Economics of Ageing*, Vol. 7(C), pp. 106–22.

Mason, Andrew et al. (2017), 'Support Ratios and Demographic Dividends: Estimates for the World', UNPD Technical Paper No. 2017/1, New York.

May, John (2017), 'The policies of family planning and programs in sub-Saharan Africa', Supplement to *Population and Development Review*, Vol. 43, pp. 308–29.

May, John, Guengant, Jean-Pierre and Barras, V. (2017), 'Demographic Challenges of the Sahel Countries', in Hans Groth and John F. May (eds), *Africa's Population: In Search of a Demographic Dividend*, Springer, Cham, pp. 165–77.

Mbacké, Cheikh (2017), 'The persistence of high fertility in sub-Saharan Africa: A comment', Supplement to *Population and Development*, Vol. 43, pp. 330–7.

Mbaye, Ahmadou Aly (2019), *Supporting Small Informal Businesses to Improve the Quality of Jobs in Africa*, Policy Brief, Africa Growth Initiative, Brookings Institution, Washington DC.

Mbaye, Ahmadou Aly, Coulibaly, Brahima S. and Gandhi, Dhruv (2019), 'Job Creation for Youth in Africa: Assessing the Potential of Industries Without Smokestacks', Working Paper No. 22, Africa Growth Initiative, Brookings Institution, Washington DC.

Mberu, Blessing U. and Reed, Holly E. (2014), 'Understanding Subgroup Fertility Differentials in Nigeria', *Population Review*, Vol. 53, No. 2, pp. 23–46.

Mberu, Blessing U. and Ezeh, Alex (2017), 'The population factor and economic growth and development in sub-Saharan Africa', *African Population Studies*, Vol. 31, No. 2, pp. 3833–44.

Mberu, Blessing U., Beguy, Donatien and Ezeh, Alex (2017), 'Internal Migration, Urbanization and Slums in Sub-Saharan Africa', in Hans Groth and John F. May (eds), *Africa's Population: In Search of a Demographic Dividend*, Springer, Cham, pp. 315–32.

Meagher, Kate (2013), 'The jobs crisis behind Nigeria's unrest', *Current History*, Vol. 112, Issue 754, pp. 169–74.

Meagher, Kate (2015), 'Leaving no one behind?: Informal economies, economic inclusion and Islamic extremism in Nigeria', *Journal of International Development*, Vol. 27, No. 6, pp. 835–55.

Meagher, Kate (2016), 'The scramble for Africans: Demography, globalisation and Africa's informal labour markets', *The Journal of Development Studies*, Vol. 52, No. 4, pp. 483–97.

Michailof, Serge (2016), *Programmed Explosion? The Potential Consequences of the Rapid Population Growth in Sub-Saharan Africa*, Konrad Adenauer Stiftung International Reports, Issue 4, pp. 41–54.

Michailof, Serge (2018), *Africanistan: Development or Jihad*, Oxford University Press.

Mo Ibrahim Foundation (2019), *Africa's Youth: Jobs or Migration?*, Ibrahim Forum Report.

Moreland, Scott and Madsen, Elizabeth Leahy (2017), 'Africa's Population: In Search of a Demographic Dividend', in Hans Groth and John F. May (eds), *Africa's Population: In Search of a Demographic Dividend*, Springer, Cham, pp. 453–67.

Moultrie, Tom (2017), 'A Case of an Almost Complete Demographic Transition', in Hans Groth and John F. May (eds), *Africa's Population: In Search of a Demographic Dividend*, Springer, Cham, pp. 87–99.

Moultrie, Tom, Sayi, Takudzwa and Timæus, Ian (2012), 'Birth intervals, postponement, and fertility decline in Africa: A new type of transition?', *Population Studies*, Vol. 66, Issue 3, pp. 241–58.

Moultrie, Tom and Timæus, Ian (2014), 'Rethinking African Fertility: The State in, and of, the Future Sub-Saharan African Fertility Decline', Paper presented to Population Association of America Conference, Boston MA, 1–3 May.

Moyo, Nelson P. (1986), 'Population policy: Do we need it? Prospects and problems', *Zimbabwe Journal of Economics*, Vol. 1, No. 3, pp. 36–40.

Mueller, Valerie and Thurlow, James (eds) (2019), *Youth and Jobs in Rural Africa: Beyond Stylized Facts*, International Food Policy Research Institute/Oxford University Press.

Myers, Norman (1989), 'Population Growth, Environmental Decline and Security Issues in Sub-Saharan Africa', in A. Hjort af Ornäs and M.A. Salih (eds), *Ecology and Politics: Environmental Stress and Security in Africa*, Scandinavian Institute of African Studies, Uppsala, pp. 211–31.

National Academies of Sciences, Engineering and Medicine (2016), *Recent Fertility Trends in Sub-Saharan Africa: Workshop Summary*, The National Academies Press, Washington DC.

Newfarmer, Richard S., Page, John M. and Tarp, Finn (eds) (2018), *Industries Without Smokestacks: Industrialization in Africa Reconsidered*, UNU-WIDER Studies in Development Economics, Oxford University Press.

Obono, Oka (2003), 'Cultural diversity and population policy', *Population and Development Review*, Vol. 29, No. 1, pp. 103–11.

Odimegwu, Clifford, Bamiwuye, Olusina S. and Adedini, Sunday A. (2015), 'Gender-based violence as a new proximate determinant of fertility in sub-Saharan Africa', *Southern African Journal of Demography*, Vol. 16, No. 1, pp. 87–121.

Odimegwu, Clifford O. et al. (2018), 'Fertility, family size preference and contraceptive use in sub-Saharan Africa: 1990–2014', *African Journal of Reproductive Health*, Vol. 22, No. 4, pp. 44–53.

Odimegwu, Clifford O. and Olamijuwon, Emmanuel O. (2018), 'Potentials for demographic dividend and rapid economic growth in Mali: What policy scenario would yield the greatest dividend?', *Population Horizons*, Vol. 15, No. 2, pp. 1–9.

OECD/Sahel and West Africa Club (2020), *Africa's Urbanisation Dynamics 2020: Africapolis, Mapping a New Urban Geography*, West African Studies, OECD Publishing, Paris.

Olamosu, Biodun and Wynne, Andy (2015), 'Africa rising? The economic history of sub-Saharan Africa', *International Socialism*, Issue 146.

Onuoha, Nelson C. and Timæus, Ian M. (1995), 'Has a fertility transition begun in West Africa?', *Journal of*

International Development, Vol. 7, No. 1, pp. 93–116.

O'Neill, Brian C. et al., (2001), 'A guide to global population projections', *Demographic Research*, Vol. 4, Art. 8, pp. 203–88.

O'Sullivan, Jane (2015), 'The Infrastructure Dividend: Conceptualising and Quantifying the Cost of Providing Capacity for Additional People', Paper presented at the seventh African Population Conference, 'Demographic Dividend in Africa: Prospects, Opportunities and Challenges', Johannesburg, 30 November–4 December, pp. 1–18.

O'Sullivan, Jane (2017), 'The Contribution of Reduced Population Growth to Demographic Dividend', Paper presented at XXVIII International Population Conference, Cape Town, 29 October–4 November 2017, pp. 1–18.

O'Sullivan, Jane (2019), 'World Population Prospects 2019 – good news or bad?', The Overpopulation Project, 26 June.

O'Sullivan, Jane and Martin, Roger (2016), 'The risk of misrepresenting the demographic dividend', N-IUSSP, 18 April.

Owino, Kwame, Wamalwa, Noah and Ivory Ndekei (2017), *How Kenya Is Failing to Create Decent Jobs*, Africa Research Institute (Counterpoints series), London.

Page, John M. (2011), 'Should Africa Industrialize?', UNU-WIDER Working Paper No. 2011/47.

Page, John M. (2012), 'Youth, Jobs, and Structural Change: Confronting Africa's "Employment Problem"', AfDB Working Paper No. 155.

Pearce, Fred (2011), *Peoplequake: Mass Migration, Ageing Nations and the Coming Population Crash*, Eden Project Books – Transworld Publishers, London.

Pison, Gilles (2017a), 'Why African families are larger than those of other continents', *The Conversation*, 11 October.

Pison, Gilles (2017b), 'Is the Earth over-populated?', *The Conversation*, 30 October.

Pison, Gilles (2017c), 'The population of the world (2017)', *Population & Societies*, No. 547, pp. 1–8.

Pison, Gilles (2019), 'The population of the world (2019)', *Population & Societies*, No. 569, pp. 1–8.

Pool, Ian (2005), 'The Way Forward: Changes in Population Structure', in *The ICPD Vision: How Far Has the 11-Year Journey Taken Us?*, Report from a UNFPA Panel Discussion at IUSSP XXV International Population Conference, Tours, July, pp. 24–39.

Pool, Ian (2007), 'Demographic dividends: Determinants of development or merely windows of opportunity?', *Ageing Horizons*, No. 7, pp. 28–35.

Population Reference Bureau (PRB), 'World Population Data Sheet' 2017, 2018, 2019, 2020, Washington DC.

Potts, Malcolm, Henderson, Cortney and Campbell, Martha (2013), 'The Sahel: A Malthusian challenge?', *Environmental and Resource Economics*, Vol. 55, pp. 501–12.

Potts, Malcolm et al. (2013), *Crisis in the Sahel*, Organizing to Advance Solutions in the Sahel (OASIS) Conference Report, Bixby Center for Population, Health & Sustainability, University of California, Berkeley.

Potts, Malcolm et al. (2015), 'Niger: Too little, too late', *International Perspectives on Sexual and Reproductive Health*, Vol. 37, No. 3, pp. 95–101.

Reader, John (1998), *Africa: A Biography of the Continent*, Penguin Books, London.

Rodrik, Dani (2016), 'An African growth miracle?', *Journal of African Economies*, pp. 1–18.

Rosling, Hans (with Ola Rosling and Anna Rosling Rönnlund), *Factfulness*, Penguin Books, London.

The Royal Society (2012), *People and the Planet*, London.

Sai, Fred T. (1988), 'Changing perspectives of population in Africa and international responses', *African Affairs*, Vol. 87, No. 347, pp. 267–76.

Sammam, Emma and Watkins, Kevin (2017), 'Africa's Opportunity: Reaping the Early Harvest of the Demographic Transition and Ensuring No One Is Left Behind', Overseas Development Institute, London.

Schoumaker, Bruno (2009), 'Stalls and Reversals in Fertility Transitions in Sub-Saharan Africa: Real or Spurious?', Document de travail No. 30, Université catholique de Louvain.

Schoumaker, Bruno (2017), 'African Fertility Changes', in Hans Groth and John F. May (eds), *Africa's Population: In Search of a Demographic Dividend*, Springer, Cham, pp. 197–211.

Schoumaker, Bruno (2019), 'Stalls in fertility transitions in sub-Saharan Africa: Revisiting the evidence', *Studies in Family Planning*, Vol. 50, No. 3, pp. 257–78.

Schoumaker, Bruno and Tabutin, Dominique (2008), 'Fertility Transitions in Sub-Saharan Africa at the Sub-national Level', Paper presented at the annual meeting of the Population Association of America, New Orleans LA, 17–19 April.

Schoumaker, Bruno and Dimbuene, Zacharie Tsala (2017), 'Stalls in Fertility Transition in Sub-Saharan Africa: Revisiting the Evidence', Paper presented at IUSSP XXVIII International Population Conference, Cape Town, 29 October–4 November.

Shapiro, David (2017), 'Linkages Between Education and Fertility in Sub-Saharan Africa', Paper presented at AFD-Sorbonne workshop 'Demographic Challenges in Africa', AFD, Paris, 23 February.

Shapiro, David (2018), 'Frustrated Fertility Goals of Well-Educated Women in Sub-Saharan Africa', Paper presented at the annual meeting of the Population Association of America, Denver CO, 26–28 April.

Shapiro, David, and Gebreselassie, Tesfayi (2007), 'Fertility Transition in sub-Saharan Africa: Falling and Stalling', Paper presented at the annual meeting of the Population Association of America, New York, 29–31 March.

Shapiro, David and Hinde, Andrew (2017a), 'The pace of fertility decline in SSA', N-IUSSP, 12 December.

Shapiro, David and Hinde, Andrew (2017b), 'On the pace of fertility decline in sub-Saharan Africa', *Demographic Research*, Vol. 37, Art. 40, pp. 1327–38.

Shapiro, David and Tenikue, Michel (2017c), 'Women's education, infant and child mortality, and fertility decline in urban and rural sub-Saharan Africa', *Demographic Research*, Vol. 37, Art. 21, pp. 669–708.

Shekar, Meera et al. (2016), 'Population and Development in the Sahel: Policy Choices to Catalyse a Demographic Dividend', World Bank Discussion Paper, Washington DC.

Short, Roger and Potts, Malcolm (eds) (2009), 'The impact of population growth on tomorrow's world', *Philosophical Transactions of the Royal Society B* (Theme Issue), Vol. 364, Issue 1532, pp. 2971–3124.

Singh, Ajit Kumar (2016), 'India's demographic dividend: A sceptical look', *Indian Journal of Human Development*, Vol. 10, No. 1, pp. 10–26.

Sippel, Lilli et al. (2011), *Africa's Demographic Challenges: How a Young*

Population Can Make Development Possible, Berlin Institute for Population and Development.

Smith, Stephen (2019), *The Scramble for Europe*, Polity Press, Cambridge.

Smith-Greenaway, Emily (2015), 'Educational attainment and adult literacy: A descriptive account of 31 sub-Saharan Africa countries', *Demographic Research*, Vol. 33, Art. 35, pp. 1015–34.

Spoorenberg, Thomas (2019), 'Forty years of fertility changes in the Sahel', *Demographic Research*, Vol. 41, Art. 46, pp. 1289–314.

Starrs, Ann et al. (2018), 'Accelerate progress – sexual and reproductive health and rights for all: Report of the Guttmacher-Lancet Commission', *The Lancet*, Vol. 391, pp. 2642–92.

Stecklov, Guy and Menashe-Oren, Ashira (2019), 'The Demography of Rural Youth in Developing Countries', Background Paper for *2019 Rural Development Report*, International Fund for Agricultural Development (IFAD) Research Series 41, Rome.

Tabutin, Dominique and Schoumaker, Bruno (2004), 'The demography of sub-Saharan Africa from the 1950s to the 2000s: A survey of changes and a statistical assessment', *Population*, Vol. 59, No. 3/4, pp. 457–556.

Tabutin, Dominique and Schoumaker, Bruno (2020), 'The demography of sub-Saharan Africa in the 21st century: Transformations since 2000, outlook to 2050', *Population*, Vol. 75, No. 2/3, pp. 165–286.

Turbat, Vincent (2017), 'The Demographic Dividend: A Potential Surplus Generated by a Demographic Transition', in Hans Groth and John F. May (eds), *Africa's Population: In Search of a Demographic Dividend*, Springer, Cham, pp. 181–95.

Turner, Adair (2009), 'Population priorities: The challenge of continued rapid population growth', *Philosophical Transactions of the Royal Society B*, Vol. 364, Issue 1532, pp. 2977–84.

UNDESA (1971), *The World Population Situation in 1970*, Population Studies No. 49, New York.

UNECA (1983), *ECA and Africa's Development 1983–2008: A Preliminary Perspective Study*, Addis Ababa.

UNECA (1990), *African Alternative Framework to Structural Adjustment Programmes for Socio-Economic Recovery and Transformation* (AAF-SAP), Addis Ababa.

UNECA (1992), *Demographic Handbook for Africa*, Addis Ababa.

UNECA (2001), *The State of the Demographic Transition in Africa*, Addis Ababa.

UNECA (2019), *Healthcare and Economic Growth in Africa*, Addis Ababa.

UNECA/OAU (1994), *Population and Development in Africa*, Addis Ababa.

UNECA/AU (2011), *Economic Report on Africa 2011 – Governing Development in Africa – the Role of the State in Economic Transformation*, Addis Ababa.

UNECA/UNFPA (2016), *The Demographic Profile of African Countries*.

UNICEF (2017), *Generation 2030 Africa 2.0*, New York.

UNPD (2002), *Completing the Fertility Transition*, Population Bulletin Special Issue Nos. 48/49, New York.

UNPD (2003), *World Population Prospects: The 2002 Revision – Highlights*, New York.

UNPD (2004), *World Population to 2300*, New York.

UNPD (2009a), *World Population Prospects: The 2008 Revision – Vol. I: Comprehensive Tables, Vol. II: Demographic Profiles*, New York.

UNPD (2009b), 'What Would It Take to Accelerate Fertility Decline in the

Least Developed Countries?', Policy Brief No. 2009/1, New York.

UNPD (2011), *World Population Prospects: The 2010 Revision – Highlights and Advance Tables, Vol. I: Comprehensive Tables, Vol. II: Demographic Profiles*, New York.

UNPD (2013a), *World Population Prospects: The 2012 Revision – Highlights and Advance Tables, Vol. I: Comprehensive Tables, Vol. II: Demographic Profiles*, New York.

UNPD (2013b), *Explaining Differences in the Projected Populations Between the 2012 and 2010 Revisions of World Population Prospects: The Role of Fertility in Africa*, Population Facts No. 2013/10, New York.

UNPD (2015a), *World Population Prospects: The 2015 Revision – Key Findings and Advance Tables, Vol. I: Comprehensive Tables, Vol. II: Demographic Profiles, Data Booklet*, New York.

UNPD (2015b), *World Fertility Patterns – Data Booklet*, New York.

UNPD (2015c), *Youth Population Trends and Sustainable Development*, Population Facts No. 2015/1, New York.

UNPD (2017a), *World Population Prospects: The 2017 Revision – Key Findings and Advance Tables, Vol. I: Comprehensive Tables, Vol. II: Demographic Profiles, Data Booklet*, New York.

UNPD (2017b), *World Fertility Report 2015*, New York.

UNPD (2017c), *The End of High Fertility Is Near*, Population Facts No. 2017/3, New York.

UNPD (2017d), *The Impact of Population Momentum on Future Population Growth*, Population Facts No. 2017/4, New York.

UNPD (2017e), *Life Expectancy at Birth Increasing in Less Developed Regions*, Population Facts No. 2017/9, New York.

UNPD (2017f), 'Methodology of the United Nations Population Estimates and Projections', Working Paper No. ESA/P/WP.250, New York.

UNPD (2017g), *Changing Population Age Structures and Sustainable Development: A Concise Report*, New York.

UNPD (2019a), *World Population Prospects: The 2019 Revision – Highlights, Data Booklet, Vol. I: Comprehensive Tables, Vol. II: Demographic Profiles*, New York.

UNPD (2019b), *World Population Prospects 2019: Methodology of the United Nations Population Estimates and Projections*, New York.

UNPD (2019c), *Fertility Among Very Young Adolescents*, Population Facts No. 2019/1, New York.

UNPD (2019d), *Potential Impact of Later Childbearing on Future Population*, Population Facts No. 2019/5, New York.

UNPD (2019e), *How Certain Are the United Nations Global Population Projections?* Population Facts No. 2019/6, New York.

UNPD (2019f), *World Population Ageing 2019 – Highlights*, New York.

UNPD (2020a), *World Fertility and Family Planning 2020 – Highlights*, New York.

UNPD (2020b), *World Population Ageing 2020 – Highlights*, New York.

Upadhyay, Ushma D. and Karasek, Deborah (2012), 'Women's empowerment and ideal family size: An examination of DHS empowerment measures in sub-Saharan Africa', *International Perspectives on Sexual and Reproductive Health*, Vol. 38, No. 2, pp. 78–89.

Urdal, Henrik (2006), 'A clash of generations? Youth bulges and political violence', *International Studies Quarterly*, Vol. 50, Issue 3, pp. 607–29.

Urdal, Henrik (2012), 'Youth Bulges and Violence' in Jack Goldstone et al., *Political Demography*, pp. 117–32.

Walle, Etienne van de and Foster, Andrew D. (1990), 'Fertility Decline in Africa: Assessment and Prospects', World Bank Technical Paper No. 125, Africa Technical Department, World Bank, Washington DC.

Walle, Etienne van de Walle and J. Knodel (1980), 'Europe's fertility transition: New evidence and lessons for today's developing world', *Population Bulletin*, Vol. 34, No. 6, pp. 3–44.

Whitty, Christopher (2015), 'The Shape of Things to Come: Future Demography Around the World', Gresham College Lecture, Museum of London, 3 February.

Williamson, Jeffrey G. (2013), 'Demographic dividends revisited', *Asian Development Review*, Vol. 30, No. 2, pp. 1–25.

World Bank (1972), *The World Bank Atlas: Population, Per Capita Product and Growth Rates*, Washington DC.

World Bank (1983), *The Demographic Situation in Burundi*, Washington DC.

World Bank (1986), *Population Growth and Policies in Sub-Saharan Africa*, Washington DC.

World Bank (1989), *Sub-Saharan Africa: From Crisis to Sustainable Growth*, Washington DC.

World Bank (2010), *Determinants and Consequences of High Fertility: A Synopsis of the Evidence*, Portfolio Reviews, Washington DC.

World Bank (2015), *More, and More Productive, Jobs for Nigeria: A Profile of Work and Workers*, Washington DC.

World Bank (2019), *World Development Report: The Changing Nature of Work*, Washington DC.

World Economic Forum (2017), *The Africa Competitiveness Report 2017: Addressing Africa's Demographic Dividend*, Geneva.

World Economic Forum (2019), 'The Sub-Saharan Africa Risks Landscape', White Paper, Geneva, September 2019.

Zeleza, Tiyambe (1991), 'Economic policy and performance in Kenya since independence', *Transafrican Journal of History*, Vol. 20, pp. 35–76.

Zinkina, Julia and Korotayev, Andrey (2014a), 'Projecting Mozambique's demographic futures', *Journal of Futures Studies*, Vol. 19, No. 2, pp. 21–40.

Zinkina, Julia and Korotayev, Andrey (2014b), 'Explosive population growth in tropical Africa: Crucial omission in development forecasts – emerging risks and way out', *World Futures*, No. 70, pp. 120–39.

Acknowledgements

My profound thanks go to Anthony Cheetham and Neil Belton for recognising the signal importance to the world of demographic trends in Africa and being willing to publish this treatment of the topic in a commercial format, to Matilda Singer, for her patience, diligent co-ordination of everything and unerring cheerfulness; and to their colleagues at Head of Zeus – Christian Duck, Ben Cracknell, Jeff Edwards, Philippa Hudson and Nic Nicholas. I am equally fortunate that Georgina Capel and her team at Georgina Capel Associates have 'had my back' for two decades. Linden Lawson brought her considerable copy-editing skills to bear on the draft; and Gregor Tims contributed some valuable insights in the early stages of research. I am also grateful to the friends and colleagues who showed interest and gave encouragement over the course of the three years this book was in the making, and to the many demographers (you know who you are) who unfailingly answered queries rapidly, helpfully and, in one particular case, at length that I had no right to expect.

Special thanks are due to Richard Smith, founder (in 2007) and Chairman of the Trustees of Africa Research Institute. It was his idea to take a close look at Africa's diverse demography; and once the research was under way his enthusiasm for the topic and support were unflagging, and his occasional suggestions always perspicacious.

List of Figures

List of Tables

Index